"Of all the sciences, political economy is that which to civilized men of today is of most practical importance"

the science of political economy

Henry George

But let none expect any great promotion of the sciences, especially in their effective part, unless natural philosophy be drawn out to particular sciences; and again unless these particular sciences be brought back again to natural philosophy. From this defect it is that astronomy, optics, music, many mechanical arts, and what seems stranger, even moral and civil philosophy and logic, rise but little above their foundations, and only skim over the varieties and surface of things, viz., because after these particular sciences are formed and divided off they are no longer nourished by natural philosophy, which might give them strength and increase; and therefore no wonder if the sciences thrive not when separated from their roots.–
BACON, *Novum Organum.*

the science of political economy

A reconstruction of its principles in clear and systematic form

Henry George

ROBERT SCHALKENBACH FOUNDATION
41 East 72nd Street, New York
1992

THE
ROBERT SCHALKENBACH
FOUNDATION

incorporated in 1925, to administer a Trust Fund left by the will of the late Robert Schalkenbach, former president of the New York Typothetae, and such other funds as may be donated to it, for the purpose of spreading among the people of this and other countries a wider acquaintance with the social and economic philosophy of Henry George.

First trade edition published by Doubleday & McClure Co., New York, 1898. Subsequent editions issued by the Robert Schalkenbach Foundation, New York, 1938, 1981. This printing 1992.

George, Henry, 1839-1897.
The science of political economy.

Originally published: New York: Schalkenbach Foundation, 1980.
Includes index.
1. Economics. I. Title
HB171.G33 1981 330.1 81-5939
ISBN O-911312-51-X AACR2

Printed in the United States of America by Sherwin/Dodge Printers
Binding by New Hampshire Bindery
Design by A.L. Morris

To
August Lewis of New York
and
Tom L. Johnson of Cleveland, Ohio,
who, of their own motion, and without suggestion
or thought of mine, have helped me to the
leisure needed to write it, I
affectionately dedicate what in
this sense is their
work

Take, since you bade it should bear,
These, of the seed of your sowing—
Blossom or berry or weed.
Sweet though they be not, or fair,
That the dew of your word kept growing;
Sweet at least was the seed.

SWINBURNE TO MAZZINI.

CONTENTS

Errata: In the footnote on page 33 referring to *A Perplexed Philosopher,* the page number in early edition is 285 as noted. In later edition it is 245.

PREFACE

to the

CURRENT EDITION / 1981

IT was as an individualist that Henry George, though with but little schooling, caught the elegant truth contained in his magnum opus, *Progress and Poverty.* A staunch believer in liberty, with a vigorous and brilliant mind, he reached out and caught the theme of that book as though plucking a bolt from the blue. His was truly an individual effort. Long after the fundamental principles came to George, he was told that they had occurred to others in previous times and other countries. That book is a work of art, excellent in its very shape and form, as in its content, and no book on economic philosophy has been more widely circulated.

By contrast, it was as an erudite citizen of the world that he wrote *The Science of Political Economy.* He was now widely read, a social philosopher of standing, comfortably at home with many of the thinkers who had come before, and blessed with the same astute mind. Yet he struggled with this book for seven years until his premature death prevented his completing it. Thus, among the book's many rich and lovely pages are a few where George's ideas seem still unhewn. The distractions of the various activities into which his fame forced him may help explain the difference. But it goes deeper than that.

The Science of Political Economy is a bigger task than the one he pursued in writing *Progress and Poverty.* George explains in his own preface how this book came about, and we know from his son's Prefatory Note how quickly the work brought him to a body of understanding which has since taken shape as a science of its own.

These pages literally teem with evidence that George was probing an area now known as General Semantics. He searches for meanings. He is aware that Adam Smith wrote, not just the *Wealth of Nations,* but a vigorous and imaginative "paper on the formation of languages." George wrestles with the meaning of "value" and "space" and "time."

Most importantly, he believes that money is a sibling of language, and that both of them are instruments of man's unique ability and willingness to exchange. *The Science of Political Economy* does not stop with the individual; it deals with his interaction with others. The individual is the unit of society, and "no opera was ever written by a committee." But that is not enough. No individual alone ever did nor ever could devise the language by which the opera could take form. And no individual could comprise the assemblage within the four walls of a theater to bring it alive.

Nothing is more evident than that the more mature man wants to bring us together, and yet above all else wants us to keep our individuality intact.

Richard Noyes
Editor, Salem Observer

February, 1981

PREFATORY NOTE

to the

ORIGINAL EDITION / 1898

THIS WORK, begun in 1891, after returning from a lecturing tour through Australia and a trip around the world, grew out of the author's long-cherished purpose to write a small text-book, which should present in brief the principles of a true political economy. This "Primer of Political Economy" was to set forth in direct, didactic form the main principles of what he conceived to be an exact and indisputable science, leaving controversy for a later and larger work.

Before proceeding far, however, the author realized the difficulty of making a simple statement of principles while there existed so much confusion as to the meaning of terms. He therefore felt impelled to change his plan, and first to present the larger work, which should recast political economy and examine and explicate terminology as well as principles; and which, beginning at the beginning, should trace the rise and partial development of the science in the hands of its founders a century ago, and then show its gradual emasculation and at last abandonment by its professed teachers—accompanying this with an account of the extension of the science outside and independently of the schools, in the philosophy of the natural order now spreading over the world under the name of the single tax.

Soon after this work had got well under way the author laid it aside to write a brochure in reply to a papal encyclical ("The

Condition of Labor," 1891), and again later to write a book exposing Mr. Herbert Spencer's recantation of principles on the land question ("A Perplexed Philosopher," 1892). Save for these interruptions, and occasional newspaper and magazine writing, and lecturing and political speaking, he devoted himself continuously to his great undertaking until he entered the mayoralty campaign, toward the close of which death came, October 29, 1897.

"The Science of Political Economy," if entirely finished as planned by the author, would have shown Book V., on Money, extended, and the nature and function of the laws of Wages, Interest and Rent fully considered in Book IV.; but the work as left was, in the opinion of its author, in its main essentials completed, the broken parts, to quote his own words a few days before his death, "indicating the direction in which my [his] thought was tending."

The author's preface is fragmentary. It bears in the manuscript a penciled date, "March 7, 1894," and is here transcribed from a condensed writing used by him in his preliminary "roughing-out" work.

Aside from the filling in of summaries in four chapter headings (indicated by foot-notes), the addition of an index, and the correction of a few obvious clerical errors, the work is here presented exactly as it was left by the author—the desire of those closest to him being that it should be given to the world untouched by any other hand.

Henry George, Jr.

New York, February 1, 1898.

PREFACE

to the

ORIGINAL EDITION / 1894

IN "Progress and Poverty" I recast political economy in what were at the time the points which most needed recasting. Criticism has but shown the soundness of the views there expressed.

But "Progress and Poverty" did not cover the whole field of political economy, and was necessarily in large measure of a controversial rather than of a constructive nature. To do more than this was at the time beyond the leisure at my command. Nor did I see fully the necessity. For while I realized the greatness of the forces which would throw themselves against the simple truth which I endeavored to make clear, I did think that should "Progress and Poverty" succeed in commanding anything like wide attention there would be at least some of the professed teachers of political economy who, recognizing the ignored truths which I had endeavored to make clear, would fit them in with what of truth was already understood and taught.

The years which have elapsed since the publication of "Progress and Poverty" have been on my part devoted to the propagation of the truths taught in "Progress and Poverty" by books, pamphlets, magazine articles, newspaper work, lectures and speeches, and have been so greatly successful as not only far to exceed what fifteen years ago I could have dared to look forward to in this time, but to have given me reason to feel that of all the men of whom I have ever heard who have attempted anything like so great a work against anything like so great odds, I have been in the result of the endeavor to arouse thought most favored.

Not merely wherever the English tongue is spoken, but in all parts of the world, men are arising who will carry forward to final triumph the great movement which "Progress and Poverty" began. The great work is not done, but it is commenced, and can never go back.

On the night on which I finished the final chapter of "Progress and Poverty" I felt that the talent intrusted to me had been accounted for—felt more fully satisfied, more deeply grateful than if all the kingdoms of the earth had been laid at my feet; and though the years have justified, not dimmed, my faith, there is still left for me something to do.

But this reconstruction of political economy has not been done. So I have thought it the most useful thing I could do to drop as far as I could the work of propaganda and the practical carrying forward of the movement to do this.

GENERAL CONTENTS.

GRAND DIVISIONS.

SUB-DIVISIONS.

CHAPTER II.

MAN, HIS PLACE AND POWERS.

SHOWING OUR RELATIONS TO THE GLOBE, AND THE QUALITIES THAT ENABLE US TO EXTEND OUR KNOWLEDGE OF IT AND OUR POWERS ON IT.

CHAPTER III.

HOW MAN'S POWERS ARE EXTENDED.

SHOWING THAT THEIR USE OF REASON WELDS MEN INTO THE SOCIAL ORGANISM OR ECONOMIC BODY.

CHAPTER IV.

CIVILIZATION—WHAT IT MEANS.

SHOWING THAT CIVILIZATION CONSISTS IN THE WELDING OF MEN INTO THE SOCIAL ORGANISM OR ECONOMIC BODY.

CHAPTER V.

THE ORIGIN AND GENESIS OF CIVILIZATION.

SHOWING THE NATURE OF REASON; AND HOW IT IMPELS TO EXCHANGE, BY WHICH CIVILIZATION DEVELOPS.

CHAPTER VI.

OF KNOWLEDGE AND THE GROWTH OF KNOWLEDGE.

SHOWING THAT THE GROWTH OF KNOWLEDGE IS BY COÖPERATION, AND THAT IT INHERES IN THE SOCIETY.

CHAPTER VII.

OF SEQUENCE, CONSEQUENCE AND LAWS OF NATURE.

SHOWING THE PROPER MEANING OF SEQUENCE AND OF CONSEQUENCE, AND WHY WE SPEAK OF LAWS OF NATURE.

CHAPTER VIII.

OF THE KNOWLEDGE PROPERLY CALLED SCIENCE.

SHOWING THAT SCIENCE DEALS ONLY WITH LAWS OF NATURE, AND THAT IN THE CURRENT POLITICAL ECONOMY THIS HAS BEEN FORGOTTEN.

CHAPTER IX.

THE ECONOMY CALLED POLITICAL ECONOMY.

SHOWING THE MEANING, UNITS AND SCOPE OF POLITICAL ECONOMY.

CHAPTER X.

THE ELEMENTS OF POLITICAL ECONOMY.

SHOWING HOW POLITICAL ECONOMY SHOULD PROCEED AND WHAT RELATIONS IT SEEKS TO DISCOVER.

CHAPTER XI.

OF DESIRES AND SATISFACTIONS.

SHOWING THE WIDTH AND IMPORTANCE OF THE FIELD OF POLITICAL ECONOMY.

CHAPTER XII.

THE FUNDAMENTAL LAW OF POLITICAL ECONOMY.

SHOWING THAT THE LAW FROM WHICH POLITICAL ECONOMY PROCEEDS IS THAT MEN SEEK TO SATISFY THEIR DESIRES WITH THE LEAST EXERTION.

CHAPTER V.

ADAM SMITH AND THE PHYSIOCRATS.

SHOWING THE RELATION BETWEEN ADAM SMITH AND THE PHYSIOCRATS.

CHAPTER VI.

SMITH'S INFLUENCE ON POLITICAL ECONOMY.

SHOWING WHAT THE "WEALTH OF NATIONS" ACCOMPLISHED AND THE COURSE OF THE SUBSEQUENT DEVELOPMENT OF POLITICAL ECONOMY.

CHAPTER VII.

INEFFECTUAL GROPINGS TOWARD A DETERMINATION OF WEALTH.

SHOWING THE OPPOSITION TO THE SCHOLASTIC ECONOMY BEFORE "PROGRESS AND POVERTY."

CHAPTER VIII.

BREAKDOWN OF SCHOLASTIC POLITICAL ECONOMY.

SHOWING THE REASON, THE RECEPTION, AND EFFECT ON POLITICAL ECONOMY OF "PROGRESS AND POVERTY."

CHAPTER IX.

WEALTH AND VALUE.

SHOWING THE REASON FOR CONSIDERING THE NATURE OF VALUE BEFORE THAT OF WEALTH.

CHAPTER X.

VALUE IN USE AND VALUE IN EXCHANGE.

SHOWING THE TWO SENSES OF VALUE; HOW THE DISTINCTION HAS BEEN IGNORED, AND ITS REAL VALIDITY; AND THE REASON FOR CONFINING THE ECONOMIC TERM TO ONE SENSE.

CHAPTER XI.

ECONOMIC VALUE—ITS REAL MEANING AND FINAL MEASURE.

SHOWING HOW VALUE IN EXCHANGE HAS BEEN DEEMED A RELATION OF PROPORTION; AND THE AMBIGUITY WHICH HAS LED TO THIS.

CHAPTER XII.

VALUE IN EXCHANGE REALLY RELATED TO LABOR.

SHOWING THAT VALUE DOES NOT COME FROM EXCHANGEABILITY, BUT EXCHANGEABILITY FROM VALUE, WHICH IS AN EXPRESSION OF THE SAVING OF LABOR INVOLVED IN POSSESSION.

CHAPTER XIII.

THE DENOMINATOR OF VALUE.

SHOWING WHAT VALUE IS, AND ITS RELATIONS.

CHAPTER XIV.

THE TWO SOURCES OF VALUE.

SHOWING THAT THERE IS A VALUE FROM PRODUCTION AND ALSO A VALUE FROM OBLIGATION.

CHAPTER XV.

THE MEANING OF WEALTH IN POLITICAL ECONOMY.

SHOWING HOW VALUE FROM PRODUCTION IS WEALTH IN POLITICAL ECONOMY.

CHAPTER XVI.

THE GENESIS OF WEALTH.

SHOWING HOW WEALTH ORIGINATES AND WHAT IT ESSENTIALLY IS.

CHAPTER XVII.

THE WEALTH THAT IS CALLED CAPITAL.

SHOWING WHAT THE WEALTH CALLED CAPITAL REALLY IS.

CHAPTER XVIII.

WHY POLITICAL ECONOMY CONSIDERS ONLY WEALTH.

SHOWING THAT POLITICAL ECONOMY, AS PROPERLY STATED, COVERS ALL THE RELATIONS OF MEN IN SOCIETY INTO WHICH IT IS NECESSARY TO INQUIRE.

CHAPTER XIX.

MORAL CONFUSIONS AS TO WEALTH.

SHOWING HOW RICH AND POOR ARE CORRELATIVES, AND WHY CHRIST SYMPATHIZED WITH THE POOR.

CHAPTER XX.

OF THE PERMANENCE OF WEALTH.

SHOWING THAT VALUES FROM OBLIGATION SEEM REALLY TO LAST LONGER THAN VALUES FROM PRODUCTION.

CHAPTER XXI.

THE RELATION OF MONEY TO WEALTH.

SHOWING THAT SOME MONEY IS AND SOME MONEY IS NOT WEALTH.

BOOK III.

THE PRODUCTION OF WEALTH.

CHAPTER I.

THE MEANING OF PRODUCTION.

SHOWING THE MEANING AND PROPER USE OF PRODUCTION.

CHAPTER II.

THE THREE MODES OF PRODUCTION.

SHOWING THE COMMON CHARACTER, YET DIFFERENT MODES OF PRODUCTION.

CHAPTER III.

POPULATION AND SUBSISTENCE.

SHOWING THAT THE THEORY OF A TENDENCY IN POPULATION TO INCREASE FASTER THAN SUBSISTENCE HAS PREVIOUSLY BEEN EXAMINED AND CONDEMNED.

CHAPTER IV.

THE ALLEGED LAW OF DIMINISHING RETURNS IN AGRICULTURE.

SHOWING WHAT THIS ALLEGED LAW IS.

CHAPTER V.

OF SPACE AND TIME.

SHOWING THAT HUMAN REASON IS ONE, AND SO FAR AS IT CAN GO MAY BE RELIED ON.

CHAPTER VI.

CONFUSION OF THE SPACIAL LAW WITH AGRICULTURE.

SHOWING THE GENESIS OF THIS CONFUSION.

CHAPTER VII.

THE RELATION OF SPACE IN PRODUCTION.

SHOWING THAT SPACE HAS RELATION TO ALL MODES OF PRODUCTION.

CHAPTER XVI.

THE SECOND FACTOR OF PRODUCTION—LABOR.

SHOWING THAT LABOR IS THE HUMAN OR ACTIVE FACTOR IN ALL PRODUCTION.

CHAPTER XVII.

THE THIRD FACTOR OF PRODUCTION—CAPITAL.

SHOWING THAT CAPITAL IS NOT A PRIMARY FACTOR, BUT PROCEEDS FROM LAND AND LABOR, AND IS A FORM OR USE OF WEALTH.

BOOK IV.

THE DISTRIBUTION OF WEALTH.

CHAPTER I.

THE MEANING OF DISTRIBUTION.

SHOWING THE MEANING AND USES OF THE WORD DISTRIBUTION; THE PLACE AND MEANING OF THE ECONOMIC TERM; AND THAT IT IS CONCERNED ONLY WITH NATURAL LAWS.

CHAPTER II.

THE NATURE OF DISTRIBUTION.

SHOWING THE FALLACY OF THE CONTENTION THAT DISTRIBUTION IS A MATTER OF HUMAN LAW; THAT THE NATURAL LAWS OF DISTRIBUTION ARE MANIFEST NOT ON WEALTH ALREADY PRODUCED, BUT ON SUBSEQUENT PRODUCTION; AND THAT THEY ARE MORAL LAWS.

BOOK V.

MONEY—THE MEDIUM OF EXCHANGE AND MEASURE OF VALUE.

CHAPTER I.

CONFUSIONS AS TO MONEY.

SHOWING THE DIVERGENCE IN COMMON THOUGHT AND AMONG ECONOMISTS AS TO MONEY.

CHAPTER II.

THE COMMON UNDERSTANDING OF MONEY.

SHOWING THAT THE COMMON USE OF MONEY IS TO BUY THINGS WITH, AND THAT ITS ESSENTIAL CHARACTER IS NOT IN ITS MATERIAL, BUT IN ITS USE.

CHAPTER III.

MEDIUM OF EXCHANGE AND MEASURE OF VALUE.

SHOWING HOW THE COMMON MEDIUM OF EXCHANGE BECOMES THE COMMON MEASURE OF VALUE, AND WHY WE CANNOT FIND A COMMON MEASURE IN LABOR.

GENERAL INTRODUCTION

For tho' the Giant Ages heave the hill
  And break the shore, and evermore
Make and break, and work their will;
  Tho' world on world in myriad myriads roll
Round us, each with different power
And other forms of life than ours,
  What know we greater than the soul!

—*Tennyson*

GENERAL INTRODUCTION.

REASON OF THIS WORK.

I SHALL try in this work to put in clear and systematic form the main principles of political economy.

The place I would take is not that of a teacher, who states what is to be believed, but rather that of a guide, who points out what by looking is to be seen. So far from asking the reader blindly to follow me, I would urge him to accept no statement that he himself can doubt, and to adopt no conclusion untested by his own reason.

This I say, not in unfelt deprecation of myself nor in idle compliment to the reader, but because of the nature and present condition of political economy.

Of all the sciences, political economy is that which to civilized men of to-day is of most practical importance. For it is the science which treats of the nature of wealth and the laws of its production and distribution; that is to say, of matters which absorb the larger part of the thought and effort of the vast majority of us—the getting of a living. It includes in its domain the greater part of those vexed questions which lie at the bottom of our politics and legislation, of our social and governmental theories, and even, in larger measure than may at first be supposed, of our philosophies and religions. It is the science to which must belong the solving of problems that at the close of a century of the greatest material and scientific development the world has yet seen, are in all civilized countries clouding the horizon of the future—the only science that can enable our civilization to escape already threatening catastrophe.

Yet, surpassing in its practical importance as political economy is, he who to-day would form clear and sure ideas of what it really teaches must form them for himself. For there is no body of accepted truth, no consensus of recognized authority, that he may without question accept. In all other branches of knowledge properly called science the inquirer may find certain fundamentals recognized by all and disputed by none who profess it, which he may safely take to embody the information and experience of his time. But, despite its long cultivation and the multitude of its professors, he cannot yet find this in political economy. If he accepts the teaching of one writer or one school, it will be to find it denied by other writers and other schools. This is not merely true of the more complex and delicate questions, but of primary questions. Even on matters such as in other sciences have long since been settled, he who to-day looks for the guidance of general acceptance in political economy will find a chaos of discordant opinions. So far indeed are first principles from being agreed on, that it is still a matter of hot dispute whether protection or free trade is most conducive to prosperity—a question that in political economy ought to be capable of as certain an answer as in hydrodynamics the question whether a ship ought to be broader than she is long, or longer than she is broad.

This is not for want of what passes for systematic study. Not only are no subjects so widely and frequently discussed as those that come within the province of political economy, but every university and college has now its professor of the science, whose special business it is to study and to teach it. But nowhere are inadequacy and confusion more apparent than in the writings of these men; nor is anything so likely to give the impression that there is not and cannot be a real science of political economy.

But while this discordance shows that he who would really acquaint himself with political economy cannot rely upon authority, there is in it nothing to discourage the hope that he who will use his own reason in the honest search for truth may attain firm and clear conclusions.

For in the supreme practical importance of political economy we may see the reason that has kept and still keeps it in dispute, and that has prevented the growth of any body of accepted and assured opinion.

Under existing conditions in the civilized world, the great struggle among men is for the possession of wealth. Would it not then be irrational to expect that the science which treats of the production and distribution of wealth should be exempt from the influence of that struggle? Macaulay has well said that if any large pecuniary interest were concerned in disputing the attraction of gravitation, that most obvious of all facts would not yet be accepted. What, then, can we look for in the teaching of a science which directly concerns the most powerful of "vested rights"—which deals with rent and wages and interest, with taxes and tariffs, with privileges and franchises and subsidies, with currencies and land-tenures and public debts, with the ideas on which trade-unions are based and the pleas by which combinations of capitalists are defended? Economic truth, under existing conditions, has not merely to overcome the inertia of indolence or habit; it is in its very nature subject to suppressions and distortions from the influence of the most powerful and vigilant interests. It has not merely to make its way; it must constantly stand on guard. It cannot safely be trusted to any selected body of men, for the same reasons that the power of making laws and administering public affairs cannot be so trusted.

It is especially true to-day that all large political questions are at bottom economic questions. There is thus introduced into the study of political economy the same disturbing element that setting men by the ears over the study of theology has written in blood a long page in the world's history, and that at one time, at least, so affected even the study of astronomy as to prevent the authoritative recognition of the earth's movement around the sun long after its demonstration. The organization of political parties, the pride of place and power that they arouse and the strong prejudices they kindle, are always inimical to the search for truth and to the acceptance of truth.

And while colleges and universities and similar institutions, though ostensibly organized for careful investigation and the honest promulgation of truth, are not and cannot be exempt from the influences that disturb the study of political economy, they are especially precluded under present conditions from faithful and adequate treatment of that science. For in the present social conditions of the civilized world nothing is clearer than that there is some deep and wide-spread wrong in the distribution, if not in the production, of wealth. This it is the office of political economy to disclose, and a really faithful and honest explication of the science must disclose it.

But no matter what that injustice may be, colleges and universities, as at present constituted, are by the very law of their being precluded from discovering or revealing it. For no matter what be the nature of this injustice, the wealthy class must, relatively at least, profit by it, and this is the class whose views and wishes dominate in colleges and universities. As, while slavery was yet strong, we might have looked in vain to the colleges and universities and accredited organs of education and opinion in our Southern States, and indeed for that matter in the North, for any admission of its injustice, so under present conditions must we look in vain to such sources for any faithful treatment of political economy. Whoever accepts from them a chair of political economy must do so under the implied stipulation that he shall not really find what it is his professional business to look for.*

In these extraneous difficulties, and not in any difficulty inherent in political economy itself, lies the reason why, to-day, after all the effort that since Adam Smith wrote has been devoted to its investigation, or presumed investigation, he who would really know what it teaches can find no consistent body of undisputed doctrine that he may safely accept; and can turn to the colleges and universities only with the certainty that, wherever else he may find the truth, he cannot find it there.

Yet, if political economy be the one science that cannot safely be left to specialists, the one science of which it is needful for all to know something, it is also the science which the ordinary man may most easily study. It requires no tools, no apparatus, no special learning. The phenomena which it investigates need not be sought for in laboratories or libraries; they lie about us, and are constantly thrust upon us. The principles on which it builds are truths of which we all are conscious, and on which in every-day matters we constantly base our reasoning and our actions. And its processes, which consist mainly in analysis, require only care in distinguishing what is essential from what is merely accidental.

In proposing to my readers to go with me in an attempt to work out the main principles of political economy, I am not asking them to think of matters they have never thought of before, but merely to think of them in a careful

* On this subject, Adam Smith's opinion of colleges and universities (Article II., Part III., Chapter I., Book V., "Wealth of Nations") may still be read with much advantage.

and systematic way. For we all have some sort of political economy. Men may honestly confess an ignorance of astronomy, of chemistry, of geology, of philology, and really feel their ignorance. But few men honestly confess an ignorance of political economy. Though they may admit or even proclaim ignorance, they do not really feel it. There are many who say that they know nothing of political economy—many indeed who do not know what the term means. Yet these very men hold at the same time and with the utmost confidence opinions upon matters that belong to political economy, such as the causes which affect wages and prices and profits, the effects of tariffs, the influence of labor-saving machinery, the function and proper substance of money, the reason of "hard times" or "good times," and so on. For men living in society, which is the natural way for men to live, must have some sort of politico-economic theories—good or bad, right or wrong. The way to make sure that these theories are correct, or if they are not correct, to supplant them by true theories, is by such systematic and careful investigation as in this work I propose.

But to such an investigation there is one thing so necessary, one thing of such primary and constant importance, that I cannot too soon and too strongly urge it upon the reader. It is, that in attempting the study of political economy we should first of all, and at every step, make sure of the meaning of the words that we use as its terms, so that when we use them they shall always have for us the same meaning.

Words are the signs or tokens by which in speech or writing we communicate our thoughts to one another. It is only as we attach a common meaning to words that we can communicate with one another by speech. And to understand one another with precision, it is necessary that each attach precisely the same meaning to the same word. Thus, two men may look on the ocean from the same place, and one honestly insist that there are three ships in sight, while the other as honestly insists that there are only two, if the one uses the word ship in its general meaning of navigable vessel, and the other uses it in its technical meaning of a vessel carrying three square-rigged masts. Such use of words in somewhat different senses is peculiarly dangerous in philosophic discussion.

But words are more than the means by which we communicate our thoughts. They are also signs or tokens in which we ourselves think—the labels of the thought drawers or pigeonholes in which we stow away the various ideas that we often mentally deal with by label. Thus we cannot think with precision unless in our own minds we use words with precision. Failure to do this is a great cause of the generation and persistence of economic fallacies.

In all studies it is important that we should attach definite meanings to the terms we use. But this is especially important in political economy. For in other studies most of the words used as terms are peculiar to that study. The terms used in chemistry, for instance, are used only in chemistry. This makes the study of chemistry harder in beginning, for the student has to familiarize himself with new words. But it avoids subsequent difficulties, for these words being used only in chemistry, their meaning is not likely to be warped by other use from the one definite sense they properly bear in chemistry.

Now the terms used in political economy are not words reserved to it. They are words in every-day use, which the necessities of daily life constantly require us to give to, and accept for, a different than the economic meaning. In studying political economy, in thinking out any of its problems, it is absolutely necessary to give to such terms as wealth, value, capital, land, labor, rent, interest, wages, money, and so on, a precise meaning; and to use them only in this—a meaning which always differs, and in some cases differs widely, from the common meaning. But not only have we all been accustomed in the first place to use these words in their common meanings; but even after we have given them as politico-economic terms a definite meaning, we must, in ordinary talk and reading continue to use and accept them in their ordinary sense.

Hence arises in political economy a liability to confusion in thought from lack of definiteness in the use of terms. The careless as to terms cannot take a step without falling into this confusion, and even the usually careful are liable to fall into confusion if at any moment they relax their vigilance. The most eminent writers on political economy have given examples of this, confusing themselves as well as their readers by the vague use of a term. To guard against this danger it is necessary to be careful in beginning, and continuously to be careful. I shall therefore in this work try to define each term as it arises, and thereafter, when using it as an economic term, try to use it in that precise sense, and in no other.

To define a word is to mark off what it includes from what it does not include—to make it in our minds, as it were, clear and sharp on its edges—so that it will always stand for the same thing or things, not at one time mean more and at another time less.

Thus, beginning at the beginnings, let us consider the nature and scope of political economy, that we may see its origin and meaning, what it includes and what it does not include. If in this I ask the reader to go with me deeper than writers on political economy usually do, let him not think me wandering from the subject. He who would build a towering structure of brick and stone, that in stress and strain will stand firm and plumb, digs for its foundation to solid rock.

Should we grudge such pains in laying the foundations of a great science, on which in its superstructure so much must rest?

In nothing more than in philosophy is it wise that we should be "like a man which built an house, and digged deep, and laid the foundation on a rock."

BOOK I.

THE MEANING OF POLITICAL ECONOMY.

Though but an atom midst immensity,
  Still I am something, fashioned by Thy hand!
I hold a middle rank 'twixt heaven and earth—
  On the last verge of mortal being stand
Close to the realms where angels have their birth,
  Just on the boundaries of the spirit-land!
The chain of being is complete in me—
  In me is matter's last gradation lost,
And the next step is spirit—Deity!
  I can command the lightning, and am dust!

—Bowring's translation of Derzhavin

CONTENTS OF BOOK I.

THE MEANING OF POLITICAL ECONOMY.

CHAPTER IV.

CIVILIZATION—WHAT IT MEANS.

CHAPTER V.

THE ORIGIN AND GENESIS OF CIVILIZATION.

CHAPTER VI.

OF KNOWLEDGE AND THE GROWTH OF KNOWLEDGE.

CHAPTER VII.

OF SEQUENCE, CONSEQUENCE AND LAWS OF NATURE.

CHAPTER VIII.

OF THE KNOWLEDGE PROPERLY CALLED SCIENCE.

PAGE

SHOWING THAT SCIENCE DEALS ONLY WITH LAWS OF NATURE, AND THAT IN THE CURRENT POLITICAL ECONOMY THIS HAS BEEN FORGOTTEN.

CHAPTER IX.

THE ECONOMY CALLED POLITICAL ECONOMY.

SHOWING THE MEANING, UNITS AND SCOPE OF POLITICAL ECONOMY.

CHAPTER X.

THE ELEMENTS OF POLITICAL ECONOMY.

SHOWING HOW POLITICAL ECONOMY SHOULD PROCEED AND WHAT RELATIONS IT SEEKS TO DISCOVER.

CHAPTER XI.

OF DESIRES AND SATISFACTIONS.

SHOWING THE WIDTH AND IMPORTANCE OF THE FIELD OF POLITICAL ECONOMY.

CHAPTER XII.

THE FUNDAMENTAL LAW OF POLITICAL ECONOMY.

CHAPTER XIII.

METHODS OF POLITICAL ECONOMY.

CHAPTER XIV.

POLITICAL ECONOMY AS SCIENCE AND AS ART.

INTRODUCTION TO BOOK I.

THE earliest, and as I think sufficient, definition of Political Economy, is, the science that treats of the nature of wealth, and of the laws of its production and distribution. But as this definition seems never to have been fully understood and adhered to by the accepted teachers of political economy, and has during late years been abandoned by those who occupy the position of official teachers in all our leading colleges and universities, let us, beginning at the beginnings, endeavor to see for ourselves just what political economy is.

CHAPTER I.

THE THREE FACTORS OF THE WORLD.

SHOWING THE CONSTITUENTS OF ALL WE PERCEIVE.

Meaning of factor; and of philosophy: and of the world—What we call spirit—What we call matter—What we call energy—Though these three may be at bottom one, we must separate them in thought—Priority of spirit.

THE word factor, in commercial use, means one who acts as agent for another. In mathematical use, it means one of the quantities which multiplied together form a product. Hence in philosophy, which may be defined as the search for the nature and relations of things, the word factor affords a fit term for the elements which bring about a result, or the categories into which analysis enables us to classify these elements.

In the world—I use the term in its philosophic sense of the aggregate or system of things of which we are cognizant and of which we ourselves are part—we are enabled by analysis to distinguish three elements or factors:

1. That which feels, perceives, thinks, wills; which to distinguish, we call mind or soul or spirit.

2. That which has a mass or weight, and extension or form; which to distinguish, we call matter.

3. That which acting on matter produces movement; which to distinguish, we call motion or force or energy.

We cannot, in truth, directly recognize energy apart from matter; nor matter without some manifestation of energy; nor mind or spirit unconjoined with matter and motion. For though our own consciousness may testify to our own essentially spiritual nature, or even at times to what we take to be direct evidence of pure spiritual existence, yet consciousness itself begins with us only after bodily life has already begun, and memory by which alone we can recall past consciousness is later still in appearing. It may be that what we call matter is but a form of energy; and it may perhaps be that what we call energy is but a manifestation of what we call mind or soul or spirit; and some have even held that from matter and its inherent powers all else originates. Yet though they may not be in fact separable by us, and though it may be that at bottom they are one, we are compelled in thought to distinguish these three as independent, separable elements, which in their actions and reactions make up the world as it is presented to our perception.

Of these from our standpoint, that which feels, perceives, thinks, wills, comes first in order of priority, for it is this which is first in our own consciousness, and it is only through this that we have consciousness of any other existence. In this, as our own consciousness testifies, is the initiative of all our own motions and movements, so far as consciousness and memory shed light; and in all cases in which we can trace the genesis of anything to its beginning we find that beginning in thought and will. So clear, so indisputable is the priority of this spiritual element that wherever and whenever men have sought to account for the origin of the world they have always been driven to assume a great spirit or God. For though there be atheistic theories, they always avoid the question of origin, and assume the world always to have been.

CHAPTER II.

MAN, HIS PLACE AND POWERS.

SHOWING OUR RELATIONS TO THE GLOBE, AND THE QUALITIES THAT ENABLE US TO EXTEND OUR KNOWLEDGE OF IT AND OUR POWERS ON IT.

Man's earliest knowledge of his habitat—How that knowledge grows, and what civilized men now know of it—The essential distinction between man and other animals—In this lies his power of producing and improving.

WE awake to consciousness to find ourselves, clothed in flesh, and in company with other like beings, resting on what seems to us a plane surface. Above us, when the clouds do not conceal them, the sun shines by day and the moon and stars by night. Of what this place is, and of our relations to it, the first men probably knew little more than is presented to us in direct consciousness, little more in fact than the animals know; and, individually, we ourselves could know little more. But the observations and reflections of many succeeding men, garnered and systematized, enable us of the modern civilization to know, and with the eyes of the mind almost to see, things to which the senses untaught by reason are blind.

By the light of this gathered knowledge we behold ourselves, the constantly changing tenants of the exterior of a revolving sphere, circling around a larger and luminous sphere, the sun, and beset on all sides by depths of space, to which we can neither find nor conceive of limits.

Through this immeasurable space revolve myriads of luminous bodies of the nature of our sun, surrounded, it is confidently inferred from the fact that we know it to be the case with our sun, by lesser, non-luminous bodies that have in them their centers of revolution.

Our sun, but one, and far from one of the largest, of countless similar orbs, is the center of light and heat and revolution to eight principal satellites (having in their turn satellites of their own), as well as to an indefinite number of more minute bodies known to us as asteroids and of more erratic bodies called comets. Of the principal satellites of the sun, the third in point of distance from it, and the fourth in point of size, is our earth. It is in constant movement around the sun, and in constant revolution on its own axis, while its satellite, the moon, also revolving on its own axis, is in constant movement around it. The sun itself, revolving too on its own axis, is, with all its attendant bodies, in constant movement around some, probably moving, point in the universe which astronomers have not yet been able to determine.

Thus we find ourselves, on the surface of a globe seemingly fixed, but really in constant motion of so many different kinds that it would be impossible with our present knowledge to make a diagram indicating its real movement through space at any point—a globe large to us, yet only as a grain of sand on the sea-shore compared with the bodies and spaces of the universe of which it is a part. We find ourselves on the surface of this ceaselessly moving globe, as passengers, brought there in utter insensibility, they know not how or whence, might find themselves on the deck of a ship, moving they know not where, and who see in the distance similar ships, whether tenanted or how tenanted they can only infer and guess. The immeasurably great lies beyond us, and about and beneath as the immeasurably small. The microscope reveals infinitudes no less startling to our minds than does the telescope.

Here we are, depth upon depth about us, confined to the bottom of that sea of air which envelops the surface of this moving globe. In it we live and breathe and are constantly immersed. Were our lungs to cease taking in and pumping out this air, or our bodies relieved of its pressure, we should die.

Small as our globe seems in the light of astronomy, it is not really of the whole globe that we are tenants, but only of a part of its surface. Above this mean surface, men have found it possible only with the utmost effort and fortitude to ascend something less than seven miles; below it our deepest mining shafts do not pierce a mile. Thus the extreme limits in depth and height to which man may occasionally adventure, though not permanently live, are hardly eight miles. In round numbers the globe is 8000 miles in diameter. Thus the skin of the thinnest-skinned apple gives no idea of the relative thinness of the zone of perpendicular distance to which man is confined. And three fourths of the surface of the globe at its junction with the air is covered by water, on which, though man may pass, he cannot dwell; while considerable parts of what remain are made inaccessible by ice. Like a bridge of hair is the line of temperature that we must keep. Investigators tell us of the existence of temperatures thousands of degrees above zero and thousands of degrees below zero. But man's body must maintain the constant level of a fraction over 98 degrees above zero. A rise or fall of seven degrees either way from this level and he dies. With the permanent rise or fall of a few more degrees in the mean temperature of the surface of the globe it would become uninhabitable by us.

And while all about us, even what seems firmest, is in constant change and motion, so is it with ourselves. These bodies of ours are in reality like the flame of a gas-burner, which has continuous and defined form, but only as the manifestation of changes in a stream of succeeding particles, and which disappears the moment that stream is cut off. What there is real and distinctive in us is that to which we may give a name but cannot explain nor easily define—that which gives to changing matter and passing motion the phase and form of man. But our bodies and our physical powers themselves, like the form and power of the gas-flame, are only passing manifestations of that indestructible matter and eternally pulsing energy of which the universe so far as it is tangible to us is made up. Stop the air that every instant is drawn through our lungs and we cease to live. Stop the food and drink that serve to us the same purpose as coal and water to the steam-engine, and, as certainly, if more slowly, the same result follows.

In all this, man resembles the other animals that with him tenant the superficies of the same earth. Physically he is merely such an animal, in form and structure and primary needs closely allied to the mammalia, with whose species he is zoölogically classified. Were man only an animal he would be but an inferior animal. Nature has not given him the powers and weapons which enable other animals readily to secure their food. Nor yet has she given him the covering which protects them. Had he like them no power of providing himself with artificial clothing, man could not exist in many of the regions he now inhabits. He could live only in the most genial and equable parts of the globe.

But man is more than an animal. Though in physical equipment he may in nothing surpass, and in some things fall below other animals, in mental equipment he is so vastly superior as to take him out of their class, and to make him the lord and master of them all—to make him veritably, of all that we may see, "the roof and crown of things." And what more clearly perhaps than all else indicates the deep gulf which separates him from all other animals is that he alone of all animals is the producer, or bringer forth, and in that sense a maker. In this is a difference which renders the distinction between the highest animal and the lowest man one not of degree but of kind, and which, linked with the animals though he be, justifies the declaration of the Hebrew Scripture, that man is created in the likeness of the All-Maker.

Consider this distinction: We know of no race of men so low that they do not raise fruits or vegetables, or domesticate and breed animals; that do not cook food; that do not fashion weapons; that do not construct habitations; that do not make for themselves garments; that do not adorn themselves or their belongings with ornamentation; that do not show at least the rude beginnings of drawing and painting and sculpture and music. In all the tribes of animated nature below man there is not the slightest indication of the power thus shown. No animal save man ever kindled a fire or cooked a meal, or made a tool or fashioned a weapon.

It is true that the squirrel hides nuts; that birds build nests; that the beaver dams streams; that bees construct combs, in which they store the honey they extract from flowers; that spiders weave webs; that one species of ants are said to milk insects of another kind. All this is true, just as it is also true that there are birds whose melody far surpasses the best music of the savage, and that on tribes below man nature lavishes an adornment of attire that in taste as well as brilliancy surpasses the meretricious adornments of primitive man.

But in all this there is nothing akin to the faculties which in these things man displays. What man does, he does by taking thought, by consciously adjusting means to ends. He does it by adapting and contriving and experimenting and copying; by effort after effort and trial after trial. What he does, and his ways of doing it, vary with the individual, with social development, with time and place and surroundings, and with what he sees others do.

But the squirrel hides its nuts; the birds after their orders build their nests, and in due time force their young to fly; the beaver constructs its dam; the bees store their honey; the spiders weave, and the ants do the work of their societies, without taking thought, without toilsomely scheming for the adapting of means to ends, without experimenting or copying or improving. What they do of such things, they do not as originators who have discovered how to do it; nor yet as learners or imitators or copyists. They do it, first as well as last, unfalteringly and unalteringly, forgetting nothing and improving in nothing. They do it, not by reason but by instinct; by an impulse inhering in their nature which prompts them without perplexity or trial on their part to go so far, but gives them no power to go farther. They do it as the bird sings or the dog barks, as the hen sits on her eggs or the chick picks its way from the shell to scratch the ground.

Nature provides for all living things beneath man by implanting in them blind, strong impulses which at proper times and seasons prompt them to do what it is necessary they should do. But to man she grants only such impellings of instinct as that which prompts the mother to press the new-born babe to her breast and the babe to suckle. With exceptions such as these, she withdraws from man her guiding power and leaves him to himself. For in him a higher power has arisen and looks out on the world—a power that separates him from the brute as clearly and as widely as the brute is separated from the clod; a power that has in it the potency of producing, of making, of causing things to be; a power that seeks to look back into a past ere the globe was, and to peer into a future when it will cease to exist; a power that looks on Nature's show with curiosity like that with which an apprentice might scan a master's work, and will ask why tides run and winds blow, and how suns and stars have been put together; a power that in its beginnings lacks the certainty and promptness of instinct, but which, though infinitely lower in degree, must yet in some sort be akin to that from which all things proceed.

As this power, which we call reason, rises in man, nature withdraws the light of instinct and leaves him to his own devices—to rise or fall, to soar above the brute or to sink lower. For as the Hebrew Scriptures have phrased it, his eyes are opened and before him are good and evil. The ability to fall, no less than the ability to rise—the very failures and mistakes and perversities of man—show his place and powers. There is among the brutes no drunkenness, no unnatural vice, no waste of effort in accomplishing injurious results, no wanton slaughter of their own kind, no want amid plenty. We may conceive of beings in the form of man, who, like these animals, should be ruled by such clear and strong instincts that among them also there would be no liability to such perversions. Yet such beings would not be men. They would lack the essential character and highest powers of man. Fitted perfectly to their environment they might be happy in a way. But it would be as the full-fed hog is happy. The pleasure of making, the joy of overcoming, the glory of rising, how could they exist for such beings? That man is not fitted for his environment shows his higher quality. In him is that which aspires—and still aspires.

Endowed with reason, and deprived, or all but deprived, of instinct, man differs from other animals in being the producer. Like them, for instance, he requires food. But while the animals get their food by taking what they find, and are thus limited by what they find already in existence, man has the power of getting his food by bringing it into existence. He is thus enabled to obtain food in greater variety and in larger quantity. The amount of grass limits the number of wild cattle, the amount of their prey limits the number of the carnivora; but man causes grasses and grains and fruits to grow where they did not grow before; he breeds animals on which he feeds. And so it is with the fulfilment of all his wants; the satisfaction of all his desires. By the use of his animal powers, man can cover perhaps as much ground in a day as can a horse or a dog; he can cross perhaps about as wide a stream. But by virtue of the power that makes him the producer he is already spanning continents and oceans with a speed, a certainty and an ease that not even the birds of most powerful wing and swiftest flight can rival.

CHAPTER III.

HOW MAN'S POWERS ARE EXTENDED.

SHOWING THAT THEIR USE OF REASON WELDS MEN INTO THE SOCIAL ORGANISM OR ECONOMIC BODY.

Extensions of man's powers in civilization—Due not to improvement in the individual but in the society—Hobbes's "Leviathan" —The Greater Leviathan—This capacity for good also capacity for evil.

MAN, as we have any knowledge of him, either in the present or in the past, is always man; differing from other animals in the same way, feeling the same essential needs, moved by the same essential desires, and possessed of the same essential powers.

Yet between man in the lowest savagery and man in the highest civilization how vast the difference in the ability of satisfying these needs and desires by the use of these powers. In food, in raiment, in shelter; in tools and weapons; in ease of movement and of transportation; in medicine and surgery; in music and the representative arts; in the width of his horizon; in the extent and precision of the knowledge at his service—the man who is free to the advantages of the civilization of to-day is as a being of higher order compared to the man who was clothed in skins or leaves, whose habitation was a cave or rude hut, whose best tool a chipped flint, whose boat a hollowed log, whose weapons the bow and arrows, and whose horizon was bounded, as to the past, by tribal tradition, and as to the present by the mountains or sea-shore of his immediate home and the arched dome which seemed to him to shut it in.

But if we analyze the way in which these extensions of man's power of getting and making and knowing and doing are gained, we shall see that they come, not from changes in the individual man, but from the union of individual powers. Consider one of those steamships now crossing the Atlantic at a rate of over five hundred miles a day. Consider the coöperation of men in gathering knowledge, in acquiring skill, in bringing together materials, in fashioning and managing the whole great structure; consider the docks, the storehouses, the branching channels of trade, the correlation of desires reaching over Europe and America and extending to the very ends of the earth, which the regular crossing of the ocean by such a steamship involves. Without this coöperation such a steamship would not be possible.

There is nothing whatever to show that the men who to-day build and navigate and use such ships are one whit superior in any physical or mental quality to their ancestors, whose best vessel was a coracle of wicker and hide. The enormous improvement which these ships show is not an improvement of human nature; it is an improvement of society—it is due to a wider, fuller union of individual efforts in the accomplishment of common ends.

To consider in like manner any one of the many and great advances which civilized man in our time has made over the power of the savage, is to see that it has been gained, and could only have been gained, by the widening coöperation of individual effort.

The powers of the individual man do not indeed reach their full limit when maturity is once attained, as do those of the animal; but, the highest of them at least, are capable of increasing development up to the physical decay that comes with age, if not up to the verge of the grave. Yet, at best, man's individual powers are small and his life is short. What advances would be possible if men were isolated from each other and one generation separated from the next as are the generations of the seventeen-year locusts? The little such individuals might gain during their own lives would be lost with them. Each generation would have to begin from the starting-place of its predecessor.

But man is more than an individual. He is also a social animal, formed and adapted to live and to coöperate with his fellows. It is in this line of social development that the great increase of man's knowledge and powers takes place.

The slowness with which we attain the ability to care for ourselves and the qualities incident to our higher gifts involve an overlapping of individuals that continues and extends the family relation beyond the limits which obtain among other mammalia. And, beyond this relation, common needs, similar perceptions and like desires, acting among creatures endowed with reason and developing speech, lead to a coöperation of effort that even in its crudest forms gives to man powers that place him far above the beasts and that tends to weld individual men into a social body, a larger entity, which has a life and character of its own, and continues its existence while its components change, just as the life and characteristics of our bodily frame continue, though the atoms of which it is composed are constantly passing away from it and as constantly being replaced.

It is in this social body, this larger entity, of which individuals are the atoms, that the extensions of human power which mark the advance of civilization are secured. The rise of civilization is the growth of this coöperation and the increase of the body of knowledge thus obtained and garnered.

Perhaps I can better point out what I mean by an illustration:

The famous treatise in which the English philosopher Hobbes, during the revolt against the tyranny of the Stuarts in the seventeenth century, sought to give the sanction of reason to the doctrine of the absolute authority of kings, is entitled "Leviathan." It thus begins:

> Nature, the art whereby God hath made and governs the world, is by the art of man, as in many other things, so in this also imitated, that it can make an artificial animal. . . . For by art is created that great Leviathan called a commonwealth or state, in Latin *civitas*, which is but an artificial man; though of greater stature and strength than the natural, for whose protection and defense it was intended; and in which the sovereignty is an artificial soul, as giving life and motion to the whole body; the magistrates and other officers of judicature and execution, artificial joints; reward and punishment, by which fastened to the seat of the sovereignty every joint and member is moved to perform his duty, are the nerves, that do the same in the body natural; the wealth and riches of all the particular members, are the strength; *salus populi*, the people's safety, its business; counselors by whom all things needful for it to know are suggested unto it, are the memory; equity and laws, an artificial reason and will; concord, health; sedition, sickness; and civil war, death. Lastly, the pacts and covenants, by which the parts of this body politic were at first made, set together, and united, resemble that fiat, or the "Let us make man," pronounced by God in the creation.

Without stopping now to comment further on Hobbes's suggestive analogy, there is, it seems to me, in the system or arrangement into which men are brought in social life, by the effort to satisfy their material desires—an integration which goes on as civilization advances—something which even more strongly and more clearly suggests the idea of a gigantic man, formed by the union of individual men, than any merely political integration.

This Greater Leviathan is to the political structure or conscious commonwealth what the unconscious functions of the body are to the conscious activities. It is not made by pact and covenant, it grows; as the tree grows, as the man himself grows, by virtue of natural laws inherent in human nature and in the constitution of things; and the laws which it in turn obeys, though their manifestations may be retarded or prevented by political action are themselves utterly independent of it, and take no note whatever of political divisions.

It is this natural system or arrangement, this adjustment of means to ends, of the parts to the whole and the whole to the parts, in the satisfaction of the material desires of men living in society, which, in the same sense as that in which we speak of the economy of the solar system, is the economy of human society, or what in English we call political economy. It is as human units, individuals or families, take their place as integers of this higher man, this Greater Leviathan, that what we call civilization begins and advances.

But in this as in other things, the capacity for good is also capacity for evil, and prejudices, superstitions, erroneous beliefs and injurious customs may in the same way be so perpetuated as to turn what is the greatest potency of advance into its greatest obstacle, and to engender degradation out of the very possibilities of elevation. And it is well to remember that the possibilities of degradation and deterioration seem as clear as the possibilities of advance. In no race and at no place has the advance of man been continuous. At the present time, while European civilization is advancing, the majority of mankind seem stationary or retrogressive. And while even the lowest peoples of whom we have knowledge show in some things advances over what we infer must have been man's primitive condition, yet it is at the same time true that in other things they also show deteriorations, and that even the most highly advanced peoples seem in some things below what we best imagine to have been as the original state of man.

CHAPTER IV.

CIVILIZATION—WHAT IT MEANS.

SHOWING THAT CIVILIZATION CONSISTS IN THE WELDING OF MEN INTO THE SOCIAL ORGANISM OR ECONOMIC BODY.

Vagueness as to what civilization is—Guizot quoted—Derivation and original meaning—Civilization and the State—Why a word referring to the precedent and greater has been taken from one referring to the subsequent and lesser.

THE word civilization is in common use. But it is used with vague and varying meanings, which refer to the qualities or results that we attribute to the thing, rather than to the thing itself the existence or possibility of which we thus assume.

Sometimes our expressed or implied test of civilization is in the methods of industry and control of natural forces. Sometimes it is in the extent and diffusion of knowledge. Sometimes in the kindliness of manners and justice and benignity of laws and institutions. Sometimes it may be suspected that we use the word as do the Chinese when they class as barbarians all humanity outside of the "Central Flowery Kingdom." And there is point in the satire which tells how men who had lost their way in the wilderness, exclaimed at length when they reached a prison: "Thank God, we are at last in civilization!"

This difficulty in determining just what civilization is, does not pertain to common speech alone, but is felt by the best writers on the subject. Thus Buckle, in the two great volumes of the general introduction to his "History of Civilization in England," which was all his untimely death permitted him to complete, gives us his view of what civilization depends on, what influences it, what promotes or retards it; but does not venture to say what civilization is. And thus Guizot, in his "General History of Civilization in Modern Europe," says of civilization itself:

> It is so general in its nature that it can scarcely be seized; so complicated that it can scarcely be unraveled; so hidden as scarcely to be discernible. The difficulty of describing it, or recounting its history, is apparent and acknowledged; but its existence, its worthiness to be described and to be recounted, is not less certain and manifest.

Yet, surely, it ought to be possible to fix the meaning of a word so common and so important; to determine the thing from which the qualities we attribute to civilization proceed. This I shall attempt, not only because I shall have future occasion to use the word, but because of the light the effort may throw on the matter now in hand, the nature of political economy.

The word civilization comes from the Latin *civis*, a citizen. Its original meaning is, the manner or condition in which men live together as citizens. Now the relations of the citizen to other citizens, which are in their conception peaceable and friendly, involving mutual obligations, mutual rights and mutual services, spring from the relation of each citizen to a whole of which each is an integral part. That whole, from membership in which proceeds the relationship of citizens to each other, is the body politic, or political community, which we name the state, and which, struck by the analogy between it and the human body, Hobbes likened to a larger and stronger man made up by the integration of individual men, and called Leviathan.

Yet it is not this political relation, but a relation like it, that is suggested in this word civilization—a relation deeper, wider and closer than the relation of the citizen to the State, and prior to it.

There is a relation between what we call a civilization and what we call a state, but in this the civilization is the antecedent and the state the subsequent. The appearance and development of the body politic, the organized state, the Leviathan of Hobbes, is the mark of civilization already in existence. Not in itself civilization, it involves and presupposes civilization.

And in the same way the character of the state, the nature of the laws and institutions which it enacts and enforces, indicate the character of the underlying civilization. For while civilization is a general condition, and we speak of mankind as civilized, half civilized or uncivilized, yet we recognize individual differences in the characteristics of a civilization, as we recognize differences in the characteristics of a state or in the characteristics of a man. We speak of ancient civilization and modern civilization; of Asiatic civilization and European civilization; of the Egyptian, the Assyrian, the Chinese, the Indian, the Aztec, the Peruvian, the Roman and the Greek civilizations, as separate things, having such general likeness to each other as men have to men, but each marked by such individual characteristics as distinguish one man from other men. And whether we consider them in their grand divisions or in their minor divisions, the line between what we call civilizations is not the line of separation between bodies politic. The United States and Canada, or the United States and Great Britain, are separate bodies politic, yet their civilization is the same. The making of the Queen of Great Britain Empress of India does not substitute the English civilization for the Indian civilization in Bengal, nor the Indian civilization for the English civilization in Yorkshire or Kent. Change in allegiance involves change in citizenship, but in itself involves no change in the civilization. Civilization is evidently a relation which underlies the relations of the body politic as the unconscious motions of the body underlie the conscious motions.

Now, as the relations of the citizen proceed essentially from the relation of each citizen to a whole—the body politic, or Leviathan, of which he is a part—is it not clear, when we consider it, that the relations of the civilized man proceed from his relations to what I have called the body economic, or Greater Leviathan? It is this body economic, or body industrial, which grows up in the coöperation of men to supply their wants and satisfy their desires, that is the real thing constituting what we call civilization. Of this the qualities by which we try to distinguish what we mean by civilization are the attributes. It does indeed, I think, best present itself to our apprehension in the likeness of a larger and greater man, arising out of and from the coöperation of individual men to satisfy their desires, and constituting, after the evolution which finds its crown in the appearance of man himself, a new and seemingly illimitable field of progress.

This body economic, or Greater Leviathan, always precedes and always underlies the body politic or Leviathan. The body politic or state is really an outgrowth of the body economic, in fact one of its organs, the need for which and appearance of which arises from and with its own appearance and growth. And from this relation of dependence upon the body economic, the body politic can never become exempt.

Why, then, it may be asked, is it that we take for the greater and precedent a word drawn from the lesser and subsequent, and find in the word civilization, which expresses an analogy to the body politic, the word that serves us as a name for the body economic? The reason of this is worth noting, as it flows from an important principle in the growth of human knowledge. Things that come first in the natural order are not always first apprehended. As the human eye looks out, but not in, so the human mind as it scans the world is apt to observe what is of the superstructure of things before it observes what is of the foundation.

The body politic is more obvious to our eyes, and, so to speak, makes more noise in our ears, than the unseen and silent body economic, from which it proceeds and on which it depends. Thus, in the intellectual development of mankind, it and its relations are noticed sooner and receive names earlier than the body economic. And the words so made part of our mental furniture, afterwards by their analogies furnish us with words needed to express the body economic and its relations when later in intellectual growth we come to recognize it. Thus it is that while the thing civilization must in the natural order precede the body politic or state, yet when in the development of human knowledge we come to recognize this thing, we take to express it and its relations words already in use as expressive of the body politic and its relations.

But without at present pursuing further that record of the history of thought that lies in the meaning of words, let us endeavor to see whence comes the integration of men into a body economic and how it grows.

CHAPTER V.

THE ORIGIN AND GENESIS OF CIVILIZATION.

SHOWING THE NATURE OF REASON; AND HOW IT IMPELS TO EXCHANGE, BY WHICH CIVILIZATION DEVELOPS.

Reason the power of tracing causal relations—Analysis and synthesis—Likeness and unlikeness between man and other animals—Powers that the apprehension of causal relations gives—Moral connotations of civilization—But begins with and increases through exchange—Civilization relative, and exists in the spiritual.

MAN is an animal; but an animal plus something more—the divine spark differentiating him from all other animals, which enables him to become a maker, and which we call reason. To style it a divine spark is to use a fit figure of speech, for it seems analogous to, if not indeed a lower form of, the power to which we must attribute the origin of the world; and like light and heat radiates and enkindles.

The essential quality of reason seems to lie in the power of tracing the relationship of cause and effect. This power, in one of its aspects, that which proceeds from effect to cause, thus, as it were, taking things apart, so as to see how they have been put together, we call analysis. In another of its aspects, that which proceeds from cause to effect, thus, as it were, putting things together, so as to see in what they result, we call synthesis. In both of these aspects, reason, I think, involves the power of picturing things in the mind, and thus making what we may call mental experiments.

Whoever will take the trouble (and if he has the time, he will find in it pleasure) to get on friendly and intimate terms with a dog, a cat, a horse, or a pig, or, still better,—since these animals, though they have four limbs like ours, lack hands,—with an intelligent monkey, will find many things in which our "poor relations" resemble us, or perhaps rather, we resemble them.

To such a man these animals will exhibit traces at least of all human feelings—love and hate, hope and fear, pride and shame, desire and remorse, vanity and curiosity, generosity and cupidity. Even something of our small vices and acquired tastes they may show. Goats that chew tobacco and like their dram are known on shipboard, and dogs that enjoy carriage-rides and like to run to fires, on land. "Bummer" and his client "Lazarus" were as well known as any two-legged San Franciscan some thirty-five or forty years ago, and until their skins had been affectionately stuffed, they were "deadheads" at free lunches, in public conveyances and at public functions. I bought in Calcutta, when a boy, a monkey which all the long way home would pillow her little head on mine as I slept, and keep off my face the cockroaches that infested the old Indiaman by catching them with her hands and cramming them into her maw. When I got her home, she was so jealous of a little brother that I had to part with her to a lady who had no children. And my own children had in New York a little monkey, sent them from Paraguay, that so endeared herself to us all that when she died from over-indulgence in needle-points and pinheads it seemed like losing a member of the family. She knew my step before I reached the door on coming home, and when it opened would spring to meet me with chattering caresses, the more prolonged the longer I had been away. She leaped from the shoulder of one to that of another at table; nicely discriminating between those who had been good to her and those who had offended her. She had all the curiosity attributed to her sex in man, and a vanity most amusing. She would strive to attract the attention of visitors, and evince jealousy if a child called off their notice. At the time for school-children to pass by, she would perch before a front window and cut monkey shines for their amusement, chattering with delight at their laughter and applause as she sprang from curtain to curtain and showed the convenience of a tail that one may swing by.

How much "human nature" there is in animals, whoever treats them kindly knows. We usually become most intimate with dogs. And who that has been really intimate with a generous dog has not sympathized with the children's wish to have him decently buried and a prayer said over him? Or who, when he saw at last the poor beast's stiffened frame, could, despite his accustomed philosophy which reserves a future life to man alone, refrain from a moment's hope that when his own time came to cross the dark river his faithful friend might greet him on the other shore? And must we say, Nay? The title by which millions of men prefer to invoke the sacred name, it is not "the All Mighty," but "the Most Merciful."

One of the most striking differences between man and the lower animals is that which distinguishes man as the unsatisfied animal. Yet I am not sure that this is in itself an original difference; an essential difference of kind. I am, on the contrary, as I come closely to consider it, inclined rather to think it a result of the endowment of man with the quality of reason that animals lack, than in itself an original difference.

For, on the one side, we see that men when placed in conditions that forbid the hope of improvement do become almost if not quite as stolidly content with no greater satisfactions than their fathers could obtain as the mere animals are. And, on the other side, we see that, to some extent at least, the desires of animals increase as opportunities for gratifying them are afforded. Give a horse lump-sugar and he will come to you again to get it, though in his natural state he aspires to nothing beyond the herbage. The pampered lap-dogs whose tails stick out from warm coats on the fashionable city avenues in winter seem to enjoy their clothing, though they could never solve the mystery of how to get it on, let alone how to make it. They come to want the daintiest food served in china on soft carpets, while dogs of the street will fight for the dirtiest bone. I know a cat in the mountains that lives in the woods all the months when leaves are green, but when they turn and die seeks the farmer's hearth. The big white puss that lies curled in the soft chair beside the stove in the hall below, and who will swell and purr with satisfaction when I scratch her head and stroke her back as I pass down, hardly dared sneak into the house a few weeks ago, but now that she finds she is welcome is content with nothing less than the softest couch and the warmest fire. And the shaggy dog that likes so well to sit in a boat and watch the water as it plashes by, makes me wonder sometimes if he would not want a nicely cushioned naphtha launch if he could make out how to get one. Even man is content with the best he can get until he begins to see he can get better. A handsome woman I have met, who puts on for ball or opera an earl's ransom in gems, and must have a cockade in her coachman's hat and bicycle tires on her carriage-wheels, will tell you that once her greatest desire was for a new wash-tub and a better cooking-stove.

The more we come to know the animals the harder we find it to draw any clear mental line between them and us, except on one point, as to which we may see a clear and profound distinction. This, that animals lack and that men have, is the power of tracing effect to cause, and from cause assuming effect. Among animals this want is to some extent made up for by finer sense-perceptions and by the keener intuitions that we call instinct. But the line that thus divides us from them is nevertheless wide and deep. Memory, which the animals share with man, enables them to some extent to do again what they have been first taught to do; to seek what they have found pleasant, and to avoid what they have found painful. They certainly have some way of communicating their impressions and feelings to others of their kind which constitutes a rudimentary language, while their sharper senses and keener intuitions serve them in some cases where men would be at fault. Yet they do not, even in the simplest cases, show the ability to "think a thing out," and the wiliest and most sagacious of them may be snared and held by devices the simplest man would with a moment's reflection "see his way through." *

Is it not in this power of "thinking things out," of "seeing the way through"—the power of tracing causal relations—that we find the essence of what we call reason, the possession of which constitutes the unmistakable difference, not in degree but in kind, between man and the brutes, and enables him, though their fellow on the plane of material existence, to assume mastery and lordship over them all?

Here is the true Promethean spark, the endowment to

* I do not of course include the animals of fairy tale, nor the superordinary dogs that Herbert Spencer's correspondents write to him about. See Herbert Spencer's "Justice," Appendix D, or my "A Perplexed Philosopher," p. 285.

which the Hebrew Scriptures refer when they say that God created man in His own image; and the means by which we, of all animals, become the only progressive animal. Here is the germ of civilization.

It is this power of relating effect to cause and cause to effect which renders the world intelligible to man; which enables him to understand the connection of things around him and the bearings of things above and beyond him; to live not merely in the present, but to pry into the past and to forecast the future; to distinguish not only what are presented to him through the senses, but things of which the senses cannot tell; to recognize as through mists a power from which the world itself and all that therein is must have proceeded; to know that he himself shall surely die, but to believe that after that he shall live again.

It is this power of discovering causal relations that enables him to bring forth fire and call out light; to cook food; to make for himself coats other than the skin with which nature clothes him; to build better habitations than the trees and caves that nature offers; to construct tools, to forge weapons; to bury seeds that they may rise again in more abundant life; to tame and breed animals; to utilize in his service the forces of nature; to make of water a highway; to sail against the wind and lift himself by the force that pulls all things down; and gradually to exchange the poverty and ignorance and darkness of the savage state for the wealth and knowledge and light that come from associated effort.

All these advances above the animal plane, and all that they imply or suggest, spring at bottom from the power that makes it possible for a man to tie or untie a square knot, which animals cannot do; that makes it impossible that he should be caught in a figure-4 trap as rabbits and birds are caught, or should stand helpless like a bull or a horse that has wound his tethering-rope around a stake or a tree, not knowing in which way to go to loose it. This power is that of discerning the relation between cause and effect.

We measure civilization in various ways, for it has various aspects or sides; various lines along which the general advance implied in the word shows itself—as in knowledge, in power, in wealth, in justice and kindliness. But it is in this last aspect, I think, that the term is most commonly used. This we may see if we consider that the opposite of civilized is savage or barbarous. Now savage and barbarous refer in common thought and implication not so much to material as to moral conditions, and are synonyms of ferocious or cruel or merciless or inhuman. Thus, the aspect of civilization most quickly apprehended in common thought is that of a keener sense of justice and a kindlier feeling between man and man. And there is reason for this. While an increased regard for the rights of others and an increased sympathy with others is not all there is in civilization, it is an expression of its moral side. And as the moral relates to the spiritual, this aspect of civilization is the highest, and does indeed furnish the truest sign of general advance.

Yet for the line on which the general advance primarily proceeds, for the manner in which individual men are integrated into a body economic or greater man, we must look lower. Let us try to trace the genesis of civilization.

Gifted alone with the power of relating cause and effect, man is among all animals the only producer in the true sense of the term. He is a producer, even in the savage state; and would endeavor to produce even in a world where there was no other man. But the same quality of reason which makes him the producer, also, wherever exchange becomes possible, makes him the exchanger. And it is along this line of exchanging that the body economic is evolved and develops, and that all the advances of civilization are primarily made.

But while production must have begun with man, and the first human pair to appear in the world, we may confidently infer, must have begun to use in the satisfaction of their wants a power essentially different in kind from that used by animals, they could not begin to use the higher forms of that power until their numbers had increased. With this increase of numbers the coöperation of efforts in the satisfaction of desires would begin. Aided at first by the natural affections, it would be carried beyond the point where these suffice to begin or to continue coöperation by that quality of reason which enables the man to see what the animal cannot, that by parting with what is less desired in exchange for what is more desired, a net increase in satisfaction is obtained.

Thus, by virtue of the same power of discerning causal relations which leads the primitive man to construct tools and weapons, the individual desires of men, seeking satisfaction through exchange with their fellows, would operate, like the microscopic hooks which are said to give its felting quality to wool, to unite individuals in a mutual coöperation that would weld them together as interdependent members of an organism, larger, wider and stronger than the individual man—the earlier and Greater Leviathan that I have called the body economic.

With the beginning of exchange or trade among men this body economic begins to form, and in its beginning civilization begins. The animals do not develop civilization, because they do not trade. The simulacra of civilization which we observe among some of them, such as ants and bees, proceed from a lower plane than that of reason—from instinct. While such organization is more perfect in its beginnings, for instinct needs not to learn from experience, it lacks all power of advance. Reason may stumble and fall, but it involves possibilities of what seem like infinite progression.

As trade begins in different places and proceeds from different centers, sending out the network of exchange which relates men to each other through their needs and desires, different bodies economic begin to form and to grow in different places, each with distinguishing characteristics which, like the characteristics of the individual face and voice, are so fine as only to be appreciated relatively, and then are better recognized than expressed. These various civilizations, as they meet on their margins, sometimes overlap, sometimes absorb, and sometimes overthrow one another, according to a vitality dependent on their mass and degree, and to the manner in which their juxtaposition takes place.

We are accustomed to speak of certain peoples as uncivilized, and of certain other peoples as civilized or fully civilized, but in truth such use of terms is merely relative. To find an utterly uncivilized people we must find a people among whom there is no exchange or trade. Such a people does not exist, and, so far as our knowledge goes, never did. To find a fully civilized people we must find a people among whom exchange or trade is absolutely free, and has reached the fullest development to which human desires can carry it. There is, as yet, unfortunately, no such people.

To consider the history of civilization, with its slow beginnings, its long periods of quiescence, its sudden flashes forward, its breaks and retrogressions, would carry me further than I can here attempt. Something of that the reader may find in the last grand division of "Progress and Poverty," Book X., entitled, "The Law of Human Progress." What I wish to point out here is in what civilization essentially and primarily consists.

But this is to be remembered: Neither what we speak of as different civilizations nor yet what we call civilization in the abstract or general has existence in the material or is directly related to rivers and mountains, or divisions of the earth's surface. Its existence is in the mental or spiritual.

CHAPTER VI.

OF KNOWLEDGE AND THE GROWTH OF KNOWLEDGE.

SHOWING THAT THE GROWTH OF KNOWLEDGE IS BY COÖPERATION, AND THAT IT INHERES IN THE SOCIETY.

Civilization implies greater knowledge—This gain comes from coöperation—The incommunicable knowing called skill—The communicable knowing usually called knowledge—The relation of systematized knowledge to the means of storing knowledge, to skill and to the economic body—Illustration from astronomy.

IN contrasting man in the civilized state with man in his primitive state I have dwelt most on the gain in the power of gratifying material desires, because such gains are most obvious. Yet as thought precedes action, the essential gain which these indicate must be in knowledge. That the ocean steamship takes the place of the hollow log, the great modern building of the rude hut, shows a larger knowledge utilized in such constructions.

To consider the nature of this gain in knowledge is to see that it is not due to improvement in the individual power of knowing, but to the larger and wider coöperation of individual powers; to the growth of that body of knowledge which is a part, or rather, perhaps, an aspect of the social integration I have called the body economic. If we could separate the individuals whose knowledge, correlated and combined, is expressed in the ocean steamship or great modern building, it is doubtful if their separate knowledge would suffice for more than the constructions and tools of the savage.

The knowledge that comes closest to the individual is what we call skill, which consists in knowing how to govern the organs directly responsive to the conscious will, so as to bring about desired results. Whoever, in mature years, has learned to do some new thing, as for instance to ride a bicycle, knows how slowly and painfully such knowledge is acquired. At first each leg and foot, each arm and hand, to say nothing of the muscles of the chest and neck, seems to need separate direction, which the conscious mind cannot give so quickly and in such order as to prevent the learner from falling off or running into what he would avoid. But as the effort is continued, the knowledge of how to direct these muscles passes from the domain of the conscious to that of the subconscious mind, becoming part of what we sometimes call the memory of the muscles, and the needed correlation takes place with the will to bring about the result, or automatically. For a while, even after one has learned to hold on and keep his wheel moving, the exertion needed will be so great and his attention will be so absorbed in this, that he can look neither to right nor to left, nor notice what he passes.

But with continued effort, the knowledge required for the proper movement of the muscles becomes so fully stored in the subconscious memory that at length the learner may ride easily, indulging in other trains of thought and noticing persons and scenery. His hard-gotten knowledge has passed into skill.

So in learning to use a typewriter. We must at first find out, and with a separate effort strike the key for each separate letter. But as this knowledge takes its place in the subconscious memory, we merely think the word, and without further conscious direction, the fingers, as we need the letters, strike their keys.

This is how all skill is gained. We may see it in the child. We may see him gradually acquiring skill in doing things that we have forgotten that we ourselves had to learn how to do. When a new man comes into the world he seems to know only how to cry. But by degrees, and evidently in the same way by which so many of us over fifty have learned to ride a bicycle, he learns to suck; to laugh; to eat; to use his eyes; to grasp and hold things; to sit; to stand; to walk; to speak; and later, to read, to write, to cipher, and so on, through all the kinds and degrees of skill.

Now, because skill is that part of knowledge which comes closest to the individual, becoming as it were a part of his being, it is the knowledge which is longest retained, and is also that which cannot be communicated from one to another, or so communicated only in very small degree. You may give a man general directions as to how to ride a bicycle or operate a typewriter, but he can get the skill necessary to do either only by practice.

As to this part of knowledge at least, it is clear that the advances of civilization do not imply any gain in the power of the individual to acquire knowledge. Not only do antiquities show that in arts then cultivated the men of thousands of years ago were as skilful as the men of to-day, but we see the same thing in our contact with people whom we deem the veriest savages, and the Australian black fellow will throw a boomerang in a way that excites the wonder of the civilized man. On the other hand, the European with sufficient practice will learn to handle the boomerang or practise any of the other arts of the savages as skilfully as they, and wild tribes to whom the horse and firearms are first introduced by Europeans become excellent riders and most expert marksmen.

It is not in skill, but in the knowledge which can be communicated from one to another, that the civilized man shows his superiority to the savage. This part of knowledge, to which the term knowledge is usually reserved, as when we speak of knowledge and skill, consists in a knowing of the relation of things to other external things, and may, but does not always or necessarily, involve a knowing of how to modify those relations. This knowledge, since it is not concerned with the government of the organs directly responsive to the conscious will, does not come as close to the individual as skill, but is held rather as a possession of the organ of conscious memory, than as a part of the individual himself. While thus subject to loss with the weakening or lapse of that organ, it is also thus communicable from one to another.

Now, this is the knowledge which constitutes the body of knowledge that so vastly increases with the progress of civilization. Being held in the memory, it is transferable by speech; and as the development of speech leads to the adoption of means for recording language, it becomes capable of more permanent storage and of wider and easier transferability—in monuments, manuscripts, books, and so on.

This ability to store and transmit knowledge in other and better ways than in the individual memory and in individual speech, which comes with the integration of individual men in the social body or body economic, is of itself an enormous gain in the advance of the sum of knowledge. But the gain in other and allied directions that comes from the larger and closer integration of individuals in the social man is greater still. Of the systematized knowledges, that which we call astronomy was probably one of the earliest. Consider the first star-gazers, who with no instrument of observation but the naked eyes, and no means of record save the memory, saw by watching night after night related movements in the heavenly bodies. How little even of their own ability to gather and store knowledge could they apply to the getting of such knowledge. For until civilization had passed its first stages, the knowledge and skill required to satisfy their own material needs must have very seriously lessened the energy that could be applied to the gaining of any other knowledge.

Compare with such an observer of the stars, the star-gazer who watches now in one of the great modern observatories. Consider the long vistas of knowledge and skill, of experiment and meditation and effort, that are involved in the existence of the building itself, with its mechanical devices; in the great lenses; in the ponderous tube so easily adjusted; in the delicate instruments for measuring time and space and temperature; in the tables of logarithms and mechanical means for effecting calculations; in the lists of recorded observations and celestial atlases that may be consulted; in the means of communicating by telegraph and telephone with other observers in other places, that now characterize a well-appointed observatory, and in the means and appliances for securing the comfort and freedom from distraction of the observer himself! To consider all these is to begin to realize how much the coöperation of other men contributes to the work of even such a specialized individual as he who watches the stars.

CHAPTER VII.

OF SEQUENCE, CONSEQUENCE AND LAWS OF NATURE.

SHOWING THE PROPER MEANING OF SEQUENCE AND OF CONSEQUENCE, AND WHY WE SPEAK OF LAWS OF NATURE.

Coexistence and succession—Sequence and consequence—Causes in series; names for them—Our direct knowledge is of spirit—Simplest perception of causal relation—Extensions of this—The causal search unsatisfied till it reaches spirit—And finds or assumes intent—Early evidences of this—Why we must assume a superior spirit.—Evidences of intent—The word nature and its implication of will or spirit—The word law—The term "law of nature."

WHETHER all our knowledge of the relations of things in the external world comes to us primarily by experience and through the gates of the senses, or whether there is some part of such knowledge of which we are intuitively conscious and which belongs to our human nature as its original endowment, are matters as to which philosophers are, and probably always will be, at variance. But into such discussions, mainly verbal as they are, it is needless for us to enter. For what concerns us here the distinctions made in ordinary perceptions and common speech will suffice.

In the phenomena presented to him, man must early notice two kinds of relation. Some things show themselves with other things, and some things follow other things. These two kinds of relation we call relations of coexistence and relations of succession or sequence. Since what continues is not so apt to attract our attention as what changes, it is probable that the first of these two relations to be noticed is that of succession. Light comes with the appearance of the luminous bodies of the firmament, and darkness with their disappearance. Night succeeds day, and day night; spring the winter, and summer the spring; the leaf, the bud; and wind and rain the heavy threatening cloud. The approach to fire is followed by a pleasant sensation as we get close enough to it, and by a most painful sensation if we get too close. The eating of some things is succeeded by satisfaction; the eating of other things by pain.

But to note the relation of things in succession does not content man. The essential quality of reason, the power of discerning causal relations, leads him to ask why one thing follows another, and in the relation of sequence to assume or to seek for a relation of con-sequence.

Let us fix in our minds the meaning of these two words. For even by usually careful writers one of them is sometimes used when the other is really meant, which brings about confusion of thought where precision is needed.

The proper meaning of sequence is that which follows or succeeds. The proper meaning of consequence is that which follows from. To say that one thing is a sequence of another, is to say that the one has to the other a relation of succession or coming after. To say that one thing is a consequence of another, is to say that the one has to the other a relation not merely of succession, but of necessary succession, the relation namely of effect to cause.

Now of the sequences which we notice in external nature, some are variable, that is to say, they do not always follow what is given as the antecedent, while some are invariable, that is to say, they always follow what is given as the antecedent. As to these invariable sequences, which we properly call consequences, we give a name to the causal connection between what we apprehend as effect and what we assume as cause by calling it a law of nature. What we mean by this term is a matter too important to be left in the uncertainty and confusion with which it is treated in the standard economic works. Let us therefore, before beginning to use the term, try to discover how it has come into use, that we may fully understand it.

When, proceeding from what we apprehend as effect or consequence, we begin to seek cause, it in most cases happens that the first cause we find, as accounting for the phenomena, we soon come to see to be in itself an effect or consequence of an antecedent which to it is cause. Thus our search for cause begins again, leading us from one link to another link in the chain of causation, until we come to a cause which we can apprehend as capable of setting in motion the series of which the particular result is the effect or consequence.

In a series of causes, what we apprehend as the beginning cause is sometimes called "primary cause" and sometimes "ultimate cause;" while "final cause," which has the meaning of purpose or intent, lies deeper still. This use of seemingly opposite names for the same thing may at first puzzle others as at first it puzzled me. But it is explained when we remember that what is first and what last in a chain or series depends upon which end we start from. Thus, when we proceed from cause towards effect, the beginning cause comes first, and is styled the "primary cause." But when we start from effect to seek cause, as is usually the case, for we can know cause as cause only when it lies in our own consciousness, the cause nearest the result comes first, and we call it the "proximate cause;" and what we apprehend as the beginning cause is found last, and we call it the "ultimate" or "efficient cause," or, at least where an intelligent will is assumed, as the all-originator, the "final cause;" while those which lie between either end of the chain are styled, sometimes "secondary," and sometimes "intermediate causes."

Now the only way in which we can hope to discover what to us is yet unknown is by reasoning to it from what to us is known. What we know most directly and immediately is that in us which feels and wills; that which to distinguish from our own organs, parts or powers we call the ego, or I; that which distinguishes us, ourselves, from the external world, and which is included in the element or factor of the world that in Chapter I. we called spirit.

Man himself, in outward and tangible form at least, is comprehended in nature, even in what, when we make the distinction between subjective and objective, we call external nature. His body is but a part of the, to us, indestructible matter, and the motion which imbues it and through which he may modify external things, is but part of the, to us, indestructible energy which existed in nature before man was, and which will remain, nothing less and nothing more, after he is gone. As I brought into the world no matter or motion, but from the time of my first tangible existence as a germ or cell have merely used the matter and motion already here, so I take nothing away when I depart. Whether, when I am done with it, my body be cremated or buried or sunk in the depths of the sea, the matter which gave it form and the energy which gave it movement do not cease to be, but continue to exist and to act in other forms and other expressions.

That which really distinguishes man from external nature; that which seems to come into the world with the dawning of life and to depart from it with death, is that whose identity I recognize as "me." through all changes of matter and motion. It is this which not only receives the impressions brought to it through the senses, but by the use of the power we call imagination contemplates itself, as one may look at his own face in a mirror. In this way the ego or I of man may reason, not only upon the phenomena of the external world as presented to it through the senses, but also upon its own nature, its own powers, and its own activities, and regard the world, external and internal, as a whole, having for its components not merely matter and energy, but also spirit.

Whatever doubts any one may entertain or profess to entertain of the existence of what we have called spirit, can come only, I think, from a confusion in words. For the one thing of which each of us must be most certain is that "I am." And it is through this assurance of our own existence that we derive certainties of all other existence.

The simplest causal relation we perceive is that which we find in our own consciousness. I scratch my head, I slap my leg, and feel the effects. I drink, and my thirst is quenched. Here we have perhaps the closest connection between consequence and cause. The feeling of head or leg or stomach, which here is consequence, transmitted through sense to the consciousness, finds in the direct perceptions of the same consciousness, the cause—an exertion of the will. Or, reversely, the conscious exertion of the will to do these things produces through the senses a consciousness of result. How this connection takes place we cannot really tell. When we get to that, the scientist is as ignorant as the savage. Yet, savage or scientist, we all know, because we feel the relation in such cases between cause and consequence.

Passing beyond the point where both cause and effect are known by consciousness, we carry the certainty thus derived to the explanation of phenomena as to which cause and effect. one or both, lie beyond consciousness. I throw a stone at a bird and it falls. This result, the fall of the bird, is made known to me indirectly through my sense of sight, and later when I pick it up, by my sense of touch. The bird falls because the stone hit it. The stone hit it because put in motion by the movement of my hand and arm. And the movement of my hand and arm was because of my exertion of will, known to me directly by consciousness.

What we apprehend as the beginning cause in any series, whether we call it primary cause or final cause, is always to us *the* cause or sufficient reason of the particular result. And this point in causation at which we rest satisfied is that which implies the element of spirit, the exertion of will. For it is of the nature of human reason never to rest content until it can come to something that may be conceived of as acting in itself, and not merely as a consequence of something else as antecedent, and thus be taken as the cause of the result or consequence from which the backward search began. Thus, in our instance, leaving out intermediate links in the chain of causation, and proceeding at once from result to ultimate cause, or sufficient reason, we say correctly that the bird fell because I hit it—that is, because I exerted in an effective way the will to hit it.

But I know, by consciousness, that in me the exertion of will proceeds from some motive or desire. And reasoning from what I know to explain what I wish to discover, I explain similar acts in others by similar desires.

So, if one man brain another by striking him with a club, or bring about his death more gradually by giving him a slow poison, we should feel that we were being played with and our intelligence insulted if on asking the cause of death we were told it was because a club struck him, or because breath failed him. We are not satisfied until we know what will was exerted to put into action the proximate causes of the result. Nor does this completely satisfy us. After we know the how, we are apt to ask the why—the purpose or motive that prompted this exertion of will. It is not till we get some answer to this that we feel completely satisfied.

And thus, we sometimes make a still shorter cut in our causal explanation, by dropping will itself, and speaking of the desire which prompts to the exertion of will as the cause of an effect. I see another walk or run or climb a tree. From what I know of the causes of my own acts, I recognize in this an exertion of will prompted by desire—the tangible manifestation of an intent; and say, he walks or runs or climbs the tree because he wants to get or do or avoid something. So when we see the bird fly, the fish swim, the mole or gopher burrow in the ground, we also recognize in their acts similar intent—the exertion of will prompted by desire.

Now, this motive or intent or purpose or desire to bring about an end, which sets an efficient cause to work, was recognized by Aristotle, and the logicians and metaphysicians who so long followed him, as properly a cause and a beginning cause, and called in their terminology the "final cause." This term has now, however, become limited in its use to the idea of purpose or intent in the mind of the Supreme Being, and the "doctrine of final causes," now largely out of fashion, is understood to mean the doctrine which, as the last or final explanation of the existence and order of the world, seeks to discover the purpose or intent of the Creator. The argument from the assumption of what are now called final causes for the existence of an intelligent Creator is called the "teleological argument," and is by those who have the vogue in modern philosophy regarded with suspicion, if not with contempt. Nevertheless, the recognition of purpose or intent as a final or beginning cause is still to be found in that homely logic that fills the common speech of ordinary people with "becauses."

How early and how strong is the disposition to seek cause in the exertion of will prompted by desire is shown in the prattle of children, in folk-lore and fairy tales. We are at first apt to attribute even to what we afterwards learn are inanimate things the exertion of will and the promptings of desire such as we find in our own consciousness, and to say, not as figures of speech, but as recognitions of cause, that the sun smiles and the clouds threaten and the wind blows for this or that purpose or with this or that intent.

And in the earliest of such recognitions we find the moral element, which belongs alone to spirit. What mother has not soothed her child by threatening or pretending to whip the naughty chair or bad stone that caused her little girl or boy to stumble, and has not held the little thing in rapt silence with stories of talking animals and thinking trees? But as we look closer, we see that the power of reason is not in animals, nor volition in sticks and stones. Yet still seeking cause behind effect, and not satisfied that we have found cause until we have come to spirit, we find rest for a while by accounting for effects that we cannot trace to will in men or animals, on the assumption of will in supersensible forms, and thus gratify the longing of the reason to discover cause, by peopling rivers and mountains and lakes and seas and trees and seasons with spirits and genii, and fairies and goblins, and angels and devils, and special gods.

Yet, in and through this stage of human thought grows the apprehension of an order and co-relation in things, which we can understand only by assuming unity of will and comprehensiveness of intent—of an all-embracing system or order which we personify as Nature, and of a great "I am" from whose exertion of will all things visible and invisible proceed, and which is the first or all-beginning cause. In every direction the effort of the reason to seek the cause of what it perceives, forces this upon the thoughtful mind.

The bird flies because it wants to fly. In this will or spirit of the bird we find an ultimate cause or sufficient reason to satisfy us so far as such action is concerned. But probably no man ever lived, and certainly no child, who, seeing the easy sweep of birds through the open highways of air, has not felt the wish to do likewise. Why does not the man also fly when he wants to fly? We answer, that while the bird's bodily structure permits of the gratification of a will to fly, the man's bodily structure does not. But what is the reason of this difference? Here we come to a sphere where we can no longer find the cause of result in the individual will. Seeking still for will, as the only final explanation of cause, we are compelled to assume a higher and more comprehensive will or spirit, which has given to the bird one bodily structure, to the man another.

Or take the man himself. The child cries because it wants to cry and laughs because it wants to laugh. But that its teeth begin to come at the proper age—is it because it wants teeth? In one sense, yes! When its teeth begin to come it begins to need teeth; or rather will shortly begin to need teeth, to fit for its stomach the more solid food it will then require. But in another, and in what we are discussing, the real sense, no! The need for teeth when they begin to come is not a need of the child as it then is, but a need of the child as it will in future be; a totally different being so far as consciousness is concerned. The yet sucking child can no more want teeth, in the sense of desiring teeth, than the adult can want to have those teeth pulled out for the sake of the pulling. The coming of teeth is not pleasant, but painful—seemingly more painful and probably more dangerous than is the pulling of teeth by modern dentistry. It is clearly not by the will of the child that we can explain the coming of teeth. Nor yet can we explain it by the will of the mother. She may desire that the child's teeth should come. But she cannot make her will effective in any larger degree than by rubbing the child's gums. Nor can the most learned physician help her further than by lancing them, should they seriously swell. To find a sufficient cause for this effect, we are compelled to assume a higher will and more comprehensive purpose than that of man; a will conscious from the very first of what will yet be needed, as well as of what already is needed.

The things that show most clearly the adaptation of means to ends, so that we can at once understand their genesis and divine their cause, are things made by man, such as houses, clothing, tools, adornments, machines; in short, what we call human productions. These, as evincing the adaptation of means to ends, have an unmistakable character. The coming upon a piece of clothing, or a brooch or ring, or tomahawk or bow, or the embers and fragments of a cooked meal, would have been as quick and even surer proof of the presence of man on his supposed desert island than were to Robinson Crusoe the footprints in the sand. For of all the beings that our senses give us knowledge of, man is the only one that in himself has the power of adapting means to ends by taking thought.

Yet, so soon as man looks out, he finds in the world itself evidences of the same power of adapting means to ends that characterize his own works. Hence, recognizing in the sum of perceptible things—exclusive of himself or rather of his essential principle or ego, but inclusive, not merely of his bodily, but also of his mental frame—a system or whole, composed of related parts, he personifies it in thought and calls it Nature.

Still, while we personify this, which is to our apprehension the greatest of systems, and give to it in our English speech the feminine gender, it is, I think, as sailors personify a ship, or engine-drivers a locomotive. That is to say, the general perception of the sum of related parts or system, that we call Nature, does not include the idea of the originating will, or first or final cause of all. That, we conceive of as something essentially distinct from Nature, though animating Nature, and give it another name, such as Great Spirit, or Creator, or God. Those who contend that Nature is all, and that there is nothing above or beyond or superior to Nature, do so, I think, by confounding two distinct conceptions, and using the word Nature as meaning what is usually distinguished by the word God.

We all, indeed, frequently use the word Nature to avoid the necessity of naming that which we feel to be unnamable, in the sense of being beyond our comprehension, and therefore beyond our power of defining. Yet I think that not merely the almost universal, but the clearest, and therefore best, perceptions of mankind, really distinguish what we call Nature from what we call God, just as we distinguish the ship, or other machine, that we personify, from the will which we recognize as exerted in its origination and being; and that at the bottom our idea is that of Pope:

> All are but parts of one stupendous whole,
> Whose body Nature is, and God the soul.

It is from this conception of Nature as expressing or as animated by the highest will, that we derive, I think, the term "law of Nature."

We come here to another instance of the application to greater things of names suggested by the less. In original meaning, the word law refers to human will, and is the name given to a command or rule of conduct imposed by a superior upon an inferior, as by a sovereign or state upon those subject to it. At first the word law doubtless referred only to human law. But when, later in intellectual development, men came to note invariable coexistences and sequences in the relations of external things, they were, of the mental necessity already spoken of, compelled to assume as cause a will superior to human will, and adapting the word they were wont to use for the highest expression of human will, called them laws of Nature.

Whatever we observe as an invariable relation of things, of which in the last analysis we can affirm only that "it is always so," we call a law of Nature. But though we use this phrase to express the fact of invariable relation, something more than this is suggested. The term itself involves the idea of a causative will. As John Stuart Mill, trained to analysis from infancy, and from infancy exempt from theological bias, says:

> The expression "law of Nature" is generally employed by scientific men with a sort of tacit reference to the original sense of the word law, namely, the expression of the will of a superior—the superior, in this instance, being the Ruler of the universe.

Thus, then, when we find in Nature certain invariable sequences, whose cause of being transcends the power of the will testified to by our own consciousness—such, for instance, as that stones and apples always fall towards the earth; that the square of a hypothenuse is always equal to the sum of the squares of its base and perpendicular; that gases always coalesce in certain definite proportions; that one pole of the magnet always attracts what the other always repels; that the egg of one bird subjected to a certain degree of warmth for a certain time brings forth a chick that later will clothe itself with plumage of a certain kind and color, and the egg of another bird under the same conditions brings forth a chick of a different kind; that at a certain stage of infancy teeth appear, and later decay and drop out; and so on through the list of invariable sequences that these will suggest—we say, for it is really all that we can say, that these sequences are invariable because they belong to the order or system of Nature; or, in short, that they are "laws of Nature."

The dog and cow sometimes look wise enough to be meditating on anything. If they really could bother their heads with such matters or express their ideas in speech, they would probably say that such sequences are invariable, and then rest. But man is impelled by his endowment of reason to seek behind fact for cause. For that something cannot come from nothing, that every consequence implies a cause, lies at the very foundation of our perception of causation. To deny or ignore this would be to cease to reason—which we can no more cease in some sort of fashion to do than we can cease to breathe.

Thus, whether civilized or uncivilized, man is compelled, of mental necessity, to look for cause beneath the phenomena that he begins really to consider, and no matter what intermediate cause he may find, cannot be content until he reaches will and finds or assumes intent. This necessity is universal to human nature, for it belongs to that quality or principle of reason which essentially distinguishes man from the brute. The notion that—

> The heathen in his blindness,
> Bows down to wood and stone,

is of the real ignorance of pretended knowledge. Beneath the belief of the savage in totems and amulets and charms and witchcraft lurks the recognition of spirit; and the philosophies that have hardened into grotesque forms of religion contain at bottom that idea of an originating will which the Hebrew Scriptures express in their opening sentence: "In the beginning God created the heaven and the earth."

To such recognition of will or spirit, reason, as it searches from effect for cause, must come before it can rest content. Beyond this, reason cannot go. Why is it that some things always coexist with other things? and that some things always follow other things? The Mohammedan will answer: "It is the will of God." The man of our Western civilization will answer: "It is a law of Nature." The phrase is different, but the answer one.

CHAPTER VIII.

OF THE KNOWLEDGE PROPERLY CALLED SCIENCE.

SHOWING THAT SCIENCE DEALS ONLY WITH LAWS OF NATURE, AND THAT IN THE CURRENT POLITICAL ECONOMY THIS HAS BEEN FORGOTTEN.

Proper meaning of science—It investigates laws of nature, not laws of man—Distinction between the two—Their confusion in the current political economy—Mason and Lalor's "Primer of Political Economy" quoted—Absurdity of this confusion—Turgot on the cause of such confusions.

SCIENCE is a word much abused just now, when all sorts of pretenders to special knowledge style themselves scientists and all sorts of ill-verified speculations are called sciences; yet it has a well-defined, proper meaning which may easily be kept in mind. Literally, the word science means knowledge, and when used to distinguish a particular kind of knowledge, should have the meaning of *the* knowledge—that is, of the highest and deepest knowledge. This is, indeed, the idea which attaches to the word. In its proper and definite meaning, science does not include all knowledge or any knowledge, but that knowledge by or in which results or phenomena are related to what we assume to be their cause or sufficient reason, and call a law or laws of nature.

As the knowledge we call skill is that part of knowledge which comes closest to the individual, being retained in the subconscious memory, and hence nearly or completely incommunicable; so, on the contrary, science properly so called is that part of knowledge which comes closer to the higher faculty of reason, being retained in the conscious memory, and hence most easily and completely communicable through the power of speech in which reason finds expression, and through the arts that are extensions of and subservient to speech, such as writing, printing and the like. Something of skill even animals may acquire. Trained dogs, trained goats, trained monkeys and trained bears are common, and even what are called trained fleas are exhibited. But it is impossible to teach an animal science, since animals lack the causal faculty by which alone science is apprehended. It is in youth, when the joints are most flexible and the muscles most supple, that skill is most readily acquired. But it is in the years that bring the contemplative mind that we most appreciate and best acquire science. And so, while the advantages of civilization do not imply increased skill, they do imply the extension of science.

With human laws what is properly called science has nothing whatever to do, unless it be as phenomena which it subjects to examination in the effort to discover in natural law their cause. Thus there may be a science of jurisprudence, or a science of legislation, as there may be a science of grammar, a science of language, or a science of the mental structure and its operations. But the object of such sciences, properly so called, is always to discover the laws of nature in which human laws, customs and modes of thought originate—the natural laws which lie behind and permanently affect, not merely all external manifestations of human will, but even the internal affections of that will itself.

Human laws are made by man, and share in all his weaknesses and frailties. They must be enforced by penalties subsequent to and conditioned upon their violation. Such penalties are called sanctions. Unless accompanied by some penalty for its violation, no act of legislative body or sovereign prince becomes law. Lacking sanction, it is merely an expression of wish, not a declaration of will. Human laws are acknowledged only by man; and that not by all men in all times and places, but only by some men—that is, by men living in the time and place where the political power that imposes them has the ability to enforce their sanctions; and not even by all of these men, but generally by only a very small part of them. Limited to the circumscribed areas which we call political divisions, they are even there constantly fluctuating and changing.

Natural laws, on the other hand, belong to the natural order of things; to that order in which and by which not only man himself but all that is, exists. They have no sanctions in the sense of penalties imposed upon their violation, and enforced subsequent to their violation; they cannot be violated. Man can no more resist or swerve a natural law than he can build a world. They are acknowledged not only by all men in all times and places, but also by all animate and all inanimate things; and their sway extends not merely over and throughout the whole earth of which we are constantly changing tenants, but over and through the whole system of which it is a part, and so far as either observation or reason can give us light, over and through the whole universe, visible or invisible. So far as we can see, either by observation or by reason, they know not change or the shadow of turning, but are the same—yesterday, to-day, to-morrow; for they are expressions, not of the mutable will of man, but of the immutable will of God.

I dwell again on the distinction between laws of nature and laws of man, because it is of the first necessity in beginning the study of political economy that we should grasp it firmly and keep it clearly in mind. This necessity is the greater, since we shall find that in the accredited economic treatises laws of nature and laws of man are confused together in what they call laws of political economy.

It is not worth while to make many quotations to show a confusion which one may see by taking up the economic work approved by college or university that first comes to his hand; but that what passes in these institutions for the science of political economy may speak for itself, I shall make one quotation.

I take for that purpose the best book I can find that puts into compact form the teachings of the scholastic economists—one that is, I think, superior in this to Mrs. Millicent Garrett Fawcett's "Political Economy for Beginners," which at the time I wrote "Progress and Poverty" seemed to me the best short statement of accepted economic teachings I then knew of. It is "The Primer of Political Economy, in Sixteen Definitions and Forty Propositions," by Alfred B. Mason and John J. Lalor (Chicago, A. C. McClurg & Co.).* Messrs. Mason and Lalor, who have since proved themselves to be men of ability, were in 1875, when they wrote the primer, fresh from a university course of political economy and a subsequent study of the approved authorities, and their primer has been widely indorsed and largely used in institutions of learning. This is the first of their sixteen definitions, and their explanation of it:

* In writing this book I have vainly tried to find some such condensation that would do for the "new-school" scholastic economy what Mrs. Fawcett and Messrs. Mason and Lalor have done for the old, and can only conclude that its teachings are too vague to permit of such condensation.

DEFINITION I.—Political Economy is the Science which teaches the laws that regulate the Production, Distribution and Exchange of Wealth.

Everything in this world is governed by law. Human laws are those made by man. All others are natural laws. A law providing for the education of children in schools is a human law. The law that children shall keep growing, if they live, until they are men and women, and shall then slowly decay and at last die, is a natural law. An apple falls from a tree and the earth moves around the sun in obedience to natural laws. The laws which regulate the production, distribution and exchange of wealth are of both kinds. The more important ones, however, are natural.

In this Messrs. Mason and Lalor aptly illustrate the essential difference between natural law and human law. But the way in which the two are mixed together as economic laws suggests the examination-paper of a Philadelphia boy more interested in hooking catfish and stoning frogs than in Lindley Murray. To the question, "Name and describe nouns?" the answer was:

Nouns are three in number and sometimes more. There are proper nouns, common nouns, bloody nouns * and other nouns. Proper nouns are the properest nouns, but common nouns are the commonest. Bloody nouns are the big ones. Other nouns are no good.

Yet ridiculous as is this confusion of human law and natural law, and absurd as is a definition that leaves one to guess which is meant by "laws," this little primer correctly gives what is to be found in the pretentious treatises it endeavors to condense—and that even in the most systematic and careful of them, as I shall hereafter have occasion to show.

It is only with the implication that by law is meant natural law, that we can say, "Everything in this world is

---

* A name given by boys in Philadelphia to large bullfrogs.

governed by law." To say, as the little summary of the scholastic political economy from which I have quoted says, that political economy is the science which teaches the laws, some of them natural laws and some of them human laws, which regulate the production, distribution and exchange of wealth, is like saying that astronomy is the science which teaches the laws, some of them laws of matter and motion and some of them Bulls of Popes and Acts of Parliament, which regulate the movements of stars and comets.

The absurdity of this is not so strikingly obvious in the ponderous treatises from which it is derived as in this little primer, because the attention of the reader is in them confused by the utter want of logical arrangement, and distracted by the shoveling in on him, as it were, of great masses of irrelevant matter, which makes it a most difficult, and with the majority of readers an utterly hopeless task to dig out what is really meant—a task usually abandoned by the ordinary reader with a secret feeling of shame at his own incapacity to follow such deep and learned men, who seem lightly to revel in what he cannot understand. The expositions of what passes for the science of political economy in our schools do indeed for the most part contain some things that really belong to science. But in far larger part what properly belongs to science is, in the literature of political economy that has grown up since his time, confused and overlaid with what Turgot, over a hundred years ago, spoke of as an art—the art, namely, "of those who set themselves to darken things that are clear to the open mind."

What this truly great Frenchman of the eighteenth century said is worth quoting, for it finds abundant and constant illustration in the writings of the professors of political economy of the nineteenth century, and especially in the latest of them:

This art consists in never beginning at the beginning, but in rushing into the subject in all its complications, or with some fact that is only an exception, or some circumstance, isolated, far-fetched or merely collateral, which does not belong to the essence of the question and goes for nothing in its solution. . . . Like a geometer who treating of triangles should begin with white triangles as most simple, in order to treat afterwards of blue triangles, then of red triangles, and so on.

If political economy is a science—and if not it is hardly worth the while of earnest men to bother themselves with it—it must follow the rules of science, and seek in natural law the causes of the phenomena which it investigates. With human law, except as furnishing illustrations and supplying subjects for its investigation, it has, as I have already said, nothing whatever to do. It is concerned with the permanent, not with the transient; with the laws of nature, not with the laws of man.

CHAPTER IX.

THE ECONOMY CALLED POLITICAL ECONOMY.

SHOWING THE MEANING, UNITS AND SCOPE OF POLITICAL ECONOMY.

The word economy—The word political—Origin of the term "political economy" and its confusions—It is not concerned with the body politic, but with the body economic—Its units, and the system or arrangement of which it treats—Its scope.

THE word economy, drawn from two Greek words, house and law, which together signify the management or arrangement of the material part of household or domestic affairs, means in its most common sense the avoidance of waste. We economize money or time or strength or material when we so arrange as to accomplish a result with the smallest expenditure. In a wider sense its meaning is that of a system or arrangement or adaptation of means to ends or of parts to a whole. Thus, we speak of the economy of the heavens; of the economy of the solar system; the economy of the vegetable or animal kingdoms; the economy of the human body; or, in short, of the economy of anything which involves or suggests the adaptation of means to ends, the coördination of parts in a whole.

As there is an economy of individual affairs, an economy of the household, an economy of the farm or workshop or railway, each concerned with the adaptation in these spheres of means to ends, by which waste is avoided and the largest results obtained with the least expenditure, so there is an economy of communities, of the societies in which civilized men live—an economy which has special relation to the adaptation or system by which material wants are satisfied, or to the production and distribution of wealth.

The word political means, relating to the body of citizens or state, the body politic; to things coming within the scope and action of the commonwealth or government; to public policy.

Political economy, therefore, is a particular kind of economy. In the literal meaning of the words it is that kind of economy which has relation to the community or state; to the social whole rather than to individuals.

But the convenience which impels us to abbreviate a long term has led to the frequent use of "economic" when "politico-economic" is meant, so that we may by usage speak of the literature or principles or terms of political economy as "economic literature," or "economic principles," or "economic terms." Some recent writers, indeed, seem to have substituted the term "economics" for political economy itself. But this is a matter as to which the reader should be on his guard, for it has been used to make what is not really political economy pass for political economy, as I shall hereafter show.

Adam Smith, who at the close of the last century gave so powerful an impulse to the study of what has since been called political economy that he is, not without justice, spoken of as its father, entitled his great book, "An Inquiry into the Nature and Causes of the Wealth of Nations;" and what we call political economy the Germans call national economy.

No term is of importance if we rightly understand what it means. But, both in the term "political economy," and in that of "national economy," as well as in the phrase "wealth of nations," lurk suggestions which may and in fact often do interfere with a clear apprehension of the ground they properly cover.

The use of the term "political economy" began at a time when the distinction between natural law and human law was not clearly made, when what I have called the body economic was largely confounded with what is properly the body politic, and when it was the common opinion in Europe, even of thoughtful men, that the production and distribution of wealth were to be regulated by the legislative action of the sovereign or state.

The first one to use the term is said to have been Antoine de Montchretien in his "Treatise on Political Economy" ("Traité de l'économie politique"), published in Rouen, France, 1615. But if not invented by them, it was given currency, some 130 or 140 years after, by those French exponents of natural right, or the natural order, who may to-day be best described as the first single-tax men. They used the term "political economy" to distinguish from politics the branch of knowledge with which they were concerned, and from this called themselves Economists. The term is used by Adam Smith only in speaking of "this sect," composed of "a few men of great learning and ingenuity in France." But although these Economists were overwhelmed and have been almost forgotten, yet of their "noble and generous system" this term remained, and since the time of Adam Smith it has come into general use as expressive of—to accept the most common and I think sufficient definition—that branch of knowledge that treats of the nature of wealth, and the laws of its production and distribution.

But the confusion with politics, which the Frenchmen of whom Adam Smith speaks endeavored to clear away by their adoption of the term "political economy," still continues, and is in fact suggested by the term itself, which seems at first apt to convey the impression of a particular kind of politics rather than of a particular kind of economy. The word political has a meaning which relates it to civil government, to the exercise of human sovereignty by enactment or administration, without reference to those invariable sequences which we call natural laws. An area differentiated from other areas with reference to this power of making municipal enactments and compelling obedience to them, we style a political division; and the larger political divisions, in which the highest sovereignty is acknowledged, we call nations. It is therefore important to keep in mind that the laws with which political economy primarily deals are not human enactments or municipal laws, but natural laws; and that they have no more reference to political divisions than have the laws of mechanics, the laws of optics or the laws of gravitation.

It is not with the body politic, but with that body social or body industrial that I have called the body economic, that political economy is directly concerned; not with the commonwealth of which a man becomes a member by the attribution or acceptance of allegiance to prince, potentate or republic; but with the commonwealth of which he becomes a member by the fact that he lives in a state of society in which each does not attempt to satisfy all of his own material wants by his own direct efforts, but obtains the satisfaction of some of them at least through the coöperation of others. The fact of participation in this coöperation does not make him a citizen of any particular state. It makes him a civilized man, a member of the civilized world—a unit in that body economic to which our political distinctions of states and nations have no more relation than distinctions of color have to distinctions of form.

The unit of human life is the individual. From our first consciousness, or at least from our first memory, our deepest feeling is, that what we recognize as "I" is something distinct from all other things, and the actual mergement of its individuality in other individualities, however near and dear, is something we cannot conceive of. But the lowest unit of which political economy treats often includes the family with the individual. For though isolated individuals may exist for a while, it is only under unnatural conditions. Human life, as we know it, begins with the conjuncture of individuals, and even for some time after birth can continue to exist only under conditions which make the new individual dependent on and subject to preceding individuality; while it requires for its fullest development and highest satisfactions the union of individuals in one economic unit.

While, then, in treating of the subject-matter of political economy, it will be convenient to speak of the units we shall have occasion to refer to as individuals, it should be understood that this term does not necessarily mean separate persons, but includes, as one, those so bound together by the needs of family life as to have, as our phrase is, "one purse."

An economy of the economic unit would not be a political economy, and the laws of which it would treat would not be those with which political economy is concerned. They would be the laws of personal or family conduct. An economy of the individual or family could treat the production of wealth no further than related to the production of such a unit. And though it might take cognizance of the physical laws involved in its agriculture and mechanics, of the distribution of wealth in the economic sense it could not treat at all, since any apportionment among the members of such a family of wealth obtained by it would be governed by the laws of individual or family life, and not by any law of the distribution of the results of socially conjoined effort.

But when in the natural course of human growth and development economic units come into such relations that the satisfaction of material desires is sought by conjoined effort, the laws which political economy seeks to discover begin to appear.

The system or arrangement by which in such conditions material satisfactions are sought and obtained may be roughly likened to a machine fed by combined effort, and producing joint results, which are finally divided or distributed in individual satisfactions—a machine resembling an old-time grist-mill to which individuals brought separate parcels of grain, receiving therefrom in meal, not the identical grain each had put in, nor yet its exact equivalent, but an equivalent less a charge for milling.

Or to make a closer illustration: The system or arrangement which it is the proper purpose of political economy to discover may be likened to that system or arrangement by which the physical body is nourished. The lowest unit of animal life, so far as we can see, is the single cell, which sucks in and assimilates its own food; thus directly satisfying what we may style its own desires. But in those highest forms of animal life of which man is a type, myriads of cells have become conjoined in related parts and organs, exercising different and complex functions, which result in the procurement, digestion and assimilation of the food that nourishing each separate cell maintains the entire organism. Brain and stomach, hands and feet, eyes and ears, teeth and hair, bones, nerves, arteries and veins, still less the cells of which all these parts are composed, do not feed themselves. Under the government of the brain, what the hands, aided by the legs, assisted by the organs of sense, procure, is carried to the mouth, masticated by the teeth, taken by the throat to the alembic of the stomach, where aided by the intestines it is digested, and passing into a fluid containing all nutritive substances, is oxygenized by the lungs; and impelled by the pumping of the heart, makes a complete circuit of the body through a system of arteries and veins, in the course of which every part and every cell takes the nutriment it requires.

Now, what the blood is to the physical body, wealth, as we shall hereafter see more fully, is to the body economic. And as we should find, were we to undertake it, that a description of the manner in which blood is produced and distributed in the physical body would involve almost, if not quite, a description of the entire physical man with all his powers and functions and the laws which govern their operations; so we shall find that what is included or involved in political economy, the science which treats of the production and distribution of wealth, is almost, if not quite, the whole body social, with all its parts, powers and functions, and the laws under which they operate.

The scope of political economy would be roughly explained were we to style it the science which teaches how civilized men get a living. Why this idea is sufficiently expressed as the production and distribution of wealth will be more fully seen hereafter; but there is a distinction as to what is called getting a living that it may be worth while here to note.

We have but to look at existing facts to see that there are two ways in which men (*i.e.*, some men) may obtain satisfaction of their material desires for things not freely supplied to them by nature.

The first of these ways is, by working, or rendering service.

The second is, by stealing, or extorting service.

But there is only one way in which man (*i.e.*, men in general or all men) can satisfy his material desires—that is by working, or rendering service.

For it is manifestly impossible that men in general or all men, or indeed any but a small minority of men, can satisfy their material desires by stealing, since in the nature of things working or the rendering of service is the only way in which the material satisfactions of desire can be primarily obtained or produced.

Stealing produces nothing; it only alters the distribution of what has already been produced.

Therefore, however it be that stealing is to be considered by an individual economy or by an economy of a political division, and with whatever propriety a successful thief who has endowed churches and colleges and libraries and soup-houses may in such an economy be treated as a public benefactor and spoken of as Antony spoke of Cæsar—

> He hath brought many captives home to Rome,
> Whose ransoms did the general coffers fill,

—a true science of political economy takes no cognizance of stealing, except in so far as the various forms of it may pervert the natural distribution, and thus check the natural production of wealth.

Yet, at the same time, political economy does not concern itself with the character of the desires for which satisfaction is sought. It has nothing to do, either with the originating motive that prompts to action in the satisfaction of material desires, nor yet with the final satisfaction which is the end and aim of that action. It is, so to speak, like the science of navigation, which is concerned with the means whereby a ship may be carried from point to point on the ocean, but asks not whether that ship may be a pirate or a missionary barque, what are the expectations which may induce its passengers to go from one place to another, or whether or not these expectations will be gratified on their arrival. Political economy is not moral or ethical science, nor yet is it political science. It is the science of the maintenance and nutriment of the body politic.

Although it will be found incidentally to throw a most powerful light upon, and to give a most powerful support to, the teachings of moral or ethical science, its proper business is neither to explain the difference between right and wrong nor to persuade to one in preference to the other. And while it is in the same way what may be termed the bread-and-butter side of politics, it is directly concerned only with the natural laws which govern the production and distribution of wealth in the social organism, and not with the enactments of the body politic or state.

CHAPTER X.

THE ELEMENTS OF POLITICAL ECONOMY.

SHOWING HOW POLITICAL ECONOMY SHOULD PROCEED AND WHAT RELATIONS IT SEEKS TO DISCOVER.

How to understand a complex system—It is the purpose of such a system that political economy seeks to discover—These laws, natural laws of human nature—The two elements recognized by political economy—These distinguished only by reason—Human will affects the material world only through laws of nature—It is the active factor in all with which political economy deals.

TO understand a complex machine the best way is first to see what is the beginning and what the end of its movements, leaving details until we have mastered its general idea and comprehended its purpose. In this way we most easily see the relation of parts to each other and to the object of the whole, and readily come to understand to the minutest movements and appliances what without the clue of intention might have hopelessly perplexed us.

When the safety bicycle was yet a curiosity even in the towns of England and the United States, an American missionary in a far-off station received from an old friend, unaccompanied by the letter intended to go with it, a present of one of these machines, which for economy in transportation had not been set up, but was forwarded in its unassembled parts. How these parts were to be put together was a perplexing problem, for neither the missionary himself nor any one he could consult could at first imagine what the thing was intended to do, and their guesses were of almost everything but the truth, until at length the saddle suggested a theory, which was so successfully followed that by the time, months afterwards, another ship brought the missing letter, the missionary was riding over the hard sand of the beach on his wheel.

In the same way an intelligent savage, placed in a great industrial hive of our civilization before some enormous factory throbbing and whirring with the seemingly independent motion of pistons and wheels and belts and looms, might, with no guide but his own observation and reason, soon come to see the what, the how and the why of the whole as a connected device for using the power obtained by the transformation of coal into heat in the changing of such things as wool, silk or cotton into blankets or piece-goods, stockings or ribbons.

Now the reason which enables us to understand the works of man as soon as we discover the reason that has brought them into existence, also enables us to interpret nature by assuming a like reason in nature. The child's question, "What is it for?"—what is its purpose or intent? —is the master key that enables us to turn the locks that hide nature's mysteries. It is in this way that all discoveries in the field of the natural sciences have been made, and this will be our best way in the investigation we are now entering upon. The complex phenomena of the production and distribution of wealth in the elaborate organization of modern civilization will only puzzle us, as the many confused and confusing books written to explain it show, if we begin, as it were, from the middle. But if we seek first principles and trace out main lines, so as to comprehend the skeleton of their relation, they will readily become intelligible.

The immense aggregate of movements by which, in civilization, wealth is produced and distributed, viewed collectively as the subject of political economy, constitute a system or arrangement much greater than, yet analogous to, the system or arrangement of a great factory. In the attempt to understand the laws of nature, which they illustrate and obey, let us avoid the confusion that inevitably attends beginning from the middle, by proceeding in the way suggested in our illustration—the only scientific way.

These movements, so various in their modes, and so complex in their relations, with which political economy is concerned, evidently originate in the exertion of human will, prompted by desire; their means are the material and forces that nature offers to man and the natural laws which these obey; their end and aim the satisfaction of man's material desires. If we try to call to mind as many as we can of the different movements that are included in the production and distribution of wealth in modern civilization—the catching and gathering, the separating and combining, the digging and planting, the baking and brewing, the weaving and dyeing, the sewing and washing, the sawing and planing, the melting and forging, the moving and transporting, the buying and selling—we shall see that what they all aim to accomplish is some sort of change in the place, form or relation of the materials or forces supplied by nature so as better to satisfy human desire.

Thus the movements with which political economy is concerned are human actions, having for their aim the attainment of material satisfactions. And the laws that it is its province to discover are not the laws manifested in the existence of the materials and forces of nature that man thus utilizes, nor yet the laws which make possible their change in place, form or relation, but the laws of man's own nature, which affect his own actions in the endeavor to satisfy his desires by bringing about such changes.

The world, as it is apprehended by human reason, is by that reason resolvable, as we have seen, into three elements or factors—spirit, matter and energy. But as these three ultimate elements are conjoined both in what we call man and in what we call nature, the world regarded from the standpoint of political economy has for its original elements, man and nature. Of these, the human element is the initiative or active factor—that which begins or acts first. The natural element is the passive factor—that which receives action and responds to it. From the interaction of these two proceed all with which political economy is concerned—that is to say, all the changes that by man's agency may be wrought in the place, form or condition of material things so as better to fit them for the satisfaction of his desires.

Between the material things which come into existence through man's agency and those which come into existence through the agency of nature alone, the difference is as clear to human reason as the difference between a mountain and a pyramid, between what was on the shores of Lake Michigan when the caravels of Columbus first plowed the waters of the Caribbean Sea and the wondrous White City, beside which in 1893 the antitypes of those caravels, by gift of Spain, were moored. Yet it eludes our senses and can be apprehended only by reason.

Any one can distinguish at a glance, it may be said, between a pyramid and a mountain, or a city and a forest. But not by the senses uninterpreted by reason. The animals, whose senses are even keener than ours, seem incapable of making the distinction. In the actions of the most intelligent dog you will find no evidence that he recognizes any difference between a statue and a stone, a tobacconist's wooden Indian and the stump of a tree. And things are now manufactured and sold as to which it requires an expert to tell whether they are products of man or products of nature.

For the essential thing that in the last analysis distinguishes man from nature can, on the material plane that is cognizable by the senses, appear only in the garb and form of the material. Whatever man makes must have for its substance preëxisting matter; whatever motion he exerts must be drawn from a preëxisting stock of energy. Take away from man all that is contributed by external nature, all that belongs to the economic factor land, and you have, what? Something that is not tangible by the senses, yet which is the ultimate recipient and final cause of sensation; something which has no form or substance or direct power in or over the material world, but which is yet the originating impulse which utilizes motion to mold matter into forms it desires, and to which we must look for the origin of the pyramid, the caravel, the industrial palaces of Chicago and the myriad marvels they contained.

I do not wish to raise, or even to refer further than is necessary, to those deep problems of being and genesis where the light of reason seems to fail us and twilight deepens into dark. But we must grasp the thread at its beginning, if we are to hope to work our way through a tangled skein. And into what fatal confusions those fall who do not begin at the beginning may be seen in current economic works, which treat capital as though it were the originator in production, labor as though it were a product, and land as though it were a mere agricultural instrument —a something on which cattle are fed and wheat and cabbages raised.

We cannot really consider the beginning of things, so far as a true political economy is forced to concern itself with them, without seeing that when man came into the world the sum of energy was not increased nor that of matter added to; and that so it must be to-day. In all the changes that man brings about in the material world, he adds nothing to and subtracts nothing from the sum of matter and energy. He merely brings about changes in the place and relation of what already exists, and the first and always indispensable condition to his doing anything in the material world, and indeed to his very existence therein, is that of access to its material and forces.

So far as we can see, it is universally true that matter and energy are indestructible, and that the forms in which we apprehend them are but transmutations from forms they have held before; that the inorganic cannot of itself pass into the organic; that vegetable life can only come from vegetable life; animal life from animal life; and human life from human life. Notwithstanding all speculation on the subject, we have never yet been able to trace the origin of one well-defined species from another well-defined species. Yet the way in which we find the orders of existence superimposed and related, indicates to us design or thought—a something of which we have the first glimpses only in man. Hence, while we may explain the world of which our senses tell us by a world of which our senses do not tell us, a world of what Plato vaguely called ideas, or what we vaguely speak of as spirit, yet we are compelled when we would seek for the beginning cause and still escape negation to posit a primary or all-causative idea or spirit, an all-producer or creator, for which our short word is God.

But to keep within what we do know. In man, conscious will—that which feels, reasons, plans and contrives, in some way that we cannot understand—is clothed in material form. Coming thus into control of some of the energy stored up in our physical bodies, and learning, as we may see in infancy, to govern arms, legs and a few other organs, this conscious will seeks through them to grasp matter and to set to work, in changing its place and form, other stores of energy. The steam-engine rushing along with its long train of coal or goods or passengers, is in all that is evident to our senses but a new form of what previously existed. Everything of it that we can see, hear, touch, taste, weigh, measure or subject to chemical tests, existed before man was. What has brought preëxisting matter and motion to the shape, place and function of engine and train is that which, prisoned in the engineer's brain, grasps the throttle; the same thing that in the infant stretches for the moon, and in the child makes mud-pies. It is this conscious will seeking the gratification of its desires in the alteration of material forms that is the primary motive power, the active factor, in bringing about the relations with which political economy deals. And while, whatever be *its* origin, this will is in the world as we know it an original element, yet it can act only in certain ways, and is subject in that action to certain uniform sequences, which we term laws of nature.

CHAPTER XI.

OF DESIRES AND SATISFACTIONS.

SHOWING THE WIDTH AND IMPORTANCE OF THE FIELD OF POLITICAL ECONOMY.

Action springs from desire and seeks satisfaction—Order of desires—Wants or needs—Subjective and objective desires—Material and immaterial desires—The hierarchy of life and of desires.

ALL human actions—at least all conscious and voluntary actions—are prompted by desire, and have for their aim its satisfaction. It may be a desire to gain something or a desire to escape something, as to obtain food or to enjoy a pleasing odor, or to escape cold or pain or a noisome smell; a desire to benefit or give pleasure to others, or a desire to do them harm or give them pain. But whether positive or negative, physical or mental, beneficent or injurious, so invariably is desire the antecedent of action that when our attention is called to any human action we feel perplexed if we do not recognize the antecedent desire or motive, and at once begin to look for it, confident that it has to the action the relation of cause to effect.

So confident, indeed, are we of this necessary causal relation between action and desire, that when we cannot find, or at least with some plausibility surmise, an antecedent desire of which the action is an expression, we will not believe that the action took place, or at the least, will not believe that it was a voluntary, conscious action, but will assume, as the older phraseology put it, that the man was possessed by some other human or extra-human will; or, as the more modern phrase puts it, that he was insane. For so unthinkable is conscious, voluntary action without antecedent desire, that we will reject the testimony of others or even the testimony of our own senses rather than believe that a conscious act can take place without motive.

And as desire is the prompter, and the satisfaction of desire is the end and aim, of all human action, all that men seek to do, to obtain or to avoid may be embraced in one term, as satisfactions, or satisfactions of desire.

But of these desires and their corresponding satisfactions, some are more primary or fundamental than others; and it is only as these desires obtain satisfaction that other desires arise and are felt. Thus the desire for air is perhaps the most fundamental of all human desires. Yet its satisfaction is under normal conditions so easily had that we usually are not conscious of it—it is in fact rather a latent than an actual desire. But let one be shut off from air, and the desire to get it becomes at once the strongest of desires, casting out for the moment all others. So it is with other desires, such as those for food and drink, the satisfaction of which is necessary to the maintenance of life and health and the avoidance of injury and pain, and which we share in common with the brute. These primary desires lie as it were beneath, or are fundamental to, the manifold desires which arise in man when they are satisfied. For, while the desires of other animals seem comparatively speaking few and fixed, the desires of man are seemingly illimitable. He is indeed the never-satisfied animal; his desires under normal conditions growing with his power of satisfying them, without assignable limit.

In the same way as we distinguish between necessities and luxuries, so do we often distinguish between what we call "wants" or "needs" and what we speak of simply as desires. The desires whose satisfaction is necessary to the maintenance of life and health and the avoidance of injury and pain—those desires, in short, which come closest to the merely animal plane—we are accustomed to call "wants" or "needs." At least this is the primary idea, though as a matter of fact we often speak of needs or wants in accordance with that usual standard of comfort which we call reasonable, and which is in a large degree a matter of habit. And thus while the satisfaction of desire of some kind is the end and aim of all human action, we recognize, though vaguely, a difference in relative importance when we say that the end and aim of human effort is the satisfaction of needs and the gratification of desires.

Without desire man could not exist, even in his animal frame. And those Eastern philosophies, of which that of Schopenhauer is a Western version, that teach that the wise man should seek the extinction of all desire, also teach that such attainment would be the cessation of individual existence, which they hold to be in itself an evil. But in fact, as man develops, rising to a higher plane, his desires infallibly increase, if not in number at least in quality, becoming higher and broader in their end and aim.

Now, of human desires and their corresponding satisfactions, some may be subjective, that is, relating to the individual mind or thinking subject; and some objective, that is, relating to the external world, the object of its thought. And by another distinction, some may be said to be immaterial, that is, relating to things not cognizable by the senses, *i.e.*, thought and feeling; and some to be material, that is, relating to things cognizable by the senses, *i.e.*, matter and energy.

There is a difference between these two distinctions, but practically it is not a large one. A subjective desire—as when I desire greater love or greater knowledge or happiness for and in my own mind—is always an immaterial desire. But it does not follow that an objective desire is always a material desire, since I may desire greater love or knowledge or happiness for and in the mind of another. Yet we have to remember: 1. That much that we are prone to consider as immaterial seems to be so only because the words we use involve a purely ideal abstraction of qualities from things they qualify, and without which they cannot exist as things really conceived. Love, knowledge or happiness presupposes something which loves, knows or feels, as whiteness presupposes a thing which is white. 2. That while such qualities as love, knowledge or happiness may be predicated of objective though immaterial things, yet, normally at least, we can have no cognizance of such an immaterial thing, or of its states or conditions, except through the material. Deprived of the senses of sight, sound, touch, taste and smell, the gates through which the ego becomes conscious of the material world, how, in any normal way, could I or you know of the love, knowledge, happiness or existence of any other such being? Except, indeed, there be some direct way in which spirit may have knowledge of spirit—a way it may be that is opened when that through the material by the gates of the senses is closed—the exclusion of the material is therefore a practical exclusion of the objective.

I speak of this for the purpose of showing how nearly the field of material desires and satisfactions, within which the sphere of political economy lies, comes to including all human desires and satisfactions. And when we consider how in man the subjective is bound in with the objective, the spiritual with the material, the importance of material desires and satisfactions to human life as a whole is even clearer. For though we may be forced to realize, as the innermost essential of man, a something that is not material; yet this spirit or soul, as in this life we know it.

is incased and imprisoned in matter. Even if subjective existence be possible without the body, the ego as we know it, deprived of touch with matter through the senses, would be condemned to what may be likened to solitary imprisonment.

As vegetable life is built, so to speak, upon inorganic existence, and the animal may be considered as a self-moving plant, plus perhaps an animal soul; so man is an animal plus a human soul, or reasoning power. And while, for reasons I have touched on, we are driven when we think of ultimate origins to consider the highest element of which we know as the originating element, yet we are irresistibly compelled to think of it as having first laid the foundation before raising the superstructure. This is the profound truth of that idea of evolution which all theories of creation have recognized and must recognize, but which is not to be confounded with the materialistic notion of evolution which has of late years been popularized among superficial thinkers. The wildest imagination never dreamed that first of all man came into being; then the animals; afterwards the plants; then the earth; and finally the elementary forces. In the hierarchy of life, as we know it, the higher is built upon the lower, order on order, and is as summit to base. And so in the order of human desires, what we call needs come first, and are of the widest importance. Desires that transcend the desires of the animal can arise and seek gratification only when the desires we share with other animals are satisfied. And those who are inclined to deem that branch of philosophy which is concerned with the gratification of material needs, and especially with the way in which men are fed, clothed and sheltered, as a secondary and ignoble science, are like a general so absorbed in the ordering and moving of his forces as utterly to forget a commissariat; or an architect who should deem the ornamentation of a façade more important than the laying of a foundation.

CHAPTER XII.

THE FUNDAMENTAL LAW OF POLITICAL ECONOMY.

SHOWING THAT THE LAW FROM WHICH POLITICAL ECONOMY PROCEEDS IS THAT MEN SEEK TO SATISFY THEIR DESIRES WITH THE LEAST EXERTION.

Exertion followed by weariness—The fact that men seek to satisfy their desires with the least exertion—Meaning and analogue—Exemplified in trivial things—Is a law of nature and the fundamental law of political economy—Substitution of selfishness for this principle—Buckle quoted—Political economy requires no such assumption—The necessity of labor not a curse.

THE only way man has of satisfying his desires is by action.

Now action, if continued long enough in one line to become really exertion, a conscious putting forth of effort, produces in the consciousness a feeling of reluctance or weariness. This comes from something deeper than the exhaustion of energy in what we call physical labor; for whoever has tried it knows that one may lie on his back in the most comfortable position and by mere dint of sustained thinking, without consciously moving a muscle, tire himself as truly as by sawing wood; and that the mere clash and conflict of involuntary or undirected thought or feeling, or its continuance in one direction, will soon bring extreme weariness.

But whatever be its ultimate cause, the fact is that labor, the attempt of the conscious will to realize its material desire, is always, when continued for a little while, in itself hard and irksome. And whether from this fact alone, or from this fact, conjoined with or based upon something intuitive to our perceptions, the further fact, testified to both by observation of our own feelings and actions and by observation of the acts of others, is that men always seek to gratify their desires with the least exertion.

This, of course, does not mean that they always succeed in doing so, any more than the physical law that motion tends to persist in a straight line means that moving bodies always take that line. But it does mean the mental analogue of the physical law that motion seeks the line of least resistance—that in seeking to gratify their desires men will always seek the way which under existing physical, social and personal conditions seems to them to involve the least expenditure of exertion.

Whoever would see this disposition of human nature exemplified in trivial things has only to watch the passers-by in a crowded street, or those who enter or depart from a frequented house. He will be instructed and perhaps not a little amused to note how slight the obstruction or semblance of obstruction that will divert their steps, and will see the principle observed by saint and sinner—by "wicked man on evil errand bent," and "Good Samaritan intent on works of mercy."

Whether it proceed from experience of the irksomeness of labor and the desire to avoid it, or further back than that, have its source in some innate principle of the human constitution, this disposition of men to seek the satisfaction of their desires with the minimum of exertion is so universal and unfailing that it constitutes one of those invariable sequences that we denominate laws of nature, and from which we may safely reason. It is this law of nature that is the fundamental law of political economy—the central law from which its deductions and explanations may with certainty be drawn, and, indeed, by which alone they become possible. It holds the same place in the sphere of political economy that the law of gravitation does in physics. Without it there could be no recognition of order, and all would be chaos.

Yet the failure clearly to apprehend this as the fundamental law of political economy has led to very serious and wide-spread mistakes as to the nature of the science; and has indeed, in spite of the vigorous assertions and assumptions of its accredited professors, prevented it from truly taking in popular esteem the place of a real science, or from long holding in scholastic circles the credit it had for a while gained. For the principle that men always seek to satisfy their desires with the least exertion, there has been substituted, from the time that political economy began to claim the attention of thoughtful men, the principle of human selfishness. And with the assumption that political economy takes into its account only the selfish feelings of human nature, there have been linked, as laws of political economy, other assumptions as destitute of validity.

To show how completely the idea has prevailed that the foundation of political economy is the assumption of human selfishness, I shall not stop to quote from the accredited writers on the subject, nor yet from those who have made of it a ground of their repugnance to the political economy that has been with justice styled "the dismal science"—such as Carlyle, Dickens or Ruskin. I take for that purpose a writer who, while he fully accepted what was at his time (1857–60) the orthodox political economy, deeming it "the only subject immediately connected with the art of government that has yet been raised to a science," and was well conversant with its literature, was not concerned with it as a controversialist, but only as a historian of the development of thought.

Buckle's understanding of political economy was that it eliminated every other feeling than selfishness. In his "Inquiry into the Influence Exercised by Religion, Literature and Government" (Vol. I., Chapter V., of his "History of Civilization in England"), he says that in the "Wealth of Nations," which he regards as "probably the most important book which has ever been written," Smith "generalizes the laws of wealth, not from the phenomena of wealth, nor from statistical statements, but from the phenomena of selfishness; thus making a deductive application of one set of mental principles to the whole set of economical facts."

And in his "Examination of the Scotch Intellect during the Eighteenth Century" (Vol. II., Chapter VI.), he returns in greater detail to the same subject. Adam Smith, he says, wrote two great books, with an interval of seventeen years between them. In both he employed the same method, that form of deduction "which proceeds by an artificial separation of facts in themselves inseparable." In the first of these, the "Theory of Moral Sentiments," he "so narrowed the field of inquiry as to exclude from it all consideration of selfishness as a primary principle, and only to admit its great antagonist, sympathy." In the second, the "Wealth of Nations," which Buckle regards as a correlative part of Smith's one great scheme, though still greater than its predecessor, Smith, on the contrary, "assumes that selfishness is the main regulator of human affairs, just as in his previous work he had assumed sympathy to be so." Or, as Buckle, later on, repeats:

> He everywhere assumes that the great moving power of all men, all interests and all classes, in all ages and in all countries, is selfishness. The opposite power of sympathy he entirely shuts out; and I hardly remember an instance in which even the word occurs in the

whole course of his work. Its fundamental assumption is, that each man exclusively follows his own interest, or what he deems to be his own interest. . . . In this way Adam Smith completely changes the premises he had assumed in his earlier work. Here, he makes men naturally selfish; formerly, he had made them naturally sympathetic. Here, he represents them pursuing wealth for sordid objects, and for the narrowest personal pleasures; formerly, he represented them as pursuing it out of regard to the sentiments of others, and for the sake of obtaining their sympathy. In the "Wealth of Nations" we hear no more of this conciliatory and sympathetic spirit; such amiable maxims are altogether forgotten, and the affairs of the world are regulated by different principles. It now appears that benevolence and affection have no influence over our actions. Indeed, Adam Smith will hardly admit common humanity into his theory of motives. If a people emancipate their slaves, it is a proof, not that the people are acted on by high moral considerations, nor that their sympathy is excited by the cruelty inflicted on these unhappy creatures. Nothing of the sort. Such inducements to conduct are imaginary and exercise no real sway. All that the emancipation proves, is, that the slaves were few in number, and, therefore, small in value. Otherwise they would not have been emancipated.

So, too, while in his former work he had ascribed the different systems of morals to the power of sympathy, he, in this work, ascribes them entirely to the power of selfishness.

This presumption, so well stated and defended by Buckle, that political economy must eliminate everything but the selfish feelings of mankind, has continued to pervade the accredited political economy up to this time, whatever may have been the effects upon the common mind of the attacks made upon it by those, who, not putting their objections into logical and coherent form, could be spoken of as sentimentalists, but not political economists. Yet, however generally the accepted writers on political economy may have themselves supposed the assumption of universal selfishness to be the fundamental principle of political economy, or how much ground they may have given for such a supposition on the part of their readers, a true political economy requires no such assumption. The primary postulate on and from which its whole structure is built is not that all men are governed only by selfish motives, or must for its purposes be considered as governed only by selfish motives; it is that all men seek to gratify their desires, whatever those desires may be, with the least exertion. This fundamental law of political economy is, like all other laws of nature, so far as we are concerned, supreme. It is no more affected by the selfishness or unselfishness of our desires than is the law of gravitation. It is simply a fact.

The irksomeness or weariness that inevitably attends all continued exertion caused earlier men to look on the necessity of labor to production as a penalty imposed upon our kind by an offended Deity. But in the light of modern civilization we may see that what they deemed a curse is in reality the impulse that has led to the most enormous extensions of man's power of dealing with nature. So true is it that good and evil are not in external things or in their laws of action, but in will or spirit.

CHAPTER XIII.

METHODS OF POLITICAL ECONOMY.

SHOWING THE NATURE OF THE METHODS OF INVESTIGATION THAT MAY BE USED IN POLITICAL ECONOMY.

Deductive and inductive schools—"New American Cyclopedia" quoted—Triumph of the inductionists—The method of induction and the method of deduction—Method of hypothesis—Bacon's relation to induction—Real error of the deductionists and the mistake of the inductionists—Lalor's Cyclopedia quoted—Result of the triumph of the inductionists—A true science of political economy must follow the deductive method—Davis's "Elements of Inductive Logic" quoted—Double assurance of the real postulate of political economy—Method of mental or imaginative experiment.

A MISCONCEPTION of the fundamental law on which a science is based must lead to divergences and confusions as the attempt to develop that science proceeds.

In the case of political economy, the result of the assumption that its fundamental principle is human selfishness is shown in disputes and confusions as to its proper method. These began shortly after it was recognized as deserving the attention of the institutions of learning, and are an increasingly noticeable feature in economic literature for some sixty or seventy years. Adam Smith and the most prominent of his successors followed the deductive method. But ere long there began to be questionings as to whether the inductive method was not the proper one. Having on their side the weight of authority, the defenders of the deductive method, or "old school" political economy, as it began to be called, held for a long time their formal position, though compelled by the incongruities of the system they were endeavoring to uphold to make damaging deductions and weakening admissions; while the opposition to them, called by various names, but generally known as inductive or "new school" economists, gathered strength.

What lay beneath this contest, which was largely verbal, and in which there was confusion on both sides, I shall have occasion to speak of hereafter; but as to how it seemed to stand in the scholastic world at the beginning of the seventh decade of our century I quote from the article "Political Economy" in the "New American Cyclopedia" (1861), which, as written by an opponent of the then orthodox school (Henry Carey Baird), with an evident desire to be entirely fair, will I think better show the actual situation at that time than anything else I can find:

> The progress thus far made in political economy has been slow and uncertain, and there is in its entire range hardly a doctrine or even the definition of an important word which is universally or even generally accepted beyond dispute. . . . Amid all their discords and disagreements it is possible to divide political economists under two general heads: those who treat the subject as a deductive science, "in which all the general propositions are in the strictest sense of the word hypothetical;" and those who treat it by the inductive or Baconian method. Of the first-named school are all the English economists and most of those of continental Europe who have acquired any reputation. As the representatives of the last, Mr. Henry C. Carey and his followers are most prominent.*

---

* As illustrating the looseness with which the words "inductive" and "deductive" have been thrown around in this discussion as to the proper method of political economy, it may be worth mentioning that the same Henry C. Carey, who is here cited as the most prominent representative of the inductive school, as opposed to the deduc-

Thus, in 1861, the deductive method, even to the view of an adherent of the opposing school, still formally held sway in the scholastic world. But at present, as the century nears its close, it has so utterly lost its hold that so far as I can discover, there is not now a prominent college or university anywhere in which the professed teachers of what is reputed to be political economy adhere to what was then called the deductive method.

Yet this triumph in scholastic opinion of the advocates of what is called the inductive method is in reality but the triumph of one set of confusions over another set of confusions, in which the determining element has been the vague consciousness that the previously authoritative political economy was not a true political economy. Where a new set of confusions is pitted against an old set of confusions, the victory must finally and for a time remain with the new; for the reason that on the old lies the burden of defending what is indefensible, while the new has for a while only the easier task of attack. What this passing phase of economic thought really shows is the utter confusion into which the whole scholastic political economy has fallen from lack of care as to first principles. In my view of the matter those who have said that the deductive method was the proper method of political economy have been right as to that, but wrong in principles from which they have made deductions; while those who contended for the inductive method have been wrong as to that, but right as to the weaknesses of their opponents.

As to the course of what has been called the science of

tive school of Smith, Ricardo and Mill, is in the biographical notice of him in the latest successor of the "New American Cyclopedia," the revised edition of "Johnson's Universal Cyclopedia" (1895), said to be "the founder of a school of political economy whose principles are anti-socialistic and more deductive than those of Smith, Ricardo and Mill."

political economy and the destructive revolution which it has of late years undergone, I shall have occasion to speak in the next book. I am here concerned in clearing only what might be a perplexity to the reader in regard to the proper methods of the real science.

The human reason has two ways of ascertaining truth. The first of these is that of reasoning from particulars to generals in an ascending line, until we come at last to one of those invariable uniformities that we call laws of nature. This method we call the inductive, or *a posteriori*. But when we have reached what we feel sure is a law of nature, and as such true in all times and places, then an easier and more powerful method of ascertaining truth is open to us—the method of reasoning in the descending line from generals to particulars. This is the method that we call the deductive, or *a priori* method. For knowing what is the general law, the invariable sequence that we call a law of nature, we have only to discover that a particular comes under it to know what is true in the case of that particular.

In the relation of priority the two methods stand in the order in which I have named them—induction being the first or primary method of applying human reason to the investigation of facts, and deduction being the second or derivative. So far as our reason is concerned, induction must give the facts on which we may proceed to deduction. Deduction can safely be based only on what has been supplied to the reason by induction; and where the validity of this first step is called in question, must apply to induction for proof. Both methods are proper to the careful investigation that we speak of as scientific: induction in its preliminary stages, when it is groping for the law of nature; deduction when it has discovered that law, and is thus able to proceed by a short cut from the general to the particular, without any further need for the more laborious and, so to speak, uphill method of induction, except it may be to verify its conclusions.

There is a further method of investigation, which consists in a combination of these two original methods of the reason, and which has been found most effective in the discovery of truth in the physical sciences. When our inductions so point to the existence of a natural law that we are able to form a surmise or suspicion of what it may prove to be, we may tentatively assume the existence of such a law, and proceed to see whether particulars will fall into place in deductions made from it. This is the method of tentative deduction, or hypothesis.

The inductive method is sometimes, as in the last quotation I have made, spoken of as the Baconian method, and the great name of Bacon has been freely used to give plausibility to what the advocates of the "new school" in political economy have called the inductive method. But whatever originality there may have been in his classifications and devices, Bacon did not invent the inductive method. It was by that method that man's reason has from the first enabled him to apprehend laws of nature that he has subsequently used as bases for deduction. It was thus that he must have learned what we are accustomed to think the simplest of nature's uniformities—such as, that after an interval a new moon succeeds the old moon; that the sun, after apparently tending to the south for a while, turns again to the north; that fire will burn, and that water will quench fire. What Bacon did was not to invent or discover the inductive method, but to formulate some rules for its application and to apply it to the investigation of fields of knowledge from which it had been long shut out by a blind reliance upon authority—by a false assumption that wiser men who had gone before had taught all there was worth knowing on certain subjects, and that there remained for those who came after nothing further to do than to make deductions from premises their predecessors had supplied.

Where the application of the inductive method was really needed in what is now called by the "new lights" the "classical" political economy was to test the premises from which its deductions were made, and to clear them of what had no better warrant than a disposition to use political economy to justify existing social arrangements. It was not needed to take the place of the deductive method, where that was applicable. For the deductive method, when applied to the further extension of what has already been validly ascertained, constitutes the most powerful means of extending knowledge that the human mind can avail itself of.

In its use of the deductive method after its premises had been settled, the classical political economy was not in error. The error that gave insecurity to its whole structure lay deeper still, in the insufficient inductions on which those premises rested. But, instead of addressing themselves to these flaws in its accepted premises, the various schools of economists generally classed as inductive have denied that there were any general principles that could with certainty be laid down as the basis for deduction. Thus, if such a question be asked them as, does free trade or protection best promote a general prosperity? or, what is the best system of land-tenure? or, what is the best system of taxation? or, what are the limits of governmental interference with industry, or trade-union regulations? no general answer can be given. It can only be said that one thing may be best in one place and time, and another in another place and time, so that the matter can be determined only by special investigations. In other words, to quote the phrase of Professor James, of the University of Pennsylvania, an adherent of the "new school" (article, "Political Economy," in Lalor's "Cyclopedia of Political Science, Political Economy and United States History," 1884), they have opposed "the theory which seeks eternally valid natural laws in economics, and which considers the natural condition of unlimited personal freedom as the only justifiable one, without regard to the needs of special times and nations."

The result, therefore, of the triumph of the "inductionists" over the "deductionists" in the accredited organs of economic teaching, has been to destroy in the "new" political economy even the semblance of coherency that it had in the "old," and to decompose it into a congeries of unrelated doctrines and unverified speculations which only its professors can presume to understand, and as to which they can dispute and quarrel with each other in the wild abandon that results from the absence of any recognized common principle.

But to me it seems clear that if political economy can be called a science at all, it must as a science, that is to say from the moment the laws of nature on which it depends are discovered, follow the deductive method of examination, using induction only to test the conclusions thus obtained. For the particulars which are included in its province are too vast and too complex to admit of any hope of bringing them into order and relation by direct induction.

To quote from the latest elementary text-book of logic of which I know, Professor Noah K. Davis's "Elements of Inductive Logic" (Harper Bros., New York, 1893), p. 197:

> The great object of the scientist is to obtain by rigid induction the laws of nature, and to follow them by rigid deduction to their consequences. A science at first wholly inductive becomes, as soon as a law has been proved, more or less deductive, and as it progresses, rising to higher and wider but fewer inductions, the deductive processes increase in number and importance, until it is no longer properly an inductive, but a deductive science. Thus, hydrostatics, acoustics, optics and electricity, commonly called inductive sciences,

have passed under the dominion of mathematics, from inductive to deductive sciences and mechanics has a like history. Celestial mechanics as founded in the "Principia" of Newton is mainly inductive, as elaborated in the "Mécanique Céleste" of Laplace, is mainly deductive. By pursuing this latter process it has multiplied its matter and reached its present high perfection. A revolution is quietly progressing in all the natural sciences. Bacon changed their method from deductive to inductive, and it is now rapidly reverting from inductive to deductive. The task of logic is to explicate and regulate these methods.

Now the law of nature which forms the postulate of a true science of political economy is not, as has been erroneously assumed, that men are invariably and universally selfish. As a matter of fact, this is not true. Nor can we abstract from man all but selfish qualities in order to make as the object of our thought on economic matters what has been called the "economic man," without getting what is really a monster, not a man.

The law of nature which is really the postulate of a true science of political economy is that men always seek to gratify their desires with the least exertion, whether those desires are selfish or unselfish, good or bad.

That this is a law of nature we have the highest possible warrant, wider in fact than we can have for any of the laws of external nature, such for instance as the law of gravitation. For the laws of external nature can be apprehended only objectively. But that it is a law of nature that men seek to gratify their desires with the least exertion, we may see both subjectively and objectively. Since man himself is included in nature, we may subjectively reach the law of nature that men seek to gratify their desires with the least exertion, by an induction derived from consciousness of our own feelings and an analysis of our own motives of action; while objectively we may also reach the same law by an induction derived from observation of the acts of others.

Proceeding from a law of nature thus doubly assured, the proper method of a political economy which becomes really a science by its correct apprehension of a fundamental law, is the method of deduction from that law, the method of proceeding from the general to the particular; for this is the method which will enable us to attain incomparably greater results. To abandon that method and resort to what the "new lights" of political economy seem really to mean by induction, would be as though we were to discard the rules of arithmetic and endeavor by direct inquiries in all parts of the world to discover how much one number added to another would make, and what would be the quotient of a sum divided by itself.

Thus, in the main, the science of political economy resorts to the deductive method, using induction for its tests. But in its more common investigations its most useful instrument is a form of hypothesis which may be called that of mental or imaginative experiment,* by which we may separate, combine or eliminate conditions in our own imaginations, and thus test the working of known principles. This is a most common method of reasoning, familiar to us all, from our very infancy. It is the great working tool of political economy, and in its use we have only to be careful as to the validity of what we assume as principles.

---

* See lecture delivered by me before the students of the University of California on "The Study of Political Economy," April, 1877, reprinted in "Popular Science Monthly," March, 1880.

CHAPTER XIV.

POLITICAL ECONOMY AS SCIENCE AND AS ART.

SHOWING THAT POLITICAL ECONOMY IS PROPERLY A SCIENCE, AND THE MEANING IT SHOULD HAVE IF SPOKEN OF AS ART.

Science and art—There must be a science of political economy, but no proper art—What must be the aim of an art of political economy—White art and black art—Course of further investigation.

THERE is found among economic writers much dispute not only as to the proper method of political economy, but also as to whether it should be spoken of as a science or as an art. There are some who have styled it a science, and some who have styled it an art, and some who speak of it as both science and art. Others again make substantially the same division, into abstract or theoretical or speculative political economy, on the one side, and concrete or normative or regulative or applied political economy, on the other side.

Into this matter, however, it is hardly worth while for us to enter at any length, since the reasons for considering a proper political economy as a science rather than an art have been already given. It is only necessary to observe that where systematized knowledge may be distinguished, as it sometimes is, into two branches, science and art, the proper distinction between them is that the one relates to what we call laws of nature; the other to the manner in which we may avail ourselves of these natural laws to attain desired ends.

This first branch of knowledge, it is clear, is in political economy the primary and most important. It is only as we know the natural laws of the production and distribution of wealth that we can previse the result of the adjustments and regulations which human laws attempt. And as whoever wishes to understand and treat the diseases and accidents of the human frame would properly begin by studying it in its normal condition, noting the position, relation and functions of the organs in a state of perfect health; so any study of the faults, aberrations and injuries which occur in the economy of society comes best after the study of its natural and normal condition.

There may be disputes as to whether there is yet a science of political economy, that is to say, whether our knowledge of the natural economic laws is as yet so large and well digested as to merit the title of science. But among those who recognize that the world we live in is in all its spheres governed by law, there can be no dispute as to the possibility of such a science.

And as there can be only one science of chemistry, one science of astronomy and one science of physiology, which, in so far as they are really sciences, must be true and invariable, so, while there may be various opinions, various teachings, various hypotheses (or in a loose and improper but exceedingly common use of the word, various theories), of political economy, there can be only one science. And it, in so far as it is really a science—that is to say, in so far as we have really discovered and related the natural laws which are within its province—must in all times and places be true and invariable. For we live in a world where the same effects always follow the same causes and where nothing is capricious, unless indeed it be that something within us which desires, wills and chooses. But this in man, that seems, to a certain extent at least, independent of the external nature that is recognized by our senses, can manifest itself only in accordance with natural laws, and can accomplish its external purposes only by using those laws.

When we shall have worked out the science of political economy—when we shall have discovered and related the natural laws which govern the production and distribution of wealth, we shall then be in position to see the effect of human laws and customs. But it does not seem to me that a knowledge of the effect which natural laws of the production and distribution of wealth bring about in the outcome of human laws, customs and efforts, can be properly spoken of as an art of political economy, or that the knowledge properly classified under the term political economy, can be divided, as some writers have attempted to divide it, into a science and an art. There is a science of astronomy, which has its applications in such arts as those of navigation and surveying; but no art of astronomy. There is a science of chemistry, which has its applications in many arts; but no art of chemistry. And so the science of political economy finds its applications in politics and its various subdivisions. But these applications can hardly be spoken of as constituting an art of political economy.

Yet if we choose, as some have done, to speak of political economy as both science and art, then the art of political economy is the art of securing the greatest production and the fairest distribution of wealth; the art whose proper object it is to abolish poverty and the fear of poverty, and so lift the poorest and weakest of mankind above the hard struggle to live. For if there be an art of political economy, it must be the noble art that has for its object the benefit of all members of the economic community.

But just as when men believed in magic they held that there was both a white magic and a black magic—an art which aimed at alleviating suffering and doing good, and an art which sought knowledge for selfish and evil ends—so, in this view, it may be said that there is a white political economy and a black political economy. Where a knowledge of the laws of the production and distribution of wealth is used to enrich a few at the expense of the many, or even where a reputed knowledge of those laws is used to bolster up such injustice, and by darkening counsel to prevent or delay the reform of it, such art of political economy, real or reputed, is truly a black art. This is the art of which the great Turgot spoke.

For our part, having seen the nature and scope of the science of political economy, for which we adopt the older definition—the science that investigates the nature of wealth and the laws of its production and distribution—let us proceed in this order, endeavoring to discover: (1) the nature of wealth; (2) the laws of its production; and then (3) the laws of its distribution. When this is done we shall have accomplished all that is necessary for a true science of political economy, as I understand it. It will not be necessary for us to consider the matter of the consumption of wealth; nor, indeed, as I shall hereafter show, is a true political economy concerned with consumption, as many of the minor economic writers have assumed it to be.

BOOK II.

—

THE NATURE OF WEALTH.

Definitions are the basis of systematic reasoning. —*Aristotle.*

The mixture of those things by speech which are by nature divided is the mother of all error.—*Hooker.*

Bacon made us sensible of the emptiness of the Aristotelian philosophy; Smith, in like manner, caused us to perceive the fallaciousness of all the previous systems of political economy; but the latter no more raised the superstructure of this science, than the former created logic. . . . We are, however, not yet in possession of an established text-book on the science of political economy, in which the fruits of an enlarged and accurate observation are referred to general principles that can be admitted by every reflecting mind; a work in which these results are so complete and well arranged as to afford to each other mutual support, and that may everywhere and at all times be studied with advantage.—*J. B. Say, 1803.*

We may cite as examples of such inchoate but yet incomplete discoveries the great "Wealth of Nations" by Adam Smith—a work which still stands out, and will ever stand out, as that of a pioneer, and the only book on political economy which displays its genius to every kind of intelligent reader. But among the specialists and the schools, this work of genius which swayed all Europe in its day, is laid upon the shelf as an antiquated affair, superseded by the smaller and duller men who have pulled his system to pieces and are offering us the fragments as a science most of whose first principles are still under dispute.—*Professor (Greek) J. P. Mahaffy, "The Present Position of Egyptology," "Nineteenth Century," August, 1894.*

CONTENTS OF BOOK II.

THE NATURE OF WEALTH.

CHAPTER VI.

SMITH'S INFLUENCE ON POLITICAL ECONOMY.

SHOWING WHAT THE "WEALTH OF NATIONS" ACCOMPLISHED AND THE COURSE OF THE SUBSEQUENT DEVELOPMENT OF POLITICAL ECONOMY.

CHAPTER VII.

INEFFECTUAL GROPINGS TOWARD A DETERMINATION OF WEALTH.

SHOWING THE OPPOSITION TO THE SCHOLASTIC ECONOMY BEFORE "PROGRESS AND POVERTY."

CHAPTER VIII.

BREAKDOWN OF SCHOLASTIC POLITICAL ECONOMY.

SHOWING THE REASON, THE RECEPTION, AND EFFECT ON POLITICAL ECONOMY OF "PROGRESS AND POVERTY."

CHAPTER IX.

WEALTH AND VALUE.

SHOWING THE REASON FOR CONSIDERING THE NATURE OF VALUE BEFORE THAT OF WEALTH.

CHAPTER X.

VALUE IN USE AND VALUE IN EXCHANGE.

SHOWING THE TWO SENSES OF VALUE; HOW THE DISTINCTION HAS BEEN IGNORED, AND ITS REAL VALIDITY; AND THE REASON FOR CONFINING THE ECONOMIC TERM TO ONE SENSE.

CHAPTER XI.

ECONOMIC VALUE—ITS REAL MEANING AND FINAL MEASURE.

SHOWING HOW VALUE IN EXCHANGE HAS BEEN DEEMED A RELATION OF PROPORTION; AND THE AMBIGUITY WHICH HAS LED TO THIS.

CHAPTER XII.

VALUE IN EXCHANGE REALLY RELATED TO LABOR.

SHOWING THAT VALUE DOES NOT COME FROM EXCHANGEABILITY, BUT EXCHANGEABILITY FROM VALUE, WHICH IS AN EXPRESSION OF THE SAVING OF LABOR INVOLVED IN POSSESSION.

CHAPTER XIII.

THE DENOMINATOR OF VALUE.

SHOWING WHAT VALUE IS, AND ITS RELATIONS.

CHAPTER XIV.

THE TWO SOURCES OF VALUE.

SHOWING THAT THERE IS A VALUE FROM PRODUCTION AND ALSO A VALUE FROM OBLIGATION.

CHAPTER XV.

THE MEANING OF WEALTH IN POLITICAL ECONOMY.

SHOWING HOW VALUE FROM PRODUCTION IS WEALTH IN POLITICAL ECONOMY.

CHAPTER XIX.

MORAL CONFUSIONS AS TO WEALTH.

SHOWING HOW RICH AND POOR ARE CORRELATIVES, AND WHY CHRIST SYMPATHIZED WITH THE POOR.

CHAPTER XX.

OF THE PERMANENCE OF WEALTH.

SHOWING THAT VALUES FROM OBLIGATION SEEM REALLY TO LAST LONGER THAN VALUES FROM PRODUCTION.

CHAPTER XXI.

THE RELATION OF MONEY TO WEALTH.

SHOWING THAT SOME MONEY IS AND SOME MONEY IS NOT WEALTH.

INTRODUCTION TO BOOK II.

SINCE political economy is the science which treats of the nature of wealth and the laws of its production and distribution, our first step is to fix the meaning that in this science properly attaches to its primary term.

I shall in the first place show the need for an exhaustive inquiry, by showing the confusion that from the time of Adam Smith has attached to this term, and the utter incoherency with regard to it into which the scholastic economy has now fallen.

I shall next try to ascertain the causes of this confusion. This will lead to a consideration of economic development, and in the absence in our literature of any intelligent history of political economy, I shall attempt briefly to trace its course, from the time of Adam Smith and his predecessors, the French economists called Physiocrats, to its virtual abandonment in the teachings of the English and American colleges and universities at the present time.

Having seen that the only point as to wealth on which the scholastic economists now agree is that it has value, and that their confusions as to wealth proceed largely from confusions as to value, I shall then try to determine the proper meaning of the term value. That fixed, we shall be in a position to fix the real meaning and relations of the term wealth, and shall proceed to do so.

Although in this book it will be seen that I am giving many chapters to a subject which preceding systematic writers have passed over in a few lines, even where, as is the case with many of them, they have not utterly ignored it, I am sure that the reader will ultimately find in the ease and certainty with which subsequent inquiries may be conducted an ample reward for the care thus taken in the beginning.

CHAPTER I.

CONFUSIONS AS TO THE MEANING OF WEALTH.

SHOWING THE FAILURE OF THE CURRENT POLITICAL ECONOMY TO DEFINE WEALTH, AND THE CONFUSIONS THEREFROM, CULMINATING IN THE ABANDONMENT OF POLITICAL ECONOMY BY ITS PROFESSED TEACHERS.

Wealth the primary term of political economy—Common use of the word—Vagueness more obvious in political economy—Adam Smith not explicit—Increasing confusion of subsequent writers—Their definitions—Many make no attempt at definition—Perry's proposition to abandon the term—Marshall and Nicholson—Failure to define the term leads to the abandonment of political economy—This concealed under the word "economic"—The intent expressed by Macleod—Results to political economy.

THE purpose of the science of political economy is, as we have seen, the investigation of the laws that govern the production and distribution of wealth in social or civilized life. In beginning its study, our first step is therefore to see what is the nature of the wealth of societies or communities; to determine exactly what we mean by the word wealth when used as a term of political economy.

There are few words in more common use than this word wealth, and in the general way that suffices for ordinary purposes we all know what we mean by it. But when it comes to defining that meaning with the precision necessary for the purposes of political economy, so as to determine what is and what is not properly included in the idea of wealth as political economy must treat of it, most of us, though we often and easily use the word in ordinary thought and speech, are apt to become conscious of indefiniteness and perplexity.

This is not strange. Indeed, it is a natural result of the transference to a wider economy of a term we are accustomed to use in a narrower economy. In our ordinary thought and speech, referring, as it most frequently does, to every-day affairs and the relations of individuals with other individuals, the economy with which we are usually concerned and have most frequently in mind is individual economy, not political economy—the economy whose standpoint is that of the unit, not the economy whose standpoint is that of the social whole or social organism; the Greater Leviathan of natural origin of which I have before spoken.

The original meaning of the word wealth is that of plenty or abundance; that of the possession of things conducive to a certain kind of weal or well-being. Health, strength and wealth express three kinds of weal or well-being. Health relates to the constitution or structure, and expresses the idea of well-being with regard to the physical or mental frame. Strength relates to the vigor of the natural powers, and expresses the idea of well-being with regard to the ability of exertion. Wealth relates to the command of external things that gratify desire, and expresses the idea of well-being with regard to possessions or property. Now, as social health must mean something different from individual health, and social strength something different from individual strength; so social wealth, or the wealth of the society, the larger man or Greater Leviathan of which individuals living in civilization are components, must be something different from the wealth of the individual.

In the one economy, that of individuals or social units, everything is regarded as wealth the possession of which tends to give wealthiness, or the command of external things that satisfy desire, to its individual possessor, even though it may involve the taking of such things from other individuals. But in the other economy, that of social wholes, or the social organism, nothing can be regarded as wealth that does not add to the wealthiness of the whole. What, therefore, may be regarded as wealth from the individual standpoint, may not be wealth from the standpoint of the society. An individual, for instance, may be wealthy by virtue of obligations due to him from other individuals; but such obligations can constitute no part of the wealth of the society, which includes both debtor and creditor. Or, an individual may increase his wealth by robbery or by gaming; but the wealth of the social whole, which comprises robbed as well as robber, loser as well as winner, cannot be thus increased.

It is therefore no wonder that men accustomed to the use of the word wealth in its ordinary sense, a sense in which no one can avoid its continual use, should be liable, unless they take great care, to slip into confusion when they come to use the same word in its economic sense. But what does seem strange is that indefiniteness, perplexity and confusion as to the meaning of the economic term wealth, are even more obvious in the writings of the professional economists who are accredited by colleges and universities and other institutions of learning with the possession of special knowledge which authorizes them to instruct their fellows on economic subjects. While as for the professional statisticians who in long arrays of figures attempt to estimate the aggregate wealth of states and nations, they seem for the most part innocent of any suspicion that what may be wealth to an individual may not be wealth to a community.*

Adam Smith, who is regarded as the founder of the modern science of political economy, is not very definite or entirely consistent as to the real nature of the wealth of nations, or wealth in the economic sense. But since his time the confusions of which he shows traces, instead of being cleared up by the writings of those who in our schools and colleges are recognized as political economists,† has become progressively so much worse confounded that in the latest and most elaborate of these treatises all attempts to define the term seem to have been abandoned.

In "Progress and Poverty" (1879), I showed the utter confusion as to wealth into which the scholastic political economy had fallen, by printing together a number of varying and contradictory definitions of its sub-term capital, as given by accredited economic writers.‡ Although I was then obliged to fix the meaning of the main term wealth in order to fix the meaning of the sub-term

* A curious, if not comical, instance of the loose way in which professed statisticians jump at conclusions is afforded in the controversy I had in "Frank Leslie's Weekly" (1883) with Professor Francis A. Walker, then superintendent of the United States Census, and which was afterwards reprinted as an appendix to the American edition of my "Social Problems."

† "Progress and Poverty," although it has already exerted a wider influence than any other economic work written since the "Wealth of Nations," is not so recognized, not being even alluded to in the elaborate history of political economy which, on account of the utter chaos into which the teachings of that science have fallen, takes in the last edition of the "Encyclopædia Britannica" the place before accorded to the science itself, and which has since been reprinted in separate form. ("A History of Political Economy," by John Kells Ingram, LL.D., Macmillan & Co., 1888.)

‡ "Progress and Poverty," Book I., Chapter II., "The Meaning of the Terms."

capital, with which I was immediately concerned, the confusion among the accredited economists has "got no better very fast," the "economic revolution" which has in the meanwhile displaced from their chairs the professors of the then orthodox political economy in order to give place to so-called "Austrians," or similar professors of "economics," having only made confusion worse confounded. Let me, therefore, in order to show in the most up-to-date way the confusion existing among scholastic economists as to the primary term of political economy, put together what definitions of the economic term wealth I can find in the works of representative and accredited economic writers since Adam Smith to the present time, placing them in chronological order as far as possible:

J. B. Say—Divides wealth into natural and social, and applies the latter term to whatever is susceptible of exchange.

Malthus—Those material objects which are necessary, useful or agreeable to man.

Torrens—Articles which possess utility and are produced by some portion of voluntary effort.

McCulloch—Those articles or products which have exchangeable value, and are either necessary, useful or agreeable to man.

Jones—Material objects voluntarily appropriated by man.

Rae—All I can find on this subject in his "New Principles of Political Economy" (1833) is that "individuals grow rich by the acquisition of wealth previously existing; nations by the creation of wealth that did not before exist."

Senior—All those things, and those things only, which are transferable, are limited in supply, and are directly or indirectly productive of pleasure or preventive of pain. . . .

Health, strength and knowledge, and the other acquired powers of body and mind, appear to us to be articles of wealth.

Vethake—All objects, immaterial as well as material, having utility, excepting those not susceptible of being appropriated, and those supplied gratuitously by nature. By the wealth of a community or nation is meant all the wealth which is possessed by the persons composing it, either in their individual or corporate capacities.

John Stuart Mill—All useful and agreeable things which possess exchangeable value; or in other words, all useful and agreeable things except those which can be obtained, in the quantity desired, without labor or sacrifice.

Fawcett—Wealth may be defined to consist of every commodity which has an exchangeable value.

Bowen—The aggregate of all things, whether material or immaterial, which contribute to comfort and enjoyment and which are objects of frequent barter and sale.

Jevons—What is (1) transferable, (2) limited in supply, (3) useful.

Mason and Lalor, 1875—Anything for which something can be got in exchange.

Leverson—The necessaries and comforts of life produced by labor.

Shadwell—All articles the possession of which affords pleasure to anybody.

Macleod—Anything whatever that can be bought, sold or exchanged, or whose value can be measured in money. . . . Wealth is nothing but exchangeable rights.

De Laveleye—Everything which answers to men's rational wants. A useful service and a useful object are equally wealth. . . . Wealth is what is good and useful—a good climate, well-kept roads, seas teeming with fish, are unquestionably wealth to a country, and yet they cannot be bought.

Francis A. Walker—All articles of value and nothing else.

Macvane—All the useful and agreeable material objects we own or have the right to use and enjoy without asking the consent of any other person. Wealth is of two general kinds—natural wealth and wealth produced by labor.

Clark—Usage has employed the word wealth to signify, first, the comparative welfare resulting from material possessions, and secondly, and by a transfer, the possessions themselves. Wealth then consists in the relative-weal-constituting elements in man's material environment. It is objective to the user, material, useful and appropriable.

Laughlin—Defines material wealth as something which satisfies a want; cannot be obtained without some sacrifice of exertion, and is transferable; but also speaks of immaterial wealth without defining it.

Newcomb—That for the enjoyment of which people pay money. The skill, business ability or knowledge which enables their possessors to contribute to the enjoyment of others, including the talents of the actor, the ability of the man of business, the knowledge of the lawyer and the skill of the physician, is to be considered wealth when we use the term in its most extended sense.

Bain—A commodity is material worked up after a design to answer to a definite demand or need, and wealth is simply the sum total of commodities.

Ruskin—This brilliant essayist and art critic can hardly be classed as a scholastically accepted political economist, and I have refrained from giving his definition of wealth in what otherwise would have been its proper place. But his "Unto this Last" (1866) consists of four essays on political economy, and the brilliant flashes of ethical truth which they like his other works contain have led many admirers to regard him as a profound economist. He is anything but complimentary to the "modern *soi-disant* science," as he calls it, against which he brings the charge that while claiming to be the science of wealth it cannot tell what wealth is. In the preface to these essays he says: "The real gist of these papers, their central meaning and aim is to give, as I believe, for the first time in plain English, a logical definition of wealth; such definition being absolutely needed for a basis of economical science." It would be well, therefore, without assuming that Ruskin in any way represents the scholastic political economy, which he likened to an astronomy unable to say what a star was, to give his definition. That definition, to use his own words is—"The possession of useful articles that we can use," or as again stated somewhat later on, "The possession of the valuable by the valiant."

The endeavor to get together these definitions of wealth by economic writers has involved considerable effort, but it is likely to be noticeable by its omissions. The fact is, that many of the best-known writers on political economy, such for instance as Ricardo, Chalmers, Thorold Rogers and Cairnes, make no attempt to give any definition of wealth. The same thing is to be said of the two volumes of Karl Marx entitled "Capital;" and also of the two volumes on the same subject by Böhm-Bawerk, which also have been translated into English, and are much quoted by that now dominant school of scholastic political economy known as the "Austrian." And while many of the writers who make no attempt to define wealth, do have a good deal to say about it, what they say is too diffused and incoherent either to quote or condense. There are many who without saying so, evidently hold the opinion thus frankly expressed by Professor Perry in his "Elements of Political Economy" (1866):

This word wealth has been the bane of political economy. It is the bog whence most of the mists have arisen which have beclouded the whole subject. From its indefiniteness and the variety of associations it carries along with it in different minds, it is totally unfit for any scientific purpose whatever. It is itself almost impossible to be defined, and consequently can serve no useful purpose in a definition of anything else. . . . The meaning of the word wealth has never yet been settled; and if political economy must wait until that work be done as a preliminary, the science will never be satisfactorily constructed. . . . Men may think, and talk, and write, and dispute till doomsday, but until they come to use words with definiteness, and mean the same thing by the same word, they reach comparatively few results and make but little progress. And it is just at this point that we find the first grand reason of the slow advance hitherto made by this science. It undertook to use a word for scientific purposes which no amount of manipulation and explanation could make suitable for that service. Happily there is no need to use this word. In emancipating itself from the word wealth as a technical term, political economy has dropped a clog, and its movements are now relatively free.

To make this exhibition of definitions as fairly representative as possible I have wished to include in it that of Professor Alfred Marshall, Professor of Political Economy in the University of Cambridge, England, whose "Principles of Economics" (of which only the first volume, issued in 1890, and containing some 800 octavo pages, has yet been published) may be considered the latest and largest, and scholastically the most highly indorsed, economic work yet published in English.

It cannot be said of him, as of many economic writers, that he does not attempt to say what is meant by wealth, for if one turns to the index he is directed to a whole chapter. But neither in this chapter nor elsewhere can I find any paragraph, however long, that may be quoted as defining the meaning he attaches to the term wealth. The only approach to it is this:

All wealth consists of things that satisfy wants, directly or indirectly. All wealth therefore consists of goods; but not all kinds of goods are reckoned as wealth.

But for the distinction between goods reckoned as wealth and goods not reckoned as wealth, which one would think was about to follow, the reader looks in vain. He merely finds that Professor Marshall gives him the choice of classifying goods into external-material-transferable goods, external-material-non-transferable goods, external-personal-transferable goods, external-personal-non-transferable goods, and internal-personal-non-transferable goods; or else into material-external-transferable goods, material-external-non-transferable goods, personal-external-transferable goods, personal-external-non-transferable goods, and personal-internal-non-transferable goods. But as to which of these kinds of goods are reckoned as wealth and which are not, Professor Marshall gives the reader no inkling, unless, indeed, he may be able to find it in Wagner's "Volkswirthschaftslehre," to which the reader is referred at the conclusion of the chapter as throwing "much light upon the connection between the economic concept of wealth and the juridical concept of rights in private property." I can convey the impression produced on my mind by repeated struggles to discover what the Professor of Political Economy in the great English University of Cambridge holds is to be reckoned as wealth, only by saying that it seems to comprise all things in the heavens above, the earth beneath and the waters under the earth, that may be useful to or desired by man, individually or collectively, including man himself with all his natural or acquired capabilities, and that all I can absolutely affirm, for it is the only thing for which I can find a direct statement, is, that "we ought for many purposes to reckon the Thames a part of England's wealth."

The same utter, though perhaps somewhat less elaborate, incoherency is shown by Professor J. Shield Nicholson, Professor of Political Economy in the great Scottish University of Edinburgh, whose "Principles of Political

Economy" appeared in first volume (less than half as big as that of Professor Marshall's) in 1893, and has not yet (1897) been succeeded by another. Looking up the index for the word "wealth" one finds no less than fifteen references, of which the first is "popular conception of," and the second "economic conception of." Yet in none of these, nor in the whole volume, though one wade through it all in the search, is anything like a definition of wealth to be found, the only thing resembling a direct statement being the incidental remark (p. 404) that "land is in general the most important item in the inventory of national wealth"—a proposition which logically is as untrue as that we ought to reckon the Thames a part of England's wealth.

Now, wealth is the object-noun, or name given to the subject-matter, of political economy, the science that seeks to discover the laws of the production and distribution of wealth in human society. It is therefore the economic term of first importance. Unless we know what wealth is, how possibly can we hope to discover how it is procured and distributed? Yet after a century of what passes for the cultivation of this science, with professors of political economy in every college, the question, "What is wealth?" finds at their hands no certain answer. Even to such questions as, "Is wealth material or immaterial?" or "Is it something external to man or does it include man and his attributes?" we get no undisputed reply. There is not even a consensus of opinion. And in the latest and most pretentious scholastic teaching the attempt to obtain any has been virtually, where not definitely, abandoned, and the economic meaning of wealth reduced to that of anything having value to the social unit.

It is clear that failure to define its subject-matter or object-noun must be fatal to any attempted science; for it shows lack of the first essential of true science. And the fate of rejection even by those who profess to study and teach it has already befallen political economy at the hands of the accredited institutions of learning.

This fact will not be obvious to the ordinary reader, for it is concealed to him under a change in the meaning of a word.

Since the term comes into our language from the Greek, the proper word for expressing the idea of relationship to political economy is "politico-economic." But this is a term too long, and too alien to the Saxon genius of our mother tongue, for frequent repetition. And so the word "economic" has come into accepted use in English, as expressing that idea. We are justified therefore, in supposing, and as a matter of fact do generally suppose when we first hear of them, that the works now written by the professors of political economy in our universities and colleges, and entitled "Elements of Economics," "Principles of Economics," "Manual of Economics," etc., are treatises on political economy. Examination, however, will show that many of these at least are not in reality treatises on the science of political economy, but treatises on what their authors might better call the science of exchanges, or the science of exchangeable quantities. This is not the same thing as political economy, but quite a different thing —a science in short akin to the science of mathematics.* In this there is no necessity for distinguishing between what is wealth to the unit and what is wealth to the whole, and moral questions, that must be met in a true political economy, may be easily avoided by those to whom they seem awkward.

A proper name for this totally different science, which the professors of political economy in so many of the lead-

* The attempts by titular professors of political economy to find mathematical expression for what they call "economics" must be familiar to those who have toiled through recent scholastic literature.

ing colleges and universities on both sides of the Atlantic have now substituted in their teaching for the science they are officially supposed to expound, would be that of "catallactics," as proposed by Archbishop Whately, or that of "plutology," as proposed by Professor Hern, of Melbourne; but it is certainly not properly "economics," for that by long usage is identified with political economy.

Both the reason for, and what is meant by, the change of title from political economy to economics, which is so noticeable in the writings of the professors of political economy in recent years, are thus frankly shown by Macleod (Vol. I., Chapter VII., Sec. 11, "Science of Economics"):

> We do not propose to make any change at all in the name of the science. Both the terms "Political Economy" and "Economic Science," or "Economics," are in common use, and it seems better to discontinue that name which is liable to misinterpretation, and which seems to relate to politics, and to adhere to that one which most clearly defines its nature and extent and is most analogous to the names of other sciences. We shall, therefore, henceforth discontinue the use of the term "political economy" and adhere to that of "economics." Economics, then, is simply the science of exchanges, or of commerce in its widest extent and in all its forms and varieties; it is sometimes called the science of wealth or the theory of value. The definition of the science which we offer is:
>
> Economics is the science which treats of the laws which govern the relations of exchangeable quantities.

Now the laws which govern the relations of exchangeable quantities are such laws as $2+2=4$; $4-1=3$; $2\times4=8$; $4\div2=2$; and their extensions.

The proper place for such laws in any honest classification of the sciences is as laws of arithmetic or laws of mathematics, not as laws of economics. And the attempt of holders of chairs of political economy to take advantage of the usage of language which has made "economic" a short word for "politico-economic" to pass off their "science of economics" as if it were the science of political economy, is as essentially dishonest as the device of the proverbial Irishman who attempted to cheat his partners by the formula, "Here's two for you two, and here's two for me too."

To this, in less than a century after Say congratulated his readers on the first establishment of chairs of political economy in universities, has the scholastic political economy come.

Professor Perry, writing thirty years ago, thought that by emancipating itself from the word wealth as a technical term, political economy would drop a clog and its movements would become relatively free. In what is now taught from the chairs of political economy in our leading colleges on both sides of the Atlantic the clog has indeed been dropped, with results which very strongly suggest the increased freedom of movement which comes from the dropping of its tail by a boy's kite. Without the clog of an object-noun, political economy as there taught has plunged out of existence, and the science of values which is taught in its place has no answer whatever to give even to questions which Professor Perry would have thought completely settled at the time he wrote.

CHAPTER II.

CAUSES OF CONFUSION AS TO THE MEANING OF WEALTH.

SHOWING THE REAL DIFFICULTY THAT BESETS THE ECONOMIC DEFINITION OF WEALTH.

Effect of slavery on the definition of wealth—Similar influences now existing—John Stuart Mill on prevalent delusions—Genesis of the protective absurdity—Power of special interests to mold common opinion—Of injustice and absurdity, and the power of special interests to pervert reason—Mill an example of how accepted opinions may blind men—Effect upon a philosophical system of the acceptance of an incongruity—Meaning of a saying of Christ—Influence of a class profiting by robbery shown in the development of political economy—Archbishop Whately puts the cart before the horse—The power of a great pecuniary interest to affect thought can be ended only by abolishing that interest—This shown in American slavery.

THE neglect of political economy in the classical world has been explained by modern economists as due to the effect of slavery in causing labor to be regarded as degrading.*

But in this a quicker and more direct effect of slavery in preventing the cultivation of political economy has been overlooked.

* See, for instance, McCulloch's "Principles of Political Economy" (1825), Part I.

Except perhaps as the crucified fomenter of a servile rebellion, the only class in which any philosopher of the ancient world might have got a hearing that could have brought his name and teachings down to us, was that wealthy class, whose riches were largely in their slaves. For in any social condition in which privilege and wealth are inequitably distributed, what Jefferson said of Jesus* must be true of all moral or economic teachers—"All the learned of His country, intrenched in its power and riches, were opposed to Him, lest His labors should undermine their advantages."

The first question which a coherent political economy must answer is, what is wealth? This, in a state of society in which the ruling class were universally slaveholders, was too delicate a question for any accredited philosopher to have fairly met. Even the most astute among them could go no further than to say, with the intellectual giant Aristotle, that wealth "is all things whose value is measured by money," or with the Roman jurist Ulpian, "that is wealth which can be bought and sold." From this point, the very point to which our modern political economy has in current scholastic teachings now come again, though there may be economies of finance and economies of exchange and economies of agriculture (there were many such among the Greeks and Romans, their agricultural economy even teaching how slaves should be sold as soon as age and infirmity began to lessen the work that could be extorted from them), there was and could be no political economy.

But this indisposition to recognize the distinction between what may be wealth to the individual and what is

---

* "Syllabus of an estimate of the merits of the doctrines of Jesus." ("The Writings of Thomas Jefferson," collected and edited by Paul Leicester Ford, Putnam's Sons, Vol. VIII., p. 227.)

wealth to the society, which has prevented the growth of any science of political economy wherever, either in the ancient or the modern world, the ownership of human beings has been an important element in the wealth of the wealthy class, has not entirely ceased to show itself with the abolition of chattel slavery. Even the men who have seen that there was a connection between the failure of the restless and powerful thinkers of the classic world to develop a political economy and their acceptance of slavery, have in their own development of political economy been unconsciously affected by a similar retarding and aberrating influence. Chattel slavery is only one of the means by which individuals become wealthy without increase in the general wealth, and as in modern civilization it has lost importance, other means to the same end have taken its place. But wherever and from whatever causes society is divided into the very rich and the very poor, the primary question of political economy, what is wealth? must be a delicate one to men sensibly or insensibly influenced by the feelings and opinions of the dominating class. For in such social conditions much that commonly passes for wealth must really be only legalized robbery, and nothing can be more offensive to those enjoying the profit of robbery than to call it by its true name.

In the preliminary remarks to his "Principles of Political Economy" John Stuart Mill says:

> It often happens that the universal belief of one age of mankind—a belief from which no one was, nor without an extraordinary effort of genius and courage, could at that time be free—becomes to a subsequent age so palpable an absurdity, that the only difficulty then is to imagine how such a thing can ever have appeared credible. It has so happened with the doctrine that money is synonymous with wealth. The conceit seems too preposterous to be thought of as a serious opinion. It looks like one of the crude fancies of childhood, instantly corrected by a word from any grown person. But let no

one feel confident that he should have escaped the delusion if he had lived at the time when it prevailed.

Let no one be confident indeed!

Yet it is a mistake to liken the absurdities of the mercantile or protective system to the crude fancies of childhood. This has never been their origin or their strength. In the petty commerce in marbles and tops that goes on among school-boys no boy ever imagined that the more he gave and the less he got in such exchange the better off he should be. No primitive people were ever yet so stupid as to suppose that they could increase their wealth by taxing themselves. Any child that could understand the proposition would see that a dollar's worth of gold could not be more valuable than a dollar's worth of anything else, as readily as it would see that a pound of lead could not be heavier than a pound of feathers. Such ideas are not the fancies of childhood. Their growth, their strength, their persistence, as we may clearly see in the newer countries of America and Australia, where they have appeared and gathered force since Adam Smith's time, is due to the growth of special interests in artificial restrictions on trade as a means of increasing individual wealth at the expense of the general wealth.

The power of a special interest, though inimical to the general interest, so to influence common thought as to make fallacies pass as truths, is a great fact without which neither the political history of our own time and people nor that of other times and peoples can be understood. A comparatively small number of individuals brought into virtual though not necessarily formal agreement of thought and action by something that makes them individually wealthy without adding to the general wealth, may exert an influence out of all proportion to their numbers. A special interest of this kind is, to the general interests of society, as a standing army is to an unorganized mob. It gains intensity and energy in its specialization, and in the wealth it takes from the general stock finds power to mold opinion. Leisure and culture and the circumstances and conditions that command respect accompany wealth, and intellectual ability is attracted by it. On the other hand, those who suffer from the injustice that takes from the many to enrich the few, are in that very thing deprived of the leisure to think, and the opportunities, education and graces necessary to give their thought acceptable expression. They are necessarily the "unlettered," the "ignorant," the "vulgar," prone in their consciousness of weakness to look up for leadership and guidance to those who have the advantages that the possession of wealth can give.

Now, if we consider it, injustice and absurdity are simply different aspects of incongruity. That which to right reason is unjust must be to right reason absurd. But an injustice that impoverishes the many to enrich the few shifts the centers of social power, and thus controls the social organs and agencies of opinion and education. Growing in strength and acceptance by what it feeds on, it has only to continue to exist to become at length so vested or rooted, not in the constitution of the human mind itself, but in that constitution of opinions, beliefs and habits of thought which we take, as we take our mother tongue, from our social environment, that it is not perceived as injustice or absurdity, but seems even to the philosopher an integral part of the natural order, with which it were as idle if not as impious to quarrel as with the constitution of the elements. Even that highest gift, the gift of reason, is in its bestowal on man subjected to his use, and the very mental qualities that enable us to discover truth may be perverted to fortify error, and are always so perverted wherever an anti-social special interest gains control of the thinking and teaching functions of society.

In this lies the explanation of the fact that looking through the vista of what we know of human history we everywhere find what are to us the most palpable absurdities enshrining themselves in the human mind as unquestionable truths—whole nations the prey of preposterous superstitions, abasing themselves before fellow-creatures, often before idiots or voluptuaries, whom their imagination has converted into the representatives of Deity; the great masses toiling, suffering, starving, that those they bear on their shoulders may live idly and daintily. Wherever and whenever what we may now see to be a palpable absurdity has passed for truth, we may see if we look close enough that it has always been because behind it crouched some powerful special interest, and that the man has hushed the questioning of the child.

This is of human nature. The world is so new to us when we first come into it; we are so compelled at every turn to rely upon what we are told rather than on what we ourselves can discover; what we find to be the common and respected opinion of others has with us such almost irresistible weight, that it becomes possible for a special interest by usurping the teaching province to make to us black seem white and wrong seem right.

Let no one indeed feel confident that he could have escaped any delusion, no matter how preposterous, that has ever prevailed among men, if he had lived when and where it was accepted. From as far back as we can see, human nature has not changed, and we have but to look around us to discover in operation to-day the great agency that has made falsehood seem truth.

Of the fact of which, in what I have quoted, John Stuart Mill speaks with reference to the doctrine that money is synonymous with wealth—the fact that accepted opinion may blind even able and courageous men—he himself, in the same book and almost in the same paragraph, gives unconscious illustration, in the timidity with which he touches the question of the nature of wealth, when it leads beyond what Adam Smith had already shown, that it was not synonymous with money. He recognizes, indeed, that what is wealth to an individual is not therefore wealth to the community or nation, and definitely states, or rather concedes, that debt, even funded debt, is no part of the wealth of the society. But the way in which he does this is suggestive. He says:

> The canceling of the debt would be no destruction of wealth, but a transfer of it; a wrongful abstraction of wealth from certain members of the community, for the profit of the government or of the taxpayers.

The gratuitous word "wrongful" shows the bias. And even this recognition that debt cannot be wealth in the economic sense is ignored in the subsequent definition of wealth.

So strongly indeed was John Stuart Mill, who seems to me a very type of intellectual honesty, under the influence of the accustomed ideas of his time and class, that although he saw with perfect clearness that the wealth that comes to individuals by reason of their monopoly of land really comes to them through force and fraud, yet he seemingly never dreamed that land was no part of national wealth. Nor yet, does he seem even to dream that the people of a country, once they had been forcibly deprived of it, could recover what he saw to be their natural right. In all the history of dead absurdities there can be no sentence more strikingly illustrative of the power of accepted opinion to hide absurdity than this of his:

> The land of Ireland, the land of every country, belongs to the people of that country. The individuals called landowners have no

right in morality and justice to anything but rent, or compensation for its salable value.

This is simply to say that the ownership of the land of Ireland gave the people who morally owned it the right to *buy* it from those who did not morally own it.

What was it that hid from this trained logician and radically minded man the patent absurdity of saying that the individuals called landowners had no right to land, except that which is the sum and expression of all exchangeable rights to land—rent?

Whoever will examine his writings will see that it was his previous acceptance of certain doctrines—doctrines with which a succession of ingenious men had endeavored to bring into semblance of logical coherence a political economy vitally defective, and which resembled the elaborate system of cycles and epicycles with which the ingenuity of astronomers previous to Copernicus had endeavored to account for the movements of the heavenly bodies.

When an incongruous substance, such for instance as a bullet, is implanted in the human body, the physical system, as soon as it despairs of its removal, sets about the endeavor to accommodate itself to the incongruity, frequently with such success that at length the incongruity is not noticed. The stout, masterful man with whom I have just now been talking, and whom you might liken to a bull if it were not for the intelligence of his face, has long carried a bullet under his skin. And men have even been known to live for years with bullets in their brains.

So, too, with philosophical systems. When an incongruity is accepted in a philosophical system, the abilities of its professors are at once set to work to accommodate other parts of the system to the incongruity, frequently with such success that philosophical systems containing fatal incongruities have been known to command acceptance for long generations. For the mind of man is even more plastic than the body of man, and the human imagination, which is the chief element in the building up of philosophical systems, furnishes a lymph more subtle than that which the blood supplies to the bodily system.

Indeed, the artificialities and confusions by which an incongruity is made tolerable to a philosophic system, for the very reason that they cannot be understood except by those who have submitted their minds to a special course of cramping, become to them a seeming evidence of superiority, gratifying a vanity like that of the contortionist who has painfully learned to walk a little way on his hands instead of his feet and to twist his body into unnatural and unnecessary positions; or like that of the conveyancer or lawyer, who has in the same way painfully learned to perform such tricks with language.

And just as the long toleration by the physical system of such an incongruity as a bullet, a tumor or a dislocation, by reason of the efforts which the system has made to reconcile to it other parts and functions, renders it more difficult of removal or remedy, so the toleration in a philosophical system of an incongruity makes its removal or remedy far more difficult to those who have bent their minds to the system as it has by ingenious men been adapted to the incongruity, than it is to those who approach the subject from first principles, and who if they may have more to learn have less to unlearn. For it is true, as Bacon said, that "a cripple in the right way may beat a racer in the wrong one. Nay, the fleeter the racer is who has once missed his way, the farther he leaves it behind."

This, I think, is what was meant in the concise but deep philosophy of Christ by such sayings as that the Kingdom of Heaven, or system of right-doing, though revealed unto babes, is hidden from those deemed wise and prudent, and that what the common people heard gladly was foolishness to the learned scribes and pharisees. With illustrations of this principle the history of accepted opinion in every time and place abounds.

It is not to the fancies of childhood that we must look for an explanation of the strength of long dominant absurdities. Michelet ("The People") truly says: "No consecrated absurdity would have stood its ground in this world if the man had not silenced the objection of the child."

But not to depart from the matter in hand: It is evident that the existence of a powerful class whose incomes could not fail to be endangered by a recognition of the fact that what makes them individually wealthy is not any part of the wealth of society, but only robbery, must from the beginning of the cultivation of political economy in modern times have beset its primary step, the determination of what the wealth of society consists of, with something of the same difficulty that prevented its development in classic times. And when the development commenced, and especially after it had been taken charge of by the colleges and universities, which as at present constituted must be peculiarly susceptible to the influence of the wealthy classes, it is evident that the efforts of able men to bring into some semblance of coherency a system of political economy destitute of any clear and coherent definition of wealth must have surrounded the subject with greater perplexities and helped powerfully to prevent the need of a definition of wealth from being felt.

This is precisely what we see when we examine the different attempts to define wealth in the economic sense, and note the increasing confusions that have attended them, culminating in the acceptance of the common meaning of the word wealth—anything that has exchangeable power—as the only meaning that can be given to the economic term; and the consequent abandonment of the possibility of a science of political economy.

Archbishop Whately, in the chapter on ambiguous terms appended to his "Elements of Logic," says in speaking of one of the ambiguities of the word wealth, that which led to the use of wealth as synonymous with money:

> The results have been fraud, punishment and poverty at home, and discord and war without. It has made nations consider the wealth of their customers a source of loss instead of profit; and an advantageous market a curse instead of a blessing. By inducing them to refuse to profit by the peculiar advantages in climate, soil or industry, possessed by their neighbors, it has forced them in a great measure to give up their own. It has for centuries done more, and perhaps for centuries to come will do more, to retard the improvement of Europe than all other causes put together.

In this, the Archbishop, though famous as a logician, "puts the cart before the horse."

These are not the effects of the confusion of a term. The confusion of the term is one of the effects of the influence upon thought of the same special interest that in its efforts to give wealth to individuals at the expense of the general wealth, has done and is doing all this.

Nor can this power of a great pecuniary interest to affect thought, and especially to affect thought in those circles of society whose opinions are most respected, ever be done away with save by the abolition of its cause—the social adjustment or institution that gives power to obtain wealth without earning it. The pecuniary interest in the ownership of slaves was never very large in the United States. But it so dominated the thought of the whole country that up to the outbreak of the civil war the term abolitionist was to good, kindly and intelligent people even in the North an expression that meant everything vile and wicked. And whatever else might have been the issue of the war, had the pecuniary interest in the maintenance of slavery remained, it would still have continued to show itself in thought. But as soon as the supplies of the slave-owning interest were cut off by the freeing of the slaves this power upon opinion vanished. Now, no preacher, professor or politician, even in the South, would think of advocating or defending slavery; and in Boston, where he narrowly escaped mobbing, stands a public statue of William Lloyd Garrison.

CHAPTER III.

WHAT ADAM SMITH MEANT BY WEALTH.

SHOWING HOW ESSENTIALLY ADAM SMITH'S PRIMARY CONCEPTION OF WEALTH DIFFERED FROM THAT NOW HELD BY HIS SUCCESSORS.

Significance of the title "Wealth of Nations"—Its origin shown in Smith's reference to the Physiocrats—His conception of wealth in his introduction—Objection by Malthus and by Macleod—Smith's primary conception that given in "Progress and Poverty"—His subsequent confusions.

IF, considering the increasing indefiniteness among professed economists as to the nature of wealth, we compare Adam Smith's great book with the treatises that have succeeded it, we may observe on its very title-page something usually unnoticed, but really very significant. Adam Smith does not propose an inquiry into the nature and causes of wealth, but "an inquiry into the nature and causes of *the wealth of nations*."

The words I here italicize have become the descriptive title of the book. This is known, not as "Adam Smith's Inquiry," or "Adam Smith's Wealth," but as "Adam Smith's Wealth of Nations." Yet these limiting words, "of nations," seem to have been little noticed and less understood by the writers who in increasing numbers for almost a hundred years have taken this great book as a basis for their elucidations and supposed improvements. Their assumption seems to be that it is wealth generally or wealth without limitation which Adam Smith treats of and which is the proper subject of political economy, and that if he meant anything by his determining words "of nations," he referred to such political divisions as England, France, Holland, etc.

Some superficial plausibility is perhaps given to this view from the fact that one of the divisions of the "Wealth of Nations," Book III., is entitled "Of the Different Progress of Opulence in Different Nations," and that in it illustrative reference is made to various ancient and modern states. But that in his choice of the limiting words "of nations" as indicating the kind of wealth into the nature and causes of which he proposed to inquire, Adam Smith referred to something other than the political divisions of mankind called states or nations, is sufficiently clear.

While he is, as I have said, not very definite and not entirely consistent in his use of the term wealth, yet it is certain that what he meant by "the wealth of nations," of the nature and causes of which he proposed to inquire, was something essentially different from what is meant by wealth in the ordinary use of the word, which includes as wealth everything that may give wealthiness to the individual considered apart from other individuals. It was that kind of wealth the production of which increases and the destruction of which decreases the wealth of society as a whole, or of mankind collectively, which he sought to distinguish from the word "wealth" in its common or individual sense by the limiting words, "of nations," in the meaning not of the larger political divisions of mankind, but of societies or social organisms.

In the body of the "Wealth of Nations" there occurs again the phrase which furnished Adam Smith the title for his ten years' work. In Book IV., speaking of those members of "the French republic of letters" who at that time called themselves and were called "Economists," but who have been since distinguished from other economists, real or pretended, by the name of Physiocrats,*—a school who might be better still distinguished as the Single Taxers of the Eighteenth Century, he says (the italics are mine):

> This sect, in their works, which are very numerous, and which treat not only of *what is properly called political economy, or of the nature and causes of the wealth of nations*, but of every other branch of the system of civil government, all follow implicitly, and without any sensible variation, the doctrines of Mr. Quesnai.

This recognition of the fact that, not wealth in the loose and common sense of the word, but that which is wealth to societies considered as wholes, or as he phrased it, "the wealth of nations," is the proper subject-matter of what is properly called political economy—shows the origin of the title Adam Smith chose for his book. He had doubtless thought of calling it a "Political Economy," but either from the consciousness that his work was incomplete, or from the modesty of his real greatness, finally preferred the less pretentious title, which expressed to his mind the same idea, "An inquiry into the Nature and Causes of the Wealth of Nations."

It has been much complained of Adam Smith that he does not define what he means by wealth. But this has been exaggerated. In the very first paragraph of the introduction to his work he thus explains what he means by the wealth of nations, the only sense of the word wealth which it is the business "of what is properly called political economy" to consider:

---

* From *physiocratie*, or government in the nature of things, or natural order, a name suggested, in 1768, by Dupont de Nemours, one of the most active of their number.

The annual labor of every nation is the fund which originally supplies it with all the necessaries and conveniences of life which it annually consumes, and which consist always either in the immediate produce of that labor, or in what is purchased with that produce from other nations.

Again, in the last sentence of this introduction he speaks of "the real wealth, the annual produce of the land and labor of the society." And in other places throughout the book he also speaks of this wealth of society or wealth of nations, or real wealth, as the produce of land and labor.

What he meant by the produce of land and labor was of course not the produce of land plus the produce of labor, but the joint produce of both—that is to say: the result of labor, the active factor of all production, exerted upon land, the passive factor of all production, in such a way as to fit it (land or matter) for the gratification of human desires. Malthus, indorsed by McCulloch and a long line of commentators upon Adam Smith, objects to his definition that "it includes all the useless products of the earth, as well as those which are appropriated and enjoyed by man." And in the same way Macleod, a recent writer whose ability to say clearly what he wants to say makes his "Elements of Economics," despite its essential defects, a grateful relief among economic writings, objects that if—

the annual produce of land and labor, either separately or combined, is wealth, then every useless product of the earth is wealth, as well as the most useful—the tares as well as the wheat. If a diver fetch a pearl oyster from the deep sea, the shell is as much the "produce of land and labor" as the pearl itself. So if a nugget of gold or a diamond is obtained from a mine, the rubbish it is found in and brought up with is as much the "produce of land and labor" as the gold or the diamond; and innumerable instances of this sort may be cited.

The communication of thought by speech would be at an end if Adam Smith could be asked to explain that the produce of labor means what the labor is exerted to get, not what it is incidentally obliged to remove in the process of getting that. Yet most of the complaints of his failure to say what he means by wealth have no better basis than these objections.

In truth whoever will attend to the obvious meaning of the word he uses will see that what Adam Smith meant by "the wealth of nations" or wealth in the sense it is to be considered in "what is properly called political economy," is in reality what in the chapter of "Progress and Poverty" entitled "The Meaning of the Terms" (Book I., Chapter II.) is given as the proper meaning of the economic term—namely, that of "natural products that have been secured, moved, combined, separated, or in other ways modified by human exertion, so as to fit them for the gratification of human desires."

Through the first and most important part of his work, this is the idea which Smith has constantly in mind and to which he constantly adheres in tracing all production of wealth to labor. But having grasped this idea of the nature of wealth without having clearly defined its relation to other ideas still lying in his mind, he falls into the subsequent confusion of also classing personal qualities and debts as wealth.

CHAPTER IV.

THE FRENCH PHYSIOCRATS.

SHOWING WHO THE FIRST DEVELOPERS OF A TRUE SCIENCE OF POLITICAL ECONOMY WERE, AND WHAT THEY HELD.

Quesnay and his followers—The great truths they grasped and the cause of the confusion into which they fell—This used to discredit their whole system, but not really vital—They were real free traders—The scant justice yet done them—Reference to them in "Progress and Poverty"—Macleod's statement of their doctrine of natural order—Their conception of wealth—Their day of hope and their fall.

THE first developers in modern times of something like a true science of political economy, or, rather (since social truths, though they may be covered up and for a while ignored, must since the origin of human society always have been here to be seen), the men who first got a hearing large enough and wide enough to bring down their names and their teachings to our times, were the French philosophers whom Adam Smith speaks of in the sentence before quoted, as the sect who "all follow implicitly, and without any sensible variation, the doctrines of Mr. Quesnai."

François Quesnai, or Quesnay, as the name is now usually spelled, a French philosopher, who, as McCulloch says, was "equally distinguished for the subtlety and originality of his understanding and the integrity and simplicity of his character," was born June 4, 1694, twenty-eight years before Adam Smith, at Mercy, some ten leagues from Paris. Beginning life in the manual labor of the farm, he was without either the advantages or, as they often prove to men of parts, the disadvantages of a scholastic education. With much effort he taught himself to read, became apprentice to a surgeon, and at length began practice for himself at Mantes, where he acquired some means and came to the knowledge of Marshal de Noailles, who spoke of him to the queen, who in her turn recommended him to the king. He finally settled in Paris, bought the place of physician to the king, and was made by the monarch his first physician. Abstaining from the intrigues of the court, he won the sincere respect of Louis XV., with whom as his first physician he was brought into close personal contact. The king made him a noble, gave him a coat of arms, assigned him apartments in the palace, calling him affectionately his thinker, and had his books printed in the royal printing-office. And around him, in his apartments in the palace of Versailles, this "King's Thinker" was accustomed to gather a group of eminent men who joined him in an aim the grandest the human mind can entertain—being nothing less than the establishment of liberty and the abolition of poverty among men, by the conformation of human laws to the natural order intended by the Creator.

These men saw what has often been forgotten amid the complexities of a high civilization, but is yet as clear as the sun at noonday to whoever considers first principles. They saw that there is but one source on which men can draw for all their material needs—land; and that there is but one means by which land can be made to yield to their desires—labor. All real wealth, they therefore saw, all that constitutes or can constitute any part of the wealth of society as a whole, or of the wealth of nations, is the result or product of the application of labor to land.

They had not only grasped this first principle—from which any true economy, even that of a savage tribe or an isolated individual, must start—but they had grasped the central principle of a true political economy. This is the principle that in the natural growth of the social organism into which men are integrated in society there is developed a fund which is the natural provision for the natural needs of that organism—a fund which is not merely sufficient for all the material wants of society, and may be taken for that purpose, its intended destination, without depriving the unit of anything rightfully his; but which must be so taken to prevent the gravest injuries to individuals and the direst disasters to the state.

This fund Quesnay and his followers styled the *produit net*—the net, or surplus, or remaining, product. They called it this, evidently because they saw it as something which remained, attached, as it were, to the control of land, after all the expenses of production that are resolvable into compensation for the exertion of individual labor are paid. What they really meant by the *produit net*, or net product, is precisely what is properly to be understood in English by the word "rent" when used in the special sense or technical meaning which it has acquired since Ricardo's time as a term of political economy. Net product is really a better term than rent, as not being so liable to confusion with a word in constant use in another sense; and John Stuart Mill, probably without thought of the Physiocrats, came very close to the perception that governed their choice of a term when he spoke of economic rent as "the unearned increment of land values."

That Quesnay and his associates saw the enormous significance of this "net product" or "unearned increment" for which our economic term is "rent," is clear from their practical proposition, the *impôt unique*, or single tax. By this they meant just what its modern advocates now mean by it—the abolition of all taxes whatever on the making, the exchanging or the possession of wealth in any form, and the recourse for public revenues to economic rent; the net or surplus product; the (to the individual) unearned increment which attaches to land wherever in the progress of society any particular piece of land comes to afford to the user superior opportunities to those obtainable on land that any one is free to use.

In grasping the real meaning and intent of the net product, or economic rent, there was opened to the Physiocrats a true system of political economy—a system of harmonious order and beneficent purpose. They had grasped the key without which no true science of political economy is possible, and from the refusal to accept which the scholastic economy that has succeeded Adam Smith is, after nearly a hundred years of cultivation, during which it has sunk into the contemptible position of "the dismal science," now slipping into confessed incompetency and rejection.

But misled by defective observation and a habit of thought that prevailed long after them, and indeed yet largely prevails (a matter to which I shall subsequently more fully allude), the Physiocrats failed to perceive that what they called the net or surplus product, and what we now call economic rent, or the unearned increment, may attach to land used for any purpose. Looking for some explanation in natural law of what was then doubtless generally assumed to be the fact, and of which I know of no clear contradiction until "Progress and Poverty" was written, that agriculture is the only occupation which yields to the landlord a net or surplus product, or unearned increment (rent), over and above the expenses of production, they not unnaturally under the circumstances hit upon a striking difference between agriculture, which grows things, and the mechanical and trading occupations, which merely change things in form, place or ownership, as furnishing the explanation for which they were in search. This difference lies in the use which agriculture makes of the generative or reproductive principle in nature.

This supposed fact, and what seemed to them the rational explanation of it, in the peculiar use made in agriculture of the principle of growth and reproduction which characterizes all forms of life, vegetable and animal, the Physiocrats expressed in their terminology by styling agriculture the only productive occupation. All other occupations, however useful, they regarded as sterile or barren, insomuch as under the fact assumed such occupations give rise to no net produce or unearned increment, merely returning again to the general fund of wealth, or gross product, the equivalent of what they had taken from it in changing the form, place or ownership of material things already in existence.

This was their great and fatal misapprehension, since it has been effectually used to discredit their whole system.

Still, it was not really a vital mistake. That is to say, it made no change in their practical proposals. The followers of Quesnay insisted that agriculture, in which they admitted fisheries and mines, was the only productive occupation, or in other words the only application of labor that added to the sum of wealth; while manufactures and exchange, though useful, were sterile, merely changing the form or place of wealth without adding to its sum. They, however, proposed no restrictions or disabilities whatever on the occupations they thus stigmatized. On the contrary, they were—what the so-called "English free traders" who have followed Adam Smith never yet have been—free traders in the full sense of the term. In their practical proposition, the single tax, they proposed the only means by which the free trade principle can ever be carried to its logical conclusion—the freedom not merely of trade, but of all other forms and modes of production, with full freedom of access to the natural element which is essential to all production. They were the authors of the motto that in the English use of the phrase "*Laissez faire!*" "Let things alone," has been so emasculated and perverted, but which on their lips was, "*Laissez faire, laissez aller,*" "Clear the ways and let things alone!" This is said to come from the cry that in medieval tournaments gave the signal for combat. The English motto which I take to come closest to the spirit of the French phrase is, "A fair field and no favor!"

It is for the reason that of all modern philosophers they not only were the first, but were really true free traders, that I dedicated to the memory of Quesnay and his fellows my "Protection or Free Trade" (1885), saying:

> By thus carrying the inquiry beyond the point where Adam Smith and the writers who have followed him have stopped, I believe I have stripped the vexed tariff question of its greatest difficulties, and have cleared the way for the settlement of a dispute which otherwise might go on interminably. The conclusions thus reached raise the doctrine of free trade from the emasculated form in which it has been taught by the English economists to the fullness in which it was held by the predecessors of Adam Smith, those illustrious Frenchmen, with whom originated the motto "*Laissez faire,*" and who, whatever may have been the confusions of their terminology or the faults of their method, grasped a central truth which free traders since their time have ignored.

These French "Economists," now more definitely known as Physiocrats, or single taxers, had got hold of what in its bearings on philosophy and politics is probably the greatest of truths; but had got hold of it through curiously distorted apprehensions. It was to them, however, like a rainbow seen through clouds. They did not see the full sweep of the majestic curve, and endeavored to piece out their lack of insight with a confused and confusing terminology. But what they did see showed them its trend, and they felt that natural laws could be trusted where attempts to order the world by human legislation would be certain to go astray.

Yet nothing better shows the importance of correct theory to the progress of truth against the resistance of powerful special interests than the complete overthrow of the Physiocrats. Their mistake in theory has sufficed to prevent, or perhaps rather to furnish a sufficient excuse to prevent the justice and expediency of their practical proposal from being considered.

I know of no English writer on the Physiocrats or their doctrines who seems to have understood them or to have had any glimmering that the truth which lay behind their theory that agriculture is the only productive occupation was an apprehension of what has since been known as the Ricardian doctrine of rent, carried out further than Ricardo carried it, to its logical results; but apprehended, as indeed Ricardo himself seems to have apprehended it, only in its relations to agriculture.

In "Progress and Poverty," after working out what I believe to be the simple yet sovereign remedy for the continuance of wide-spread poverty amid material progress, I thus, in the chapter entitled "Indorsements and Objections" (Book VIII., Chapter IV.), refer to the Physiocrats:

> In fact, that rent should, both on grounds of expediency and justice, be the peculiar subject of taxation, is involved in the accepted doctrine of rent, and may be found in embryo in the works of all economists who have accepted the law of Ricardo. That these principles have not been pushed to their necessary conclusions, as I have pushed them, evidently arises from the indisposition to endanger or offend the enormous interest involved in private ownership in land, and from the false theories in regard to wages and the cause of poverty which have dominated economic thought.
>
> But there has been a school of economists who plainly perceived, what is clear to the natural perceptions of men when uninfluenced by habit—that the revenues of the common property, land, ought to be appropriated to the common service. The French Economists of the last century, headed by Quesnay and Turgot, proposed just what

I have proposed, that all taxation should be abolished save a tax upon the value of land. As I am acquainted with the doctrines of Quesnay and his disciples only at second hand through the medium of the English writers, I am unable to say how far his peculiar ideas as to agriculture being the only productive avocation, etc., are erroneous apprehensions, or mere peculiarities of terminology. But of this I am certain from the proposition in which his theory culminated—that he saw the fundamental relation between land and labor which has since been lost sight of, and that he arrived at practical truth, though, it may be, through a course of defectively expressed reasoning. The causes which leave in the hands of the landlord a "produce net" were by the Physiocrats no better explained than the suction of a pump was explained by the assumption that nature abhors a vacuum; but the fact in its practical relations to social economy was recognized, and the benefit which would result from the perfect freedom given to industry and trade by a substitution of a tax on rent for all the impositions which hamper and distort the application of labor, was doubtless as clearly seen by them as it is by me. One of the things most to be regretted about the French Revolution is that it overwhelmed the ideas of the Economists, just as they were gaining strength among the thinking classes, and were apparently about to influence fiscal legislation.

Without knowing anything of Quesnay or his doctrines, I have reached the same practical conclusion by a route which cannot be disputed, and have based it on grounds which cannot be questioned by the accepted political economy.

The best English account of the Physiocratic views that I now know of is that given by Henry Dunning Macleod, in his "Elements of Economics" (1881). He seems to have no notion of the truth that lay at the bottom of a mistake that has caused their great services to be all but forgotten, and which I shall take opportunity in a subsequent book more fully to explain. To him it is "simply incomprehensible how men of the ability of the Physiocrats could maintain that a country could not be enriched by the labor of artisans and by commerce." This he styles "one of those aberrations of the human intellect which we can only wonder at and not explain." But nevertheless he awards them the honor of being the founders of the science of political economy, declares that in spite of their errors "they are entitled to imperishable glory in the history of mankind," and gives in his own language an outline of their doctrine, from which (Book I., Chapter V., Sec. 3) I take the following:

The Creator has placed man upon the earth with the evident intention that the race should prosper, and there are certain physical and moral laws which conduce in the highest degree to ensure his preservation, increase, well-being, and improvement. The correlation between these physical and moral laws is so close that if either be misunderstood, through ignorance or passion, the others are also. Physical nature, or matter, bears to mankind very much the relation which the body does to the soul. Hence the perpetual and necessary relation of physical and moral good and evil on each other.

Natural justice is the conformity of human laws and actions to natural order, and this collection of physical and moral laws existed before any positive institutions among men. And while their observance produces the highest degree of prosperity and well-being among men, the non-observance or transgression of them is the cause of the extensive physical evils which afflict mankind.

If such a natural law exists, our intelligence is capable of understanding it; for, if not, it would be useless, and the sagacity of the Creator would be at fault. As, therefore, these laws are instituted by the Supreme Being, all men and all states ought to be governed by them. They are immutable and irrefragable, and the best possible laws: therefore necessarily the basis of the most perfect government, and the fundamental rule of all positive laws, which are only for the purpose of upholding natural order, evidently the most advantageous for the human race.

The evident object of the Creator being the preservation, the increase, the well-being, and the improvement of the race, man necessarily received from his origin not only intelligence, but instincts conformable to that end. Every one feels himself endowed with the triple instincts of well-being, sociability, and justice. He understands that the isolation of the brute is not suitable to his double nature, and that his physical and moral wants urge him to live in the society of his equals in a state of peace, good-will, and concord.

He also recognizes that other men, having the same wants as himself, cannot have less rights than himself, and therefore he is bound to respect this right, so that other men may observe a similar obligation towards him.

These ideas—the product of reason, the necessity of work, the necessity of society, and the necessity of justice—imply three others—liberty, property, and authority, which are the three essential terms of all social order.

How could man understand the necessity of labor to obey the irresistible instinct of his preservation and well-being, without conceiving at the same time that the instrument of labor, the physical and intellectual qualities with which he is endowed by nature, belongs to him exclusively, without perceiving that he is master and the absolute proprietor of his person, that he is born and should remain free?

But the idea of liberty cannot spring up in the mind without associating with it that of property, in the absence of which the first would only represent an illusory right, without an object. The freedom the individual has of acquiring useful things by labor supposes necessarily that of preserving them, of enjoying them, and of disposing of them without reserve, and also of bequeathing them to his family, who prolong his existence indefinitely. Thus liberty conceived in this manner becomes property, which may be conceived in two aspects as it regards movable goods on the earth, which is the source from which labor ought to draw them.

At first property was principally movable; but when the cultivation of the earth was necessary for the preservation, increase, and improvement of the race, individual appropriation of the soil became necessary, because no other system is so proper to draw from the earth all the mass of utilities it can produce; and, secondly, because the collective constitution of property would have produced many inconveniences as to sharing of the fruits, which would not arise from the division of the land, by which the rights of each are fixed in a clear and definite manner. Property in land, therefore, is the necessary and legitimate consequence of personal and movable property. Every man has, then, centered in him by the laws of Providence, certain rights and duties; the right of enjoying himself to the utmost of his capacity, and the duty of respecting similar rights in others. The perfect respect and protection of reciprocal rights and duties conduces to production in the highest degree, and the obtaining the greatest amount of physical enjoyments.

The Physiocrats, then, placed absolute freedom, or property—as the fundamental right of man—freedom of Person, freedom of Opinion, and freedom of Contract, or Exchange; and the violation of these as contrary to the law of Providence, and therefore the cause of all evil to man. Quesnay's first publication, "Le Droit Naturel," contains an inquiry into these natural rights; and he afterwards, in another called "General Maxims of the Economical Government of an Agricultural Kingdom," endeavored to lay down in a series of thirty maxims, or fundamental general principles, the whole bases of the economy of society. The 23d of these declares that a nation suffers no loss by trading with foreigners. The 24th declares the fallacy of the doctrine of the balance of trade. The 25th says: "Let entire freedom of commerce be maintained; for the regulation of commerce, both internal and external, the most sure, the most true, the most profitable to the nation and to the state, exists in entire freedom of competition." In these three maxims, which Quesnay and his followers developed, was contained the entire overthrow of the existing system of Political Economy; and notwithstanding certain errors and shortcomings, they are unquestionably entitled to be considered as the founders of the science of Political Economy.

Wealth, in the economic sense of the wealth of societies, or the wealth of nations, Macleod goes on to state, the Physiocrats held to consist exclusively of material things, drawn from land—to man the source of all material things—by the exertion of labor, and possessing value in exchange, or exchangeability; a distinction which they recognized as essentially different from, and not necessarily associated with, value in use or usefulness. That man can neither create nor annihilate matter they repeated again and again in such phrases as: "Man can create nothing," and "Nothing can come out of nothing." They expressly excluded land itself and labor itself, and all personal capacities and powers and services, from the category of wealth, and were far ahead of their time in deriving the essential quality of money from its use in serving as a medium of exchange, and in including all usury laws in the restrictions that they would sweep away.

That these men rose in France, and as it were in the very palace of the absolute king, just as the rotten Bourbon dynasty was hastening to its fall, is one of the most striking of the paradoxes with which history abounds.

Never, before nor since, out of the night of despotism gleamed there such clear light of liberty.

They were deluded by the idea—the only possibility in fact, under existing conditions of carrying their views into effect in their time—that the power of a king whose predecessor had said, "I am the state!" might be utilized to break the power of other special interests, and to bring liberty and plenty to France, and through France to the world.

They had their day of hope, and almost it must have seemed of assured triumph, when in 1774, three months before Quesnay's death, Turgot was made Finance Minister of Louis XVI., and at once began clearing the ways by cutting the restrictions that were stifling French industry. But they leaned on a reed. Turgot was removed. His reforms were stopped. The pent-up misery of the masses, which they had been so largely instrumental in showing utterly repugnant to the natural order, burst into the blind madness of the great revolution. The Physiocrats were overthrown, many of them perishing on the guillotine, in prison or in exile. In the reaction which the excesses of that revolution everywhere produced among those most influencing thought, the propertied and the powerful, the Physiocrats were remembered merely by their unfortunate misapprehension in regarding agriculture as the only productive occupation.

France will some day honor among the noblest the centuries have given her the names of Quesnay, and Gournay, and Turgot, and Mirabeau, and Condorcet, and Dupont, and their fellows, as we shall have in English, intelligent explanations, if not translations of their works. But, probably for the reason that France has as yet felt less than the English and Teutonic and Scandinavian nations the influence of the new philosophy of the natural order, best known as the Single Tax, the teachings of these men seem at present, even in France, to be practically forgotten.

CHAPTER V.

ADAM SMITH AND THE PHYSIOCRATS.

SHOWING THE RELATION BETWEEN ADAM SMITH AND THE PHYSIOCRATS.

Smith and Quesnay—The "Wealth of Nations" and Physiocratic ideas—Smith's criticism of the Physiocrats—His failure to appreciate the single tax—His prudence.

ON the continental trip he made between 1764 and 1766, after resigning his Glasgow professorship of moral philosophy to accompany as tutor the young Duke of Buccleuch, Adam Smith made the personal acquaintance of Quesnay and some of the "men of great learning and ingenuity," who regarded the "King's Thinker" with an admiration "not inferior to that of any of the ancient philosophers for the founders of their respective systems," and was, while in Paris, a frequent and welcome visitor at the apartments in the palace, where, unmindful of the gaieties and intrigues of the most splendid and corrupt court of Europe that went on but a floor below them, this remarkable group discussed matters of the highest and most permanent interest to mankind.

This must have been a fruitful time in Adam Smith's intellectual life. During this time the almost unknown Scottish tutor, notable among his few acquaintances for his fits of abstraction, must have been mentally occupied with the work which ten years after was to begin a fame that for more than a century has kept him at the very head of economic philosophers and in the first rank of the permanently illustrious men of his generation.

Upon this work he entered immediately after his return from the continent, in the leisure afforded him by the ample pension that the trustees of the Duke had agreed should continue until he could be provided with a profitable government place. The Duke himself, on coming to his majority and estates, seems to have made no effort to release himself from this payment by securing such a place for the man whom he always continued to regard with respect and affection, thinking doubtless that its duties, however nearly nominal, might somewhat interfere with his freedom to devote himself to his long work. And when, the "Wealth of Nations" having been at last published, its author was appointed by Lord North to be one of the Commissioners of Customs in Scotland—an appointment which seems to have been due to the gratitude of the Premier for hints received from that book as to new sources of taxation rather than to any pressure of the Buccleuch interest, and which raised the simple-mannered student to comparative opulence—the Duke insisted on making no change in his payment, but continued the pension for life.

The "liberal and generous system" of the French Economists could not fail to appeal powerfully to a man of Adam Smith's disposition, and the "Wealth of Nations" bears ample evidence of the depth of the opinion he in one place expresses in terms, that this system, "with all its imperfections, is perhaps the nearest approximation to the truth that has yet been published upon the subject of political economy." It was indeed his original intention as stated to his friend and biographer, Professor Dugald Stewart, to dedicate to Quesnay the fruits of his ten years' application. But the French philosopher died in 1774, two years before the Scotsman's great work saw the light. Thus it appeared without any indication of an intention which, had it been expressed, might, in the bitter prejudice soon afterwards aroused against the Physiocrats by the outbreak of the French Revolution, have seriously militated against its usefulness.

The resemblance of the views expressed in this work to those held by the Physiocrats has, however, been noticed by all critics, and both on the side of their opponents and their advocates there have not been wanting intimations that Smith borrowed from them. But while he must have been eminently ready to absorb any idea that commended itself to his mind, there is no reason to regard these views as not originally Adam Smith's own. The keenness of observation and analysis, the vigor of imagination and solidity of learning, that characterize the "Wealth of Nations" are shown in the "Theory of the Moral Sentiments," written before Smith had left the University of Glasgow, and which indeed led to the invitation that he should accompany the young nobleman on his trip. They are shown as well in the paper on the formation of languages, and the papers on the principles which lead and direct philosophical inquiry, as illustrated in the history of various sciences, which are usually published with that work. It appears from the "Theory of the Moral Sentiments" that Adam Smith was even then meditating some such a book as the "Wealth of Nations," and there is no reason to suppose that without knowledge of the Physiocrats it would have been essentially different.

It is a mistake to which the critics who are themselves mere compilers are liable, to think that men must draw from one another to see the same truths or to fall into the same errors. Truth is, in fact, a relation of things, which is to be seen independently because it exists independently.

Error is perhaps more likely to indicate transmission from mind to mind; yet even that usually gains its strength and permanence from misapprehensions that in themselves have independent plausibility. Such relations of the stars as that appearance in the north which we call the Dipper or Great Bear, or as that in the south which we call the Southern Cross, are seen by all who scan the starry heavens, though the names by which men know them are various. And to think that the sun revolves around the earth is an error into which the testimony of their senses must cause all men independently to fall, until the first testimony of the senses is corrected by reason applied to wider observations.

In what is most important, I have come closer to the views of Quesnay and his followers than did Adam Smith, who knew the men personally. But in my case there was certainly no derivation from them. I well recall the day when, checking my horse on a rise that overlooks San Francisco Bay, the commonplace reply of a passing teamster to a commonplace question, crystallized, as by lightning-flash, my brooding thoughts into coherency, and I there and then recognized the natural order—one of those experiences that make those who have had them feel thereafter that they can vaguely appreciate what mystics and poets have called the "ecstatic vision." Yet at that time I had never heard of the Physiocrats, or even read a line of Adam Smith.

Afterwards, with the great idea of the natural order in my head, I printed a little book, "Our Land and Land Policy," in which I urged that all taxes should be laid on the value of land, irrespective of improvements. Casually meeting on a San Francisco street a scholarly lawyer, A. B. Douthitt, we stopped to chat, and he told me that what I had in my little book proposed was what the French "Economists" a hundred years before had proposed.

I forget many things, but the place where I heard this, and the tones and attitude of the man who told me of it, are photographed on my memory. For, when you have seen a truth that those around you do not see, it is one of the deepest of pleasures to hear of others who have seen it. This is true even though these others were dead years before you were born. For the stars that we of to-day see when we look were here to be seen hundreds and thousands of years ago. They shine on. Men come and go, in their generations, like the generations of the ants.

This pleasure of a common appreciation of truth not yet often accepted, Adam Smith must have had from his intercourse with the Physiocrats. Widely as he and they may have differed, there was yet much that was common in their thought. He was a free trader as they were, though perhaps not so logical and thorough-going. And though differing in temper and widely differing in conditions, both were bent on struggling against what must have seemed at the time insuperable difficulties.

Adam Smith's knowledge of, and admiration for, the Physiocrats must at least have affected his thought and expression, sometimes by absorption and sometimes perhaps by reaction. But no matter how much of his economic views were original with him and how much he imbibed consciously or unconsciously from them, it is certain that his political economy, as far as it goes on all fours, is the system of natural order proclaimed by them.

What Adam Smith meant by the wealth of nations is in most cases, and wherever he is consistent, the material things produced from land by labor which constitute the necessities and conveniences of human life; the aggregate *produce* of society, using the word produce as expressive of the sum of material results, in the same way that we speak of agricultural produce, of factory produce, of the produce of mines, or fisheries, or the chase. Now this is what the Physiocrats meant by wealth, or as they sometimes termed it, the gross product of land and labor.

But this is also, as I shall hereafter show, the primary or root meaning of the word wealth in its common use. And whoever will read Smith's "Considerations Concerning the First Formation of Languages," originally published with his "Moral Sentiments," in 1759, will see from his manner of tracing words to their primary uses, that whenever he came to think of it, he would have recognized the original and true meaning of the word wealth to be that of the necessities and conveniences of human life, brought into being by the exertion of labor upon land.

The difference between Smith and the Physiocrats is this:

The Physiocrats, on their part, clearly laid down and steadily contended that nothing that did not have material existence, or was not produced from land, could be included in the category of the wealth of society. Adam Smith, however, with seeming inadvertence, has fallen in places into the inconsistency of classing personal qualities and obligations as wealth. This is probably attributable to the fact that what it seemed to him possible to accomplish was much less than what the Physiocrats aimed at. The task to which he set himself, that in the main of showing the absurdity and impolicy of the mercantile or protective system, was sufficiently difficult to make him comparatively regardless of speculations that led far beyond it. With the disproval of the current notion that the wealth of nations consists of the precious metals, his care as to what is and what is not a part of that wealth relaxed. He went with the Physiocrats in their condemnation of the attempts of governments to check commerce, but stopped both where they had carried the idea of freeing all production from tax or restraint to the point of a practical proposition, and where they had fallen into obvious error. He neither proposed the single tax nor did he fall into the mistake of declaring agriculture the only productive occupation. That there is a natural order he saw; and that to this natural order our perceptions of justice conform, he also saw. But that involved in this natural order is a provision for the material needs of advancing society he seems never to have seen.

Whether Adam Smith's failure to grasp the great truth that the French "Economists" perceived, though "as through a glass, darkly," was due to their erroneous way of stating it, or to some of those environments of the individual mind which seem on special points to close its powers of perception, there is no means that I know of for determining. Adam Smith saw that the Physiocrats must be wrong in regarding manufactures and exchanges as sterile occupations, but he did not see the true answer to their contention, the answer that would have brought into the light of a larger truth that portion of truth they had wrongly apprehended. The answer he makes to them in Book IV., Chapter IX., of the "Wealth of Nations" could hardly have been entirely satisfactory to himself. In this he does not venture to contend that the labor of artificers, manufacturers and merchants is as productive of wealth *as* the labor of agriculturists. He only contends that it is not to be considered as utterly sterile, and that "the revenue of a trading and manufacturing country must, other things being equal, always be much greater than that of one without trade and manufactures," because "a smaller quantity of manufactured produce purchases a great quantity of rude produce." That he himself, indeed, regarded agriculture as at least the most productive of occupations is shown directly in other places in his great work.

And there is one part of this answer that is extremely unsatisfactory and utterly out of its author's usual temper. No one better than Adam Smith could see the fallacy of comparing a philosopher who declared that the political body would thrive best under conditions of perfect liberty and perfect justice with a physician who "imagined that the health of the human body could be preserved only by a certain precise regimen of diet and exercise." And that he should resort to an illustration which depended for its effect upon such a *suppressio veri* to explain or emphasize his dissent from a man whom he esteemed so highly as Quesnay, shows a latent uncertainty. Both in quality and in temper of mind, Smith seems the last of men to use such an argument except in despair of finding a better one.

There are passages in the "Wealth of Nations" where Adam Smith checks his inquiry with a suddenness that shows an indisposition to venture on ground that the possessing classes would deem dangerous. But in nothing he left after him (just before his death he destroyed all manuscripts he did not wish published), is there an indication that he was more than puzzled by the attempt of the Physiocrats to explain the great truth that they saw with wrong apprehension. He clearly perceived that "the produce of labor constitutes the natural recompense or wages of labor," and that it was the appropriation of land that had deprived the laborer of his natural due. But he had evidently never looked further into the phenomena of rent than to see that "the landlords, like all other men, love to reap where they never sowed." He passes over the great subject of the relations of men to the land they inhabit, as though the appropriation by a few of what nature has provided as the dwelling-place and storehouse of all must now be accepted as if it were a part of the natural order. And so, indeed, in his times and conditions it must have appeared to him.

Even if Adam Smith had seen the place of the single tax in the natural order, as the natural means for the supply of the natural needs of civilized societies, prudence might well have suggested that his inquiry should not be carried so far. I mean, not merely that prudence of the individual which impelled Copernicus to withhold until after his death any publication of his discovery of the movement of the earth about the sun; but that prudence of the philosopher which, from a desire to do the utmost that he can for Truth and Justice in his own time, may prevent him from advancing a larger measure of truth than his own time can receive.

In that part of the eighteenth century when the Physiocrats dreamed that they were on the verge of carrying their great reform and Smith wrote painfully his "Wealth of Nations," there was a wide difference between the conditions of France and Scotland.

Sheltered under the friendship of a king whose dynasty had reduced the great feudal landlords to servitors and courtiers; seeking with the aphorism, "Poor peasants, poor kingdom; poor kingdom, poor king," to arouse the strongest power in the state to the relief of the most downtrodden; cherishing the hope that the emancipation of man might be accomplished by the short and royal road of winning the mind and conscience of a young and amiable sovereign, the French philosophers might have some prospect of getting a hearing in their advocacy of the single tax. But, on the other side of the Channel, the "landed interest," gorged with the spoil of Church and Crown and peasants and clansmen, reigned supreme. For a solitary man of letters to have attacked this supreme power in front would have been foolishness.

That Adam Smith, "all-round man" that he was, possessed both the prudence of the man and the prudence of the philosopher, is shown by the fact that he managed to do what he did, without arousing in greater degree the ire of the defenders of vested wrongs. Whoever will intelligently read the "Wealth of Nations" will find it full of radical sentiment, an arsenal from which lovers of liberty and justice may still draw weapons for victories remaining to be won. Yet its author was a college professor, traveling tutor of a duke, held a lucrative government position and died Lord Rector of Glasgow University.

For the present times at least, the Scotsman succeeded where the Frenchman failed. It is he, not Quesnay, who has come down to us as the "father of political economy."

This position is recognized even by economists who differ from what they deem his school. Thus Professor James, of the University of Pennsylvania, himself belonging to the "new school," says of Adam Smith in the article "Political Economy" in Lalor's Cyclopedia, 1884:

> All theories and development of the preceding ages culminate in him, all lines of development in the succeeding ages start from him. His work has been before the public over one hundred years, and yet no second book has been produced that deserves to be compared with it in originality and importance. The subsequent history of the science is mainly the history of attempts to broaden and deepen the foundation laid by Adam Smith, to build the superstructure higher and render it more solid.

It is for this reason that I take Adam Smith's "Wealth of Nations" as the great landmark in the history of Political Economy.

CHAPTER VI.

SMITH'S INFLUENCE ON POLITICAL ECONOMY.

SHOWING WHAT THE "WEALTH OF NATIONS" ACCOMPLISHED AND THE COURSE OF THE SUBSEQUENT DEVELOPMENT OF POLITICAL ECONOMY.

Smith, a philosopher, who addressed the cultured, and whose attack on mercantilism rather found favor with the powerful landowners —Not entirely exempt from suspicion of radicalism, yet pardoned for his affiliation with the Physiocrats—Efforts of Malthus and Ricardo on respectabilizing the science—The fight against the corn-laws revealed the true beneficiaries of protection, but passed for a free-trade victory, and much strengthened the incoherent science—Confidence of its scholastic advocates—Say's belief in the result of the colleges taking up political economy—Torrens's confidence—Failure of other countries to follow England's example—Cairnes doubts the effect of making it a scholastic study —His sagacity proved by the subsequent breakdown of Smith's economy—The true reason.

ADAM SMITH was not a propagandist or a politician, as were the Physiocrats. He was simply a philosopher, addressing primarily a small, comfortable and cultured class, whose sympathies and feelings were identified with the existing social order, and he wielded a power which requires the fruition of time and the opening of opportunity for its culmination in action—a power which men of affairs are in its first beginnings apt to underrate.

When the first few copies of my "Progress and Poverty" were printed in an author's edition in San Francisco, a large landowner (the late General Beale, proprietor of the Tejon Ranch, and afterwards United States Minister to Austria), sought me to express the pleasure with which he had read it as an intellectual performance. This, he said, he had felt at liberty to enjoy, for to speak with the freedom of philosophic frankness, he was certain my work would never be heard of by those whom I wished it to affect.

In the same way, but to a much greater degree, the small class whom alone the "Wealth of Nations" could first reach were able to enjoy its greatness as an intellectual performance that widened the circle of thought. Few of them were disturbed by any fear of its ultimate effect on special interests. At that time a popular press was not yet in existence, and books of this kind were addressed only to the "superior orders." The House of Commons, the nominal representative of the unprivileged in Great Britain, was filled by the appointees of the great landowners; and the oligarchy that ruled in the British Islands was really stronger than the similar class under the absolute monarchy of France. It was only a few years before the publication of the "Wealth of Nations" that the landlord's right of pit and gallows, *i.e.*, of life and death, had been abolished in Scotland, not as a matter of justice, but by purchase, as a matter of dynastic expediency; and workmen in coal-pits and salt-works were still virtually slaves, being formally denied the right of *habeas corpus.*

Adam Smith had avoided arousing antagonism from the landed interests. And in turning the aggressive side of the new science against the mercantile system, as he styled what has since been known as the protective system, he found favor with, rather than excited prejudice among, the cultured class—the only class to which such a book as his could at that time be addressed. Such a class, under the conditions then existing in Great Britain, is apt to feel contempt tinged with anger for traders beginning to aspire towards sharing the power and place of "born masters of the soil." Thus the indignation with which he speaks of how "the sneaking arts of underling tradesmen are erected into political maxims for the conduct of a great empire," and with which he compares "the capricious ambition of kings and ministers"—"the violence and injustice of the rulers of mankind, for which, perhaps, the nature of human affairs can scarce afford a remedy," with "the impertinent jealousy, the mean rapacity, the monopolizing spirit of merchants and manufacturers who neither are nor ought to be the rulers of mankind," could not fail to strike a sympathetic chord in the spirit then intellectually as politically dominant in Great Britain. This would render unnoticed the quiet way in which he shows that "superiority of birth" is but "an ancient superiority of fortune"* and attributes the difference between the philosopher and the street porter to the difference in the accidents under which they have been placed.

Yet with the outbreak of the French Revolution the radicalism of the "Wealth of Nations" did not pass entirely unnoticed. A note appended by Dugald Stewart, in 1810, to the second edition of the biography of Adam Smith, first read before the Royal Society of Edinburgh in 1793, explains as a reason why he had in the first edition confined himself to a much more general view of the "Wealth of Nations" than he had once intended, that:

> The doctrine of a free trade was itself represented as of a revolutionary tendency; and some who had formerly prided themselves on an intimacy with Mr. Smith, and on their zeal for the propagation of his liberal system, began to call in question the expediency of subjecting to the disputations of philosophers the arcana of state policy and the unfathomable wisdom of the feudal ages.

---

* "Wealth of Nations," Book V.. Chapter II., Part II.

And William Playfair, in his annotated edition of the "Wealth of Nations" (London, 1805), deems it necessary to apologize for Smith's sympathy with the Physiocrats by declaring that "the real fact is that Dr. Smith, as well as many of the Economists themselves, was ignorant of the secret belonging to the sect"—that "simply pretending to reduce to practice the Economical Table, they were silently laboring to overturn the thrones of Europe." This ignorance, since it was shared at the same time by "a monarch of such eminent abilities and penetration" as the great Frederick of Prussia, Playfair thinks may be well pardoned to Dr. Smith. And pardoned it was. Or rather the objections made to Dr. Smith on the score of radicalism attracted so little attention that it is only by delving in forgotten literature that any trace of them can be found. The larger fact is that Adam Smith, opening the study of political economy at a lower level than the Physiocrats, found less resistance, and his book began to secure so permanent a recognition for the new science that its continuance to our time is properly traced to him as its founder rather than to them.

In 1798, five years after Stewart read his biography of Smith before the Royal Society of Edinburgh, and eight years after the author of the "Wealth of Nations," lamenting with his last breath that he had done so little, was laid to rest in the Edinburgh Cannongate, the English clergyman Malthus brought forward his famous theory of population. This at once, like "a long-felt want," took its place in the crystallizing system of political economy which Smith had brought into shape, and which, if it was lacking in a clear and consistent definition of wealth, was not on that account objectionable to the spirit of the learned institutions which soon began to make its teaching a function of their official faculties. A few years after Malthus came Ricardo, to correct mistakes into which Smith had fallen as to the nature and cause of rent, and to formulate the true law of rent; but to do this by laying stress on the fact that rent would increase as the necessities of increasing population forced cultivation to less and less productive land, or to less and less productive points on the same land.

Thus, the theory of wages into which Adam Smith fell when, as though fearful of the radical conclusions to which it must lead, he suddenly abandons his true perception that "the produce of labor constitutes the natural recompense or wages of labor," to consider the master as providing from his capital the wages of his workmen, together with the theory of the tendency of population to increase faster than subsistence, and the apprehension of the theory of rent as resulting from the forcing of exertion to less and less productive land, with what was deemed its corollary, "the law of diminishing productiveness in agriculture," became cardinal doctrine. These linking with and buttressing each other, in what soon became the accepted system of political economy as developed from the "Wealth of Nations," did away effectually with any fear that the study of natural laws of the production and distribution of wealth might be dangerous to the great House of Have. For in this way political economy was made to serve the purpose of an assumed scientific demonstration that the shocking contrasts in the material conditions of men which our advancing civilization presents, result not from the injustice and mistakes of human law, but from the immutable law of Nature—the decrees of the All-originating, All-maintaining Spirit.

So far from showing any menace to the great special interests, a political economy, so perverted, soon took its place with a similarly perverted Christianity to soothe the conscience of the rich and to frown down discontent on the part of the poor. In text-books and teachings from which Adam Smith's recurring perceptions of the natural equality of men were eliminated, it became indeed "the dismal science." It was held by its admirers that it needed only to be sufficiently taught them to convince even the "lower orders," that things as they are are things as they ought to be, except perhaps that "the monopolizing spirit of merchants and manufacturers," and "the sneaking arts of underling tradesmen" should no longer be permitted to be erected into maxims for governmental interferences with trade.

Thus as the system of political economy presented by Adam Smith began to attract the attention of the thoughtful and cultured, it did not meet the resistance it would have encountered had the special interests which it threatened been really those of the growing class of merchants and manufacturers. On the other hand, the apparent turning of its aggressive side against merchants and manufacturers prevented the powerful landed interest from perceiving fully its relation to their own monopoly until it had gained the weight of recognized philosophic authority.

Now the course of social development in the civilized world generally, but particularly in Great Britain, in the era of steam which immediately followed Adam Smith, was enormously to increase the relative social weight of the mercantile and manufacturing classes. But when, fifty years after the death of Adam Smith, what he called the mercantile system came into political issue in the agitation for the repeal of the corn-laws, it was not among merchants and manufacturers, but in the power of the landed interest, that the strong defense of this system was seen to lie. The repeal of the corn-laws was carried against the strenuous resistance of the landowners by a combination of merchants and manufacturers with the working-classes, urged by bitter discontent and growing aspirations. But it was not carried until it became evident to the more thoughtful that if the agitation went on it would be sure to lead to an inquiry into the right by which a few individuals called landowners, claimed the land of the British Islands as *their* property.

The truth is that merchants and manufacturers, as merchants and manufacturers, are not the ultimate beneficiaries of the protective system, and that mercantile interests can long profit by it only when sheltered behind some special monopoly. This has been shown in the United States, where the owners of coal and mineral and timber and sugar land have constituted the backbone of the political strength that has carried protection to such monstrous length.

The repeal of the English corn-laws passed in Great Britain for a victory of free trade as far as it was practicable to carry free trade. And in scholastic circles in that country and in the United States, and throughout the civilized world that took its intellectual impulse from England, it greatly increased the hopefulness of the professed economists.

Thus strengthened by this powerful impulse, there continued to grow up under the sanction and development of a series of able and authoritatively placed men, whose efforts were devoted to smoothing away difficulties and covering up incongruities, an accredited system of political economy which found its most widely accepted expounder in John Stuart Mill, and reached perhaps its highest point of authority in scholastic circles about or shortly after the centennial of the publication of the "Wealth of Nations." Yet it was as wanting in coherence as the image that Nebuchadnezzar saw in his dream. It contained much real truth well worked out. But this was conjoined with fallacies which could not stand examination. The attempt to define its object-noun, wealth, and the sub-term of wealth, capital, made them much more indefinite and confused than they had been left by Adam Smith. And it was never attempted to bring together what were given as the laws of the distribution of wealth, as that would have shown at a glance their want of relation.

This political economy had no real hold on common thought, and was regarded even by ordinarily intelligent men as a scholastic or esoteric science. But it was spoken of by its professors with the utmost confidence as an assured science, and their belief in its success was greatly increased.

From the beginning until well past the middle of the nineteenth century the temper of the recognized expounders of the political economy which took shape from Adam Smith's foundation was hopeful and confident. They believed they had hold of a true science, which needed only development to be universally recognized.

In what was printed as the introduction to the first American edition of Jean Baptiste Say's treatise on political economy *—which being translated into English and widely circulated on both sides of the Atlantic became for a long time, in the United States at least, perhaps the most popular of the expositions of the science that Adam Smith had founded—Say points out certain difficulties that political economy must have to encounter: "that opinions in political economy are not only maintained by vanity, but by the self-interest enlisted in the maintenance of a vicious order of things;" that "writers are found who possess the lamentable faculty of composing articles for journals, pamphlets and even whole volumes upon subjects which, according to their own confession, they do not understand;" and that "such is the indifference of the public

* The original work was published in 1803. But this introduction bears internal evidence of having been written not earlier than 1814.

that they rather prefer trusting to assertions than be at the trouble of investigating them."

But he continues:

Everything, however, announces that this beautiful, and above all, useful science, is spreading itself with increasing rapidity. Since it has been perceived that it does not rest upon hypothesis, but is founded upon observation and experience, its importance has been felt. It is now taught wherever knowledge is cherished. In the universities of Germany, of Scotland, of Spain, of Italy, and of the north of Europe, professorships of political economy are already established. Hereafter this science will be taught in them, with all the advantages of a regular and systematic study. Whilst the University of Oxford proceeds in her old and beaten track, within a few years that of Cambridge has established a chair for the purpose of imparting instruction in this new science. Courses of lectures are delivered in Geneva and various other places; and the merchants of Barcelona have, at their own expense, founded a professorship on political economy. It is now considered as forming an essential part of the education of princes; and those who are called to that high distinction ought to blush at being ignorant of its principles. The Emperor of Russia has desired his brothers, the Grand Dukes Nicholas and Michael, to pursue a course of study on this subject under the direction of M. Storch. Finally, the Government of France has done itself lasting honor by establishing in this kingdom, under the sanction of public authority, the first professorship of political economy.

This hopefulness as to what was to be accomplished by the regular and systematic study of political economy pervaded for a long time all economic writings. Even when it was necessary to admit that the unanimity that had been confidently expected had not come, it was always just about to come.

Thus Colonel Torrens, in the introduction to his "Essay on the Production of Wealth," says in 1821:

In the progress of the human mind, a period of controversy among the cultivators of any branch of science must necessarily precede the period of unanimity. With respect to political economy, the period of controversy is passing away, and that of unanimity rapidly approaching. Twenty years hence there will scarcely exist a doubt respecting any of its fundamental principles.

With the great defeat of protection in 1846, the confidence of political economists became even greater than before. But the predictions that the example of Great Britain in abolishing protective duties would be quickly followed throughout the civilized world—predictions based on the assumption that this partial victory for freedom had been won by the advance of an intelligent political economy, were not realized; and fostered by such tremendous political events as the great fight between the American States and the Franco-German war, a wave of reaction in favor of protection seemed to sweep over pretty nearly all the civilized world outside of Great Britain.

And while in the scholastic world, of the English-speaking countries at least, the triumph of Adam Smith's opposition to the principles of the mercantile system seemed to have established firmly an accepted science of political economy, and chairs for its teaching formed an indispensable adjunct of every institution of education, the real incoherencies which had been slurred over began more and more to show themselves.

In 1856 Professor J. E. Cairnes, delivering in Dublin University on the Whately Foundation a series of lectures afterwards reprinted under the title of "The Character and Logical Method of Political Economy," quoted what he called the unlucky prophecy of Torrens, made in 1821, that the period of controversy had passed and that of unanimity was rapidly approaching, and that in twenty years from then there would scarcely exist a doubt respecting any of the fundamental principles of political economy. Professor Cairnes did this only to give point to a statement that fundamental questions "are still vehemently debated, not merely by sciolists and smatterers. who may always be expected to wrangle, but by the professed cultivators and recognized expounders of the science," and that:

> So far from the period of controversy having passed, it seems hardly yet to have begun—controversy, I mean, not merely respecting propositions of secondary importance, or the practical application of scientific doctrines (for such controversy is only an evidence of the vitality of a science, and is a necessary condition of its progress), but controversy respecting fundamental principles which lie at the root of its reasonings, and which were regarded as settled when Colonel Torrens wrote.

Cairnes continues with a passage, which as showing a perception by a leading professor of political economy of the effect of the establishment of professorships, from which Say a generation before had hoped so much and from which up to this very time so much continued as it still continues to be hoped by those who know no better, is worth my quoting:

> When Political Economy had nothing to recommend it to public notice but its own proper and intrinsic evidence, no man professed himself a political economist who had not conscientiously studied and mastered its elementary principles; and no one who acknowledged himself a political economist discussed an economic problem without constant reference to the recognized axioms of the science. But when the immense success of free trade gave experimental proof of the justice of those principles on which economists relied, an observable change took place both in the mode of conducting economic discussions and in the class of persons who attached themselves to the cause of political economy. Many now enrolled themselves as political economists who had never taken the trouble to study the elementary principles of the science; and some, perhaps, whose capacities did not enable them to appreciate its evidence; while even those who had mastered its doctrines, in their anxiety to propitiate a popular audience, were too often led to abandon the true grounds of the science, in order to find for it in the facts and results of free trade a more popular and striking vindication. It was as if mathematicians, in order to attract new adherents to their ranks, had consented to abandon the method of analysis, and to rest the truth of their formulas on the correspondence of the almanacs with astro-

nomical events. The severe and logical style which characterized the cultivators of the science in the early part of the century has thus been changed to suit the different character of the audience to whom economists now addressed themselves. The discussions of Political Economy have been constantly assuming more of a statistical character; results are now appealed to instead of principles; the rules of arithmetic are superseding the canons of inductive reasoning; till the true course of investigation has been well-nigh forgotten, and Political Economy seems in danger of realizing the fate of Atalanta.

At the present time it is clearly to be seen that the worst fears of Cairnes have been more than realized. The period of controversy instead of having passed, had indeed, it has since been proved, hardly then begun. The accelerating tendency since his time as in the period of which he then spoke, has been away from, not towards, uniformity; controversy has become incoherence, and what he then thought to be the science of political economy has been destroyed at the hands of its own professors.

But while Cairnes realized the true drift of a tendency that most of his contemporaries did not understand, and saw the real effect of a study of political economy for the purpose of filling professorships and writing books, he did not see the real cause which so much faster and farther than he could have imagined has given sober reality to his more than half-rhetorical prediction. The reason of the constantly increasing confusion of the scholastic political economy has lain in the failure of the so-called science to define its subject-matter or object-noun. Statistics cannot aid us in the search for a thing until we know what it is we want to find. It is the Tower of Babel over again. Men who attempt to develop a science of the production and distribution of wealth without first deciding what they mean by wealth cannot understand each other or even understand themselves.

CHAPTER VII.

INEFFECTUAL GROPINGS TOWARD A DETERMINATION OF WEALTH.

SHOWING THE OPPOSITION TO THE SCHOLASTIC ECONOMY BEFORE "PROGRESS AND POVERTY."

Illogical character of the "Wealth of Nations"—Statements of natural right—Spence, Ogilvie, Chalmers, Wakefield, Spencer, Dove, Bisset—Vague recognitions of natural right—Protection gave rise to no political economy in England, but did elsewhere—Germany and protectionist political economy in the United States—Divergence of the schools—Trade-unionism in socialism.

THE "Wealth of Nations" won great vogue by its striking qualities and its prudence in avoiding antagonism with landowners. It made a nucleus around which the scholastic classes could rally, assuming that they were teaching a science of political economy, without seriously hurting any powerful interest. What Smith had done was after all an evasion—a settlement which left the cardinal principles unsettled. He had shown how greatly the division of labor increases the productiveness of labor, and without daring to go too far had shown that to leave labor unrestricted would increase the annual product. He had in short turned the aggressive side of the science against the protective, or, as he styled it, the mercantile system, thus putting on its feet a political economy which taught a sort of free trade that did not seriously object to taxes on labor and the products of labor for raising the revenues of government.

What wealth, or its sub-term, capital, was, Smith did not really say, nor yet did he make clear the division of their joint produce between the human factor and the natural factor, nor venture to show what was the cause and warrant of poverty. In political economy as he left it there were no axioms—nothing that would correlate and hold together. But such was his genius and prudence, and his adaptability to the temper of his time, that he got a hearing where more daring thinkers failed, and a science of political economy began to grow on his foundations. Malthus by giving a scientific semblance to a delusion which tallied with popular impressions, and Ricardo by giving form to a scientific interpretation of rent, soon provided what passed for axioms, one of which was wrong, and the other of which was wrongly or at least inadequately stated. While between them, all was left at sea.

Yet such was the feeling that there ought to be a political economy, and so agreeable to the ruling class was what was offered as such, that chairs for the study of it began to multiply. They were of course filled by men who taught what they had learned, with the constant pressure on them of the class dominant in all colleges—a class which, whatever be the faults of a political economy, are disposed to accept things as they are as the best order of things possible, and to view with intense opposition any radical change that would provoke real discussion. And as nearly every professor of political economy thought it incumbent on him to write a text-book, or at least to do something to show a reason for his existence, there was much going over old ground and picking out of small differences, but no questioning of anything that could arouse vital debate. And given a state of society in which the many were poor and the few were rich, any attempt to point out a true political economy, if it got attention, would inevitably arouse much debate.

Thus in fact political economy, as it found teachers and professors and the standing of a science, was to the class who had appropriated land as belonging to them exclusively a very comfortable doctrine. It applied the doctrine of "letting things alone," without any suggestion of the question of how things came to be. It was, as it was styled by Clement C. Biddle, the American translator of Say, "the liberal doctrine that the most active, general and profitable employments are given to the industry and commerce of every people by allowing to their direction and application the most perfect freedom *compatible with the security of property*." As to what constitutes property there was no dispute. And if one did not look too closely, and beyond the usages of the times, in the more advanced European nations there could be no dispute. Property? Why property was of course what was susceptible of ownership. Any fool would know that!

Nor after the surrender of the Peel ministry, in time to prevent it, was any question of the sanction of property raised. English slavery had disappeared in its last forms before the nineteenth century began, and though the question of the ownership of slaves in the tropical colonies, and finally in the Southern United States, was likely if continuously debated to bring up the larger question, this did not appeal to the feelings of the people. So it was settled for the time, as to the colonies by the device of buying off the slave-owners at public expense; and in the United States by the arbitrament of war.

The question of the validity of property was never really raised in England until after the publication of "Progress and Poverty" began to call it up. But the attention which that has aroused has since brought to light some definite utterances, which show, as I take it, that the doctrines of the French Physiocrats would have found hospitable reception in Great Britain had it been possible at the time to have really made them known.

Thus H. M. Hyndman has dug up from the British Museum a lecture by Thomas Spence, delivered before the Philosophical Society of Newcastle, on November 8, 1775, a year prior to the publication of the "Wealth of Nations," and for which the Society, as Spence puts it, did him "the honor" to expel him. In this lecture Spence declares that all men "have as equal and just a property in land as they have in liberty, air, or the light and heat of the sun," and he proposes what now would be again called "the single tax"—that the value of land should be taken for all public expenses, and all other taxes of what ever kind and nature should be abolished. He draws a glowing picture of what humanity would be if this simple but most radical reform were adopted. But so much against the wishes of all that had authority was he, that his proposal was utterly forgotten until dug out of its burial-place more than a century after.

So, in 1889, D. C. Macdonald, a single-tax man, and a solicitor of Aberdeen, dug out of the Advocates' Library of Edinburgh, and the British Museum, in London, copies of a book printed in 1782 by William Ogilvie, Professor of Humanities in King's College, Aberdeen, entitled "An Essay on the Right of Property in Land, with Respect to its Foundation in the Law of Nature, its Present Establishment by the Municipal Laws of Europe, and the Regulations by which it might be Rendered More Beneficial to the Lower Ranks of Mankind." Professor Ogilvie, though he makes no reference to any other authority than that of Moses, had evidently some knowledge of the Physiocrats, and most unquestionably declares that land is *a birthright which every citizen still retains.* He advocates the taxation of land, with the entire abolition of all other taxes, though, as if despairing of so radical a reform, he proposes some palliatives such as allotments to actual settlers, leases, etc. He doubtless saw the utter hopelessness of making the fight under existing conditions, for it seems probable that his book was never published, only a few copies being printed for private circulation by the author.

Among the scholastically accepted writers in the first thirty years of the century are two who seem to have some glimmerings of the truth perceived by the Physiocrats, of the relations between land and labor, though in a curiously distorted way. Dr. Chalmers, who was a divinity professor in the University of Edinburgh, and a strong Malthusian, contended that the owners of land ultimately paid all taxes levied on labor, and contended that titles (which he regarded as so much retained by the state for beneficial purposes) should be maintained. All others he would have ultimately abolished, and the revenues of the state ultimately raised from the value of land. This, he thought, would be simpler and better, and avoid much dispute, "relieving government from the odium of taxes which so endanger the cause of order and authority." He was a stanch supporter of primogeniture, opposed to anything which aimed at the division of the land, and would have the country enjoy the spectacle of a noble and splendid aristocracy, of which the younger branches should be supported by places of at least £1000 a year in the public services. And, while he would have the landlords pay all taxes, he thought it "wholesome and befitting that they should have the political ascendancy also." For "the lords of the soil, we repeat, are naturally and properly the lords of the ascendant." Chalmers was a good example of the toadying spirit of so many of the Scottish ministers. He afterward joined in the disruption of the Kirk by the Free Kirk movement. Yet, in spite of his obsequience, he did not succeed in popularizing the single tax with the

British aristocracy, who fought the repeal of the corn-laws as long as they could. He passed as an economist almost into oblivion.

Another curious example of the perversion of the doctrine of the relation between land and labor was given by Edward Gibbon Wakefield, who visited this country in its more democratic days in the first quarter of the century, ere the natural result of our thoughtless acceptance of land and true property as alike wealth, and our desire to get in the first place an owner for land had begun to show so fully its effects. He was impressed with the difference between the society growing up here and that to which he had been used, and viewing everything from the standpoint of those accustomed to look on the rest of mankind as created for their benefit, he deemed the great social and economic disadvantage of the United States to be "the scarcity of labor." To this he traces the rudeness of the upper class—its want of those refinements, enjoyments and delicacies of life, common to the aristocracy of England. How could an English gentleman emigrate to a country where he might actually have to black his own boots, and where no one could count on a constant supply of labor ready to accept as a boon any opportunity to perform the most menial and degrading service? He saw, as Adam Smith before him saw, that this "scarcity of labor" came from the cheapness of land where the vast area of the public domain was open for settlement at nominal prices. Without the slightest question that the land was made for landlords, and that laborers were intended to furnish a supply of labor for the upper classes, he wished the new countries which England had yet to settle to be socially, politically and economically newer Englands; and, without waiting for the slower process of speculation, he wished to bring about in these new countries such salutary "scarcity of employment" as would give cheap and abundant labor from the very start of settlement. He, therefore, proposed that land should not be given, but sold at the outset, at what he called a sufficient price—a price high enough to make laborers work for others until they had acquired the fund necessary to pay a price for what nature offered without money and without price. The money received by the state in this way he proposed to devote in paying the passage of suitable and selected immigrants. This would give from the start two classes of immigrants to settle the great waste places which England still retained, especially in Australia and New Zealand—the better class, who would pay their own expenses, and buy from the government their own land, which would at first have a value; and the assisted class, who, being selected from the best workers in the old country, would at once be able to supply all the required labor. Thus the new country where this plan was adopted would from the first, while wages were still enough higher than in England to make working-men, especially if assisted, desire to go there, offer the inducement to a wealthy and cultivated class of a "reasonable" and ready supply of labor, and save them from such hardships from the lack of it as made the United States so unattractive to the "better class" of Englishmen.

This plan was very attractive to the more wealthy and influential class of Englishmen concerned in, or thinking of, emigrating to the newer colonies, and was finally adopted by the corporation concerned in settling West Australia, and afterwards the other Australian colonies. But even its obvious inferences never affected the teaching of political economy.

In 1850 two works appeared in England, which, though neither of them was from the ranks of the scholastic economists, were both premonitions of a coming demand for a political economy which would take some consideration of the interest of the masses. One of these was by Herbert

Spencer, then young and unknown, and was entitled "Social Statics, or The Conditions Essential to Human Happiness Specified, and the First of Them Developed." Chapter IX. of this book, "The Right to the Use of the Earth," is a telling denial of what the economists of Smith's school had quietly assumed could not be questioned, the validity of property in land. It got no attention in England, having been noticed in the "British Quarterly Review" only in 1876, when his sociological works began first to be heard of. It was however reprinted in the United States in 1864, with a note by the author, and when, about 1877, Appleton & Co., of New York, became the American publishers of his philosophical writings, they reprinted this with his other works, and on the strength of them it began to get into circulation.

This was the only work of the kind I knew of when writing "Progress and Poverty;" and in "A Perplexed Philosopher" (1892), I have given a full account of it, and of Mr. Spencer's shifting repudiation and final recantation of what he had said in denial of property in land.

In the same year (1850) appeared in London "The Theory of Human Progression and Natural Probability of a Reign of Justice." It was published anonymously and dedicated to Victor Cousin of France. The argument of "The Theory of Human Progression" is that there is a probability of the reign of justice on earth, or millennium, foretold by Scriptural prophecy. One of his primary postulates is the inspiration of the Bible and the divinity of the founder of the Christian religion, which in his view is Scottish Presbyterianism, and which he treats as the true religion, all others being false. But, though adhering to the doctrine of the fall of man, who is by nature vile and wicked, he is an evolutionist in believing in the natural necessary advance of mankind by the progress of knowledge, or to use his phrase, by the progress of correct credence in the natural order and necessary sequence of the sciences, to a reign of justice, in which is to grow a reign of benevolence.

The elements of correct credence as he enunciates them (p. 94) are:

1. The Bible.
2. A correct view of the phenomena of material nature.
3. A correct philosophy of the mental operations.

The three things which he links together as respectively cause and effect, involving the conditions of society, are (p. 120):

Knowledge and freedom.
Superstition and despotism.
Infidelity and anarchy.

And the four propositions which best give an idea of the scope of his work and the course of his thought are (p. 160):

1. On the sure word of divine prophecy we anticipate a reign of justice on the earth.

2. That a reign of justice necessarily implies that every man in the world shall at some future time be put in possession of all his rights.

3. That the history of civilized communities shows us that the progression of mankind in a political aspect is from a diversity of privileges toward an equality of rights.

4. That one man can have a privilege only by depriving another man or many other men of a portion of their rights. Consequently that a reign of justice will consist in the destruction of every privilege, and in the restitution of every right.

These propositions are extended to twenty-one main propositions and twelve sub-propositions, but they are all involved in the first four. The tenth sub-division of the twentieth proposition and the twenty-first proposition as a whole are, however, well worth quoting as giving an idea of the character of the man and his thought:

> . . . Knowledge does necessarily produce change, as much as heat necessarily produces change; and where knowledge becomes more and more accurate, more and more extensive, and more and more generally diffused, change must necessarily take place in the same ratio and entail with it a new order of society, and an amended condition of man upon the globe. Wherever, then, the unjust interests of the ruling classes are required to give way before the progress of knowledge and those ruling classes peremptorily refuse to allow the condition of society to be amended, the sword is the instrument which knowledge and reason may be compelled to use; for it is not possible, it is not within the limits of man's choice, that the progress of society can be permanently arrested when the intellect of the masses has advanced in knowledge beyond those propositions, of which the present condition is only the realization.
>
> 21. We posit, finally, that the acquisition, scientific ordination, and general diffusion of knowledge will necessarily obliterate error and superstition, and continually amend the condition of man upon the globe, until his ultimate condition shall be the best the circumstances of the earth permit of. On this ground we take up (what might in other and abler hands be an argument of no small interest, namely) the natural probability of a millennium, based on the classification of the sciences, on the past progress of mankind, and on the computed evolution of man's future progress. The outline alone of this argument we shall indicate, and we have no hesitation in believing that every one who sees it in its true light will at once see how the combination of knowledge and reason must regenerate the earth and evolve a period of universal prosperity which the Divine Creator has graciously promised, and whose natural probability we maintain to be within the calculation of the human reason.

The book which, so far as my knowledge goes, "The Theory of Human Progression" most nearly resembles in motive, scope and conclusions is Herbert Spencer's "Social Statics," published in the same year, though evidently without knowledge of each other. Both seem to have little knowledge of and make slight reference to writers on political economy—Spencer referring in one place to Smith, Mill and Chalmers, while Dove quotes no authority later than Moses. Both go largely over the same ground, and both reach substantially the same practical conclusion; both assert the same grand doctrine of the natural rights of men, which is the essence of Jeffersonian democracy and the touchstone of true reform; both declare the supremacy of a higher law than human enactments, and both believe in an evolutionary process which shall raise men to higher and nobler conditions. Both express clearly and well the fundamental postulates of the single tax, and both are of course absolute free traders. Spencer devotes more space to the land question, and more elaborately proves the incompatibility of private ownership of land with the moral law, and declares the justice and necessity of appropriating rent for public revenues without saying anything of the mode; while Dove dwells at more length on the wickedness and stupidity of tariffs, excises and the other modes of raising revenues from taxes on the products of labor, and clearly indicates taxation as the method of appropriating rent for public purposes. But while the English agnostic might have regarded the Scottish Calvinist as yet in the bonds of an utterly unscientific superstition, there is one respect in which the vigor and courage of Dove's thought shines superior to Spencer's. Spencer, after demonstrating the absolute invalidity of any possible claim to the private ownership of land, goes on to say that great difficulties must attend the resumption by mankind at large of their rights to the soil; that had we to deal with the parties who originally robbed the human race of their heritage, we might make short work of the matter; but that unfortunately most of our present landowners are men who have either mediately or immediately given for their estates equivalents of honestly earned wealth, and that to "justly estimate and liquidate the claims of such is one of the most intricate problems society will one day have to solve."

But the orthodox Presbyterian utterly refuses thus to bend the knee to Baal in the slightest concession. While he is not more clear than Spencer in demonstrating that landowners as landowners have no rights whatever, there is not one word in his book that recognizes in any way their claims. On the contrary, he declares that slavery is man-robbery, and that the £20,000,000 compensation given by the British Parliament to the West India planters on the emancipation of their slaves was an act of injustice and oppression to the British masses, and (p. 139) adds:

> No man in the world and no association in the world could ever have an equitable right to tax a laborer for the purpose of remunerating a man-robber; and, although the measure is now past and done with, we very much question whether some analogous cases will not be cleared up by the mass of the nation ere many years pass over the heads of Englishmen. When the question of landed property comes to a definite discussion there may be little thought of compensation.

Yet neither in England nor in the United States, where an edition seems to have been published in Boston at the expense of Senator Sumner, did Dove get any attention, and I never heard of it until after the publication of "Progress and Poverty," when, in Ireland in 1882, I was presented with a copy by Charles Eason, head of the Dublin branch of the great news-publishing house of Smith & Sons.

In 1854 appeared another book by Patrick Edward Dove, in which the authorship of "The Theory of Human Progression" was announced—"The Elements of Political Science, in two books: first, on Method, second, on Doctrine." And in 1856 appeared a third book, "The Logic of the Christian Faith," being a dissertation on skepticism, pantheism, the *a priori* argument, the *a posteriori* argument, the intuitional argument and revelation, also under title of the author, and with a dedication to Charles Sumner, Senator of the United States, who, without his knowledge, had procured a republication of Dove's first book in Boston, being moved thereto doubtless by its vigorous words on slavery.

In 1859 appeared in London "The Strength of Nations," by Andrew Bisset, who has since (1877) published "The History of the Struggle for Parliamentary Government in England," a review of the systematic attempt of the families of Plantagenet, Tudor and Stuart to enslave the English people, which is mainly occupied with the attempt of Charles I., the resistance to it, and his final execution. "The Strength of Nations" very suggestively calls attention to the fact that feudal tenures were conditioned on the payment of rent or special services to the state, and thus the much-lauded abolition of what was left of the feudal incidents by the Long Parliament was a relief of the landholders of the payment of what measured at present prices would suffice for the whole expenditure of England, and the saddling of it on general taxation; and that from this dates the beginning of the English national debt.

These books have produced very little effect upon political economy, and some of them have passed out of print without any perceptible effect at all It is likely that there were others in addition to what I have mentioned, and it is certain that there were others that occasionally found their way into print which irregularly and spasmodically expressed some touch of the idea formulated in lines of the Wat Tyler rising:

> When Adam delved and Eve span,
> Who was then a gentleman?

Some notion of the incongruity of the idea that a small fraction of mankind were intended to eat, and eat luxuriously without working, and another and far larger portion to have nothing but work to enable them to eat, and be compelled to beg as a boon the opportunity to do that, runs in broken flashes through much of the reform literature. But in political economy as it up to 1880 existed all such questioning was tabooed, and the utmost that could be found in any of the writers recognized by the schools was a timid suggestion that the future unearned increment of land values might sometime be recognized as belonging to the community, a proposition that, though it amounted to nothing whatever, as landlords were ready to sell land for what would give them any unearned increment not yet in sight, caused John Stuart Mill who had been giving some adhesion to it to be looked on askance by some, as an awful radical.

The struggle for the repeal of the corn-laws in England did not lead to any development of a protectionist political economy. Books and pamphlets enough were written in favor of protection, but they were merely appeals to old habits of thought and vulgar prejudices, and the forces in favor of repeal carried them down. Elsewhere, however, it was different. On the Continent the conditions under which the tentative victory of free trade was won in England were lacking. Cut up into hostile nations, burdened with demands for revenue, the mercantile system got a practical hold that could not be broken by the half-hearted measures of its English opponents, and the gleam of hope which came with the English-French treaty negotiated between Cobden and Napoleon III. was destroyed by the tremendous struggles which followed the fall of the latter. In Germany the outburst of national feeling which followed the struggles with France and the unification of German states gave rise to a school of German economists who taught a national economy, in which under various names, such as romantic, inductive and national, protectionism was advocated.

When it came to making peace between England and the United States after the War of Independence, the

American Commissioners were instructed to stipulate for a complete free trade between the two countries. They failed in this, owing to the prevalence of the protective sentiment in Great Britain at the time. When the Articles of Confederation gave way to the Constitution, the need for an independent source of revenue took the easy means of laying a Federal tariff upon foreign productions, though free trade between the States was guaranteed; and the growth of selfish interests caused by and promotive of a constantly increasing demand for greater revenue built up a strong party in favor of protection, which had its way when the slavery question taking sectional shape put the States in which protectionism was dominant in control of the government with the secession of the South. This interest sought warrant in a scheme of political economy, and found it in drawing from the German economists and in the writings of Henry C. Carey of Philadelphia, whose theory in many respects differed from the English philosophy, noticeably in its advocacy of protection. In America this protectionist semblance of a political economy had its chief seat in the University of Pennsylvania, and the support of a powerful party in which the ideas of Jefferson were opposed by those of Hamilton; while in Great Britain the works of Carlyle and the course of modern study and development had in scholastic circles popularized the German.

Among the schools, moreover, there was a divergence which began to assume greater proportions as the success of the anti-corn-laws struggle began to be shown in the accomplishment of all that any of its advocates dared to propose. This took shape in a contention as to value, which inclined to emphasize the fact that the admission that some immaterial things were conceded to be wealth destroyed the ability to keep any immaterial things having value out of that category, and consequently that wealth in the common sense was the only thing to be considered in political economy, which was really a science of exchanges. With the efforts of Jevons, Macleod and others this began to make way, and naturally affiliated with the historical, the inductive, the socialistic and other protectionist schools which grew from the Continental teachings. Instead of working for greater directness and simplicity, it really made of political economy an occult science, in which nothing was fixed, and the professors of which, claiming superior knowledge, could support whatever they chose to.

During the century another form of protectionism had been growing up, originating in England, but gaining adherents everywhere. Like the others, it recognized no difference between land and products of labor, counting them all as wealth, and aimed by main strength at improvement in the conditions of labor. Recognizing the workers as a class naturally separate from employers, it aimed to unite the laborers in combinations, and to invoke in their behalf the power of the state to impose restrictions, shorten hours, and in various ways to serve their interests at the expense of the primarily employing class. The German mind, learned, bureaucratic and incomprehensible, put this in the form of what passed for a system in Karl Marx's ponderous two volumes entitled "Capital," written in England in 1867, but published in German and not translated into English until after his death in 1887. Without distinguishing between products of nature and the products of man, Marx holds that there are two kinds of value—use value and exchange value—and that through some alchemy of buying and selling the capitalist who hires men to turn material into products gets a larger value than he gives. Upon this economic proposition of Marx (it can hardly be called a theory), or others similar to it, political schemes with slight variations have been promulgated after the manner of political platforms.

Under the name of socialism, a name which all such movements have now succeeded in appropriating, all such plans are embraced. We sometimes hear of "scientific socialism," as something to be established, as it were, by proclamation, or by act of government. In this there is a tendency to confuse the idea of science with that of something purely conventional or political, a scheme or proposal, not a science. For science, as previously explained, is concerned with natural laws, not with the proposal of man—with relations which always have existed and always must exist. Socialism takes no account of natural laws, neither seeking them nor striving to be governed by them. It is an art or conventional scheme like any other scheme in politics or government, while political economy is an exposition of certain invariable laws of human nature. The proposal which socialism makes is that the collectivity or state shall assume the management of all means of production, including land, capital and man himself; do away with all competition, and convert mankind into two classes, the directors, taking their orders from government and acting by governmental authority, and the workers, for whom everything shall be provided, including the directors themselves. It is a proposal to bring back mankind to the socialism of Peru, but without reliance on divine will or power. Modern socialism is in fact without religion, and its tendency is atheistic. It is more destitute of any central and guiding principle than any philosophy I know of. Mankind is here; how, it does not state; and must proceed to make a world for itself, as disorderly as that which Alice in Wonderland confronted. It has no system of individual rights whereby it can define the extent to which the individual is entitled to liberty or to which the state may go in restraining it. And so long as no individual has any principle of guidance it is impossible that society itself should have any. How such a combination could be called a science, and how it should get a following, can be accounted for only by the "fatal facility of writing without thinking," which the learned German ability of studying details without any leading principle permits to pass, and by the number of places which such a bureaucratic organization would provide. However, through government repression and its falling in with trade-union notions it has made great headway in Germany, and has taken considerable hold in England.

This was the condition of things at the beginning of the eighth decade of the century, when the English political economy, the only economy making any pretensions to a science, received from a newer and freer England what has proved a fatal blow.

CHAPTER VIII.

BREAKDOWN OF SCHOLASTIC POLITICAL ECONOMY.

SHOWING THE REASON, THE RECEPTION, AND EFFECT ON POLITICAL ECONOMY OF "PROGRESS AND POVERTY."

"Progress and Poverty"—Preference of professors to abandon the "science" rather than radically change it, brings the breakdown of scholastic economy — The "Encyclopædia Britannica"—The "Austrian school" that has succeeded the "classical."

IN January, 1880, preceded in 1879 by an author's edition in San Francisco, appeared my "Progress and Poverty," and it was followed later in the same year by an English edition and a German edition, and in 1882 by cheap paper editions both in England and the United States. The history of the book is briefly this: I reached California by sea in the early part of 1858, and finally became an editorial writer. In 1869 I went East on newspaper business, returning to California in the early summer of 1870. John Russell Young was at that time managing editor of the *New York Tribune*, and I wrote for him an article on "The Chinese on the Pacific Coast," a question that had begun to arouse attention there, taking the side popular among the working-classes of the Coast, in opposition to the unrestricted immigration of that people. Wishing to know what political economy had to say about the causes of wages, I went to the Philadelphia

Library, looked over John Stuart Mill's "Political Economy," and accepting his view without question, based my article upon it. This article attracted attention, especially in California, and a copy I sent from there to John Stuart Mill brought a letter of commendation.

While in the East, the contrast of luxury and want that I saw in New York appalled me, and I left for the West feeling that there must be a cause for this, and that if possible I would find out what it was. Turning over the matter in my mind amid pretty constant occupation, I at length found the cause in the treatment of land as property, and in a pamphlet which I took an interval of leisure to write, "Our Land and Land Policy" (San Francisco, 1871), I stated it. Something like a thousand copies of this were sold; but I saw that to command attention the work must be done more thoroughly, and refraining from any effort to press it at the East until I knew more, I engaged with others in starting (December, 1871) a small San Francisco daily paper, which occupied my attention, though I never forgot my main purpose, until December, 1875, when, becoming entangled with an obligation to a rich man (U. S. Senator John P. Jones), whose note we had at his own request taken, I went out penniless. I then asked the Governor (Irwin), whom I had supported, for a place that would give me leisure to devote myself to thoughtful work. He gave me what was much of a sinecure, and which has now been abolished—the position of State Inspector of Gas-meters. This, while giving, though irregularly, enough to live on, afforded ample leisure. I had intended to devote this to my long-cherished plan; and after some time spent in writing and speaking, with intervals of reading and study, I brought out "Progress and Poverty" in an author's edition, in August, 1879.

In this book I took the same question that had perplexed me. Stating the world-wide problem in an introductory chapter, I found that the explanation of it given by the accepted political economy was that wages are drawn from capital, and constantly tend to the lowest amount on which labor will consent to live and reproduce, because the increase in the number of laborers tends naturally to follow and overtake any increase in capital. Examining this doctrine in Book I., consisting of five chapters, entitled "Wages and Capital," I showed that it was based upon misconceptions, and that wages were not drawn from existing capital, but produced by labor. In Book II., "Population and Subsistence," I devoted four chapters to examining and disproving the Malthusian theory. Then in Book III., "The Laws of Distribution," I showed (in eight chapters) that what were given as laws did not correlate, and proceeded to show what the laws of rent, interest and wages really were. In Book IV. (four chapters), I proved that the effect of material progress was to increase the proportion of the product that would go to rent. In Book V. (two chapters), I showed this to be the primary cause of paroxysms of industrial depression, and of the persistence of poverty amid advancing wealth. In Book VI., "The Remedy" (two chapters), I showed the inadequacy of all remedies for industrial distress short of a measure for giving the community the benefit of the increase of rent. In Book VII. (five chapters), I examined the justice; in Book VIII. (four chapters), the exact relation and practical application of this remedy; and in Book IX. (four chapters), I discussed its effect on production, on distribution, on individuals and classes, and social organization and life; while in Book X. (five chapters), I worked out briefly the great law of human progress, and showed the relation to this law of what I proposed. The conclusion (one chapter), "The Problem of Individual Life," is devoted to the problem that arises in the heart of the individual.

This work was the most thorough and exhaustive examination of political economy that had yet been made, going over in the space of less than six hundred pages the whole subject that I deemed it necessary to explain, and completely recasting political economy. I could get no one to print the work except my old partner in San Francisco, William M. Hinton, who had gone into the printing business, and who had sufficient faith in me to make the plates. I sold this author's edition in San Francisco at a good price, which almost paid for the plates, and sent copies to publishers in New York and London, offering to furnish them with plates. With the heavy expense met, Appleton & Co., of New York, undertook its printing, and though I could get no English publisher at the time, before the year of first publication was out they got Kegan Paul, Trench & Co. to undertake its printing in London. In the meantime, before publishing this book, I had delivered a lecture in San Francisco which led to the formation of the Land Reform Union of San Francisco, the first of many similar movements since.

"Progress and Poverty" has been, in short, the most successful economic work ever published. Its reasoning has never been successfully assailed, and on three continents it has given birth to movements whose practical success is only a question of time. Yet though the scholastic political economy has been broken, it has not been, as I at the time anticipated, by some one of its professors taking up what I had pointed out; but a new and utterly incoherent political economy has taken its place in the schools.

Among the adherents of the scholastic economy, who had been claiming it as a science, there had been from the time of Smith no attempt to determine what wealth was; no attempt to say what constituted property, and no attempt to make the laws of production or distribution correlate and agree, until there thus burst on them from a fresh man, without either the education or the sanction of the schools, on the remotest verge of civilization, a reconstruction of the science, that began to make its way and command attention. What were their training and laborious study worth if it could be thus ignored, and if one who had never seen the inside of a college, except when he had attempted to teach professors the fundamentals of their science, whose education was of the mere common-school branches, whose *alma mater* had been the forecastle and the printing-office, should be admitted to prove the inconsistency of what they had been teaching as a science? It was not to be thought of. And so while a few of these professional economists, driven to say something about "Progress and Poverty," resorted to misrepresentation, the majority preferred to rely upon their official positions in which they were secure by the interests of the dominant class, and to treat as beneath contempt a book circulating by thousands in the three great English-speaking countries and translated into all the important modern languages. Thus the professors of political economy seemingly rejected the simple teachings of "Progress and Poverty," refrained from meeting with disproof or argument what it had laid down, and treated it with contemptuous silence.

Had these teachers of the schools frankly admitted the changes called for by "Progress and Poverty," something of the structure on which they built might have been retained. But that was not in human nature. It would not have been merely to accept a new man without the training of the schools, but to admit that the true science was open to any one to pursue, and could be successfully continued only on the basis of equal rights and privileges. It would not merely have made useless so much of the knowledge that they had laboriously attained, and was their title to distinction and honor, but would have converted them and their science into opponents of the tremendous pecuniary interests that were vitally concerned in supporting the justification of the unjust arrangements which gave them power. The change in credence that this would have involved would have been the most revolutionary that had ever been made, involving a far-reaching change in all the adjustments of society such as had hardly before been thought of, and never before been accomplished at one stroke; for the abolition of chattel slavery was as nothing in its effects as compared with the far-reaching character of the abolition of private ownership of land. Thus the professors of political economy, having the sanction and support of the schools, preferred, and naturally preferred, to unite their differences, by giving up what had before been insisted on as essential, and to teach what was an incomprehensible jargon to the ordinary man, under the assumption of teaching an occult science, which required a great study of what had been written by numerous learned professors all over the world, and a knowledge of foreign languages. So the scholastic political economy, as it had been taught, utterly broke down, and, as taught in the schools, tended to protectionism and the German, and to the assumption that it was a recondite science on which no one not having the indorsement of the colleges was competent to speak, and on which only a man of great reading and learning could express an opinion.

The first evidence of the change was given in the "Encyclopædia Britannica," which in Vol. XIX. of the ninth edition, printed in 1886, discarded the dogmatic article on the science of political economy, which had been printed in previous editions, and on the plea that political economy was really in a transition state, and a dogmatic treatise would not be opportune, gave the space instead to an article on the science of political economy by Professor

J. K. Ingram, which undertook to review all that had been written about it, and was almost immediately reprinted in an 8vo volume with an introduction by Professor E. J. James, of the University of Pennsylvania, the leading American protectionist institution of learning.

This confession that the old political economy was dead was written in the "good God, good devil," or historical style, and consisted in a notice of the writers on political economy, from the most ancient times, through a first, a second and a third modern phase, to the coming or historical phase.

Adam Smith is put down as leading in the third modern school—the system of natural liberty. Among the predecessors of Smith are reckoned the French Physiocrats, whose proposition for a single tax on the value of land is related to their doctrine of the productiveness of agriculture and the sterility of manufactures and commerce, "which has been disposed of by Smith and others, and falls to the ground with the doctrine on which it was based;" and Smith himself is treated as a respectable "has-been," whose teachings must now give way to the wider criticism and larger knowledge of the historical school. Writers of France, Spain, Germany, Italy and northern nations are referred to in the utmost profusion, but there is no reference whatever to the man or the book that was then exerting more influence upon thought and finding more purchasers than all the rest of them combined, an example which has been followed to this day in the elaborate four-volume "Dictionary of Political Economy," edited by R. H. Inglis Palgrave.

This action was enough. The encyclopædias and dictionaries printed since have followed this example of the Britannica. Chambers, which was the first to print a new and revised edition, and Johnson's, which soon followed, concluded in 1896, discarded what they had previously printed as the teaching of political economy for articles in the style of the Britannica's; while the new dictionaries are repeatedly giving place to the jargon which has been introduced as economic terms.

As for the University of Pennsylvania, the great authority of American scholastic protectionism, it may be said that it soon after relegated to a back seat its Professor of Political Economy, Professor Robert Ellis Thompson, a Scotsman, who had been up to that time teaching the best scientific justification of protectionism that could be had, and has put in his place the Professor E. J. James already spoken of, and thrown its whole influence and resources into the teaching of protection by the Anglicized historical and inductive method, under a new though rarely mentioned name. The new science speaks of the "science of economics" and not of "political economy;" teaches that there are no eternally valid natural laws; and, asked if free trade or protection be beneficial or if the trusts be good or bad, declines to give a categorical answer, but replies that this can be decided only as to the particular time and place, and by a historical investigation of all that has been written about it. As such inquiry must, of course, be left to professors and learned men, it leaves the professors of "economics," who have almost universally taken the places founded for professors of "political economy," to dictate as they please, without any semblance of embarrassing axioms or rules. How this lends itself to an acquiescence in the views or whims of the wealthy class, dominant in all colleges, the University of Pennsylvania, controlled in the interests of protectionists for revenue only, was the first to find out, but it has been rapidly and generally followed.

Such inquiry as I have been able to make of the recently published works and writings of the authoritative professors of the science has convinced me that this change has been general among all the colleges, both of England and the United States. So general is this scholastic utterance that it may now be said that the science of political economy, as founded by Adam Smith and taught authoritatively in 1880, has now been utterly abandoned, its teachings being referred to as teachings of "the classical school" of political economy, now obsolete.

What has succeeded is usually denominated the Austrian school, for no other reason that I can discover than that "far kine have long horns." If it has any principles, I have been utterly unable to find them. The inquirer is usually referred to the incomprehensible works of Professor Alfred Marshall of Cambridge, England, whose first 764-page volume of his "Principles of Economics," out in 1891, has not yet given place to a second; to the ponderous works of Eugen V. Böhm-Bawerk, Professor of Political Economy, first in Innsbruck and then at Vienna, "Capital and Interest" and "The Positive Theory of Capital," translated by Professor William Smart of Glasgow; or to Professor Smart's "Introduction to the Theory of Value on the Lines of Menger, Wieser and Böhm-Bawerk," or to a lot of German works written by men he never heard of and whose names he cannot even pronounce.

This pseudo-science gets its name from a foreign language, and uses for its terms words adapted from the German—words that have no place and no meaning in an English work. It is, indeed, admirably calculated to serve the purpose of those powerful interests dominant in the colleges under our organization, that must fear a simple and understandable political economy, and who vaguely wish to have the poor boys who are subjected to it by their professors rendered incapable of thought on economic subjects. There is nothing that suggests so much what Schopenhauer ("Parerga and Paralipomena") said of the works of the German philosopher Hegel than what the professors have written, and the volumes for mutual admiration which they publish as serials:

> If one should wish to make a bright young man so stupid as to become incapable of all real thinking, the best way would be to commend to him a diligent study of these works. For these monstrous piecings together of words which really destroy and contradict one another so causes the mind to vainly torment itself in the effort to discover their meaning that at last it collapses exhausted, with its capacity for thinking so completely destroyed that from that time on meaningless phrases count with it for thoughts.

It is to this state that political economy in the teachings of the schools, which profess to know all about it, has now come.

CHAPTER IX.

WEALTH AND VALUE.

SHOWING THE REASON FOR CONSIDERING THE NATURE OF VALUE BEFORE THAT OF WEALTH.

The point of agreement as to wealth—Advantages of proceeding from this point.

WE have seen the utter confusion that exists among economists as to the nature of wealth, and have sufficiently shown its causes and results. Let us return now to the question we have in hand, and that must first be settled before we can advance on solid ground: What is the meaning of wealth as an economic term?

The lack of definiteness and want of consistency as to the nature of the wealth of nations, with which Adam Smith began, have in the hands of his accredited successors resulted in confusion so much worse confounded that the only proposition as to wealth on which we may say that all economists are agreed is that all wealth has value. But as to whether all that has value is wealth, or as to what forms of value are wealth and what not, there is wide divergence. And if we consider the definitions that are given in accepted works either of the term wealth or of the sub-term of wealth, capital, it will be seen that the confusions as to the nature of wealth which they show seem to proceed from confusions as to the nature of value

It is quite possible, I think, to fix the meaning of the term wealth without first fixing the meaning of the term value. This I did in "Progress and Poverty," where my purpose in defining the meaning of wealth was to fix the meaning of its sub-term, capital, in order to see whether or not it is true that wages are drawn from capital. But as in the present work, being a treatise on the whole subject of political economy, it will be necessary to treat independently of the nature of value, it will, I think, be more conducive to orderly and concise arrangement to consider the nature of value before proceeding definitely to the consideration of the nature of wealth.

And since minds that have been befogged by accepted confusions may be more easily opened to the truth by pointing out in what these confusions consist, and how they originate, this mode of proceeding to a determination of the nature of wealth through an examination of the nature of value will have the advantage of meeting on the way the confusions as to value which in the minds of the students of the scholastic economy have perplexed the idea of wealth.

CHAPTER X.

VALUE IN USE AND VALUE IN EXCHANGE.

SHOWING THE TWO SENSES OF VALUE; HOW THE DISTINCTION HAS BEEN IGNORED, AND ITS REAL VALIDITY; AND THE REASON FOR CONFINING THE ECONOMIC TERM TO ONE SENSE.

Importance of the term value—Original meaning of the word—Its two senses—Names for them adopted by Smith—Utility and desirability—Mill's criticism of Smith—Complete ignoring of the distinction by the Austrian school—Cause of this confusion—Capability of use not usefulness—Smith's distinction a real one—The dual use of one word in common speech must be avoided in political economy—Intrinsic value.

THE term value is of most fundamental importance in political economy; so much so that by some writers political economy has been styled the science of values. Yet in the consideration of the meaning and nature of value we come at once into the very quicksand and fogland of economic discussion—a point which from the time of Adam Smith to the present has been wrapped in increasing confusions and beset with endless controversy. Let us move carefully, even at the cost of what may seem at the moment needless pains, for here is a point from which apparently slight divergences may ultimately distort conclusions as to matters of the utmost practical moment.

The original and widest meaning of the word "value" is that of worth or worthiness, which involves and expresses the idea of esteem or regard.

But we esteem some things for their own qualities or for uses to which they may be directly put, while we esteem other things for what they will bring in exchange. We do not distinguish the kind or reason of regard in our use of the word esteem, nor yet is there any need of doing so in our common use of the word value. The sense in which the word value is used, when not expressed in the associated words or context, is for common purposes sufficiently indicated by the conditions or nature of the thing to which value is attributed. Thus, the one word value has in common English speech two distinct senses. One is that of usefulness or utility—as when we speak of the value of the ocean to man, the value of the compass in navigation, the value of the stethoscope in the diagnosis of disease, the value of the antiseptic treatment in surgery; or when, having in mind the merits of the mental production, its quality of usefulness to the reader or to the public, we speak of the value of a book.

The other and, though derived, utterly distinct sense of the word value, is that of what is usually, and for most purposes even of political economy, sufficiently described as exchangeability or purchasing power—as when we speak of the value of gold as greater than that of iron; of a book in rich binding as being more valuable than the same book in plain binding; of the value of a copyright or a patent; or of the lessening in the value of steel by the Bessemer process, or in that of aluminium by the improvements in extraction now going on.

The first sense of the word value, which is that of usefulness, the quality that a thing may have of ministering directly to human needs, was distinguished by Adam Smith as "value in use."

The second sense of the word value, which is that of worth in transfer or trade, the quality that a thing may have of ministering indirectly to human desire through its exchangeability for other things, was distinguished by Adam Smith as "value in exchange."

Adam Smith's words are (Book I., Chapter IV.):

> The word "value," it is to be observed, has two different meanings, and sometimes expresses the utility of some particular object, and sometimes the power of purchasing other goods which the possession of that object conveys. The one may be called "value in use;" the other, "value in exchange." The things which have the greatest value in use have frequently little or no value in exchange; and, on the contrary, those which have the greatest value in exchange have frequently little or no value in use. Nothing is more useful than water; but it will purchase scarce anything; scarce anything can be had in exchange for it. A diamond, on the contrary, has scarce any value in use, but a very great quantity of goods may frequently be had in exchange for it.

These two terms, adopted by Adam Smith, as best expressing the two distinct senses of the word value, at once took their place in the accepted economic terminology, and have since his time been generally used.

But though the terms of distinction which he used have been from the first accepted, this has not been the case with the distinction itself. From the first, his successors and commentators began to question its validity, declaring that nothing could have exchange value for which there was not demand; that demand implied some kind of utility or usefulness, and hence that what has value in exchange must also have value in use; and that Smith had been led into confusion by a disposition to import moral distinctions into a science that knows nothing of moral distinctions. This view has been generally, so far indeed as I know universally, accepted by political economists.*

* There is a latent confusion in the use of a word to which I must here call attention, as I have in previous writings slipped into this

Thus, John Stuart Mill (whom I take as the best exponent of the scholastically accepted political economy up to the time when the Austrian or psychological school began to become the "fad" of confused professors), begins his treatment of value by pointing out that "the smallest error on that subject infects with corresponding error all our other conclusions, and anything vague or misty in our conceptions of it creates confusion and uncertainty in everything else." And he thus proceeds ("Principles of Political Economy," Book III., Chapter I., Sec. 1):

We must begin by settling our phraseology. Adam Smith, in a passage often quoted, has touched upon the most obvious ambiguity of the word "value;" which, in one of its senses, signifies usefulness, in another, power of purchasing; in his own language, value in use and value in exchange. But (as Mr. De Quincey has remarked) in illustrating this double meaning, Adam Smith has himself fallen into another ambiguity. Things (he says) which have the greatest value in use have often little or no value in exchange; which is true, since that which can be obtained without labor or sacrifice will command no price, however useful or needful it may be. But he proceeds

---

use myself. The word "utility" correctly expresses the idea of what gives value in use—the quality of usefulness. And the word "desirability" is sometimes used by economists to express the contrasted idea, of what gives value in exchange, the quality of being desired, though not necessarily satisfying a need or useful purpose. Such use seems convenient and has some sanction in economic writing, and I see that I have fallen into it in Part I., Chapter V., of my "A Perplexed Philosopher," where I say:

"If we inquire what is the attribute or condition concurring with the presence, absence or degree of value attaching to anything—we see that things having some form of utility or desirability, are valuable or not valuable, as they are hard or easy to get."

Yet in reality such use of the word is not correct. There is a difficulty in using the word "desirability" in distinction to "utility." "Utility" means the capability of being used, and by analogy "desirability" should mean the capability of being desired. Yet if it did, it would not be the word we need to contrast with utility. For words of distinction must be words of restriction, as are "utility"

to add, that things which have the greatest value in exchange, as a diamond for example, may have little or no value in use. This is employing the word "use," not in the sense in which political economy is concerned with it, but in that other sense in which use is opposed to pleasure. Political economy has nothing to do with the comparative estimation of different uses in the judgment of a philosopher or of a moralist. The use of a thing, in political economy, means its capacity to satisfy a desire, or serve a purpose. Diamonds have this capacity in a high degree, and unless they had it, would not bear any price. Value in use, or, as Mr. De Quincey calls it, "teleologic" value, is the extreme limit of value in exchange. The exchange value of a thing may fall short, to any amount, of its value in use; but that it can ever exceed the value in use implies contradiction; it supposes that persons will give, to possess a thing, more than the utmost value which they themselves put upon it, as a means of gratifying their inclinations.

The word "value," when used without adjunct, always means, in political economy, value in exchange.

---

or "usefulness"—expressing a capability in some things which other things do not have. "Desirability," however, even if it had or we could give it the sense of capability of being desired, would not be a word of restriction, since anything without exception may be desired, and what we really want is not a word which expresses the capability of being desired, but the fact of being desired. "Desirability" in its well-established use, however, does *not* mean the capability of being desired, as "utility" means the capability of being used. When we say that a thing is desirable or undesirable, we do not mean that it may or may not be desired, nor that it is or is not desired, but that it ought or ought not to be desired. Thus, a desirable exchange or trade is an exchange which, with reference to the party considered, will prove a good one. An undesirable exchange is one that will to the party considered prove a bad one. So we speak of a desirable book, horse, beverage, food, medicine, appetite, habit, thought, feeling or gratification, with reference to an ultimate benefit or injury to the person or persons specially considered or to mankind generally. So, indeed, we may speak even of a desirable or undesirable desire. The reason why there is no word in the English language which expresses the idea I wish to express, and which if at liberty to coin a word I should call "desiredness," is that the one word, "value," serving in common speech for both senses, there is no common need for it.

Here is a queer settlement of phraseology. Let us pick out the positive statements. They are: That Adam Smith was wrong in saying that things which have the greatest value in exchange, as a diamond, may have little or no value in use, because the use of a thing in political economy, which knows nothing of any moral estimate of uses, means its capacity to satisfy a desire or serve a purpose—a capacity which diamonds have in high degree, and unless they had it would not have any value in exchange ("bear any price"). Value in use is the highest possible ("extreme limit of") value in exchange. The exchange value of a thing can never exceed the use value of a thing. To suppose that it could implies a contradiction—that persons will give to possess a thing more than its utmost use value to them ("value which they themselves put upon it as a means of gratifying their inclinations").

In this there is a complete identification of value in use, utility or usefulness, with value in exchange, exchangeability or purchasing power. What then becomes of Mill's other statement in the same paragraph? If Adam Smith was wrong in saying that the exchange value of a thing may be more than its use value, how could he be right in saying that the exchange value of a thing may be less than its use value? If value in use is the highest limit of value in exchange, is it not necessarily the lowest limit? If diamonds derive their exchange value from their capacity to satisfy a desire or serve a purpose, do not beans? If value in exchange means merely value in use, why does Mr. Mill distinguish between the two senses of the word value, that of usefulness, and that of purchasing power? Why does he tell us that the word value, when used without adjunct, always means in political economy value in exchange? Why keep up a distinction where there is really no difference?

In this identification of utility with "desiredness" (which I have merely quoted Mill to illustrate, for it began immediately after Adam Smith, and was well rooted in the current political economy long before Mill, as he indeed declares, saying in the first paragraph of his treatment of values, "Happily there is nothing in the laws of value which remains for the present or any future writer to clear up; the theory of the subject is complete") is the beginning of that theory of value as springing from marginal utilities of which Jevons was the first English expounder, and which has been carried to elaborate development by what is known as the Austrian or psychological school. This school, setting aside all distinction between value in use and value in exchange, makes value without distinction an expression of the intensity of desire, thus tracing it to a purely mental or subjective origin. In this theory the intensity of the desire of the bread-eater to eat bread fixes the extreme or marginal utility of bread. This again fixes the utility of the products of which bread is made—flour, yeast, fuel, etc.—and of the tools used in making it—ovens, pans, etc.—and again of the natural materials used in making these products, and finally of the land and labor.

But all this elaborate piling of confusion on confusion originates, as we may see in Mill, in a careless use of words. Nothing indeed could more strikingly illustrate the need of the warning as to the use of words in political economy which I endeavored to impress on the reader in the introductory chapter of this work than the spectacle here presented of the author of the most elaborate work on logic in the English language falling into vital error in what he himself declares to be a most fundamental question of political economy, from failure to apprehend a distinction in the meaning of two common words. Yet here plainly enough is the source of Mill's acceptance of what much inferior thinkers to Adam Smith had deemed a correction of the great Scotsman. The gist of his argument is that the capability of "a use," in the sense of satisfying a desire or serving a purpose, is identical with usefulness. But this is not so. Every child learns long before he reaches his teens that the capability of a use is not usefulness. Here, for instance, is a dialogue such as every one who has gone to an old-fashioned primary school or mixed as a boy with boys must have heard time and again:

First Boy—What's the use of that crooked pin you're bending?

Second Boy—What's the use! Its use is to lay it on a seat some fellow is just going to sit down on, and to make him jump and squeal, and to hear the teacher charging around while you're busy studying your lesson, and don't know anything about what's the matter.

This is certainly a use; but would any one, even a school-boy, attribute usefulness to such a use?

So, the wearing of nose-rings by some savages; the tattooing of their bodies by other savages, and by sailors; the squeezing of their waists by civilized women; the monstrous structures into which the hair of fashionable European ladies was built in the last century; the hooped skirts worn during a part of this; the pitiful distortion practised on the feet of upper-class female infants by the Chinese, are all uses. But do they therefore imply usefulness?

Again, the thumb-screws brought from Russia by Drummond and Dalziel, when they were sent to Scotland by Charles II. to force Episcopacy upon the Covenanters, had "a use." The racks which the English captors of the ships of the Spanish Armada were said to have found in those vessels, intended, as was believed, for the purpose of converting English Protestants to the true faith of Rome, had also a capacity of satisfying a devilish desire. They had unquestionably at that time value in exchange, and indeed, if still in existence, would have value in exchange now, for they would be purchased for museums; and I do not see how they could at that time have been refused, or if in existence, could now be refused, a place in any category of articles of wealth. But were they useful articles? No one would now say so. There were, it is true, at that time some people who might have contended for their usefulness. But consider the supposition under which alone this claim for their usefulness could have been made, for it points to an essential distinction between the meaning of usefulness and that of mere capacity for use. The thumb-screws and racks could have been considered as useful only on the assumption that the eternal salvation of men, their exemption from endless torture, depended on their acceptance of certain theological beliefs, and therefore that the rooting out of schism and heresy, even by the use of temporal torture, was conducive to the true welfare and final happiness of the generality of mankind.

To consider this is to see that what is really the essential idea of usefulness, of that quality of a thing which Adam Smith distinguished as utility or value in use, is, not the capability of any use, but the capability of use in the satisfaction of the natural, normal and general desires of men.

And in this Adam Smith, following the Physiocrats, recognized a distinction that he did not create, and that no confusions of current economic teaching can eradicate; a distinction that does not come from the refinements of philosophers or moralists, but that rests on common perceptions of the human mind—the distinction, namely, between things which in themselves or in their uses conduce to well-being and happiness and the things which in themselves or in their uses involve fruitless effort or ultimate injury and pain. The capacity of satisfying some desire, no matter how idle, vicious or cruel, is indeed all that is necessary to exchangeability or value in exchange. But to give usefulness or value in use something more is necessary, and that is the capacity to satisfy, not any possible desire, but those desires which we call needs or wants, and which, lying lower in the order of desires, are felt by all men.*

Value in use and value in exchange may and often do attach to the same things, and, as a matter of fact, doubtless the great majority of things having value in exchange have also value in use. But this connection is not necessary, and the two qualities have no relation whatever to each other. A thing may have use value in the highest degree, yet very little exchange value or none at all. A thing may have exchange value in very high degree and little or no use value. Air has the highest value in use, as without air we could not live a minute. But this supreme utility does not give air exchange value. The Bambino of Rome or the Holy Coat of Treves could probably be exchanged, as similar venerated objects have been at times exchanged, for enormous sums; but the use value of the one is that of a wax doll baby, that of the other an old rag. The two qualities of value in use and value in exchange are as essentially different and unrelatable as are weight and color, though as we sometimes speak of heavy browns and light blues, so do we in common speech use the word value now to express one of these qualities and now the other. The quality of value in use is an intrinsic or inherent quality attaching to the thing itself, and giving to it fitness to satisfy man's needs. It cannot have value in use except it has that, and as it has that, no matter what be its value in exchange. And its use value is the same whether much can be obtained for it in exchange or "no one would pick it up." The quality of value in exchange, on the other hand, is not intrinsic or inherent.

---

* As explained in Book I., Chapter XI.

There is, to be sure, a special sense in which, comformably to usage, we may speak in certain cases of an intrinsic value as applying to the part of the value which comes wholly from the estimate of man, and where in reality inherent or intrinsic value cannot exist. The cases in which we do this are cases in which we wish to distinguish between the exchange value which a thing may have in a higher or more valuable form and that exchange value which still remains if it were reduced to a lower or less valuable form. Thus, a silver pitcher or a United States silver coin would lose exchange value if beaten into ingots; or a coil of lead pipe or a ship's anchor and cable would lose in exchange value if melted into pigs. Yet they would retain the exchange value of the metal from which they were made. This value in exchange which would remain in a lower form we are accustomed to speak of as "intrinsic value." But in using this term we should always remember its merely relative sense. Value in the economic sense, or value in exchange, can never really be intrinsic. It refers not to any property of the thing itself, but to an estimate that is placed on it by man—to the toil and trouble that men will undergo to acquire possession of it, or the amount of other things costing toil and trouble that they will give for it.

Nor is there any common measure in the human mind between usefulness and exchangeability. Whether we most esteem a thing for the intrinsic qualities that give it usefulness, or for its intrinsic quality of commanding other things in exchange, depends upon conditions.

A daring fellow recently crossed from the coast of Norway to the United States in a sixteen-foot boat. Supposing him to come to New York, and one of our hundredfold millionaires, in the fashion of an Arabian Nights' Sultan, to say to him: "If you will make a trip at my direction you may fill up your boat at my expense with anything you choose to take from New York, regardless of its cost." What would he fill it up with? That could not be answered in a word, as it would entirely depend upon where the millionaire wanted him to go. If he were merely to cross the North River from New York to Jersey City, he would disregard value in use and fill up with what had the highest value in exchange, in comparison to bulk and weight—gold, diamonds, paper money. To carry the more of these he would leave out everything having value in use that he could get along without for an hour or two—even to extra sails, anchor, sea-drag, compass, a morsel of food or a drink of water. But if he were to cross the Atlantic again, his first care would be for things useful in the management of his boat and the maintenance of his own life and comfort during the long months of danger and solitude before he could hope again to reach land. He would regard value in use, disregarding value in exchange. If he had not lost the prudence which, no less than daring, is required successfully to make such a trip, it may well be doubted whether he would not prefer to carry its weight in fresh water than to take a single diamond or gold piece and prefer another can of biscuit or condensed beef to the last bundle of thousand-dollar notes that he might take instead.

Adam Smith was right. The distinction between value in use and value in exchange is an essential one. It is so clear and true and necessary that, as we have seen, John Stuart Mill could not refrain from partially recognizing it in the very breath in which he had eliminated it altogether, and the later economists who have carried the confusion which he expresses to a point of more elaborate confusion are also compelled to recognize it the moment they get out of the fog of ill-understood words. Despite all attempts to confuse and obliterate them, "value in use" and "value in exchange" must still hold their place in economic terminology. The terms themselves are perhaps not the happiest that might be chosen. But so long have they now been used that it would be difficult to substitute anything in their place. It is only necessary to do what Adam Smith could hardly have deemed necessary—point out what they really mean. They were taken indeed by him from common speech, and still retain the great advantage to any economic term of being generally intelligible.

In common speech the one word value, as I have already said, usually suffices to express either value in use or value in exchange. For which sense of the word value is meant is ordinarily indicated with sufficient clearness either by the context or by the situation or nature of the thing spoken of. But in cases where there is no indication thus supplied, or the indication is not sufficiently clear, the use of the word "value" will at once provoke a question equivalent to "Do you mean value for use or value for exchange?"

Thus, if a man says to me, "That is a valuable dog, he saved a child from drowning;" I know that the value he means is value in use. If he says, however, "That is a valuable dog, his brother brought a hundred dollars;" I know that he has in mind value in exchange. Even where he says simply, "That is a valuable dog," there is generally some indication that enables me to tell what sense of value he has in mind. If there is none, and I am interested enough to care, I ask for it by such question as "Why?" or "What for?"

In economic reasoning, however, the danger of using one word to represent two distinct and often contrasted ideas is very much greater than in common speech, and if the word is to be retained, one of its senses must be abandoned. Of the two meanings of the word value, the first, that of value in use, is not called for, or called for only incidentally in political economy; while the second, that of value in exchange, is called for continually, for this is the value with which political economy deals. To economize the use of words, while at the same time avoiding liability to misunderstanding and confusion, it is expedient, therefore, to restrict the use of the word value, as an economic term, to the meaning of value in exchange, as was done by Adam Smith, and has since his time generally been followed; and to discard the use of the single word value in the sense of value in use, substituting for it where there is occasion to express the idea of value in use, and the close context does not clearly show the limitation of meaning, either the term "value in use" or some such word as usefulness or utility. This I shall endeavor to do in this work—using hereafter the single term value, as meaning purchasing power or "value in exchange."

CHAPTER XI.

ECONOMIC VALUE—ITS REAL MEANING AND FINAL MEASURE.

SHOWING HOW VALUE IN EXCHANGE HAS BEEN DEEMED A RELATION OF PROPORTION; AND THE AMBIGUITY WHICH HAS LED TO THIS.

The conception of value as a relation of proportion—It is really a relation to exertion—Adam Smith's perception of this—His reasons for accepting the term value in exchange—His confusion and that of his successors.

VALUE, as an economic term, means, as we have seen, what in defining it from the other sense of the word value, is known as value in exchange, or exchangeability. And to this meaning alone I shall, when using the word value without adjunct, hereafter confine it.

But from what does this quality of value in exchange, or exchangeability, proceed? And by what may we measure it?

As to this the current teachings of political economy are, that value, the quality or power of exchangeability, is a relation between each exchangeable thing and all other exchangeable things. Thus, it is said, there can be no general increase or decrease of values, since what one valuable thing may gain in exchange power, some other valuable thing or things must lose; and what one loses some other or others must gain. In other words, the relation of value being a relation of ratio or proportion, any change in one ratio must involve reverse changes in other ratios, since the sum total of ratios can neither be increased nor diminished. There may be increase or decrease of value in any one or more things, as compared with any other one or more things; but no increase or decrease in all values at once. All prices, for instance, may increase or diminish, because price is a relation of exchangeability between all other exchangeable things and one particular exchangeable thing, money; and increase or decrease of price (greater or less exchangeability of other things for money) involves correlatively decrease or increase of the exchangeability of money for other things. But increase or decrease in value generally (*i.e.*, all values) is a contradiction in terms.

This view has a certain plausibility. Yet to examine it is to see that it makes value dependent on value without possibility of measurement except arbitrarily and relatively, by comparing one value with another; that it leaves the idea of value swimming, as it were, in vacancy, without connection or fixed starting-point, such as we attach to all other qualities of relation, and without which any definite idea of relation is impossible.

Thus, such qualities as size, distance, direction, color, consanguinity and the like are only comprehensible and intelligible to us by reference to some fixed starting-point, to which and not to all other things having the same quality the relation is made. Size and distance, for instance, are comprehended and intelligibly expressed as relations to certain measures of extension, such as the barleycorn, the foot, the meter, diameters of the earth, or diameters of the earth's orbit; direction, as a relation to the radii of a sphere, which, proceeding from a central point, would include all possible directions; color, as a relation to the order in which certain impressions are received through the human eye; consanguinity, as a relation in blood to the primary blood-relationship, that between parent and child; and so on.

Now, has not also the idea of value some fixed starting-point, by which it becomes comprehensible and intelligible, as have all other ideas of relation?

Clearly it has. What the idea of value really springs from, is not the relation of each thing having value to all things having value, but the relation of each thing having value to something which is the source and natural measure of all value—namely, human exertion, with its attendant irksomeness or weariness.

Adam Smith saw this, though he may not have consistently held to it, as was the case with some other things he clearly saw for a moment, as through a rift in clouds which afterwards closed up again. In the first paragraphs of Chapter V., Book I., "Wealth of Nations," he says:

> Every man is rich or poor according to the degree in which he can afford to enjoy the necessaries, conveniences and amusements of human life. But after the division of labor has once thoroughly taken place, it is but a very small part of these with which a man's own labor can supply him. The far greater part of them he must derive from the labor of other people, and he must be rich or poor according to the quantity of that labor which he can command, or which he can afford to purchase. The value of any commodity, therefore, to the person who possesses it, and who means not to use or consume it himself, but to exchange it for other commodities, is equal to the quantity of labor which it enables him to purchase or command. Labor, therefore, is the real measure of the exchangeable value of all commodities.
>
> The real price of everything, what everything really costs to the man who wants to acquire it, is the toil and trouble of acquiring it. What everything is really worth to the man who has acquired it, and who wants to dispose of it or exchange it for something else, is the toil and trouble which it can save to himself, and which it can impose upon other people. What is bought with money or with goods is purchased by labor, as much as what we acquire by the toil of our

own body. That money or those goods indeed save us this toil. They contain the value of a certain quantity of labor, which we exchange for what is supposed at the time to contain the value of an equal quantity. Labor was the first price, the original purchase money that was paid for all things. It was not by gold or by silver, but by labor, that all the wealth of the world was originally purchased; and its value, to those who possess it, and who want to exchange it for some new productions, is precisely equal to the quantity of labor which it can enable them to purchase or command.

Wealth, as Mr. Hobbes says, is power. But the person who either acquires or succeeds to a great fortune, does not necessarily acquire or succeed to any political power, either civil or military. His fortune may perhaps afford him the means of acquiring both, but the mere possession of that fortune does not necessarily convey to him either. The power which that possession immediately and directly conveys to him is the power of purchasing; a certain command over all the labor, or over all the produce of labor which is then in the market. His fortune is greater or less precisely in proportion to the extent of this power; or to the quantity of other men's labor, or, what is the same thing, of the produce of other men's labor which it enables him to purchase or command. The exchangeable value of everything must always be precisely equal to the extent of this power which it will convey to its owner.

This is perfectly clear, if we attend only to the meaning Adam Smith puts upon the words he uses somewhat loosely. The sense in which he uses the word labor is that of exertion, with its inseparable attendants, toil and trouble. What he means by price, is cost in toil and trouble, as he indeed incidentally explains,* and by wealth

* "Price," as an economic term, has come to mean value in terms of money, or at least in terms of one particular commodity; but Adam Smith did not make this distinction. He uses the word "price" sometimes where he means "cost," and sometimes where he means "value." This use of price for value he once in a while indicates, as where, in Chapter VI., he speaks of "price or exchangeable value," but in general he leaves it to inference. Where it is necessary for him to make the distinction between what we now call value and what we now call price, he usually speaks of the one as "real price" and of the other as "nominal price," meaning by "real price" value in labor, and by "nominal price" value in money.

he evidently means the products or tangible results of human exertion. What he says is that value is the equivalent of the toil and trouble of exertion, and that its measure is the amount of toil and trouble that it will save to the owner or enable him by exchange to induce others to take for him.

And he again repeats this statement a little further on in the same book:

> Equal quantities of labor, at all times and places, may be said to be of equal value to the laborer. In his ordinary state of health, strength and spirits; in the ordinary degree of his skill and dexterity, he must always lay down the same portion of his ease, his liberty, and his happiness. The price which he pays must always be the same, whatever may be the quantity of goods which he receives in return for it. Of these indeed it may sometimes purchase a greater and sometimes a smaller quantity; but it is their value which varies, not that of the labor which purchases them. At all times and places that is dear which it is difficult to come at, or which it costs much labor to acquire; and that cheap which is to be had easily, or with very little labor. Labor alone, therefore, never varying in its own value, is alone the ultimate and real standard by which the value of all commodities can at all times and places be estimated and compared. It is their real price; money is their nominal price only. . . . Labor, therefore, it appears evidently, is the only universal, as well as the only accurate measure of value, or the only standard by which we can compare the values of different commodities at all times and at all places.

How then is it that Adam Smith, when he needed a term which should express the second sense of the word value, did not adopt a phrase that would bring out the fundamental meaning of value in this sense, such, for instance, as "value in toil," or "value in exertion," or "value in labor;" but instead of any of them chose a phrase, "value in exchange," which refers directly to only a secondary and derivative meaning?

The reasons he himself gives, in what immediately follows the first two paragraphs I have quoted:

But though labor be the real measure of the exchangeable value of all commodities, it is not that by which their value is commonly estimated. It is often difficult to ascertain the proportion between two different quantities of labor. The time spent in two different sorts of work will not always alone determine this proportion. The different degrees of hardship endured, and of ingenuity exercised, must likewise be taken into account. There may be more labor in an hour's hard work than in two hours' easy business; or in an hour's application to a trade which it cost ten years' labor to learn, than in a month's industry at an ordinary and obvious employment. But it is not easy to find any accurate measure either of hardship or ingenuity. In exchanging, indeed, the different productions of different sorts of labor for one another, some allowance is commonly made for both. It is adjusted, however, not by any accurate measure, but by the higgling and the bargaining of the market, according to that sort of rough equality which, though not exact, is yet sufficient for carrying on the business of common life.

Every commodity, besides, is more frequently exchanged for, and thereby compared with, other commodities than with labor. It is more natural therefore to estimate its exchangeable value by the quantity of some other commodity, than by that of the labor which it can purchase. The greater part of people, too, understand better what is meant by a quantity of a particular commodity than by a quantity of labor. The one is a plain and palpable object; the other an abstract notion, which, though it can be made sufficiently intelligible, is not altogether so natural and obvious.

There are here two reasons assigned for the choice of the term "value in exchange," to denote what Smith saw with perfect, though only momentary clearness, really to mean "value in exertion," or in the phraseology he uses, "value in labor."

The first, and it is a weighty one, is that the term "value in exchange" was already familiar, and would be best understood in bringing out the distinction he wished to dwell upon—the difference between value in the economic sense and "value in use."

The second, which indicates a confusion in the philosopher's own mind—the swiftness with which the clouds drifted over the star he had just seen—is that he could think of nothing by which to measure the toil and trouble of exertion except time of application, which he truly saw could only measure quantity and not quality—that is to say, duration, not intensity. He failed to recognize the obvious fact that if the toil and trouble of exertion dispensed with be the measure of value, then, correlatively, value must be the real measure of the toil and trouble of that exertion, and that the something he was seemingly looking for—some material thing or attribute which, as a yardstick measures length and a standard weight measures mass, should, independently of "the higgling of the market," measure the toil and trouble of exertion—is not to be found, because it cannot exist, the only possibility of such a measurement lying in "the higgling of the market." For since toil and trouble, which constitute the resistance to exertion, are subjective feelings which cannot be objectively recognized until brought, through their influence upon action, into the objective field, there is no way of measuring them except by the inducement that will tempt men to undergo them in exertion, which can be determined only by competition or "the higgling of the market."

So, for a good reason and a bad reason, Adam Smith, for the purpose of expressing the economic sense of the word value, chose the term "value in exchange." It would be too much to say that he made a bad choice, especially considering his time and the main purpose he had in mind, which was to show the absurdity of what was then called the mercantile system, and has since been re-christened the protective system. But the ambiguity involved in the term "value in exchange" has been a stumbling-block in political economy from his day to this, and, indeed, to the ambiguity concealed in his own chosen term Adam Smith himself fell a victim. Or perhaps, rather, it should be said, that the ambiguity of the term allowed him to retain confusions that were already in his mind, save when in the paragraphs just quoted he momentarily brushed them away, only to have them recur again. It will be noticed that, in these paragraphs, Smith clearly distinguishes between labor and commodities, evidently meaning by commodities things produced by labor; and that he seems clearly to understand by wealth the products of labor. But in other places he drops into the confusion of treating labor itself as a commodity, and of classing personal qualities, such as industry, skill, knowledge, etc., as articles of wealth; just as, in Chapter VIII., he clearly sees and correctly states the true origin and nature of wages where he says: "The produce of labor constitutes the natural recompense or wages of labor," only almost immediately to abandon it and proceed to treat wages as supplied from the capital of the employer.

Adam Smith was never called upon to revise or in any way to reconsider the statement of his great book as to the nature of value, the discussion on the subject having arisen since his death. His successors in political economy have been with few exceptions, not men of original thought, but the mere imitators, compilers and straw-splitters who usually follow a great work of genius. They have, without looking further, accepted the term used by him, "value in exchange," not merely in the same way that he accepted it, as a convenient, because a readily understood, name for a quality, but as expressing the nature of that quality. Thus Adam Smith's explanation of the essential relation of value to the exertion of labor has been virtually, if not utterly, ignored. And from looking further than exchangeability for an explanation of the nature of value, these succeeding economists have been dissuaded and debarred not only by certain facts not understood, such as the fact that many things having value do not originate in labor, and by erroneous conceptions, such as that which treats labor itself as a commodity; but by a greatly effective, though doubtless in most cases a very vague recognition of the fact that danger to existing social institutions would follow any too searching an inquiry into the fundamental principle of value. A world of ingenuity has been expended and monstrous books have been written that it will tire a man to read and almost make him doubt his own sanity to try to understand, to solve the problem of the fundamental nature of value in exchange. Yet they have resulted in what are but ponderous elaborations of confusion, for the good and sufficient reason that the essence or foundation of what we call value in exchange does not lie in exchangeability at all, but in something from which exchangeability springs—the toil and trouble attendant upon exertion.

Let me endeavor, even at some length, to prove this in a succeeding chapter, for most vital and far-reaching economic issues are involved in this settlement of the meaning of a term.

CHAPTER XII

VALUE IN EXCHANGE REALLY RELATED TO LABOR.

SHOWING THAT VALUE DOES NOT COME FROM EXCHANGEABILITY, BUT EXCHANGEABILITY FROM VALUE, WHICH IS AN EXPRESSION OF THE SAVING OF LABOR INVOLVED IN POSSESSION.

Root of the assumption that the sum of values cannot increase or diminish—The fundamental idea of proportion—We cannot really think of value in this way—The confusion that makes us imagine that we do—The tacit assumption and reluctance to examine that bolster the current notion—Imaginative experiment shows that value is related to labor—Common facts that prove this—Current assumption a fallacy of undistributed middle—Various senses of "labor"—Exertion positive and exertion negative—Re-statement of the proposition as to value—Of desire and its measurement—Causal relationship of value and exchangeability—Imaginative experiment showing that value may exist where exchange is impossible—Value an expression of exertion avoided.

FROM the assumption that economic value is not merely what we have found it convenient to call value in exchange, but in reality is exchangeability—a quality of power by which the owner of a valuable thing may, by surrendering his ownership to some one else, obtain from him by similar transfer the ownership of another valuable thing—value is thought of as proceeding from value, and existing in a circle of which each part must have a relation of proportion or ratio to all other parts. It is this that gives axiomatic semblance to the proposition that while there may be increase or decrease in some values, this must always involve reversely decrease or increase in some other values, and hence that increase or decrease of all values, or of the sum of values, is impossible. If value be really a relation of proportion, this indeed is self-evident.

But is value really a relation of proportion or ratio? What is the fundamental idea of proportion or ratio? Is it not that of the relation of the parts of a whole to that whole? When we use such a phrase as one-eighth we mean the relation of a part represented as one of eight equal partitions to a whole represented by one. When we use such a phrase as 10 per cent. we mean a relation of a part represented by ten of 100 equal partitions to a whole represented by 100. So such propositions as $\frac{1}{8}+\frac{1}{8}=\frac{1}{4}$; or $.153+.147=.3$; or $4 : 8 :: 6 : 12$; or $5\%+4\%=9\%$, depend for their validity upon the relations of the proportions spoken of to a whole or totality, which is the sum of all possible proportions. That there cannot be increase or decrease in all proportions follows from the axiom that a whole is equal to the sum of its parts.

But if value be a relation of proportion or ratio, what is the whole which it implies? How shall we express this totality? Or by what calculus shall we fix the relations of its parts, the numberless and constantly changing articles of value? Might we not as well try to think of or express the relation of each particular hair of our heads to the sum of the hairs in the heads of all humanity?

The truth is that we cannot think of value in this way, nor do we really try to, and the more ingenious and elaborate the attempts that have been made to give something like solid support and logical coherency to the prevailing theory that value is really nothing more than exchangeability only the more clearly show its utter inadequacy. Thus the latest and most elaborate of these attempts, that of the Austrian or psychological school, which has been of recent years so generally accepted in the universities and colleges of the United States and England, and which derives value from what it calls "marginal utilities," is an attempt to emulate in economic reasoning the stories told of East Indian jugglers, who throwing a ball of thread into the air, pull up by it a stouter thread, then a rope, and finally a ladder, on which they ascend until out of sight, and then—come down again!

For whoever will work his way through the perplexities of their reasoning will find that the adherents of this school derive the value of pig-iron, for instance, or even of iron ore in the vein, from the willingness of consumers to pay for higher and more elaborate products into the production of which iron enters, deriving that willingness from a mental estimate on the part of consumers of the utility of these products to them. Thus, as coolly as such stories of Indian jugglers ignore the law of gravitation, do they ignore that law which to political economy is what gravitation is to physics, the law that men seek to satisfy their desires with the least exertion—a law from which proceeds the universal fact that as a matter of exchange no one will pay more for anything than he is obliged to.

These elaborate attempts to link value on utility, and utility on individual will or perception, in order to find a support for the idea of value, only show that there is no resting-place in the supposition that value proceeds from exchangeability, and can only be relative to other values. The plausibility of this supposition comes from confusion in the use of a simple word.

Of all words in common use in the English tongue the word "thing" is the widest. It includes whatever may be an object of thought—an atom or a universe; a fact or a fancy; what comes into consciousness through our senses and what constitutes the peopling and furniture of our dreams; that which analysis cannot further resolve and that which has no other coherence than a verbal habit or mistake. But this comprehensiveness of the word we are sometimes apt to forget, or not fully to keep in mind, and to use such phrases as "all things" or "anything" when we really have in mind only things of one particular kind.

When we wish to test the proposition that value is a relation of exchangeability between valuable things, we usually proceed to make a mental experiment with some few valuable things, for it would be impossible to take them all, and tiresome to attempt it. For the things selected for this experiment we are apt, as examination and observation will show, and as is evident in the writings of economists, to take such things as are most widely known and commonly exchanged, turning the particular into the general when required, by the formula, expressed or implied, "and other valuable things." Thus, for instance, we think of money, or as the most widely known representative of money, a piece of gold, and say to ourselves: "Here is a piece of gold. Why is it valuable? It is that it can be exchanged for wheat, hardware, cotton goods and other valuable things. If it could not be so exchanged it would have no value, and the measure of its value is the value of the wheat, hardware, cotton goods and other valuable things for which it is exchangeable. If the relation of exchangeability alters so that for the same piece of gold one can obtain more wheat, hardware, cotton goods and other valuable things, the value of the gold rises, and that of the other valuable things falls. If the relation of exchangeability alters so that the piece of gold will exchange for less of these things, the value of the gold falls and that of the other things rises." Then, we reverse the standpoint of examination, taking in turn wheat, hardware or cotton goods, as representative of a particular instance of value, and gold, as representing other valuable things; and seeing that their value depends upon their exchangeable relation in the same way as that of gold in our first experiment, we conclude that value is indeed a relation of exchangeability, and that that is the beginning and end of it.

Thus, that value depends on value, and springs from value and can only be measured by value—that is, by the selection of some particular article having value, from which relatively and empirically the value of other articles may be measured—seems to us perfectly clear, and we accept the doctrine that there can be no general increase or decrease in values, as if it were but another statement of the axiom that a whole is equal to the sum of its parts, and consequently that *all* those parts can never be increased or diminished at the same time. The habitual use of money as a common measure of value is apt to prevent any realization of the fact that we are reasoning in a circle.

I think I have correctly described the line of reasoning which makes the derivation of value from exchangeability so plausible. I do not of course mean to say that labor is never taken into account. It is often expressly mentioned and always implied to be one of the valuable things in the category of valuable or exchangeable things. But the weight of the examination is, I think, always thrown upon such things as I have named—things resulting from the exertion of labor; while labor itself is passed over lightly as one of the "other valuable things," and attention never rests upon it.

And, furthermore, I am inclined to think that there always lurks in this examination—which is in reality an examination of the relative value of products of labor—the tacit assumption that the quantity of the valuable things (thought of as products of labor) existing at the specific moment presumed in the examination is a fixed quantity, so that there can be no exchange between those possessed of valuable things (*i.e.*, products of labor) and those possessed of no valuable things (*i.e.*, no products of labor). This, I think, is the case even where there is an assumption of giving the value of labor a place in the category of considered values, for what the reputed economists since Smith have called the "value of labor" is in reality the value of the products of labor paid to laborers in wages, which has been usually assumed to come from a (at any given moment) fixed quantity, capital. And on another side, any rigorous examination of the nature of value has been prevented by the universal disposition of economists, not really questioned until "Progress and Poverty" was published, to slur over the nature of the value of land, and practically to assume, what was indeed the common assumption, that it was of the same origin as the value attaching to such things as gold, wheat, hardware, cotton goods or similar products of labor.

That it takes two to make an exchange, as certainly as "it takes two to make a quarrel," is clear. But that value in one person's hands does not, as is impliedly or expressly taught in economic works, necessarily involve the existence of value in the hands of others, may be seen by another imaginative experiment:

Let us imagine some remote and as yet undiscovered island, where men still live as in the Biblical account our first parents lived before the Fall, taking their food from never-failing trees, quenching their thirst from ample and convenient springs, sleeping in the balmy air, and without thought of clothing, even of aprons of fig-leaves. The power of exerting labor they would of course possess, as Adam and Eve possessed it from the first; but of that exertion itself and of the toil it involves, we may imagine them as ignorant as Adam and Eve in their first estate are supposed to have been. On that island there would clearly be no value. Yet if valuable articles were brought there, would they necessarily lose their value? Could they be parted with only by gift, and would there be no possibility of exchanging them?

Imagine, now, a ship containing such merchandise as would tempt the fancy of a primitive people to come in sight of the island and cast anchor. Would exchange between the ship's people and the islanders be impossible because of the lack on the part of the islanders of anything having value? By no means. If nothing else would suffice, the offer of bright cloths and looking-glasses would surely tempt the Eves, if it did not the Adams; and though never exerted before, the islanders would exert their power of labor to fill the ship with fruit or nuts or shells, or whatever else of the natural products of the island their exertion could procure, or to pull her on the beach so that she might be calked, or to fill and roll her water-casks. There was nothing of value in the island before the ship came. Yet the exchanges that would thus take place would be the giving of value in return for value; for on the part of the islanders value that did not exist before would be brought into existence by the conversion of their labor power through exertion into wealth or services. There would thus be what so many of our economists say is impossible, a general increase of values. Even if we suppose the islanders to relapse into their former easy way of living when their visitors sailed off, there would still remain on the island, where there was no value before, some things having value, and this value would attach to these things until they were destroyed or so long as such desire as would prompt any of the islanders to render labor in exchange for them remained. On the other side, the value that the ship would carry off would certainly be not less than the value she contained on arrival, and in all probability would be much more.

Now the way thus illustrated is the way in which the value that attaches to the greater number of valuable things originates. I do not mean merely to say that this was the way of the first appearance of value among men, but that it is the way in which the value that attaches to what are properly articles of wealth *now* originates. I do not mean merely to say, as Adam Smith said, that it was "by labor that all the wealth of the world *was* originally purchased." I mean to say that it is by labor that it is *now* purchased.

Nothing, indeed, can be clearer than this. Even in the richest of civilized countries, the ultimate purchasers of the greater mass of valuable things, are not those who have in store valuable things that they can give in exchange. The great body of the people in any civilized society consist of what we call the working-class, who live almost literally from hand to mouth, and who have in their possession at any one time little, or practically nothing, of value. Yet they are the purchasers of the great body of articles of value. Where does the value which they thus exchange for value which is already in concrete form come from? Does it not come from the conversion of their labor power, through exertion, into value? Is not the exchange which is constantly going on, the exchange of the potentiality of labor, or *raw* labor power for labor power that by that transfer has already been converted into value? In common phrase, they exchange their labor for commodities.

How does this fact—the fact that the great body of valuable things pass into the hands of those who have no value to give for them except as they make valuable what before had no value, and are consumed, by being eaten, drunk, burned up or worn out, by them—consort with the theory that value is a relation of exchangeability between valuable things, and that there can be no general increase or decrease of values? Does it not utterly invalidate the theory? Must there not be a constant increase of value to make up for the constant destruction of value. and in spite of it, to permit such growth of aggregate values as we see going on in progressive countries? And in times when the ability to convert labor into values is checked by what we call "want of employment" and great numbers of workers are idle, is there not a clear lessening of the sum of values, a general decrease in values, as compared with the times when there is what we call "abundance of employment," and the great majority of them are at work, turning labor power through exertion into value?

The truth is that current theories of value have resulted from the efforts of intelligent men to mold into a semblance of coherency teachings built upon fundamental incoherencies. Let me point out what gives them plausibility, the fallacy involved in the inclusion of labor as an "other valuable thing," while the real stress of the examination is laid upon the relative values of such things as gold, wheat, hardware and cotton goods—things that are products of labor. It is a fallacy which our habit of speaking of the buying and selling and exchanging of labor, and our habit of thinking of the value of labor as we think of the value of gold or wheat or hardware or cotton goods, conceals from attention, but which is in reality a fallacy of the kind named by the old logicians "the fallacy of undistributed middle."

Here we come to another instance of the care needed in political economy in the use of words. By the word "labor" we sometimes mean the power of laboring—as when we speak of the exertion of labor, or of labor being employed, or of labor being idle or wasting. Sometimes we mean the act of laboring—as when we speak of the irksomeness or toil of labor, or of the results or products of labor. Sometimes we mean the results of laboring—as is the case in most or all of the instances in which we speak of buying, selling or exchanging labor—the real thing bought, sold or exchanged being the results of laboring, that is to say, wealth or services. And sometimes, again, we mean the persons who do labor or the persons who have the power and the willingness to labor.

It is clear that labor in the first-mentioned sense of the word, that of the power or ability of laboring, is not an exchangeable thing and cannot come into any category of values. It resides in the individual body and cannot be taken out of that body and transferred to another, any more than can sight or hearing, or wisdom or courage or skill. I may avail myself of another's skill, courage or wisdom, of his hearing or of his sight, by getting him to exert them for my benefit. And so I may avail myself of another's ability to labor by getting him to do me services, or to produce things which I am to own. But the power of laboring he cannot give, nor I receive. While there are results of its expenditure that may be transferred, the power itself is intransferable, and therefore unexchangeable.

Now the failure to keep in mind these different senses of the word labor, the failure to distribute the term, as the logicians would say, operates to shut off inquiry as to whether the cause of value is not to be found in labor. For since in some senses labor is thought of as having value in exchange, the term, without distinction as to its various senses, is apt to pass in our minds into the category of exchangeable things, with gold or wheat or hardware or cotton goods, or "other products of labor;" and thus the question is unconsciously begged.

But, when we realize that, in whatever other sense of the word we may say that labor is a valuable thing, we must carefully exclude the sense of labor power, or ability to labor, a confusion is cleared up which has made the search for the true nature of what we call value in exchange a fruitless "swinging round a circle." For since value does not exist in labor power, but does appear where that power takes tangible form through exertion, the fundamental relation of value must be a relation to exertion.

But a relation to exertion in what sense? A relation to exertion positively, or a relation to exertion negatively?

I exchange gold for silver, let us say. In this I give something positively and receive something positively. I get rid of gold and acquire silver. The other party to the exchange gets rid of silver and acquires gold. But when I exchange gold for exertion or toil, do I get rid of gold and acquire toil, and does he get rid of toil and acquire gold? Clearly not. No one wants exertion or toil; all of us want to get rid of it. It is not exertion in a positive sense which is the object of exchange, but exertion in a negative sense; not exertion given or imposed, but exertion avoided or saved; or, to use the algebraic form, the relation of the quality of value is not to plus-exertion, but to minus-exertion. Value, in short, is equivalent to the saving of exertion or toil, and the value of anything is the amount of toil which the possession of that thing will save the possessor, or enable him, to use Adam Smith's phrase, "to impose upon other people," through exchange. Thus, it is not exchangeability that gives value; but value that gives exchangeability. For since it is only by exertion that human desires can be satisfied (those cravings or impulses that can be satisfied without exertion not rising to the point of desire) whatever will dispense its owner from the toil and trouble of exertion in the satisfaction of desire in that acquires exchangeability.

Let me put the proposition in another form:

The current theory is that it is when and because a thing becomes exchangeable that it becomes valuable. My contention is that the truth is just the reverse of this, and it is when and because a thing becomes valuable that it becomes exchangeable.

It is not the toil and trouble which a thing *has* cost that gives it value. It may have cost much and yet be worth nothing. It may have cost nothing and yet be worth much. It is the toil and trouble that others are *now* willing, directly or indirectly, to relieve the owner of, in exchange for the thing, by giving him the advantage of the results of exertion, while dispensing him of the toil and trouble that are the necessary accompaniments of exertion. Whether I have obtained a diamond, for instance, by years of hard toil or by merely stooping to pick it up—a movement which can hardly be called an exertion, since it is in itself but a gratification of curiosity which does not involve irksomeness—has nothing whatever to do with its value. That depends upon the amount of toil and trouble that others will undergo for my benefit in exchange for it; or what amounts to the same thing, which they will dispense me of in the satisfaction of my desire, by giving me things in exchange, for which others will undergo toil and trouble.

That which may be had without the toil and trouble of exertion has no value. That for which the desire to possess is not strong enough to prompt to the toil and trouble of exertion has likewise no value. But everything having value, has that value only when, where and to the degree that its possession will, without exertion on the part of its possessor, satisfy through exchange a desire that prompts to exertion.

In other words, the value of a thing is the amount of laboring or work that its possession will save to the possessor.

Desire itself, which is the prompter to exertion, cannot be measured, as the most recent school of pseudo-economists attempt vainly to measure it. It is a quality or affection of the will or individual Ego, which, being in its nature subjective, can have no objective measurement until it passes through action into the field of objective existence. Even in the individual it is not a fixed quality or affection, but resembles more the illumination produced by a movable search-light, which, as it brings one object in the landscape into focus, throws another into shade. All that we can say of it is that it has a certain scale or order of appearance, so that when the more primitive desires that we call "wants" or "needs" slumber in satisfaction, other desires appear; or as they are enkindled again, these others disappear.

But desire impels to action, as what we call energy or force impels to movement. And while we can no more measure desire in itself than we can measure force in itself, we can measure it in the same way that we measure energy or force—by the resistance it will overcome. Now, while the resistance to movement is inertia—probably resolvable into gravitation and chemical affinities; so the resistance to the gratification of desire is the toil and trouble of exertion. It is this that is expressed by and measured in values.

To repeat: Since the desire for material satisfactions is universal among men, and the only way in which these satisfactions can be obtained from Nature is by exertion, which men always seek to avoid, whatever will satisfy desire without calling for exertion is for that reason desired of itself, not for its own uses, but because it affords the means of gratifying other desires, and thus becomes exchangeable whenever the existence of others than its owner makes exchange possible. Normally, at least, value and exchangeability are thus always associated and seemingly identical. But in the causal relationship, value comes first. That is to say, it is not true, as economists since the time of Adam Smith have erroneously taught, that a thing is valuable because it is exchangeable. On the contrary, it is exchangeable because it is valuable. Exchange is in fact the mutual transfer of value. Of all other qualities of things, value is the only quality of which exchange takes note.

A little use of imaginative experiment will make it clear that what we call value in exchange is in reality not dependent on exchangeability, but may exist when exchange is impossible.

A Robinson Crusoe during his period of isolation could make no exchanges, for there was no one with whom he could exchange, and it was only the hope of being sometime discovered and relieved that could have prompted him to take his pieces of eight ashore. Yet, as this hope faded it is not true that his estimate of the different things he possessed would be entirely based on their utility to him, and that he would have no sense of the relation which we call value in exchange. Even if the hope of being sometime relieved had entirely disappeared from his thought, something essentially the same as value in exchange would be brought out in his mind by any question of getting or saving one of two or more things. Of several things to him equally useful, which he might find in the wreck of his ship or on the shore line under conditions which would enable him to secure but one; or of several equally useful to him, which were threatened by a deluge of rain or an incursion of savages, it is evident that he would "set the most store by" that which would represent to him the greatest effort to replace. Thus, in a tropical island his valuation of a quantity of flour, which he could replace only by cultivating, gathering and pounding the grain, would be much greater than that of an equal quantity of bananas, which he might replace at the cost of plucking and carrying them; but on a more northern island this estimate of relative value might be reversed.

And so all things which to get or retain would require of him toil would come to assume in his mind a relation of value distinct from and independent of their usefulness, a relation based on the greater or less degree of exertion that their possession would enable him to avoid in the gratification of his desires.

It is this relation which lies at the bottom of value in the economic sense, or value in exchange. In the last analysis value is but an expression of exertion avoided.

To sum up:

Value in exchange, or value in the economic sense, is worth in exertion. It is a quality attaching to the ownership of things, of dispensing with the exertion necessary to secure the satisfaction of desire, by inducing others to take it. Things are valuable in proportion to the amount of exertion which they will command in exchange, and will exchange with each other in that proportion.

The value of a thing in any given time and place is the largest amount of exertion that any one will render in exchange for it. But as men always seek to gratify their desires with the least exertion, this is the lowest amount for which a similar thing can otherwise be obtained.

But while value means always the same quality—that of dispensing with exertion in the satisfaction of desire—yet there are various sources from which this quality originates. These may be broadly divided into two—that which originates in the toil and trouble involved in production, and that which originates in obligation to undergo toil and trouble for the benefit of another. The failure to note this difference in the sources of value is the cause of great perplexity.

CHAPTER XIII.

THE DENOMINATOR OF VALUE.

SHOWING WHAT VALUE IS, AND ITS RELATIONS.

What value is—The test of real value—Value related only to human desire—This perception at the bottom of the Austrian school—But its measure must be objective—How cost of production acts as a measure of value—Desire for similar things and for essential things—Application of this principle—Its relation to land values.

VALUE in the economic sense or value in exchange is, as we have seen, worth in exchange. It is a quality attaching to the ownership of things, of dispensing with the exertion necessary to secure the satisfaction of desire, by inducing others to take it in return for them. Things are valuable in proportion to the amount of exertion that they will thus command, and will exchange with each other in that proportion.

The value of a thing in any time and place is thus the largest amount of exertion that any one will render in exchange for it. And since men always seek to gratify their desires with the least exertion this is, or always tends to be, the lowest amount for which such a thing can otherwise be obtained.

This of course is not to say that whatever anything may exchange for is its value. In individual and especially in unaccustomed transactions the point at which any particular exchange takes place may considerably vary. But that our idea of value assumes a normal point, and what this point really is, may be seen in common speech. Thus we frequently say of the exchange of a certain thing that it brought less than its value, or that it brought more than its value. Now in this, which we refer to as a real or true value, differing from the assumption of value in the particular exchange, we mean something more definite than customary or habitual value, for this, as in our times we know, is subject in regard to particular things to considerable and not infrequent changes. What we really mean by this real value, and what is its true test, we show in the way we attempt to prove that a thing was exchanged at more or less than its value. We say that a thing was exchanged at less than its value *because* some one else would have given more for it. Or that a thing was exchanged at more than its value *because* some one else would have given the same thing for a less return. And so what we deem the point of real value, or actual equivalence, we speak of as market value, from the old idea of the market or meeting place of those who wish to make exchanges, where competition or the higgling of the market brings out the highest bidding or the lowest offering in transactions of exchange. And when we wish to ascertain the exact value of a thing we offer it at auction or in some other way subject it to competitive offers.

Thus I am justified in saying that the value of a thing in any time and place is the largest amount of exertion that any one will render in exchange for it; or to make the estimate from the other side, that it is the smallest amount of exertion for which any one will part with it in exchange.

Value is thus an expression which, when used in its proper economic sense of value in exchange, has no direct relation to any intrinsic quality of external things, but only to man's desires. Its essential element is subjective, not objective; that is to say, lying in the mind or will of man, and not lying in the nature of things external to the human will or mind. There is no material test for value. Whether a thing is valuable or not valuable, or what may be the degree of its value, we cannot really tell by its size or shape or color or smell, or any other material quality, except so far as such investigations may enable us to infer how other men may regard them. For the point of equivalence or equation that we express or assume when we speak of the value of a thing is a point where the desire to obtain in one mind so counterbalances in its effect on action the desire to retain in another mind that the thing itself may pass in exchange from the possession of one man to the possession of another with mutual willingness.

Now this fact that the perception of value springs from a feeling of man, and has not at bottom any relation to the external world—a fact that has been much ignored in the teachings and expositions of accepted economists—is what lies at the bottom of the grotesque confusions which, under the name of the Austrian school of political economy, have within recent years so easily captured the teachings of pretty much all the universities and colleges in the English-speaking world.

Vaguely feeling that there was something wrong in the accepted theory of value, they have taken the truth that value is not a quality of things but an affection of the human mind towards things, and attempted at the risk of fatal consequences to the ancient landmarks of English speech to account for, classify and measure value through what is and ever must remain the subjective—that is to say, pertaining to the individual Ego.

The fault of all this is that it begins at the wrong end. What is subjective is in itself incommunicable. A feeling so long as it remains merely a feeling can be known only to and can be measured onlv by him who feels it

It must come out in some way into the objective through action before any one else can appreciate or in any way measure it. Even if we ourselves may measure the strength of a desire while it is as yet merely felt, we can make no one else adequately understand it until it shows itself in action.

Value has of course its origin in the feeling of desire. But the only measure of desire it can afford is akin to the rough and ready way of measuring sorrow which was proposed at a funeral by the man who said: "I am sorry for the widow to the amount of five dollars. How much are the rest of you sorry?" Now, what value determines is not how much a thing is desired, but how much any one is willing to give for it; not desire in itself, but what the elder economists have called effective demand—that is to say, the desire to possess, accompanied by the ability and willingness to give in return.

Thus it is that there is no measure of value among men save competition or the higgling of the market, a matter that might be worth the consideration of those amiable reformers who so lightly propose to abolish competition.

It is never the amount of labor that has been exerted in bringing a thing into being that determines its value, but always the amount of labor that will be rendered in exchange for it. Nevertheless, we properly speak of the value of certain things as being determined by the cost of production. But the cost of production that we thus refer to is not the expenditure of labor that has taken place in producing the identical thing, but the expenditure of labor that would now be required to produce a similar thing—not what the thing itself has cost, but what such a thing would now cost.

The desire to obtain, which renders men willing to undergo exertion, is, save in rare cases, not the desire for an identical thing, but the desire for a similar thing. Thus, a desire for wheat is not a desire for certain particular grains of wheat; but a desire for wheat generally, or for wheat of a certain kind. So a desire for coats, or knives, or drinking-glasses or so on, is, save in very rare cases, not a desire for particular, identical things, but a desire for similar things. Now, the value of a thing in any given time and place is the largest amount of labor that any one will render (or cause others to render) in exchange for it. But as men always seek to gratify their desires with the least exertion, this highest amount of labor which any one will give for a similar thing in any time and place, tends always to be the lowest amount for which such a thing can in any other way be obtained.

Thus the point of equation between desire and satisfaction, or as we usually say, between demand and supply, tends in a case of things that can be produced by labor to the cost of production—that is to say, not what the production of the thing has cost, but the present cost of producing a similar thing. Desire remaining, whatever increases the amount of labor that must be expended to obtain similar things by making them will thus tend to increase the value of existing things; and whatever tends to decrease the cost of obtaining similar things by making them will tend to decrease the value of existing things.

But there are some cases in which the desire for a product of labor is not a desire for a similar thing, but for a particular and identical thing. Thus, when that great genius and great toady, Sir Walter Scott, carried off a wine-glass from which George IV. had drunk, it was to satisfy a desire not for a similar glass, but for that particular glass, which had been honored by the lips of royalty. Where such a desire is felt by only one person or one economic unit, as where I or my family may value a chair or table or book which once belonged to some one we loved, our valuation is analogous to value in use, and does not affect its economic or exchange value, except perhaps as it might make us loath to part with it at its true exchange value. But where more than one person or unit has this desire, which is the case where the possession of a particular article comes to gratify ostentation, it acquires an exchange value which is not limited by the cost of producing a similar thing. Thus, an original picture of a dead master, or an original copy of an old edition of a book, which identically cannot now be produced by any amount of exertion, may have a value not limited by the cost of production, and this may rise to any height to which sentiment or ostentation may carry desire.

The cases I have here taken to illustrate the principle have but small practical application, though they are continually called to attention, and any theory of value must include them. But the principle itself has the widest and most important applications, which steadily increase in importance with the growth of civilization. The value that attaches to land with the growth of civilization is an example of the same principle which governs in the case of a picture by a Raphael or Rubens, or an Elgin marble. Land, which in the economic sense includes all the natural opportunities of life, has no cost of production. It was here before man came, and will be here, so far as we can see, after he has gone. It is not produced. It was created.

And it was created and still exists in such abundance as even now far to exceed the disposition and power of mankind to use it. Land as land, or land generally—the natural element necessary to human life and production—has no more value than air as air. But land in special, that is, land of a particular kind or in a particular locality, may have a value such as that which may attach to a particular wine-glass or a particular picture or statue; a value which unchecked by the possibility of production has no limit except the strength of the desire to possess it.

This attaching of value to land in special—that is to say, land in particular localities with respect to population—is not merely a most striking feature in the progress of modern civilization, but it is, as I shall hereafter show, a consequence of civilization, lying entirely within the natural order, and furnishing perhaps the most conclusive proof that the intent of that order is the equality of men. If left by just municipal laws to its natural development, the strength of the desire to use particular land can never become the desire to use land generally, and can never rise to the point of lowering wages by compelling workers to give for the use of land any part of what is the natural and just earnings of their labor. But where land is monopolized and the resort of population to unmonopolized land is shut out either by legal restriction or social conditions, then the desire to use particular land may be based upon the desire to use land generally, or land the natural element; and its strength, measured in the only way in which we can measure the strength of a desire, the willingness to undergo toil and trouble for its gratification, may become when pushed to full expression, nothing less than the strength of the desire for life itself, for land is the indispensable prerequisite to life, and "all that a man hath will he give for his life."

But in every case the value of land, consisting in the amount of exertion that can be commanded from those who desire to use it by those who have the power of giving or refusing consent to its use, is in the nature of an obligation to render service rather than in that of an exchange of service.

CHAPTER XIV.

THE TWO SOURCES OF VALUE.

SHOWING THAT THERE IS A VALUE FROM PRODUCTION AND ALSO A VALUE FROM OBLIGATION.

Value does not involve increase of wealth—Value of obligation—Of enslavement—Economic definition of wealth impossible without recognition of this difference in value—Smith's confusion and results—Necessity of the distinction—Value from production and value from obligation—Either gives the essential quality of commanding exertion—The obligation of debt—Other obligations—Land values most important of all forms of value from obligation—Property in land equivalent to property in men—Common meaning of value in exchange—Real relation with exertion—Ultimate exchangeability is for labor—Adam Smith right—Light thrown by this theory of value.

WE now come to a point of much importance. For it is to the failure to note what I wish in this chapter to point out that the confusions that have so perplexed the terms value and wealth in the study of political economy have arisen.

It is usually, if not indeed invariably assumed in all standard economic works that the conversion of labor power through exertion into services or wealth is the only way in which value originates.

Yet what we have already seen is enough to show us that this cannot be so.

It is not the exertion that a thing has cost, in past time, that gives it value, but the exertion that its possession will in future time dispense with, for even the immediate is in strictness future. Thus value may be created by mere agreement to render exertion, or by the imposition of such obstacles to the satisfaction of desire as will necessitate a greater exertion for the attainment of the satisfaction. In the same way, the value of some things may be increased, or sometime perhaps produced, without the production of real wealth; or even by the destruction of real wealth.

For instance: I with another may agree to exchange, but consummate in the present but one side of the full exchange, substituting for the other side an agreement or obligation to complete it in the future. That is to say, I may give or receive things having present value in return for an obligation to render labor or the results or representatives of labor at some definite or indefinite future time. Or, both of us may exchange similar obligations. The obligations thus created may, and frequently do, at once assume value and become exchangeable for exertion or the results of exertion. Or, a government or joint-stock company may issue obligations of the same kind, in the form of bonds or stock, which may at once assume a value dependent as in the case of an individual upon the strength of the belief that the obligations will be faithfully redeemed, irrespective of any counter payment or obligation.

There is in all this no increase of wealth; but there is a creation of value—a value arising out of obligation and dependent entirely upon expectation, but still a value—an exchangeable quantity, the possession of which could command through exchange other valuable things.

Or, again: Suppose the discoverers of the Isle of Eden, we have imagined, to have been of the same kidney as the Spanish discoverers of America, and instead of tempting the islanders to work for them by exciting their desire for new satisfactions, had compelled them to work by whipping, or killing them if they refused. The discoverers might thus have carried off, as the Spanish conquistadors carried off, what readily, exchanging for exertion in other parts of the world, would there have great value—not merely precious metals or stones, woods or spices—but even the natives themselves. For carried to any country where the power to compel them to work was by municipal law transferable, these human beings would have value, just as the ability to compel their service in their native island would have value.

Now in Individual Economy, which takes cognizance only of the relations of the individual to other individuals, there is no difference between these two kinds of value. Whether an individual has the power of commanding exertion from others because he has added to the general stock, or simply because he holds the power of demanding exertion from others makes no difference to him or to them. In either case he gets and they give.

But in political economy, which is the economy of the Society or the aggregate, there is a great difference. Value of the one kind—the value which constitutes an addition to the common stock—involves an addition to the wealth of the community or aggregate, and thus is wealth in the politico-economic sense. Value of the other kind—the value which consists merely of the power of one individual to demand exertion from another individual—adds nothing to the common stock, all it effects is a new distribution of what already exists in the common stock, and in the politico-economic sense, is not wealth at all.

In the development of political economy from Adam Smith these two and totally different kinds of values have been confused in one word. Smith started in by recognizing as value that which added to wealth, but he afterwards, and with seeming carelessness included as value that which adds to the wealth of the individual, but adds nothing whatever to the wealth of the community. This consorted with the common idea that the wealth of a community is the sum of the wealth of individuals, and enabled all that has value to the individual to be included as politico-economic wealth. It consorted as wealth with the disposition of the wealthy class to give a moral sanction to whatever was to them superiority, and has thus been perpetuated by economist after economist.

But it was impossible to treat as one and the same quality a value that added to the wealth of the community and a value that did not, and yet to make a politico-economic definition of wealth. This therefore has been the point on which the political economy founded by Adam Smith has been constantly at sea. It could not be a political economy until it had defined wealth, and it could not define wealth until it had recognized a distinction between two kinds of value.

This difficulty might have been avoided in the beginning by giving to the two kinds of value separate names, but the word value has so long been used for both, that the best a science of political economy can do now, is to distinguish between value of the one kind and value of the other kind.

This however it is necessary to attempt. The best thing I can do is to distinguish value, not as one, but as of two kinds.

By a clear distinction, the various ways in which value may originate, embrace (1) the value which comes from the exertion of labor in such a way as to save future exertion in obtaining the satisfaction of desire; and, (2) the value which comes from the acquisition of power on the part of some men to command or compel exertion on the part of others, or, which is the same thing, from the imposition of obstacles to the satisfaction of desire that render more exertion necessary to the production of the same satisfaction.

Value arising in the first mode may be distinguished as "value from production," and value arising in the second mode may be distinguished as "value from obligation"—for the word obligation is the best word I can think of to express everything which may require the rendering of exertion without the return of exertion.

Value in the sense of exchange value, the only sense in which it can be properly used in political economy, since this has now been fixed by usage, is one and the same quality, just as the water that flows through the outlet of the Nile or Mississippi is one and the same stream. But as we distinguish the sources of these waters as the White Nile and the Blue Nile, or as the Upper Mississippi, the Missouri, the Ohio, etc., so we may distinguish as to origin, between value from production and value from obligation. The mere recognition that there is such a difference in the origins of value would of itself do much to extricate political economy from the utter maze into which a century of cultivation has brought it in the closing years of the nineteenth century.

But while making this distinction it must be remembered that the essential character of value is always that of equivalence to exertion in the satisfaction of desire. The value of a thing, in short, is the amount of toil and trouble which it will save to the possessor (as in the case of a Crusoe), or (as is the usual case) others may be willing to undertake in exchange for it. This is not necessarily the toil and trouble which the purchaser will agree in his own person to undergo, but the toil and trouble which he had power to command or to induce others to undergo, and of which he can thus dispense the seller in the attainment of his desire. No matter how this quality attaches to them, whether by value from production, or by value from obligation, things have value when, so long, and so far, as they will purchase exemption from toil and trouble in the attainment of desire.

That "debt is slavery" is not merely a metaphorical expression. It is literally true in this, that debt involves, though it may be in limited degree, the same obligation of rendering exertion without return as does slavery. When under the form of exchange I receive services or commodities from another, asking him to forego the receipt on his part of what I should by the terms, expressed or implied, of our exchange, receive in return from him, I assume an obligation, though probably to a limited extent and with limited sanctions, to render to him labor, or the results of labor, without, so far as it goes, any return on his part. Such a debt may be a mere debt of conscience, which he may have no means of proving, or have no legal means of collecting, even if he could prove it; or it may be a mere debt of honor, which is the name we give to debt held morally binding, but which the municipal law may refuse to help us to collect; or it may be witnessed by other persons or writings, or by the assignment of releases of specific things as in mortgages; or by the agreements of others to pay if I do not, as is the case of negotiable notes. But while all this may affect the ease with which I may dispose of my obligation to another and the value I can get in return for it, the essential principle of these different forms of obligation is the same. It is the same in so far as it goes as the obligation to render exertion, as that which gave their exchangeable value to slaves, and which is in fact the type of all debts of obligation.

The term "value from obligation" will at once be recognized as including an immense body of the values dealt with by banks, stock exchanges, trust companies, or held by private individuals, and which are commonly known as obligations or securities. But it may require a little reflection to see how much else there is having value which is really value from obligation. All debts and claims of whatever kind, whether they be what the lawyers call choses in action or mere debts of honor or good faith unrecognized by law, all special privileges and franchises, patents, and the beneficial interests known as good-will, in so far as they have value, have it as value from obligation. The value of slaves wherever slavery exists—and only a few years ago the market value of slaves in the United States was estimated in round numbers at three thousand million dollars—is clearly a value of obligation, springing not from production, but from the obligation imposed on the slave to work for the master. So too with the value of public pensions and the incumbency of profitable offices and places, when they are made matters of bargain and sale, which is in some cases yet done in England and which is I fear to a still larger extent yet done in the United States, though surreptitiously, as it is habitually done in China where "civil service reform" has for centuries prevailed.

In English newspapers one may yet occasionally read advertisements for the sale of advowsons for the cure of souls. The exchange value that they have is of course from obligation. Up to a few years ago there were similar advertisements for the sale of commissions in the army and navy. These are but survivals of an earlier and perhaps clearer type of nomenclature. The value they have is clearly a value from obligation. And the same thing is true under more modern forms, of rights given by protective duties, by civil-service regulations, and franchises, and patents, and forms of good-will. All these things have value only as "value from obligation."

Among the valuable assessments of the large landholders of feudal times was the right of holding markets, of keeping dove-cotes, of succeeding in certain instances to the property of tenants; or of grinding grain, of coining money, of collecting floatwood, etc. The values of these were clearly "values from obligation." But that they have passed insensibly into the single right of exacting a rent for the use of land is proof that the value of this right—the right, as it is called, of private ownership of land—is in reality a "value from obligation."

These ways of giving an additional value to things already in existence or of bringing out value in things which may have no more tangible existence than an act of mind, a verbal promise, a paper note, an act of legislature, a decision of court or a common habit or custom, are clearly of totally different origin and nature from the ways in which value originates by the expenditure of labor in the production of wealth or services, and readily to distinguish them we need a classifying name. It is because the word obligation best consorts with existing customs, and best expresses the common character of the element distinct from production that gives value, that I speak of value from obligation as distinct from value from production. For the common character of all that I am here speaking of is that their possession enables the possessor to command or compel others to render exertion without any return of exertion on his part to them. This power to command labor without the return of labor constitutes on the other side an obligation, and it is this that gives value.

Thus a verbal promise, a bank-account, a promissory note, or any other instrument of indebtedness, an annuity, an insurance policy, things which frequently have value, derive that value from the fact that they express an obligation fixed, unfixed or merely contingent to render exertion to the holder or assignee without return. Thus value may be increased sometimes even by the destruction of valuable things, as the Dutch East India Company kept up the value of spices in Europe by destroying great quantities of spices in the islands where they grew; and as our "protective" tariff makes certain things more valuable in the United States than they would otherwise be by imposing fines and penalties on bringing them into the country; or as strikes, as we have recently seen in Australia, in England and in America, may increase the value of coal or other products; or as a drought, which causes great loss of the corn crop over wide areas, may increase the value of corn, or as a war which lessens the supply of cotton in England may increase the value of cotton there.

All such additions to value are of "value from obligation," which can no more affect the general stock than can what Jack wins from Tom in a game of cards.

But the most important of these additions to value which do not increase wealth are unquestionably to be found in land value, the form of value from obligation which in the progress of mankind to civilization tends most rapidly to increase, and which has already in the modern world assumed perhaps more than the relative importance that slavery once held in the ancient world. In an England or a United States, or any other highly civilized country, this importance is already so great that the selling value of the land is the selling value of all improvements and personal property, in short of all "value from production;" while it is the one thing which the natural progress of society, in short all improvements of whatever kind, tend constantly to augment. Yet this value is not a part of wealth in the economic sense. It can have, so far as the individual is concerned, none of the moral sanctions of property. It rightfully belongs to no individual or individuals but to the community itself. Considered by the vulgar as the highest form and very type of wealth, land in reality is to the political economist not wealth at all.

And this is the reason that neither by Adam Smith nor by those who succeeded him, however much they may have differed as to tweedledum and tweedledee, has the true character and dual nature of value been realized. For to recognize that is to come to the conclusion of the Physiocrats that, in the economic sense, land is not wealth. And this involves a revolution, albeit to society a beneficent revolution, greater than the world has yet seen.

Yet it is perfectly clear. Let us go back in thought to our imaginary Isle of Eden, and suppose that its discoverers, instead of making merchandise of the inhabitants themselves, had done at once what the American missionaries have done gradually in the Hawaiian Islands—made themselves owners of the land of the island, and with power to enforce their claim by punishment, had forbidden any islander to pluck of a tree or drink of a spring without their permission. Land before valueless would at once become valuable, for the islanders having nothing else to give would be compelled to render exertion, or the products of exertion, for the privilege of continuing in life.

And that this quality attaching to things, of purchasing by exchange exemption from the toil and trouble in the attainment of desire, is what is commonly meant by value in exchange a little analysis will show. "The value of a thing is just what you can get for it," is a saying, current among men who have never bothered their heads with political economy, which concisely expresses the conception of value. A thing has no value for which nothing can be got in exchange, and it has value when, so long as, and to the degree that, it may be exchanged for some other thing or things.

But all things having value cannot be exchanged for all other things having value. I could not, for instance, exchange a million dollars' worth of cheese-cakes for a building worth a million dollars. What then is the one thing for which all things having value must directly or indirectly exchange? We are apt to ignore that question, because we habitually think of value in terms of money, which serves us as a flux for the exchange of all values, and because we are apt to think of labor as a valuable thing, without distinguishing the different senses in which we use the word. But if we press the question, we see that everything having value must be ultimately exchangeable into human exertion, and that it is in this that its value consists. There are some valuable things that cannot readily, and some that it is practically impossible to exchange for exertion—such, for instance, as an equatorial telescope, a locomotive, a steamship, a promissory note or bond of large amount, or a bank-note or greenback of high denomination. But they derive their value from the fact that they can be exchanged for things that can in turn be exchanged for exertion.

Money itself derives its power of serving as a medium or flux of exchanges from the fact that it is of all things that which is most readily exchangeable for exertion, and it utterly loses value when it ceases to be exchangeable for exertion. This we have seen in the United States in the case of the Continental currency, in the case of the notes of broken State banks and in the case of the Confederate currency. Thus value ends as it begins, with the power of commanding exertion, and is always measured by that power.

Again, as before, we find that Adam Smith was right in the clear though evanescent gleam that he got of the nature of value. Value in the economic sense is not a mere relation of exchangeability between valuable things, which, save relatively, as between one particular thing and another particular thing, can neither increase nor diminish. The real relation of value is with human exertion, or rather with the toil and trouble that are the inseparable adjuncts of exertion; and the true and absolute value of anything, that which makes it comparable with that of any or all other things in all times and places, is the difficulty or ease of acquiring it. That is of high value which is hard to get; that is of low value which is easy to get; while that which may be had without exertion and that which no one will undergo exertion to get are of no value at all. Cheapness or low value is the result of abundance; dearness or high value the result of scarcity. The one means that the satisfactions of desire may be obtained with little effort, the other that they can be obtained only with much effort. Thus there may be general increase or decrease of value as clearly and as truly as there may be general scarcity or general abundance.

The recognition of this simple theory of value will enable us as we proceed to clear up with ease and certainty many points which have perplexed the economists who have ignored it, and are to their students stumbling-blocks, which make them doubt whether any real science of political economy is possible. In its light all the complex phenomena of value and exchange become clear, and are seen to be but illustrations of that fundamental law of the human mind which impels men to seek the gratification of their desires with the least exertion.

Whatever increases the obstacles, natural or artificial, to the gratification of desire on the part of the ultimate users or consumers of things, thus compelling them to expend more exertion or undergo more toil and trouble to obtain those things, increases their value; whatever lessens the exertion that must be expended or the toil and trouble that must be undergone, decreases value. Thus, wars, tariffs, pirates, public insecurity, monopolies, taxes and restrictions of all kinds, which render more difficult the satisfaction of the desire for certain things, increase their value, and discoveries, inventions and improvements which lessen the exertion required for bringing things to the satisfaction of desire, lessen their value.

Here we may see at once the clear solution of a question which has perplexed and still perplexes many minds —the question whether the artificial increase of values by governmental restriction is or is not in the interest of the community. When we regard value as a simple relation of exchangeability between exchangeable things, there may seem room for debate. But when we see that its relation is to the toil and trouble which must be undergone by ultimate users in the satisfaction of desire, there is no room for debate. Scarcity may be at times to the relative interest of the few; but abundance is always to the general interest.

CHAPTER XV.

THE MEANING OF WEALTH IN POLITICAL ECONOMY.

SHOWING HOW VALUE FROM PRODUCTION IS WEALTH IN POLITICAL ECONOMY.

Wealth as fixed in "Progress and Poverty"—Course of the scholastic political economy—The reverse method of this work—The conclusion the same—Reason of the disposition to include all value as wealth—Metaphorical meanings—Bull and pun—Metaphorical meaning of wealth—Its core meaning—Its use to express exchangeability—Similar use of money—Ordinary core meaning the proper meaning of wealth—Its use in individual economy and in political economy—What is meant by increase of wealth—Wealth and labor—Its factors nature and man—Wealtb their resultant—Of Adam Smith—Danger of carrying into political economy a meaning proper in individual economy—Example of "money"—"Actual wealth" and "relative wealth"—"Value from production" and "value from obligation"—The English tongue has no single word for an article of wealth—Of "commodities"—Of "goods"—Why there is no singular in English—The attempt to form one by dropping the "s" and Anglo-German jargon.

WE are now in a position to fix the meaning of wealth as an economic term.

In "Progress and Poverty," which I desired to make as brief as possible, and where my main purpose was to fix the meaning of the word capital, I fixed the meaning of the word wealth directly, as "natural products so secured, moved, combined or altered by human labor as to fit them for human satisfaction." This also was the way in which, as I understand it, the Physiocrats, who came substantially to the same conclusion, had defined it. But the scholastic political economists, instead of either discovering for themselves or taking my hint, continued on the road by which Adam Smith had avoided saying finally what wealth was. They continued to discuss the word value, so confused in its various senses, in such manner as to give not only no conclusion as to the real meaning of wealth, but finally to actually destroy political economy itself.

Thus the confusion into which, after more than a hundred years of cultivation, the teaching of political economy has fallen as to the meaning of its principal term—a confusion which is in reality even greater than in ordinary speech, that makes no pretensions to exactness in the use of the word—is clearly due to confusions as to the meaning of the term value. The scholastic development of political economy since Adam Smith has not only confused the distinction between value in use and value in exchange, but it has tended to cover up the vital distinction between the two sources of value in exchange; that originating in the storing up of labor, and that originating in what I have called obligation—often power, devoid of moral right, to compel the expenditure of labor.

This is the condition in which the orthodox political economy now is. It has not only *not* discovered what its principal term, wealth in the economic sense, really is, but it has so confounded other terms as to give little light on the search.

In this work therefore I have adopted a different method from that employed in "Progress and Poverty." Finding it necessary to discuss the meaning of the term value in a fuller way than I had before done, and seeing that in the current political economy the only consensus of opinion was that all wealth had value, I adopted a method the reverse of that of "Progress and Poverty," and instead of beginning with wealth, began with value. Commencing with Adam Smith and inquiring what was meant by value, I found that in value were included two absolutely different things, namely, the quality of value from production, and the quality of value from obligation, one of which kinds of value resulted in wealth and the other of which did not. Now, value from production, which is the only kind of value which gives wealth, consists in application of labor in the production of wealth which adds to the common stock of wealth. Wealth, therefore, in political economy consists in natural products so secured, moved, combined or altered by human labor as to fit them for human satisfaction. Value from obligation, on the other hand, though a most important element of value, does not result in increase in the common stock, or in the production of wealth. It has nothing whatever to do with the production of wealth, but only with the distribution of wealth, and its proper place is under that heading.

Thus in the way I have in this work adopted, that of proceeding analytically from value, we come to precisely the same conclusion as that reached in "Progress and Poverty," where we proceeded directly and by deduction —we come to the result that wealth in the politico-economic sense consists in natural substances that have been so secured, moved, combined or altered by human labor as to fit them for human satisfaction. Such substances are wealth and always have value. When they cease to have value they of course cease to be wealth.

Thus, proceeding by the way adopted in this work, we reach precisely the same conclusion as to wealth as by the way adopted in my previous work. The advantages of adopting this mode here are that a conclusion reached by the methods familiar to the students of the schclastic political economy can with difficulty be ignored by them, and that in going in this way over the subject of value much has been seen both for the present and the future that was necessary to a full treatise on the science of political economy and that may elsewhere be dispensed with.

I wish therefore particularly to call the attention of the reader to what has been here done. Not that I hope that anything that I can do, unaccompanied or unsucceeded by a great change in general conditions, can long keep down the disposition which this tendency of political economy that I have alluded to shows.

As there is a reason for everything, in the mental world as truly as in the physical world, so there is a reason for this disposition to include in the term wealth everything that has value, without regard to the origin of that value. It springs at bottom from the desire on the part of those who dominate the accredited organs of education and opinion (who wherever there is inequality in the distribution of wealth are necessarily the wealthy class) to give to the mere legal right of property the same moral sanction that justly attaches to the natural right of property, or at the very least to ignore anything that would show that the recognition of a legal right may involve the denial of a moral right. As the defenders of chattel slavery, and those who did not wish to offend the slave power, not long since dominant in the United States, were obliged to stop their examination of ownership with purchase, assuming that the purchase of a slave carried with it the same right of ownership as did the purchase of a mule or of a bale of cotton, so those who would defend the industrial slavery of to-day, or at least not offend the wealth power, are obliged to stop their examination of the nature of wealth with value, assuming that everything that has value is therefore wealth, thus involving themselves and leaving their students in a fog of confusions as to the nature of the thing whose laws they profess to examine.

But to whomsoever wishes really to understand political economy there is now no difficulty in coming to a clear and precise determination of the nature of wealth, whichever way he may elect to begin.

The power of the imagination, nay even that power of recognizing likeness and unlikeness, in which perception itself consists, always expands by metaphor the primary or fundamental meaning of a word in common use, and it is by reason of this, even more than by the adoption of new root words, that a language grows in copiousness, flexibility and beauty. Thus such words as light and darkness, sunshine and rain, to eat and to drink, are put by metaphor and simile to a multiplicity of uses in common speech. We speak of the light of hope, or the light that beats upon a throne, or the light of events; of a dark purpose, or a dark saying, or a darkened intellect; of the sunshine of love or prosperity, or of a sunny countenance; of a rain of bullets, or a rain of misfortunes, or a rain of questions or epithets; of a ship eating into the wind, of rust eating iron, or of a man eating his own words; of a sword drinking blood, or of a lover drinking in the looks, words or actions of a loved one. But such use of words in common speech causes no confusion as to their original and fundamental meaning, the core from which all figurative use of them proceeds. The broad humor of the Irish bull comes from our prompt recognition of the difference between core meaning and figurative meaning; and the offensiveness of the deliberate pun, from the impertinence of the implied assumption that we will not quickly recognize this difference.

Now, in common speech the word wealth takes on such figurative meanings as do all other words in common use. We speak of the night's wealth of stars, of a poet's wealth of imagery, of an orator's wealth of expression, of a woman's wealth of hair, of a student's wealth of knowledge, or of the wealth of resource of a general, a statesman or an inventor; of a porcupine's wealth of quills or a bear's wealth of fur. But such uses of the word wealth impose no difficulty. They are merely metaphorical expressions of abundance. So, too, it is with what is called natural wealth. We speak of rich ore and poor ore, of rich land and poor land, of a naturally rich country and a naturally poor country; of a wealth of forest or mines or fisheries; of a wealth of lakes or rivers, or a wealth of beautiful scenery. But where anything more than abundance is expressed in such uses of the word wealth it is that of natural opportunity, or that of utility, or value in use, with which in its fundamental sense wealth has nothing to do. With that fundamental or core meaning of the word wealth, from which all such figurative uses spring, is inextricably blended the idea of human production. Whatever exists without man's agency, was here before he came, and will, so far as we can see, be here after he is gone; or whatever is included in man himself, however well the figurative use of the word wealth may serve to express its abundance or usefulness, cannot be wealth in the fundamental or core meaning of the word.

So, too, is the still more common use of the word wealth to express the power of exchangeability or of commanding exertion. As commonly used the word wealth when applied to the possessions of an individual includes all purchasing power, and is indeed in most cases synonymous with exchange value. But this use of the word is really representative, like the similar use we make of the word money. We say that a man has so much money, or so many dollars or pounds, without meaning, or being understood as meaning, that he has in his possession so much actual money. We mean only that he has what would exchange for so much money. Such representative use of the word money or of the terms of money does not, in every-day affairs, in the least confuse us as to the real meaning of the word. If asked to explain what money is, no one would think of saying that sheep and ships, and lands and houses are money, although he is in the constant habit of speaking of their possession as the possession of money.

So it is with the common use of the word wealth. Many things are commonly spoken of as wealth which we all know, in the true and fundamental meaning of the word, are not wealth at all.

If you take an ordinarily intelligent man whose powers of analysis have not been muddled by what the colleges call the teaching of political economy, and ask him what he understands at bottom by wealth, it will be found at last, though it may require repeated questioning to eliminate metaphor and representation, that the kernel of his idea of wealth is that of natural substances or products so changed in place, form or combination by the exertion of human labor as to fit them or fit them better for the satisfaction of human desire.

This, indeed, is the true meaning of wealth, the meaning of what I have called "value from production." It is the meaning to which in political economy the word wealth must be carefully restricted. For political economy is the economy of communities or nations. In the economy of individuals, to which our ordinary speech usually refers, the word wealth is commonly applied to anything having an exchange value as between individuals. But when used as a term of political economy the word wealth must be limited to a much more definite meaning. Many things are commonly spoken of as wealth in the hands of the individual, which in taking account of collective or general wealth cannot be included. Such things having exchange value, are commonly spoken of as wealth, since as between individuals or between sets of individuals they represent the power of obtaining wealth. But they are not really wealth, inasmuch as their increase or decrease does not affect the sum of wealth. Such are bonds, mortgages, promissory notes, bank-bills, or other stipulations for the transfer of wealth. Such are franchises, which represent special privileges, accorded to some and denied to others. Such were slaves, whose value represented merely the power of one class to appropriate the earnings of another class. Such are lands or other natural opportunities, the value of which results from the acknowledgment in favor of certain persons of an exclusive legal right to their use, and the profit of their use, and which represents only the power thus given to the mere owner to demand a share of the wealth produced by use. Increase in the value of bonds, mortgages, notes or bank-bills cannot increase the wealth of a community that includes as well those who promise to pay as those who are entitled to receive. Increase in the value of franchises cannot increase the wealth of a community that includes those who are denied special privileges as well as those who are accorded them. The enslavement of a part of their number could not increase the wealth of a people, for more than the enslavers gained the enslaved would lose. Increase in land values does not represent increase in the common wealth, for what landowners gain by higher prices the tenants or ultimate users, who must pay them, are deprived of. And all this value which, in common thought and speech, in legislation and law, is undistinguished from wealth, could, without the destruction or consumption of anything more than a few drops of ink and a piece of paper, be utterly annihilated. By enactment of the sovereign political power debts might be canceled, franchises abolished or taken by the state, slaves emancipated, and land returned to the general usufructuary ownership of the whole people, without the aggregate wealth being diminished by the value of a pinch of snuff, for what some would lose others would gain. There would be no more destruction of wealth than there was creation of wealth when Elizabeth Tudor enriched her favorite courtiers by the grant of monopolies or when Boris Godoonof made Russian peasants merchantable property.

All articles of wealth have value. If they lose value, they cease to be wealth. But all things having value are not wealth, as is erroneously taught in current economic works.* Only such things can be wealth the production of which increases and the destruction of which decreases the aggregate of wealth. If we consider what these things are, and what their nature is, we shall have no difficulty in defining wealth.

When we speak of a community increasing in wealth—as when we say that England has increased in wealth since the accession of Victoria, or that California is now a wealthier country than when it was a Mexican territory—we do not mean to say that there is more land, or that the natural powers of the land are greater, for the land is the same and its natural powers are the same. Nor yet do we mean that there are more people in the same area, for when we wish to express that idea we speak of increase of population. Nor yet do we mean that the debts or dues owing by some of these people to others of their number have increased. But we mean that there is an increase of certain tangible things, having a value that comes from production, such as buildings, cattle, tools, machinery,

---

* See, for instance, a book used as a text-book in many of the American and English colleges, the "Political Economy," by Francis A. Walker, third edition, New York, 1888, Sec. 7. "Wealth comprises all articles of value and nothing else."

agricultural and mineral products, manufactured goods, ships, wagons, furniture and the like. The increase of such things is an increase of wealth; their decrease is a lessening of wealth; and the community that, in proportion to its numbers, has most of such things is the wealthiest community. The common character of these things is that of natural substances or products which have been adapted by human labor to the satisfaction of human desire.

Thus, wealth, as alone the term can be used in political economy, consists of natural products that have been secured, moved or combined, so as to fit them for the gratification of human desires. It is, in other words, labor impressed upon matter in such a way as to store up, as the heat of the sun is stored up in coal, its power to minister to human desires. Nothing that nature supplies to man without the expenditure of labor is wealth; nor yet does the expenditure of labor result in wealth unless there is a tangible product which retains the power of ministering to desire; nor yet again can man himself, nor any of his powers, capabilities or acquirements, nor any obligation to bestow labor or yield up the products of labor from one to another, constitute any part of wealth. Nature and man—or, in economic terminology, land and labor—are the two necessary factors in the production of wealth. Wealth is the resultant of their joint action.

And though Adam Smith nowhere formally defined wealth, being mainly occupied with showing that it did not consist exclusively in money or the precious metals; and though incidentally he fell into confusion in regard to it, yet, as may be seen from the passages in the "Wealth of Nations" before quoted,* this was his idea of wealth when he came to look at it directly—the idea of products

* Page 28.

of labor, still retaining the power, impressed on them by labor, of ministering to human desire.

Now in our common use of the word wealth we make no distinction between the various kinds of things that have value, as to the origin of that value, but class them all together under the one word, wealth, speaking of the sum of value which an individual may have at his command as his wealth, or sometimes as his money. This metaphorical use of words is so embedded in common speech that it would be hopeless to object to it in common usage.

So far indeed as such use of the word wealth is confined to the province of individual economy, the relations of man to man, no harm whatever results. But as I said in the introductory, of all the sciences, political economy is that which comes closest to the thought of the masses of men. All men living in society have some sort of political economy, even though they do not recognize it by that name; and no matter how much they may profess ignorance, there is nothing as to which they less feel ignorance. From this comes a danger that the loose use of a word in common thought, where it does no harm, may be insensibly transferred to thought on economic questions, where it may do great harm.

To take an example: Our common habit of estimating possessions in terms of money does no harm whatever, so long as it is confined to the sphere of individual affairs, in which that use has grown up. When, sticking strictly to the idea of the individual, we speak of a man owning or making or obtaining so much money, we are perfectly well understood, both in our own minds and by others, as meaning not really money, but money's-worth. Yet, in passing insensibly into the field of political economy, this habit of speaking of money's-worth as money gave enormous strength to what Adam Smith called the mercantile system of political economy, or what is now called the protective system—a system which has for centuries molded the polity of nations of the European civilization, and which, though now more than a hundred years after the publication of the "Wealth of Nations," still continues largely to mold it. Both on this account and on account of other delusions which have taken root in the sphere of economic thought from the habit of commonly using the word money as synonymous with money's-worth, it is to be wished there were some word or phrase in common use that would express the distinction even when not absolutely necessary, between actual money and money's-worth.

The occasional use of some such distinction in common speech between wealth and wealth's-worth is even more to be wished for. There is more danger of injurious confusion from the insensible transference to the economic sphere of the vague uses of the word wealth which suffice for the individual sphere than is the case with similar common uses of the word money. And although the scholastic political economists have been since the time of Adam Smith largely alive to the confusions introduced into political economy by treating money and money's-worth as synonymous, and thus, so far as their influence has reached, helped to guard against any danger from the transference of the common use of the word money to economic thought; the sanction of the most respectable colleges and universities is now given to uses of the economic term wealth in a way that only conscious metaphor permits in common speech.

Now since our metaphorical use of the word wealth in the sense of wealth's-worth or value is so deeply rooted, it is to be wished that in common speech, or at least wherever common speech tends into the province of political economy, as it continually does, we should distinguish between true wealth and metaphorical or representative wealth, by the use of such words as "actual wealth"* and "relative wealth," meaning by the one that which is actually wealth, as being a product of labor, and by the other that which is not in itself wealth, although, possessing value, it will exchange for wealth. Yet this would be too much to try, and I think all may be had that it is possible to gain by clearly showing, as I have tried to do, that there are two kinds of value, one the value from production that adds to wealth, and the other the value from obligation that does not.

The sum of wealth in civilized society consists of things of many different kinds having the common character of holding in store, as it were, the ability of labor to minister to desire. Yet there is in English no single word which will clearly and definitely express the idea of an article of wealth, nor has the usage of economists yet fairly adapted any single word to that meaning as an economic term.

The word "commodity" will serve in many cases. But while it would be hard to speak of such an article of wealth as a railroad, a bridge, a massive building, or the result of the plowing of a field as a commodity, there are other things, usually accounted commodities, since they have value in exchange, that are not properly articles of wealth—such as lands, bonds, mortgages, franchises, etc.

The word "goods" as commonly used also comes near to the idea of "articles of wealth." But it has connotations if not limitations which make its meaning too narrow fully to express the idea. And even if these were set aside, as they are by a friend of mine, the wife of the superintendent of a Western zoölogical garden, who, coming to New York with her husband on the annual trip

---

* With a certain justification which will be indicated in the next chapter the lawyers have already appropriated the term "real estate," or real wealth, to what is in greater part not wealth at all.

he makes to buy wild animals, jokingly speaks of "shopping for menagerie goods," there would still remain an insuperable difficulty. "Goods," in the meaning of articles of wealth, has in English no singular, and it is impossible to make any, because the singular form of the same word already holds the place with a different meaning. While we cannot speak of "a single goods," still less can we make a singular by dropping the "s." Even though usage should confirm our speaking of the stock of a dealer in wild animals as goods, it would be to destroy the well-established use of the word to speak of a tiger, a hyena or a cobra-de-capello as "a good."

In its most general use "good" is an adjective, expressing a quality which can be thought of only as an attribute of a thing. As a noun, "good" does not mean a tangible thing at all, but a state or condition or quality of being. To try to force either a noun of accepted meaning or an adjective of accepted meaning to do duty as the singular of a noun of totally different meaning is to injure our English tongue, both as a vehicle of intelligible speech and an instrument of precise thought.

To what confusions of thought as well as of speech the attempt to force a singular of the word "goods" leads, may be seen in recent university text-books of political economy, such as that of Professor Marshall of Cambridge University, England. Whoever tries to discover what they mean by wealth will find himself struggling with a jargon in which he will have more difficulty in recognizing his mother tongue than in pigeon-English—a jargon of such terms as "material goods" and "immaterial goods," "internal goods" and "external goods," "free goods" and "economic goods," "personal goods" and "collective goods," "transferable goods" and "non-transferable goods," with occasional bursts of such thunderous sound as "external-material-transferable goods," "internal-non-transferable goods," "material-external-non-transferable goods" and "personal-external-transferable goods," with all their respective singulars.

There is in English no singular of the word "goods," and the reason is that there is no need for one, since when we want to express the idea of a single item or article in a lot of goods, it is better to use the specific noun, and to speak of a needle or an anchor, a ribbon or a blanket, as the case may be; and where I shall have occasion to speak of a single item of wealth, without reference to kind, or of the plural forms of the same idea, I shall speak of an article or of articles of wealth.

CHAPTER XVI.

THE GENESIS OF WEALTH.

SHOWING HOW WEALTH ORIGINATES AND WHAT IT ESSENTIALLY IS.

Reason of this inquiry—Wealth proceeds from exertion prompted by desire, but all exertion does not result in wealth—Simple examples of action, and of action resulting in wealth—"Riding and tying"—Sub-divisions of effort resulting in increments of wealth—Wealth essentially a stored and transferable service—Of transferable service—The action of reason as natural, though not as certain and quick as that of instinct—Wealth is service impressed on matter—Must be objective and have tangible form.

IT is so all-important that we should know precisely and certainly just what the chief factor of political economy, wealth, is, so that we may hereafter be in no doubt whatever about it but may confidently reason from our knowledge of its nature, that I propose to reinforce all that has been said by showing just how wealth originates and what in essence it actually is.

Wealth is a result of human exertion. But all human exertion does not result in wealth. Not merely is there failure and misadventure in the application of effort to the production of wealth, but the production of wealth is not the only purpose of human effort.

All human actions proceed from desire and have their aim and end in the satisfaction of desire. But if we consider those actions of men which aim at material satisfactions, we see that there is a distinction as to the way in which satisfaction is sought. In some the satisfaction sought is direct and immediate. In others it is indirect and delayed.

To put myself in imagination in the position of my most remote ancestor: I am moved by the desire we call hunger or appetite, or it is aroused in me by the sight of a tree laden with fruit. I pluck and eat the fruit, and am satisfied. Or I feel the desire called thirst, and stooping down to a spring, I drink, and am again satisfied. Action and satisfaction are in such cases confined to the same person, and the connection between them is direct and immediate.

Or, my wife is with me. She feels the same desires; but is not tall enough to pluck the fruit and cannot as well climb a tree or so readily stoop to the spring. So, impelled by that primordial impulse that ordains that the desire of the man shall be to the woman no less than the desire of the woman to the man, I pluck fruit that she may eat, and hollowing my hands give her to drink. In this case the action is on the part of one person; the satisfaction proceeding from the action is obtained by another.* This transfer of the direct result of action we speak of as a service rendered and received. But the connection between action and satisfaction is still direct and immediate, the causal relation between the two having no intermediate link.

These two examples are types of the ways in which many of our actions attain satisfaction. These are the ways in which in nearly all cases the animals satisfy their desires. If we except the storing and hiving animals, and

* There is of course on my part both a desire and a satisfaction—a desire that her desires may be satisfied and a satisfaction when they are satisfied. But these are secondary, the primary end and aim of my action being the satisfaction of her desires.

the almost accidental cases in which a predatory animal kills a victim too large to be consumed at once, there is nothing in their actions which goes beyond the direct and immediate satisfaction of desire. The cow that has browsed all day or the bird that has brought worms to her young has done nothing towards the satisfaction of desire that will recur to-morrow.

In such cases there is no suggestion of anything we would call wealth. And in a world where all human desires were satisfied in this direct and immediate way there would be no wealth, no matter how great the activities of man or how abundant the spontaneous offerings of nature for the satisfaction of his desires.

But man is a reasoning being, who looks beyond the immediate promptings of desire, and who adapts means to ends. An animal would merely eat of the fruit or drink of the spring to the full satisfaction of present desire. But the man bethinking himself of the recurrence of desire might, after satisfying his immediate desire, carry off with him some of the fruit to insure a like satisfaction on the morrow, or with a still longer prevision plant its kernel with a view to satisfaction in future years. Or with a view to the future satisfaction of thirst, he might enlarge the spring or scoop out a vessel in which to carry water, or dig a channel or construct a pipe. In such cases action would be spent not in the direct and immediate satisfaction of desire, but in the doing of what might indirectly and in the future aid in satisfying desire.

In these cases is something which did not exist in the previous cases, and which, save among the storing animals, has nothing analogous to it in animal life.* This something is wealth. It consists of natural substances or products, so changed in place, form or combination by the exertion

* Page 15.

of human labor as better to fit them for the satisfaction of human desires.

The essential character of wealth is that of the embodiment or storage in material form of action aiming at the satisfaction of desire, so that this action obtains a certain permanence—a capability of remaining for a time as at a stopping-place, whence it may be taken, either to yield satisfaction to desire, or to be carried forward towards the satisfaction of desire requiring yet more effort.

Where two men wishing to travel over a determined road have between them but one horse, they frequently "ride and tie." That is, John rides forward for a certain space, leaving Jim to follow on foot. He then ties the horse, pushing forward himself on foot. When Jim comes up, he unties the horse, and in his turn rides forward for some distance past John, and then tying the horse again for John to take, pushes forward. And so on to the journey's end. In this tying of the horse, so that he may be taken and ridden forward again, is something analogous to the way in which effort towards the satisfaction of desire is fixed or tied up in wealth, from which it may be taken for the gratification of desire, or for the purpose of being carried forward by additional effort to a point where it may serve to gratify desires requiring larger effort.

Thus, for the satisfaction of desire by the eating of bread, effort must first be expended to grow the grain; then to harvest it; then to grind it into flour; then to bake the flour into bread. At each of these stages (and they may be sub-divided) there is an increment of wealth: that is to say, some part of the effort required to reach the point of yielding the final satisfaction has been accomplished, and is tied or stored in concrete form, so that what has been gained towards the final result may be utilized in the remaining stages of the process. Grain is an article of wealth expressing the effort necessary in growing and harvesting, in such form that it may be from thence carried forward to the satisfaction of desire, either by feeding it to domestic animals, converting it into starch or alcohol, etc., or by turning it into flour and making bread. Flour again is an article of wealth embodying the effort necessary to the production of grain and the further effort required in grinding; and bread an article of wealth embodying that and the additional effort required in baking, in a form in which consumption (in this case eating) will give the satisfaction to desire of which bread is capable.

The idea of wealth cannot be reduced to that of satisfaction, since, even when the intent and the result of the effort is the satisfaction of a desire on the part of the expender of the effort, there is necessarily an intermediate step, in which the expended effort pauses or is stored up for an interval in concrete form, and whence it may be released not merely to satisfy the desire of the expender of the effort, but that of another as well. If I pluck fruit to-day for the satisfaction of to-morrow's appetite, the satisfaction I then obtain when eating it would not be to me then the direct result of an effort, but would yield me satisfaction as the result of a service—a service of which I myself would be the direct beneficiary, but still no less truly a service than it would be in the case of my wife were she the recipient of the satisfaction obtained by eating it.

Thus if we wish to bring the idea of wealth into a larger generalization, the term of widest inclusiveness that we could select would be a word which would express the idea of service without limitation as to mode. The essential idea of wealth is really that of service embodied in material form, and all our enjoying of wealth, or exchanging of wealth, or giving of wealth, or obtaining of wealth, is really at bottom the enjoying or exchanging or giving or obtaining of service, a word which involves the possibility of distinction in person between the exertor of effort and the recipient of the final satisfaction, which is its aim.

Service of some sort is essential to life, as it may well be doubted if even in what the microscope may show us of the lowest rounds of life's ladder there is anything that comes into life and maintains life self-contained and self-sufficing.

But the first and simplest form of service, that in which the recipient gets directly the satisfaction brought about by the action (and to which for the sake of distinction the term service should be reserved), though it is capable of being given, received and exchanged, is so capable only within very narrow limits, since the action is spent in such direct service and is over and done, whereas in action resulting in wealth the action is not spent, but is stored or tied in intermediate and material form, to be spent in gratification when required. In direct service the power of human action to satisfy human desire is like the exertion of the power of electricity in the lightning-flash or the spark of the Leyden jar. But in indirect service, through the medium of wealth, the action remains unused for a time in readily exchangeable form, whence it may be called forth for use, as the power of electricity remains in transportable and exchangeable form in the storage battery. So narrow indeed are the limits to the exchange of direct service for direct service that though this sometimes takes place even in our highest civilization, it is clear that were it the only mode in which the action of one person could be used in procuring satisfaction to another, nothing like what we call civilization could exist, nor indeed do I think that human life, in any stage in which we know it, could continue.

I may black your boots with the understanding that you shall in return shave my face, or gratify you by telling a story on condition that you shall gratify me by singing a song, and the possibilities of such exchange may be somewhat widened by the understanding that though I black your boots or tell you the story to-day, you may give me the shave or sing the song at a future time, and do this either for me or for any one whom I may present to receive in my place the promised service. But manifestly the exchange of services that may take place in that way is as nothing compared with the exchange that becomes possible when service is embodied in concrete form in wealth and may be passed from hand to hand and used at will in the satisfaction of desire.

By this transmutation of labor into wealth the exchange even of such services as cannot be transmuted into wealth, since they must be rendered directly to the person, is much facilitated. I desire, for instance, such service from another as the carrying of a bag or message, or the conveyance of myself and luggage from one place to another by cab, or stage, or train. There is no equivalent service on my part desired by those for whose services I wish, nor if there was could I stop to render it; but by the intervention of wealth the satisfaction of desire on both sides becomes possible, and the exchange is completed there and then; those from whom I obtain the service receiving from me some article of wealth or representative of wealth which they can in turn exchange either for wealth or for direct services from others. It is thus, and only thus, that the great body of exchanges of direct services that take place in civilization becomes possible. Indeed, without wealth it is difficult to see how men could avail themselves of one another's powers to a much greater extent than do the animals; for that some animals exchange services, whoever has watched monkeys reciprocally ridding each other of fleas must have realized. Wealth is produced by man and consequently there could be no wealth in the world until after man came, just as bees must have preceded the honey which they make. But though man has no wealth-making instinct as the bees have a honey-making instinct, yet reason supplies its place, and man produces wealth just as naturally and certainly as the bees make honey—so naturally and so certainly that save in unnatural and temporary conditions, men destitute of all forms of wealth have never been found.

The essential idea of wealth being that of exertion impressed on matter, or the power of rendering service stored in concrete form, to talk of immaterial wealth as some professed economists now talk, is as much a contradiction in terms as it would be to talk of square circles or triangular squares. Nothing can be really an object of wealth that is not tangible to the senses. Nor in the strict sense of the term, can wealth include any natural substance, or form, or power, unmodified by man's exertion, nor any human power or capacity of exertion. To talk of natural wealth, or to talk of human skill, knowledge or energy as included in wealth is also a contradiction in terms.

CHAPTER XVII.

THE WEALTH THAT IS CALLED CAPITAL.

SHOWING WHAT THE WEALTH CALLED CAPITAL REALLY IS

Capital is a part of wealth used indirectly to satisfy desire—Simple illustration of fruit—Wealth permits storage of labor—The bull and the man—Exertion and its higher powers—Personal qualities cannot really be wealth or capital—The taboo and its modern form—Common opinion of wealth and capital.

AS we have seen, all wealth is not devoted in consumption to the satisfaction of desire. Much of it is devoted to the production of other forms of wealth. That part of wealth so devoted to the production of other wealth is what is properly called capital.

Capital is not a different thing from wealth. It is but a part of wealth, differing from other wealth only in its use, which is not directly to satisfy desire, but indirectly to satisfy desire, by associating in the production of other wealth.

I have spoken of wealth as the concrete result, the tangible embodiment, by change wrought in material things, of labor exerted towards the satisfaction of desire, without as yet having reached or completely reached the point of satisfaction, consumption.

Now, if this concrete result of labor, wealth, be used, not in directly satisfying desire by consumption, but for the purpose of obtaining more wealth, it becomes in that use what we term capital. It is wealth devoted not to the final use of wealth, the satisfaction of desires, but turned aside, as it were, to pass through another stage, by which more wealth may be secured and the final possibilities of satisfaction increased.

To return to the simplest illustration given in the chapter treating of wealth: The man who, finding a fruit-tree, plucks and eats, spends his labor in the most direct and primitive form, that of satisfying desire. His desire is for the moment satisfied, but the labor he has exerted is all spent; no result remains which will help to the future satisfaction of desire.

But if not content with the satisfaction of present desire he carries off some of the fruit to where he may in the future more conveniently obtain it, he has in this gathered fruit a concrete result of the expenditure of labor. His labor expended in the gathering and removal of the fruit which he retains has been as it were stored up, as energy may be stored up by bending a bow or raising a stone, to be utilized again at a future time. This stored-up labor, concretely in this case—this gathered and transported fruit, is wealth, and will retain this character of wealth or stored-up labor, until it is (1) consumed, by being applied to the gratification of desire; or (2) destroyed, as by decay, the ravages of insects or animals, or some other change which takes away its potency of aiding in the satisfaction of desire.

But the man who has thus obtained the possession of wealth by gathering fruit and carrying it to a more convenient place may utilize its potency of ministering to desire in different ways. Let us suppose him to divide this wealth, this gathered fruit, into three portions. One portion he will eat as he feels desire; another portion he will give to some other man in exchange for some other form of wealth; and the third portion he will plant in order that in the future he may more readily and more abundantly satisfy his desire for such fruit.

All three of these portions are alike wealth. But the first portion is merely wealth; its use is the final use of all wealth—the satisfaction of desire. But the second and third portions are not simply wealth—they are capital; their use is in obtaining more or other wealth, which in its turn may be used for the satisfaction of desire.

In other words, all capital is wealth; but all wealth is not capital. Capital is wealth applied to the production of more or other wealth. It is stored labor, not applied by one further step to the ultimate end and aim of all labor, the satisfaction of desire; but in the production of more wealth to the further storage of labor.

By the storage of labor, which is involved in the production of wealth, it becomes possible for man to change the time in which a given exertion shall be utilized in the satisfaction of desire, thus greatly increasing the sum of satisfactions which given exertion may procure. And by the using of wealth as capital, which is the calling of past exertion to the service of present exertion, he is enabled to concentrate exertion upon a given point, at a given time, and to call in, as it were by the way, forces of nature which far transcend in their power those which nature has put at his use in the human frame.

To illustrate: Nature gives to the bull in his massive skull and sharp horns a weapon of offense by which almost the whole strength of his frame may be concentrated upon one or two narrow points, thus utilizing the maximum of force upon the minimum of resistance. She has given to man no such weapon, for his clenched fist, the nearest approach to the horns of the bull his bodily resources furnish, is a far inferior weapon. But by turning his labor into capital in the shape of a spear he is enabled on occasion to concentrate nearly the whole force of his body upon an even narrower point than can the bull; and by turning labor into capital in the form of a bow or crossbow or sling, he may exert in one instant the force that can be accumulated during longer intervals of time; and finally, as the result of many transmutations of labor into capital, he can exert in the rifle chemical forces more potent than any of the forces of which the energies of his own body give him command.

Wealth, in short, is labor, which is raised to a higher or second power, by being stored in concrete forms which give it a certain measure of permanence, and thus permit of its utilization to satisfy desire in other times or other places. Capital is stored labor raised to a still higher or third power by being used to aid labor in the production of fresh wealth or of larger direct satisfactions of desire.

It is likewise to be observed that capital being a form of wealth—that is to say, wealth used for the purpose of aiding labor in the production of more wealth or greater satisfactions—nothing can be capital that is not wealth, and the term capital is subject to all the restrictions and limitations that apply to the term wealth. Personal qualities such as knowledge, skill, industry, are qualities of labor and can never be properly treated as capital. While in common speech it may be permissible to speak in a metaphorical sense of such qualities as capital, meaning thereby that they are susceptible of yielding to their possessors advantages akin to the advantages given by capital, yet to transfer this metaphorical use of speech to economic reasoning is, as many ponderous treatises will testify, provocative of fundamental confusion.

And so, while the possession of slaves, of special privileges, of public debts, of mortgages, or promissory notes, or other things of the kind I have spoken of in treating of spurious wealth, may in the hands of the individual possessor be equivalent to the possession of capital, they can constitute no part of real capital. All the public debts of the world do not add in the slightest degree to the capital of the world—are incapable of aiding by one iota in the production of wealth; while the greater part of what figures in our official reports as capital invested in railroads, etc., is in reality nothing but the inflation of expectation. Capital in the economic sense is a tangible, material thing—matter changed in place, form or condition, so as to fit it for human uses, and applied to aiding labor in the production of wealth or direct satisfactions.

To recur to our first simple illustration: A high chief of the Hawaiian Islands in the old heathen days might, on discovering a tree laden with fruit, have eaten his fill and then laid the tree under taboo. He might thus have obtained for himself something of the same advantages that he would have obtained by carrying some of the fruit to a more convenient place, for the inhibition upon others might have led some of them, in return for the privilege of taking it, to consent to bring him some. But the result would not have been the same to the community as a whole. His Laziness could have obtained the fruits of labor, but only by virtually taking the labor of others.

And so the son of an Hawaiian missionary, who in the legal ownership of land holds the Christian equivalent of the old heathen power of taboo, may in return for the privilege of permitting others to apply labor to his land compel them to bring him wealth or capital. The possession of this power so far as he himself is concerned is equivalent to the possession of wealth or capital, but not so to the community. It implies no addition to the sum of production or to the power of future production. It implies merely a power of affecting the distribution of what may already by other agencies be produced.

This fact that part of what is really wealth is capital, and that what is not wealth is not capital, is so clear that it is really recognized in ordinary speech if we pay attention to the core, or original meaning of the words. As I say in "Progress and Poverty," when speaking of capital (Book I., Chapter II., "The Meaning of the Terms"):

If the articles of actual wealth existing at a given time in a given community were presented *in situ* to a dozen intelligent men who had never read a line of political economy, it is doubtful if they would differ in respect to a single item, as to whether it should be accounted capital or not. Money which its owner holds for use in his business or in speculation would be accounted capital; money set aside for household or personal expenses would not. That part of a farmer's crop held for sale or for seed, or to feed his help in part payment of wages, would be accounted capital; that held for the use of his own family would not be. The horses and carriage of a hackman would be classed as capital; but an equipage kept for the pleasure of its owner would not. So, no one would think of counting as capital the false hair on the head of a woman, the cigar in the mouth of a smoker, or the toy with which a child is playing; but the stock of a hair-dealer, of a tobacconist, or the keeper of a toy-store, would be unhesitatingly set down as capital. A coat which a tailor had made for sale would be accounted capital; but not the coat he had made for himself. Food in the possession of a hotel-keeper or a restaurateur would be accounted capital; but not the food in the pantry of a housewife, or in the lunch-basket of a workman. Pig-iron in the hands of the smelter, or founder, or dealer, would be accounted capital; but not the pig-iron used as ballast in the hold of a yacht. The bellows of a blacksmith, the looms of a factory, would be capital; but not the sewing-machine of a woman who does only her own work; a building let for hire, or used for business or productive purposes; but not a homestead. In short, I think we should find that now, as when Dr. Adam Smith wrote, "that part of a man's stock which he expects to yield him a revenue is called his capital." And, omitting his unfortunate slip as to personal qualities, and qualifying somewhat his enumeration of money, it is doubtful if we could better list the different articles of capital than did Adam Smith in the passage which in the previous part of this chapter I have condensed.

Now, if, after having thus separated the wealth that is capital from the wealth that is not capital, we look for the distinction between the two classes, we shall not find it to be as to the character, capabilities, or final destination of the things themselves, as has been vainly attempted to draw it, but it seems to me that we shall find it to be as to whether they are or are not in the possession of the consumer.* Such articles of wealth as in themselves, in their uses, or in their products, are yet to be exchanged are capital; such articles of wealth as are in the hands of the consumer are not capital. Hence, if we define capital as *wealth in course of exchange*, understanding exchange to include, not merely the passing from hand to hand, but also such transmutations as occur when the reproductive or transforming forces of nature are utilized for the increase of wealth, we shall, I think, comprehend all the things that the general idea of capital properly includes, and shut out all it does not. Under this definition, it seems to me, for instance, will fall all such tools as are really capital. For it is as to whether its services or uses are to be exchanged or not which makes a tool an article of capital; or merely an article of wealth. Thus the lathe of a manufacturer used in making things which are to be exchanged is capital; while the lathe kept by a gentleman is not. Thus wealth used in the construction of a railroad, a public telegraph line, a stage-coach, a theater, a hotel, etc., may be said to be placed in the course of exchange. The exchange is not effected all at once, but little by little, with an indefinite number of people. Yet there is an exchange, and the "consumers" of the railroad, the telegraph line, the stage-coach, theater or hotel, are not the owners, but the persons who from time to time use them.

Nor is this definition inconsistent with the idea that capital is that part of wealth devoted to production. It is too narrow an understanding of production which confines it merely to the making of things. Production includes not merely the making of things, but the bringing of them to the consumer. The merchant or storekeeper is thus as truly a producer as is the manufacturer or farmer, and his stock or capital is as much devoted to production as is theirs. But it is not worth while now to dwell upon the functions of capital, which we shall be better able to determine hereafter. Nor is the

---

* Money may be said to be in the hands of the consumer when devoted to the procurement of gratification, as, though not in itself devoted to consumption, it represents wealth which is; and thus what in the previous paragraph I have given as the common classification would be covered by this distinction, and would be substantially correct. In speaking of money, in this connection, I am, of course, speaking of coin, for although paper money may perform all the functions of coin it is not wealth, and cannot therefore be capital.—["Progress and Poverty," Book I., Chapter II.]

definition of capital I have suggested of any importance. I am not writing a text-book, but only attempting to discover the laws which control a great social problem, and if the reader has been led to form a clear idea of what things are meant when we speak of capital my purpose is served.

But before closing this digression let me call attention to what is often forgotten—namely, that the terms "wealth," "capital," "wages," and the like, as used in political economy, are abstract terms and that nothing can be generally affirmed or denied of them that cannot be affirmed or denied of the whole class of things they represent. The failure to bear this in mind has led to much confusion of thought, and permits fallacies, otherwise transparent, to pass for obvious truths. Wealth being an abstract term, the idea of wealth, it must be remembered, involves the idea of exchangeability. The possession of wealth to a certain amount is potentially the possession of any or all species of wealth to that equivalent in exchange. And consequently, so of capital.

CHAPTER XVIII.

WHY POLITICAL ECONOMY CONSIDERS ONLY WEALTH.

SHOWING THAT POLITICAL ECONOMY, AS PROPERLY STATED, COVERS ALL THE RELATIONS OF MEN IN SOCIETY INTO WHICH IT IS NECESSARY TO INQUIRE.

Political economy does not include all the exertions for the satisfaction of material desires; but it does include the greater part of them, and it is through value that the exchange of services for services is made—Its duty and province.

POLITICAL economy has been defined, and I think sufficiently, as "the science which treats of the nature of wealth and the laws of its production and distribution." The object-noun or subject-matter of political economy is therefore wealth. Now, as we have already seen, wealth is not the only result of human exertion, nor is it indeed the end and aim and final cause of human exertion. That is not reached until wealth is spent or consumed in satisfaction of desire. Wealth itself is in fact only a halting-place or storehouse on the way between prompting desire and final satisfaction; a point at which exertion, journeying towards the satisfaction of desire, remains for a time stored up in concrete form, and from whence it may be called forth to yield the satisfaction which is its ultimate aim. And there are exertions aiming at the satisfaction of desire which do not pass through the form of wealth at all.

Why then should political economy concern itself merely with the production and distribution of wealth? Is not the proper object of the science the production and distribution of human satisfactions, and would not this definition, while including wealth, as material satisfactions through material services, also include services that do not take concrete form?

My answer is that I am not engaged in laying out a new science, but only endeavoring to explain and straighten out one that has been already much pursued. I wish, therefore, as far as possible, to follow old roads and to use accustomed terms, only swerving from them where they clearly lead to error, of which there are indeed instances enough.

And further than this, I think that reflection will show that a consideration of the production and distribution of wealth will include about all that there is any practical use of considering of the production and distribution of satisfactions.

While wealth does not include the sum of all exertions for the satisfaction of material desires, it does include what in a highly civilized society are the far greater part of them, and is, as it were, the exchange point or clearing-house where the transfer of services devoted not to the production of wealth, but to the direct procurement of satisfactions, is made.

Thus the barber, the singer, the physician, the dentist, the actor, do not produce wealth, but direct satisfactions. But not only are their efforts which are expended in this way mainly devoted to the procurement of wealth, which they get in exchange for their services, but any exchange between themselves of services for services takes place through the medium of wealth. That is to say, the actor does not pay his barber in recitations, or the singer pay his physician in tones, nor yet reversely does the barber or physician often pay in shaves or medical advice for the satisfaction of hearing, acting or singing. Each habitually exchanges his services for wealth or the representative of wealth, and exchanges this for other services that he may desire. Thus in civilized society it is only in rare and exceptional cases that there is any direct exchange of services for services. To this we may add that the laws which govern the production and distribution of services are essentially the same as those which govern the production and distribution of wealth. Thus we see that all the ends of political economy may be reached if its inquiry be an inquiry into the nature of wealth and the laws that govern its production and distribution.

Political economy has a duty and a province of its own. It is not and it cannot be the science of everything; for the day in which any one scheme can include the whole province of human knowledge has long passed, and must with the increase of human knowledge further recede. Even to-day the science of politics, though closely related, is, as I conceive it, clearly distinct from the science of political economy, to say nothing of the almost numberless other schemes which treat of man's relations to other individuals and to the relations with which he is brought in contact.

CHAPTER XIX.

MORAL CONFUSIONS AS TO WEALTH.

SHOWING HOW RICH AND POOR ARE CORRELATIVES, AND WHY CHRIST SYMPATHIZED WITH THE POOR.

The legitimacy of wealth and the disposition to regard it as sordid and mean—The really rich and the really poor—They are really correlatives—The good sense of Christ's teaching.

AS to the desire for wealth in the politico-economic sense, as I have described it, there is nothing sordid or mean. Wealth, on the contrary, is a perfectly legitimate object of desire and effort. To obtain it is simply to increase the powers of the individual over nature, and is prompted by the same essentially noble desire as in any way to increase our powers or our knowledge, or in any way to raise ourselves above the level of the mere animal, from which we start; while no one can increase his own wealth in the common sense by increasing value from production, without at the same time doing something for every one else.

How then is it that wealth is so widely regarded askance by our moral perceptions; that we are told that we should not seek it, and hardly even use it; that the highest expressions of our deepest knowledge look at it so contemptuously, if not repugnantly, and that political economy, which is the science of the nature, production and exchange of wealth, should be so widely regarded as a selfish and hard science?

If we go into this question at all we must go deeper than has yet, I think, been done.

There is a distinction on which our examination of wealth and value may throw light, the distinction we commonly make between the rich and the poor. We mean by a rich man a man who is possessed of much having value, that is to say, of much wealth or of much power of commanding wealth or services from others. And by a poor man we mean a man who possesses little or nothing of such values. But where is the line of division between rich and poor? There is no line distinctly recognized in common thought, and a man is called rich or poor according to the standard of average comfort prevailing in the society or rather the grade of society in which the estimate is made. Among Connemara peasants, as in the song, a woman of three cows might be esteemed wealthy; while among Esquimaux, as in Mark Twain's story, the possession of a few iron fish-hooks might be as convincing a proof of riches as the loading of a Christian woman with diamonds by an American millionaire. There are circles of human life in New York City in which no man would be deemed poor who could see his way to a night's lodging and a breakfast in the morning, and there are other circles in which a Vanderbilt could say that a man possessed of only a million dollars could with economy live as comfortably as though he were rich.

But is there not some line the recognition of which will enable us to say with something like scientific precision that this man is rich and that man is poor; some line of possession which will enable us truly to distinguish between rich and poor in all places and conditions of society; a line of the natural, mean, or normal possession, below which in various degrees is poverty, and above which in varying degrees is wealthiness? It seems to me that there must be. And if we stop to think of it, we may see that there is.

If we set aside for the moment the narrower economic meaning of service, by which direct service is conveniently distinguished from the indirect service embodied in wealth, we may resolve all the things which indirectly satisfy human desire into one term, service; just as we resolve fractions into a common denominator. Now, is there not a natural or normal line of the possession or enjoyment of service? Clearly there is. It is that of equality between giving and receiving. This is the equilibrium which Confucius expressed in the golden word of his teaching that in English we translate into "reciprocity." Naturally the services which a member of a human society is entitled to receive from other members are the equivalents of those he renders to others. Here is the normal line from which what we call wealthiness and what we call poverty take their start. He who can command more service than he need render, is rich. He is poor, who can command less service than he does render or is willing to render; for in our civilization of to-day we must take note of the monstrous fact that men willing to work cannot always find opportunity to work. The one has more than he ought to have; the other has less. Rich and poor are thus correlatives of each other; the existence of a class of rich involving the existence of a class of poor, and the reverse; and abnormal luxury on the one side and abnormal want on the other have a relation of necessary sequence. To put this relation into terms of morals, the rich are the robbers, since they are at least sharers in the proceeds of robbery; and the poor are the robbed.

This is the reason, I take it, why Christ, who was not really a man of such reckless speech as some Christians deem Him to have been, always expressed sympathy with the poor and repugnance of the rich. In His philosophy it was better even to be robbed than to rob. In the kingdom of right-doing which He preached, rich and poor would be impossible, because rich and poor in the true sense are the results of wrong-doing. And when He said, "It is easier for a camel to pass through the eye of a needle than for a rich man to enter the kingdom of heaven!" He simply put in the emphatic forms of Eastern metaphor a statement of fact as coldly true as the statement that two parallel lines can never meet.

Injustice cannot live where justice rules, and even if the man himself might get through, his riches—his power of compelling service without rendering service—must of necessity be left behind. If there can be no poor in the kingdom of heaven, clearly there can be no rich!

And so it is utterly impossible in this, or in any other conceivable world, to abolish unjust poverty, without at the same time abolishing unjust possessions. This is a hard word to the softly amiable philanthropists who, to speak metaphorically, would like to get on the good side of God without angering the devil. But it is a true word nevertheless.

CHAPTER XX.

OF THE PERMANENCE OF WEALTH.

SHOWING THAT VALUES FROM OBLIGATION SEEM REALLY TO LAST LONGER THAN VALUES FROM PRODUCTION.

Value from production and value from obligation—The one material and the other existing in the spiritual—Superior permanence of the spiritual—Shakespeare's boast—Mæcenas's buildings and Horace's odes—The two values now existing—Franchises and land values last longer than gold and gems—Destruction in social advance—Conclusions from all this.

IN making the distinction between values from production that really constitute wealth in political economy, and values from obligation, which are not really wealth at all, and may at best be classified as "relative wealth" in contradistinction to "real wealth," there is an important and to our usual ways of thinking an unexpected difference to be mentioned between them with relation to permanence and to the effect of the progress of society upon their value.

Value from production, or real wealth, consists of material things. These things are taken as it were by labor from the reservoirs of nature, and by virtue of their materiality tend back to those reservoirs again from the moment they are taken, just as water, taken from the ocean, tends back to the ocean. The great body of wealth is, indeed, produced for a purposed consumption that involves immediate destruction. And since I think we may properly speak in a different sense of the consumption of a book by reading it, or of a picture or statue by looking at it, even the parts not subject to purposed and almost immediate destruction, are subject to destruction by the action of the elements, by mechanical and chemical disintegration, and finally by being lost. Indeed, the far greater part of material things if not absolutely all of them, after they have been brought into existence, require the constant exertion of labor to keep them in existence and prevent their relapsing into nature's reservoirs again.

But things having a value which does not come from the exertion of labor and which represents only the power given by human law, agreement or custom of appropriating the proceeds of exertion, have their real existence in the human mind or will, the spiritual element of man. The papers which we use in transferring them, or proclaiming them, or evidencing them, are not the things themselves, but mere aids to memory. The essence of a debt is not the due-bill or promissory note, but a moral obligation or mental agreement; the essence of a franchise is not the written charter or engrossed act of legislature, but the will of the sovereign, theoretically supposed to be the will of all; the ownership of land is not in the title-deeds, but in the same sovereign will or supposed general agreement.

As the spiritual part of man—mind, will and memory—continues the same while the matter of which his body is composed is continually passing, so a mental impression, recorded by tradition, belief or custom in what may be styled the social mentality, may endure while physical changes wrought by man are lost. It is probable that the oldest records of man's presence on the earth are to be found in words yet current, and that nursery rhymes and children's games antedate the most massive monuments. It was no idle boast of Shakespeare that his verse would outlast marble and brass. The stately buildings raised by the powerful prime minister of Augustus Cæsar have failed to perpetuate his memory; but far further than his world extended, the name of Mæcenas yet lives for us in the odes of Horace.

Now, in the same way, the values which cannot be included in the category of wealth are as a class much more enduring than the values which are properly so included. We of the modern civilization generally limit the time during which debts, promissory notes, and similar obligations of the individual can be legally enforced. But there are devices by which a value which is in reality but an obligation to render future labor may be continued for longer periods; while many values of similar nature we treat as perpetual, as is the case with public debts, with some franchises, and with exclusive rights to land. These may retain their value unimpaired, while the value of the great body of articles of wealth lessens and disappears.

How little of the wealth in existence in England two hundred years ago exists now! And the infinitesimal part that still exists has been maintained in existence only by constant care and toil. But stock in the public debt of England incurred then still retains value. So do perpetual pensions granted to their favorites and lemans by English kings long dust. So do advowsons, rights of fishery and market, and other special privileges. While such franchises as that of the New River Company, and the right to the exclusive use of land in many places have enormously increased in value. These things have cost no care or trouble to maintain. On the contrary, they have been sources of continual revenue to their owners—have enabled their owners to call continually upon generation after generation of Englishmen to undergo toil and trouble for their benefit. Yet their value, that is to say their power of continuing to do this, remains still, not merely unimpaired, but in many cases enormously increased.

Of all articles of value from production those which longest retain the quality of value are precious metals and gems. In the coin and jewelry passing from hand to hand in the exchanges of modern civilization there are doubtless some particles of metal and some precious stones that had value at the very dawn of history and have retained it ever since. But these are rare and indistinguishable exceptions. So far as we can see with any certainty, the quality of value has longer and more constantly attached to the ownership of land, which is not an article of wealth, than to any other valuable thing. The little piece of land in the Sabine hills, which Mæcenas gave to Horace, had doubtless been bought and sold and exchanged for centuries before that, and has, I doubt not, a value to this day. And so, certainly, with some of the building sites of Rome. Through all the mutations in the fortunes of the Imperial City, some of them have doubtless continually held a value, sometimes lower and sometimes higher. It is this permanence of value which has led the lawyers to distinguish property in land, though it is not wealth at all, as real estate or real property. Its value remains so long as population continues around it and custom or municipal law guarantees the special privilege of appropriating the profits of its use.

And between articles of wealth and things of the nature of special privileges, like franchises and property in land, which though having value are not wealth, there is still another very important distinction to be noted. The general tendency of the value attached to the one is to decrease and disappear with social advance. The general tendency of the value attaching to the other is to increase.

For social advance, involving, as it does, increase of population, extensions of exchange and improvement of the arts, tends constantly, by lessening the cost of production, steadily to reduce the value of the great body of articles of wealth already in existence, and having value from production. In some cases indeed the effect of social advance is suddenly and utterly to destroy these values. The value of almost all the products of labor has been of late years steadily and largely reduced in this way, while the value of much costly machinery has been and still is being destroyed by discoveries, inventions and improvements, which render their use in production antiquated. But the growth of population and the augmentations of the productive power of labor increase enormously the value of such special privileges as franchises and land-ownership in the highways and centers of social life.

It will be seen from our analysis, as indeed from observation, that the amount of wealth at any time existing is very much less than is usually assumed. The vast majority of mankind live not on stored wealth, but on their exertion. The vast majority of mankind, even in richest civilized countries, leave the world as destitute of wealth as they entered it.

It is the constant expenditure of labor that alone keeps up the supply of wealth. If labor were to cease, wealth would disappear.

And while this fact, that value from mere obligation has a permanence which does not belong to value from production, may have a bearing upon speculations too deep to be entered on here, and suggests perhaps truth on the part of those who say that the material universe may be a mere reflex and correspondence of the moral and mental universe, and that we may find reality not in what we call life, but in what we call death, and while it may make comprehensible the resurrection from the dead which to many has been most perplexing, it has immediate bearing on many things to which any consideration of the true nature and bearings of wealth comes close if it does not closely touch.

CHAPTER XXI.

THE RELATION OF MONEY TO WEALTH.

SHOWING THAT SOME MONEY IS AND SOME MONEY IS NOT WEALTH.

Where I shall treat of money—No categorical answer can yet be given to the question whether money is wealth—Some money is and some is not wealth.

THE subject of money, in my view of the matter, properly belongs to this Book, which treats of the nature of wealth. But the subject is at the time I write so complicated and confused by current discussions, especially in the United States, as to require for its complete elucidation a fullness of treatment that would too much expand this Book. And, moreover, these current discussions of what is and what ought to be money involve principles which do not find their proper place in the discussion of the nature of wealth, but which will be treated in the succeeding books on Production and Distribution. For these reasons, I shall postpone the full treatment of Money until after the laws of Production and the laws of Distribution have been discussed. But one question is certain to occur to the reader which must be answered here—the question, "Is money wealth?"

To this no categorical answer can be given, for the reason that what we properly call money is in all countries in our present stage of civilization of essentially different kinds. Some of the money in use to-day is wealth, and some of it is not wealth. Some, such for instance as the gold coins of the United States and England, is wealth to the full amount of its circulating value. Some, such as the silver, copper and bronze coins of the same countries, is wealth, but not wealth to the full extent of its circulating value. While some, such as the paper money, which now constitutes so large a part of the money of the civilized world, is not wealth at all. For, as we have seen, nothing is wealth in the economic sense, unless and in so far as the value which attaches to it is a value of production. The value arising from obligation constitutes no part of the wealth of nations.

BOOK III.

THE PRODUCTION OF WEALTH

CONTENTS OF BOOK III.

THE PRODUCTION OF WEALTH.

CHAPTER I.

THE MEANING OF PRODUCTION

SHOWING THE MEANING AND PROPER USE OF PRODUCTION.

CHAPTER II.

THE THREE MODES OF PRODUCTION.

SHOWING THE COMMON CHARACTER, YET DIFFERENT MODES OF PRODUCTION.

CHAPTER III.

POPULATION AND SUBSISTENCE.

SHOWING THAT THE THEORY OF A TENDENCY IN POPULATION TO INCREASE FASTER THAN SUBSISTENCE HAS PREVIOUSLY BEEN EXAMINED AND CONDEMNED.

CHAPTER IV.

THE ALLEGED LAW OF DIMINISHING RETURNS IN AGRICULTURE.

SHOWING WHAT THIS ALLEGED LAW IS.

CHAPTER V.

OF SPACE AND TIME.

SHOWING THAT HUMAN REASON IS ONE, AND SO FAR AS IT CAN GO MAY BE RELIED ON.

CHAPTER VI.

CONFUSION OF THE SPACIAL LAW WITH AGRICULTURE.

SHOWING THE GENESIS OF THIS CONFUSION.

CHAPTER VII.

THE RELATION OF SPACE IN PRODUCTION.

SHOWING THAT SPACE HAS RELATION TO ALL MODES OF PRODUCTION.

CHAPTER VIII.

THE RELATION OF TIME IN PRODUCTION.

SHOWING THAT ALL MODES OF PRODUCTION HAVE RELATION TO TIME.

CHAPTER IX.

COÖPERATION—ITS TWO WAYS.

SHOWING THE TWO WAYS OF COÖPERATION.

CHAPTER X.

COÖPERATION—ITS TWO KINDS.

SHOWING THE TWO KINDS OF COÖPERATION, AND HOW THE POWER OF THE ONE GREATLY EXCEEDS THAT OF THE OTHER.

CHAPTER XI.

THE OFFICE OF EXCHANGE IN PRODUCTION.

SHOWING THAT IN MAN THE LACK OF INSTINCT IS SUPPLIED BY THE HIGHER QUALITY OF REASON, WHICH LEADS TO EXCHANGE.

CHAPTER XII.

OFFICE OF COMPETITION IN PRODUCTION.

SHOWING THAT COMPETITION BRINGS TRADE, AND CONSEQUENTLY SERVICE, TO ITS JUST LEVEL.

CHAPTER XIII.

CHAPTER XIV.

ORDER OF THE THREE FACTORS OF PRODUCTION.

SHOWING THE AGREEMENT OF ALL ECONOMISTS AS TO THE NAMES AND ORDER OF THE FACTORS OF PRODUCTION.

CHAPTER XV.

THE FIRST FACTOR OF PRODUCTION—LAND.

SHOWING THAT LAND IS THE NATURAL OR PASSIVE FACTOR IN ALL PRODUCTION.

CHAPTER XVI.

THE SECOND FACTOR OF PRODUCTION—LABOR.

SHOWING THAT LABOR IS THE HUMAN OR ACTIVE FACTOR IN ALL PRODUCTION.

CHAPTER XVII.

THE THIRD FACTOR OF PRODUCTION—CAPITAL.

SHOWING THAT CAPITAL IS NOT A PRIMARY FACTOR, BUT PROCEEDS FROM LAND AND LABOR, AND IS A FORM OR USE OF WEALTH.

CHAPTER I.[1]

THE MEANING OF PRODUCTION.

SHOWING THE MEANING AND PROPER USE OF PRODUCTION.

Production a drawing forth of what before exists—Its difference from creation—Production other than of wealth—Includes all stages of bringing to be—Mistakes as to it.

THE word production comes from the Latin, *pro*, before, and *ducere*, to draw, and its literal meaning is a drawing forth.

Production, as a term of political economy, means a drawing forth by man; a bringing into existence by the power of man. It does not mean creation, the proper sense of which is the bringing into existence by a power superior to that of man—that power namely which to escape negation our reason is compelled to postulate as the final cause of all things.

A solar system, a world with all the substances and powers therein contained, soil, water and air, chemical affinities, vital forces, the invariable sequences which we term natural laws, vegetables and animals in their species as they exist irrespective of the modifying influence of man, and man himself with his natural powers, needs and impulses, we properly speak of as created. How precisely

[1] No introduction or motto supplied for Book III. in MS.—H. G., JR.

they came to be, and what and whence the originating impulse, we cannot tell, and probably in the sphere to which we are confined in this life can never know. All we can say with certainty, is that they cannot have been brought into existence by any power of man; that they existed before man was, and constitute the materials and forces on which his existence depends and on which and from which all his production is based. Since they cannot have come from what we call matter alone; nor from what we call energy alone; nor yet from any union of these two elements alone, they must proceed primarily from that originating element that in the largest analysis of the world that reason enables us to make we distinguish from matter and energy as spirit.

Nothing that is created can therefore in the politico-economic sense be said to be produced. Man is not a creator; he has no power of originating things, of making something out of nothing. He is a producer; that is to say a changer, who brings forth by altering what already is. All his making of things, his causing things to be, is a drawing forth, a modification in place or relation, and in accordance with natural laws which he neither originated nor altered, of what he finds already in existence. All his production has as its substratum what he finds already in the world; what exists irrespective of him. This substratum or nexus, the natural or passive factor, on which and by which the human or active factor of production acts, is in the terminology of political economy called land.

It is to be noted that when used as a term of political economy the word "production" has in some respects a narrower, and in some respects a wider, meaning than is often, in common use properly enough, attached to it. Since the production with which political economy primarily deals is the production of wealth, the economic term production refers to that. But it is important to bear in mind that the production of wealth is not the only kind of production.

I have alluded to this fact before in Chapter XVIII. of Book II. Let me speak of it again.

I black my boots; I shave my face; I take a violin and play on it, or expend effort in learning to do so; I write a poem; or observe the habits of bees; or try to make an hour pass more agreeably to a sick friend by reading to him something which arouses and pleases his higher nature. In such ways I am satisfying wants or gratifying desires, cultivating powers or increasing knowledge, either for myself or for others. But I am not producing wealth. And so, those who in the coöperation of efforts in which civilization consists devote themselves to such occupations—boot-blacks, barbers, musicians, teachers, investigators, surgeons, nurses, poets, priests—do not, strictly speaking, take part in the production of wealth. Yet it may be misleading to speak of them as non-producers, without care as to what is really meant. Though not producers of wealth, they are yet producers, and often producers of the highest kind. They are producers of utilities and satisfactions; and as such are not only producers of that to which wealth is but a means, but may indirectly aid in the production of wealth itself.

On the other hand there is something we should note.

In common speech, the word production is frequently used in a sense which distinguishes the first from the later stages of wealth-getting; and those engaged in the primary extractive or formative processes are often styled producers, as distinguished from transporters or exchangers. This use of the word production may be convenient where we wish to distinguish between separable functions, but we must be careful not to import it into our habitual use of the economic term. In the economic meaning of the term production, the transporter or exchanger, or any one engaged in any sub-division of those functions, is as truly engaged in production as is the primary extractor or maker. A newspaper-carrier or the keeper of a news-stand would for instance in common speech be styled a distributor. But in economic terminology he is not a distributor of wealth, but a producer of wealth. Although his part in the process of producing the newspaper to the final receiver comes last, not first, he is as much a producer as the paper-maker or type-founder, the editor or compositor or press-man.

For the object of production is the satisfaction of human desires, that is to say it is consumption; and this object is not made capable of attainment, that is to say, production is not really complete, until wealth is brought to the place where it is to be consumed and put at the disposal of him whose desire it is to satisfy.

Thus, the production of wealth in political economy includes transportation and exchange. The distribution of wealth, on the other hand, has in economic phraseology no relation to transportation or exchange, but refers, as we shall see when we come to treat of it, to the division of the results of production.

This fact has been ignored by the great majority of professed economists who with few exceptions treat of exchange under the head of the distribution of wealth instead of giving it its proper place under the head of the production of wealth.

CHAPTER II.

THE THREE MODES OF PRODUCTION.

SHOWING THE COMMON CHARACTER, YET DIFFERENT MODES OF PRODUCTION.

Production involves change, brought about by conscious will—Its three modes: (1) adapting, (2) growing, (3) exchanging—This the natural order of these modes.

ALL production results from human exertion upon external nature, and consists in the changing in place, condition, form or combination of natural materials or objects so as to fit them or more nearly fit them for the satisfaction of human desires. In all production use is made of natural forces or potencies, though in the first place, the energy in the human frame is brought under the direct control of the conscious human will.

But production takes place in different ways. If we run over in mind as many examples as we can think of in which the exertion of labor results in wealth—either in those primary or extractive stages of production in which what before was not wealth is made to assume the character of wealth; or in the later or secondary stages, in which an additional value or increment of wealth is attached to what has already been given the character of wealth—we find that they fall into three categories or modes.

The first of these three modes of production, for both reason and tradition unite in giving it priority, is that in which, in the changes he brings about in natural substances and objects, man makes use only of those natural forces and potencies which we may conceive of as existing or manifesting themselves in a world as yet destitute of life; or perhaps it might afford a better illustration to say, in a world from which the generative or reproductive principle of life had just departed, or been by his condition rendered unutilizable by man. These would include all such natural forces and potencies as gravitation, heat, light, electricity, cohesion, chemical attractions and repulsions—in short, all the natural forces and relations, that are utilized in the production of wealth, below those incident to the vital force of generation.

We can perhaps best imagine such a separation of natural forces by picturing to ourselves a Robinson Crusoe thrown upon a really desert island or bare sand key, in a ship abundantly supplied with marine stores, tools and food so dried or preserved as to be incapable of growth or reproduction. We might also, if we chose, imagine the ship to contain a dog, a goat, or indeed any number of other animals, provided there was no pairing of the sexes. We cannot, in truth, imagine even a bare sand key, in which there should be no manifestation of the generative principle, in insects and vegetables, if not in the lower forms of fish and bird life, but we can readily imagine that our Robinson might not understand, or might not find it convenient, to avail himself of such manifestations of the reproductive principle. Yet without any use of the principle by which things may be made to grow and increase, such a man would still be able to produce wealth, since by changing in place, form or combination what he found already in existence in his island or in his ship, he could fit them to the satisfaction of his desires. Thus he could produce wealth just as De Foe's Robinson Crusoe, whose solitary life so many of us have shared in imagination, produced wealth when he first landed, by bringing desirable things from the wrecked ship to the safety of the shore before destructive gales came on, and by changing the place and form of such of them as were fit for his purpose, making himself a cabin, a boat, sails, nets, clothes, and so on. In the same way, he could catch fish, kill or snare birds, capture turtles, take eggs, and convert the food-material at his disposal into more toothsome dishes. Thus without growing or breeding anything he could get by his labor a living, until death, or the savages, or another ship came.

For this mode of production, which is mechanical in its nature, and consists in the change in place, form, condition or combination of what is already in existence, it seems to me that the best term is "adapting."

This is the mode of production of the fisherman, the hunter, the miner, the smelter, the refiner, the mechanic, the manufacturer, the transporter; and also of the butcher, the horse-breaker or animal-trainer, who is not also a breeder. We use it when we produce wealth by taking coal from the vein and changing its place to the surface of the earth; and again when we bring about a further increment of wealth by carrying the coal to the place where it is to be consumed in the satisfaction of human desire. We use this mode of production when we convert trees into lumber, or lumber into boards; when we convert wheat into flour, or the juice of the cane or beet into sugar; when we separate the metals from the combinations in which they are found in the ores, and when we unite them in new combinations that give us desirable alloys, such as brass, type-metal, Babbitt metal, aluminum, bronze, etc.; or when by the various processes of separating and re-combining we produce the textile fabrics, and convert them again into clothes, sails, bags, etc.; or when by bringing their various materials into suitable forms and combinations, we construct tools, machines, ships or houses. In fact, all that in the narrower sense we usually call "making," or, if on a large scale, "manufacturing," is brought about by the application of labor in this first mode of production—the mode of "adapting."

In the Northwest, however, they speak sometimes of "manufacturing wheat;" in the West of "making hogs," and in the South of "making cotton" (the fiber) or "making tobacco" (the leaf). But in such local or special sense the words manufacturing or making are used as equivalent to producing. The sense is not the same, nor is the suggested action in the same mode, as when we properly speak of flour as being manufactured, or of bacon, cotton cloth or cigars being made. Wonderful machines are indeed constructed by man's power of adaptation. But no extension of this power of adaptation will enable him to construct a machine that will feed itself and produce its kind. His power of adapting extended infinitely would not enable him to manufacture a single wheat-grain that would sprout, or to make a hog, a cotton-boll or a tobacco-leaf. The tiniest of such things are as much above man's power of adapting as is the "making" of a world or the "manufacture" of a solar system.

There is, however, another or second mode of production. In this man utilizes the vital or reproductive force of nature to aid him in the producing of wealth. By obtaining vegetables, cuttings or seeds, and planting them; by capturing animals and breeding them, we are enabled not merely to produce vegetables and animals in greater quantity than Nature spontaneously offers them to our taking, but, in many cases, to improve their quality of adaptability to our uses. This second mode of production, the mode in which we make use of the vital or generative power of nature, we shall, I think, best distinguish from the first, by calling it "growing." It is the mode of the farmer, the stock-raiser, the florist, the bee-keeper, and to some extent at least of the brewer and distiller.

And besides the first mode, which we have called "adapting," and the second mode, which we have called "growing," there is still a third mode in which, by men living in civilization, wealth is produced. In the first mode we make use of powers or qualities inherent in all material things; in the second we make use of powers or qualities inherent in all living things, vegetable or animal. But this third mode of production consists in the utilization of a power or principle or tendency manifested only in man, and belonging to him by virtue of his peculiar gift of reason—that of exchanging or trading.

That it is by and through his disposition and power to exchange, in which man essentially differs from all other animals that human advance goes on, I shall hereafter show. Yet not merely is it through exchange that the utilization in production of the highest powers both of the human factor and the natural factor becomes possible, but it seems to me that in itself exchange brings about a perceptible increase in the sum of wealth, and that even if we could ignore the manner in which it extends the power of the other two modes of production, this constitutes it, in itself, a third mode of production. In the Yankee story of the two school-boys so cute at a trade that when locked in a room they made money by swapping jack-knives, there is the exaggeration of a truth. Each of the two parties to an exchange aims to get, and as a rule does get, something that is more valuable to him than what he gives—that is to say, that represents to him a greater power of labor to satisfy desire. Thus there is in the transaction an actual increase in the sum of wealth, an actual production of wealth. A trading-vessel, for instance, penetrating to the Arctic, exchanges fish-hooks, harpoons, powder and guns, knives and mirrors, green spectacles and mosquito-nets for peltries. Each party to the exchange gets in return for what costs it comparatively little labor what would cost it a great deal of labor to get by either of the other modes of production. Each gains by the act. Eliminating transportation, which belongs to the first mode of production, the joint wealth of both parties, the sum of the wealth of the world, is by the exchange itself increased.

This third mode of production let us call "exchanging." It is the mode of the merchant or trader, of the storekeeper, or as the English who still live in England call him, the shopkeeper; and of all accessories, including in large measure transporters and their accessories.

We thus have as the three modes of production:

(1) ADAPTING;
(2) GROWING;
(3) EXCHANGING.

These modes seem to appear and to assume importance in the development of human society much in the order here given. They originate from the increase of the desires of men with the increase of the means of satisfying them under pressure of the fundamental law of political economy, that men seek to satisfy their desires with the least exertion. In the primitive stage of human life the readiest way of satisfying desires is by adapting to human use what is found in existence. In a later and more settled stage it is discovered that certain desires can be more easily and more fully satisfied by utilizing the principle of growth and reproduction, as by cultivating vegetables and breeding animals. And in a still later period of development, it becomes obvious that certain desires can be better and more easily satisfied by exchange, which brings out the principle of coöperation more fully and powerfully than it could obtain among unexchanging economic units.

CHAPTER III.

POPULATION AND SUBSISTENCE.

SHOWING THAT THE THEORY OF A TENDENCY IN POPULATION TO INCREASE FASTER THAN SUBSISTENCE HAS PREVIOUSLY BEEN EXAMINED AND CONDEMNED.

The Malthusian theory—Discussed in "Progress and Poverty."

IN proceeding to consider the laws of the production of wealth it would be expedient first to consider any natural law, if such there should be, which would limit the operation of man in production. In the Malthusian theory the scholastic political economy has held that there is a law of nature that produces a tendency in population to increase faster than subsistence. This, coming as it did in the formative period of the institution of the science, was really the bulwark of the long-accepted political economy, which gave to the wealthy a comfortable theory for putting upon the Originating Spirit the responsibility for all the vice, crime and suffering, following from the unjust actions of men, that constitute the black spot of our nineteenth-century civilization. Falling in with the current doctrine that wages are determined by the ratio between capital and labor, deriving support from the principle brought prominently forward in current discussions of the theory of rent, that past a certain point the application of capital and labor to land yields a diminishing return, and harmonizing with the theory of the development of species by selection, it became of the utmost importance, and for a long time imposed even upon well-disposed and fair-minded men a weight of authority of which they could not rid themselves. But in "Progress and Poverty" I devoted to it an entire Book, consisting of four chapters. In this, with what follows, I so disposed of the theory that it is not necessary to go over the reasoning again, but can refer to my previous work those who may wish to inquire as to the nature, grounds and disproof of that theory.

As the space of that work did not allow me to go over the whole scope of political economy, but only to cover its more salient points, it will be well here to examine, what I did not do thoroughly in that work, the doctrine of the law of diminishing returns in agriculture. Since this doctrine has not yet to my knowledge been questioned, it will be well to do this thoroughly.

CHAPTER IV.

THE ALLEGED LAW OF DIMINISHING RETURNS IN AGRICULTURE.

SHOWING WHAT THIS ALLEGED LAW IS.

John Stuart Mill quoted as to the importance, relations and nature of this law—The *reductio ad absurdum* by which it is proved—Contention that it is a misapprehension of the universal law of space.

BEFORE proceeding to the subject of coöperation it is necessary to consider, if but to clear the way, what is treated in standard economic works since the time of Adam Smith as the most important law of production, and indeed of political economy as a whole. This is what is called "The Law of Diminishing Production," or more fully and exactly, "The Law of Diminishing Returns in Agriculture." Of it John Stuart Mill ("Principles of Political Economy," Book I., Chapter XII., Sec. 2) says:

> This general law of agricultural industry is the most important proposition in Political Economy. Were the law different nearly all the phenomena of the production and distribution of wealth would be other than they are.

This view of the importance of "the law of diminishing returns in agriculture" pervades the standard political economies, and is held by the most recent scholastic writers, such as Professor Walker of the United States and Professor Marshall of England, as by Mill and his predecessors. It arises from the relation of this alleged law to current apprehensions of the law of rent, and especially from the support which it seems to give to the Malthusian doctrine that population tends to outrun subsistence—a support to which the long acceptance of that doctrine is due.

Thus, as the necessary consequence of this "law of diminishing returns in agriculture," John Stuart Mill in Book I., Chapter XIII., Sec. 2, of his "Principles of Political Economy," says:

> In all countries which have passed beyond a rather early stage in the progress of agriculture, every increase in the demand for food, occasioned by increased population, will always, unless there is a simultaneous improvement in production, diminish the share which on a fair division would fall to each individual. . . . From this, results the important corollary, that the necessity of restraining population is not, as many persons believe, peculiar to a condition of great inequality of property. A greater number of people cannot, in any given state of civilization be collectively so well provided for as a smaller. The niggardliness of nature, not the injustice of society, is the cause of the penalty attached to overpopulation. An unjust distribution of wealth does not even aggravate the evil, but at most causes it to be somewhat earlier felt. It is in vain to say, that all mouths which the increase of mankind calls into existence bring with them hands. The new mouths require as much food as the old ones, and the hands do not produce as much.

As to the law itself, from which such tremendous consequences are confidently deduced—consequences which put us to the mental confusion of denying the justice of the Creator, and assuming that the Originating Spirit is so poor a contriver as to be constantly doing what any mere human host would be ashamed to be guilty of, bringing more guests to his table than could be fed—it is thus stated by Mill:

> After a certain and not very advanced stage in the progress of agriculture; as soon, in fact, as mankind have applied to cultivation

with any energy, and have brought to it any tolerable tools; from that time it is the law of production from the land, that in any given state of agricultural skill and knowledge, by increasing the labor, the produce is not increased in equal degree; doubling labor does not increase the produce; or to express the same thing in other words, every increase of produce is obtained by a more than proportional increase in the application of labor to the land.

This law of diminishing returns in agriculture it is further explained applies also to mining, and in short to all the primary or extractive industries, which give the character of wealth to what was not before wealth, but not to those secondary or subsequent industries which add an additional increase of wealth to what was already wealth. Thus since the law of diminishing productiveness in agriculture does not apply to the secondary industries, it is assumed that any increased application of labor (and capital) in manufacturing for instance, would continue to yield a proportionate and more than proportionate return. And as conclusive and axiomatic proof of this law of diminishing productiveness in agriculture, it is said that were it not for this peculiar law, and were it, on the contrary (as it is assumed it would be without it), the fact that additional application of labor would result in a proportionately increased production from the same land, one single farm would suffice to raise all the agricultural produce required to feed the whole population of England, of the United States or any other country, or of course, of the whole world, by mere increase in the application of labor.

This proposition seems to have been generally accepted by professional economists as a valid *reductio ad absurdum*, and to have carried the same weight in the common thought as has the similar proposition of the general Malthusian doctrine that *if* increasing population did not find increasing difficulty in getting subsistence. mankind would in a little while be able only to find standing-room on one another's heads.

But analysis will show that this logical structure, which economic writers have deemed so strong and on which they have so confidently built, rests upon an utter misapprehension; that there is in truth no special law of diminishing productiveness applying to agriculture, or to the extractive occupations, or to the use of natural agents, which are the various ways which the later writers have of sometimes stating what the earlier writers called the law of diminishing productiveness in agriculture; and that what has been misapprehended as a special law of diminishing returns in agriculture is in reality a general law, applying as well to manufacturing and exchanging as to agriculture, being in fact nothing less general than the spacial law of all material existence and movement—inorganic as well as organic.

This will appear if we consider the relation of space to production. But to do this thoroughly and at the same time to clear the way for considerations which may prove of importance in other parts of this work, I propose to begin by endeavoring to fix the meaning and nature of space and time.

CHAPTER V.

OF SPACE AND TIME.

SHOWING THAT HUMAN REASON IS ONE, AND SO FAR AS IT CAN GO MAY BE RELIED ON.

Purpose of this work—Of metaphysics—Danger of thinking of words as things—Space and time not conceptions of things but of relations of things—They cannot, therefore, have independent beginning or ending—The verbal habit which favors this idea—How favored by poets and by religious teachers—How favored by philosophers—Of Kant—Of Schopenhauer—Mysteries and antinomies that are really confusions in the meaning of words—Human reason and the eternal reason—"Philosophers" who are really word-jugglers.

MY purpose in this work is to explain the science of political economy so clearly that it may be understood by any one of common ability who will give to it reasonable attention. I wish therefore to avoid, as far as possible, everything that savors of metaphysics. For metaphysics, which in its proper meaning is the science of the relations recognized by human reason, has become in the hands of those who have assumed to teach it, a synonym for what cannot be understood, conveying to common thought some vague notion of a realm beyond the bounds of ordinary reason, into which common sense can venture only to shrink helpless and abashed.

Yet to trace to their root confusions involved in current economic teachings and to clear the ground for a coherent political economy, it is necessary to fix the real meaning of two conceptions which belong to metaphysics, and which are beset by confusions that have not only disturbed the teaching of political economy, but of philosophy in the higher sense. These conceptions are those of space and time.

All material existence is in space and in time. Hence, the production of wealth, which in all its modes consists in the bringing about by human exertion of changes in the place or relation of material things, so as to fit them for the satisfaction of human desire, involves both space and time.

This may seem like a truism—a fact so self-evident as not to need statement. But much disquisition has been wasted and much confusion caused by the failure of economists to keep this in mind. Hence, to start from firm foundations, we must see clearly what is really meant by space and time. Here we come into the very heart of metaphysics, at a point where the teachings of what passes for the highest philosophy are most perplexed and perplexing.

In asking ourselves what we really mean by space and time, we must have a care, for there is a danger that the habitual use of words as instruments of thought may lead to the error of treating what they express as objects of thought, or things, when they really express not things, but only the qualities or relations of things. This is one of those sources of error which Bacon in his figurative classification called Idols of the Forum. Though a word is a thing, in the sense that its verbal form may be made an object of thought, yet all words are not things in the sense of representing to the mind what apart from mere verbal form may be made an object of thought. To clothe in a form of words which the eye and ear may distinguish from other words, yet which in their meaning involve contradictions, is not to make a thing, which in itself, and aside from that mere verbal form, can be thought of. To give a name to a form of words implying contradictions is to give name to what can be thought of only verbally, and which in any deeper sense than that is a negation—that is to say, a no thing, or nothing.

Yet this is the trick of much that to-day passes for the most profound philosophy, as it was the trick of Plato and of much that he put into the mouth of Socrates. To try it, make up a word signifying opposite qualities, such as "lowhigh" or "squareround," or a phrase without thinkable meaning, such as a "fourth dimension of space." In this it will be wisest to use a tongue which being foreign to the vernacular is suggestive of learning. Latin or Greek, has long been used for this purpose, but among English-speaking people German will now do as well if not better, and those who call themselves Theosophists have taken Sanskrit or what they take to be Sanskrit very satisfactorily. Now, if you have the external associations of superior penetration, and will persist for a while in seeming to treat your new word or phrase as if you were really making it an object of deep thought, you will soon have others persuading themselves to think that they also can think of it, until finally, if it get the scholastic vogue, the man frank enough to say that he can get no meaning from it will be put down as an ignorant fellow whose education has been neglected. This is really the same trick as standing on a street and gazing into the sky, as if you saw something unusual there, until a crowd gathers to look also. But it has made great reputations in philosophy.

Now, in truth, when we come to analyze our apprehensions of space and time, we see that they are conceptions, not of things in themselves existing, but of relations which things in themselves existing may hold to each other—space being a relation of extension or place between one thing and other things, such as far or near, hither or thither; and time being a relation of succession between one thing and other things, such as before or after, now and then. To think of space we must necessarily think of two points in place, and to make the relation of extension between them intelligible to our minds, we must also think of a third point which may serve as a measure of this relation. To think of time we must necessarily think of two points in appearance or disappearance, and to make this relation of sequence between them intelligible to our minds, we must also think of some third point which may serve as a measure of this relation.

Since space and time are thus not existences, but expressions of the relation to each other of things thought of as existing, we cannot conceive of their having beginning or ending, of their creation or annihilation, as apart from that of the things whose relation they express. Space being a relation of extension between things in place, and time a relation of succession between things in order of appearance or duration, the two words properly express relations which, like the relations of form and number with which mathematics deals in its two branches of geometry and arithmetic, are expressive of actual relation wherever the things they relate to have actual existence, and of potential relation wherever the things they relate to have merely potential existence. We cannot think of a when or where in which a whole was not equal to the sum of its parts, or will ever cease to be; or in which the lines and angles of a square were not, or can ever cease to be, equal to each other; or in which the three angles of a triangle were not, or can ever cease to be, equal to two right angles. Nor yet can we think of a when or where in which twice one did not make two, or can ever cease to do so; and twice two did not, or will ever cease to, make four. In the same way it is utterly impossible for us to think of a when or where in which space and time could begin or could end, as apart from the beginning or ending of the things whose relations to each other they express. To try to think of space and time without a presumption of things whose relations to each other are thus expressed, is to try to think of shadow without reference to substance. It is to try to think of a no thing, or nothing—a negation of thought.

This is perfectly clear to us when we attach an article to the noun and speak of "a space" or "the space," or of "a time" or "the time," for in such speech the relation of one thing or set of things to another thing or set of things is expressed by some such preposition as "from," "before," "after" or "when." But when the noun is used without the article, and men speak of space by itself and time by itself without any word of particularization or preposition of relation, the words have by the usage of our English tongue the meaning of all space or space in general, or all time or time in general. In this case the habit of regarding words as denoting things in themselves existing is apt to lead us to forget that space and time are but names for certain relations in which things stand to each other, and to come to regard them as things which in themselves, and apart from the things whose relationship they express, can become objects of thought. Thus, without analyzing the process, we come to accept in our minds the naked words as representing some sort of material existences—vaguely picturing space as a sort of atmosphere or ether, in which all things swim, and time an ever-flowing current which bears all things on.

From this mode of mental picturing we are apt to assume that both space and time must have had beginning, before which there was no space and no time; and must have limits, beyond which neither space nor time can be. But when we try to think of this beginning or of these limits, we think of something which for the moment we assume to be the first or farthest of existing things. Yet no matter how far we may carry this assumption, we at the same moment see that it may be carried further still. To think of anything as first, involves the possibility of thinking of something before that, to which our momentary first would become second. To think of an utmost star in the material universe, involves the possibility of thinking of another star yet further still.

Thus in the effort to grasp such material conceptions of time and space they inevitably elude us. From trying to think of what are only names for relations which things have to each other as if they were things in themselves, we come to a point not merely of confusion, but of negation—a conflict of absolutely opposing ideas resembling that brought about in the minds of the unwary by the schoolmen's question as to what would happen did an irresistible force meet an immovable body.

Now, this way of using the nouns space and time without an article, as though they mean things in themselves existing, has been much favored by the poets, whose use of words is necessarily metaphorical and loose. And it has been much favored by the teachers of religion, whose endeavor to embody spiritual truths tends to poetical expression, and who have been prone in all ages to make no distinction between the attribution to the higher power of what transcends our knowledge and of what is opposed to our reason—assuming the repugnance of human reason to accept the contradictions to which they give the name of mysteries to be proofs of its weakness.

Thus the habit of trying to think of space and time as things in themselves and not merely relations of things, has been embedded in religious literature, and in our most susceptible years we hear of beings who know not space or time, and of whens and wheres in which space and time are not. And as the child recoils from the impossible attempt to think of the unthinkable and strives in vain to picture a when or where in which space and time have not been, or shall cease to be, he is hushed into silence by being told that he is impiously trying to measure with the shallow plummet of human reason the infinite depths of the Divine Mind.

But the disposition of the theologians to find an insolvable mystery in the contradiction that follows the attempt to think of space and time not as relations but as independent existences, has been followed or perhaps anticipated by philosophers who in the use of meaningless words, as though to them they really conveyed coherent ideas, have assumed what has passed for superior penetration. They (or at least those of them who have looked down upon the theologians with contempt) have not, it is true, called the inevitable conflict in thought which arises when we try mentally to treat of what is really a relation as though it were in itself a thing, a divine mystery. But they have recognized this conflict as something inherent, not in confusion of words, but in the weakness of human reason—which human reason they themselves pretend to go behind and instruct.

Kant, whose ponderous incomprehensibility is a striking example of what (whether it was before him or because of him) seems to have become a peculiarly German facility for inventing words handy for philosophic juggling, dignified this point of assumed necessary conflict by calling it an "antinomy," which term suggesting in its derivation the idea of a conflict of laws, was employed by him to mean a self-contradiction or mutual destruction of unavoidable conclusions of the human reason; a what must be thought of, yet cannot be thought of. Thus the word antinomy in the scholastic philosophy that has followed Kant takes the place of the word mystery in the theological philosophy, as covering the idea of a necessary irreconcilability of human reason.

Kant, for instance, tells us that space and time are forms of human sensibility, which, as well as I can understand him, means that our mental nature imposes upon us the wearing of something like colored glasses, so that when *we* consider things they always seem to us to be in space and in time; but that this is merely their appearance to us, and that "things in themselves," that is, things as they really exist outside of our sensibility or apprehension of them, or as they would be apprehended by "pure reason" (*i.e.*, some reason outside of human reason), are not in space and time at all.

In a passage I have already quoted, the much more readable Schopenhauer speaks of the destruction of the capacity for thinking which results from the industrious study of a logomachy made up by monstrous piecings together of words which abolish and contradict one another. But of this very thing, Schopenhauer himself with all his strength and brilliancy is a notable example. His industrious study of Kant had evidently reduced him to that state of mind of which he speaks, where "hollow phrases count with it for thoughts." His whole philosophy is based on Kant's "Critique of Pure Reason," which he speaks of as "the most important phenomenon that has appeared in philosophy for two thousand years," and a thorough understanding of which he declares in the beginning and over and over again to be absolutely necessary to an understanding of his own works. Likening the effect of Kant's writings on the mind to which they truly speak to that of the operation for cataract on a blind man, he adds:

The aim of my own work may be described by saying that I have sought to put into the hands of those upon whom that operation has been successfully performed a pair of spectacles suitable to eyes that have recovered their sight—spectacles to whose use that operation is the absolutely necessary condition.

And through these spectacles of "The Fourfold Root of the Principle of Sufficient Reason" and the chief work to which that is preliminary, "The World as Will and Idea," Schopenhauer introduces us into what seems to natural reason like a sort of philosophic "Alice in Wonderland." If I can understand a man who seems to have a peculiar gift of lucid expression wherever it is applied to understandable things, and whose writings are illumined by many acute observations and sagacious reflections, this world in which I find myself and which from the outside is so immense, so varied, so wonderful, is from the inside, nothing but "I, myself"—my idea, my presentment, my will; and space and time are only in my seeming, appearances imposed upon me by the forms of my consciousness. I behold, for instance, a kitten, which by and by becomes a cat and has kittens of its own, and at the same time or at different times and places I see or remember to have seen many cats—tom-cats, pussy-cats, kitty-cats, black, white, gray, mottled and tortoise-shell cats, in different stages of age, from little cats whose eyes are not yet opened to decrepit cats that have lost their teeth. But in reality, on the inside of things as it were, there is only one cat, always existent without reference to time and space. This eternal cat is the idea of a cat, or cat idea, which is reflected in all sorts of guises in the kaleidoscopic facets of my apprehension. And as with cats, so with all things else in which this infinite and varied world presents itself to me —planets and suns, plants and trees, animals and men, matter and forces, phenomena and laws. All that I see, hear, touch, taste, smell or otherwise apprehend—all is mirage, presentment, delusion. It is all the baseless fabric of a vision, the self-imposed apprehensions of the evil dream, containing necessarily more pain than pleasure, in which what we call life essentially consists; yet which he who suffers in it cannot escape by suicide, since that only brings him into life again in other form and circumstance; but from which the truly wise man must seek relief by starving himself to death without wanting to die; or in other words by conquering "the will to live," the only road to the final goal of annihilation or Nirvana, to which all life ultimately tends.

And this philosophy of negation, this nineteenth-century Buddhism without the softening features of its Asiatic prototype, that makes us but rats in an everlasting trap, and substitutes for God an icy devil, is the outcome of the impression made upon a powerful and brilliant but morbid mind by "the industrious study of a logomachy made up by monstrous piecings together of words which abolish and contradict one another," that strives to turn human reason as it were inside out and consider in the light of what is dubbed "pure reason" the outside-in of things.

The fact is, that this seemingly destructive conflict of thought that theologians call a mystery and philosophers call an antinomy—and which there must be very many of my readers who like myself can remember puzzling over in childhood in questionings of what might be beyond the limits of space and time, and what was before God was, and what might be after space and time had ceased—is not in reality a failure of reason, but a confusion in the meaning of words. When we remember that by space and time we do not really mean things having existence but certain relations to each other of things that have existence, the mystery is solved and the antinomy disappears in the perception of a verbal confusion—a confusion of the same kind as perplexes those who try to think at once of an irresistible force and an immovable body, two terms which being mutually exclusive cannot together exist.

There is a riddle about what a boy said, sometimes given among young people playing conundrums, which if not heard before, is almost certain to make the whole party "give it up," after trying all sorts of impossible answers, since its true and only possible answer, "The boy lied," is so obvious that they do not think of it.

We may be wise to distrust our knowledge; and, unless we have tested them, to distrust what we may call our reasonings; but never to distrust reason itself.

Even when we speak of lunacy or madness or similar mental afflictions as the loss of reason, analysis I think will show that it is not reason itself that is lost, but that those powers of perception and recollection that belong to the physical structure of the mind have become weakened or broken or dislocated, so that the things with which the reason deals are presented to it imperfectly or in wrong place or relation.

In testing for glasses an optician will put on you lenses through which you will see the flame of a candle above or below or right or left of its true position, or as two where there is only one. It is so with mental diseases.

And that the powers with which the human reason must work are limited and are subject to faults and failures, our reason itself teaches us as soon as it begins to examine what we find around us and to endeavor to look in upon our own consciousness. But human reason is the only reason that men can have, and to assume that in so far as it can see clearly it does not see truly, is in the man who does it not only to assume the possession of a superior to human reason, but it is to deny the validity of all thought and to reduce the mental world to chaos. As compared with the eternal reason which is manifested in the relations which we call laws of nature our human reason is clearly shallow and narrow; but that it is a perception and recognition of this eternal reason is perhaps the deepest fact of our certainty. Not as yet dreaming that this earth which seems to our first perceptions to be so firmly fixed could be in constant motion, men did not for a long time perceive what a closer and wider use of reason now shows to be the case, that the earth revolves around the sun, not the sun around the earth, and spoke with literal meaning of sunrise and sunset. But as to the phenomena of day and night, and as to the proximate cause of these phenomena being in the relations of sun and earth towards each other, they were not deceived.

As for the philosophers since Kant or before him who profess to treat space and time as mere conditions of human perception, mental glasses, as it were, that compel us to recognize relations that do not in truth exist, they are mere jugglers with words, giving names such as "the absolute," "the unconditioned," "the unknowable" to what cannot be thought of, and then proceeding to treat them as things, and to reason with them and from them.

CHAPTER VI.

CONFUSION OF THE SPACIAL LAW WITH AGRICULTURE.

SHOWING THE GENESIS OF THIS CONFUSION.

What space is — The place to which man is confined — Extension a part of the concept "land"—Perception is by contrast—Man's first use of land is by the mode of "adapting"—His second, and for a long time most important, use is by "growing"—The third, on which civilization is now entering, is "exchanging"—Political economy began in the second, and "growing" still attracts most attention—The truth and error of the Physiocrats—The successors of Smith, while avoiding the error of the Physiocrats, also ignored their truth; and with their acceptance of the Malthusian theory, and Ricardo's explanation of rent as relating to agricultural land, they fell into, and have continued the habit of treating land and rent as agricultural—Difficulty of the single tax in the United States.

THE laws of our physical being, to which I have already called attention (Book I., Chapter II.), confine us within narrow limits to that part of the superficies of our sphere where the ocean of air enveloping it meets the solid surface. We may venture temporarily a little below the solid surface, in caves and vaults and shafts and tunnels; and a little above it, on trees, or towers, or in balloons or aërial machines, if such be yet constructed; but with these temporary aërial extensions of our habitat, which of themselves require not only a preliminary but a recurring use of the solid surface of the earth, it is to that solid surface that our material existence and material production are confined. Physically we are air-breathing, light-requiring land animals, who for our existence and all our production require place on the dry surface of our globe. And the fundamental perception of the concept land—whether in the wider use of the word as that term of political economy signifying all that external nature offers to the use of man, or in the narrower sense which the word usually bears in common speech, where it signifies the solid surface of the earth—is that of extension; that of affording standing-place or room.

But a fundamental perception is not always a first perception. Weight is a fundamental perception of air. But we realize this only by the exertion of reason, and long generations of men have lived, feeling the weight of air on every part of their bodies during every second of their lives from birth to death, without ever realizing that air has weight. Perception is by contrast. What we always perceive neither attracts attention nor excites memory until brought into contrast with non-perception.

Even in the now short Atlantic trip the passenger becomes so accustomed to the constant throb of the engines as not to notice it, but is aroused by the silence when it stops. The visitor in a nail-mill is so deafened that speech seems impossible; but the men working there are said to talk to each other without difficulty and to find conversation hard when they get again into the comparative silence of the street. In later years, I have at times "supped with Lucullus," without recalling what he gave me to eat, whereas I remember to this day the ham and eggs of my first breakfast on a canal-packet drawn by horses that actually trotted; how sweet hard-tack, munched in the middle watch while the sails slept in the trade-wind, has tasted; what a dish for a prince was sea-pie on the rare occasions when a pig had been killed or a porpoise harpooned; and how good was the plum-duff that came to the forecastle only on Sundays and great holidays. I remember as though it were an hour ago, that talking to myself rather than to him, I said to a Yorkshire sailor on my first voyage, "I wish I were home, to get a piece of pie." I recall his expression and tone, for they shamed me, as he quietly said, "Are you sure you would find a piece of pie there?" Thoughtless as the French princess who asked why the people who were crying for bread did not try cake, "Home" was associated in my mind with pie of some sort—apple or peach or sweet potato or cranberry or mince—to be had for the taking, and I did not for the moment realize that in many homes pie was as rare a luxury as plums in our sea-duff.

Thus, while the fundamental quality of land is that of furnishing to men place on which they may stand or move, or rest things on, this is not the quality first noticed. As settlers in a wooded country, where every foot of land must be cleared for use, come to regard trees as a nuisance to be got rid of, rather than as the source of value that in the progress of civilization they afterwards become, so in that rude stage of social development which we are accustomed to think of as the primary condition of mankind, where the mode of expending labor in production which most attracts attention is that we have called "adapting," land would be esteemed rich or poor according to its capacity of yielding to labor expended in this first mode, the fruits of the chase.

In the next higher stage of social development, in which that second mode of production, which we have called "growing," begins to assume most importance in social life, that quality of land which generally and strongly attracts attention is that which makes it useful in agriculture, and land would be esteemed rich or poor according to its capacity for yielding to labor expended in the breeding of animals and raising of crops.

But in the still higher stage of social development which what we now call the civilized world is entering, attention begins to be largely given to the third mode of production, which we have called "exchanging," and land comes to be considered rich or poor according to its capacity of yielding to labor expended in trading. This is already the case in our great cities, where enormous value attaches to land, not because of its capacity to provide wild animals to the hunter, nor yet because of its capacity to yield rich crops to the grower, but because of its proximity to centers of exchange.

That the development of our modern economy began in what was still mainly the second stage of social development, when the use of land was usually regarded from the agricultural point of view, is it seems to me, the explanation of an otherwise curious way of thinking about land that has pervaded economic literature since the time of the Physiocrats, and that still continues to pervade the scholastic political economy—a way of thinking that leads economic writers to treat land as though it were merely a place or substance on which vegetables and grain may be grown and cattle bred.

The followers of Quesnay saw that there is in the aggregate production of wealth in civilization an unearned increment—an element which cannot be attributed to the earnings of labor or capital—and they gave to this increment of wealth, unearned so far as individuals are concerned, the name of product net or surplus product. They rightly traced this unearned or surplus product to land, seeing that it constituted to the owners of land an income or return which remained to them after all expenditure of labor and investment of capital in production had been paid for. But they fell into error in assuming that what was indeed in their time and place the most striking and prominent use of land in production, that of agriculture, was its only use. And finding in agriculture, which falls into that second mode of production I have denominated "growing," the use of a power of nature, the germinative principle, essentially different from the powers utilized in that first mode of production I have denominated "adapting," they, without looking further, jumped to the conclusion that the unearned increment of wealth or *surplus net* sprang from the utilization of this principle. Hence they deemed agriculture the only productive occupation, and insisted in spite of the absurdity of it that manufactures and commerce added nothing to the sum of wealth above what they took from it, and that the agriculturist or cultivator was the only real producer.

This weakness in the thinking of the Physiocrats and the erroneous terminology that it led them to use, finally discredited their true apprehensions and noble teachings, unpalatable as they necessarily were to the powerful interests who seemingly profit by social injustice, until the rise with the publication of "Progress and Poverty" of the new Physiocrats, the modern Single Taxers as they now call themselves and are being called.

But the economists who succeeded Adam Smith, while they avoided the error into which the Physiocrats had fallen, avoided as well the great truth of which this had been an erroneous apprehension, and greedily accepting the excuse which the Malthusian theory offered for putting upon the laws of God the responsibility for the misery and vice that flow from poverty, they fell into and have continued the habit of regarding land solely from the agricultural point of view, thus converting what is really the spacial law of all production into an alleged law of diminishing production in agriculture. Even Ricardo, who truly though very narrowly explained the law of rent, shows in all his arguments and illustrations an inability to free himself from thinking of land as relating only to agriculture, and of rent only as agricultural rent. And although in England the relative importance of agriculture has during all this century steadily and rapidly declined, the habit of thinking of land as a place or substance for agricultural operations is still kept up. Not merely is the law of diminishing production in agriculture still taught as a special law of nature in the latest works treated as authoritative in colleges and universities, but in speaking of land and of rent, most English writers will be found to have really in mind agricultural land or agricultural rent.

What is true of England is true of the United States except so far as the influence of the single tax has been felt. But the greatest difficulty which the single tax propaganda meets in the United States is the wide-spread idea, sedulously fostered by those who should know better, that non-agricultural workers have no interest in the land question and that concentrating taxes on land values means increasing the taxes of farmers. To fostering this fallacy all the efforts of the accredited organs of education are directed.

CHAPTER VII.

THE RELATION OF SPACE IN PRODUCTION.

SHOWING THAT SPACE HAS RELATION TO ALL MODES OF PRODUCTION.

Matter being material, space must have relation to all production—This relation readily seen in agriculture—The concentration of labor in agriculture tends up to a certain point to increase and then to diminish production—But it is a misapprehension to attribute this law to agriculture or to the mode of "growing"—It holds in all modes and sub-divisions of these modes—Instances: of the production of brick, of the mere storage of brick—Man himself requires space—The division of labor as requiring space—Intensive and extensive use of land.

PRODUCTION in political economy means the production of wealth. Wealth, as we have seen, consists in material substances so modified by human labor as to fit them for the satisfaction of human desires. Space, therefore, which has relation to all matter, must have relation to all production.

This relation of space to all production may be readily seen in agriculture, which is included in that mode of production we have called "growing." In this, the concentration of labor in space tends up to a certain point to increase the productiveness of labor; but the point of greatest productiveness attained, any further concentration of labor would tend to decrease productiveness. Thus, if a Robinson Crusoe, having a whole island on which to expend his labor, were to plant potatoes, each cutting a hundred yards apart from every other cutting, he would necessarily waste so much labor in planting, cultivating and gathering the crop that the return compared with his exertion would be very small. He would get a much larger return were he to concentrate his labor by planting his potatoes closer; and this increase would continue as he continued to exert his labor in lesser space, until his plants became too crowded, and the growth of one would lessen or prevent that of another. While if he continued the experiment so far as to put all his cuttings in one spot he would get no greater return than he might have had from the planting of one, and perhaps no return at all.

This spacial law of production holds good of course in labor exerted conjointly, as in labor exerted individually. On a given area, the application of labor to the growth of a crop or the breeding of animals may sometimes be increased with advantage, the exertion of two men producing more than twice as much as the exertion of one man; that of four men, more than twice as much as the exertion of two; and so on. But this increase of production with increased application of labor to any given area cannot go on indefinitely. A point is reached at which the further application of labor in the given area, though it may for a time result in a greater aggregate production, yields a less proportionate production, and finally a point is reached where the further application of labor ceases even to increase the aggregate result.

It is misapprehended appreciation of this law in so far as it applies to agricultural production, which has led to the formulation and maintenance in economic teaching of what is called "the law of diminishing productiveness in agriculture." But the law is not peculiar to agriculture nor to the second mode of production which I have called "growing." It is true that this mode of production consists in the utilization in aid of labor of the power of reproduction which characterizes life, and that living things in their growth and expansion require more space than things destitute of life. The plants that we grow require space below the surface of the ground in which to expand their roots and drink in certain constituents, and space above the surface in which to expand their leaves and drink in air and light. And the animals that we breed require space for their necessary movements. But though the spacial requirements of living things may be relatively greater than those of things not living, they are no less absolute in the one case than in the other. That two material things cannot exist in the same space is no more true of brutes than of beets, nor of beets than of bricks.

In every form or sub-division of its three modes the exertion of human labor in the production of wealth requires space; not merely standing or resting space, but moving space—space for the movements of the human body and its organs, space for the storage and changing in place of materials and tools and products. This is as true of the tailor, the carpenter, the machinist, the merchant or the clerk, as of the farmer or stock-grower, or of the fisherman or miner. One occupation may require more elbow-room or tool-room or storage-room than another, but they all alike require space, and so must come to a point where any gain from concentrating labor in space ceases, and further concentration results in a proportionate lessening of product, and finally in an absolute decline. The same law, first of increasing and then of diminishing returns, from the concentration of labor in space, which the first exponents of the doctrine of diminishing returns in agriculture say is peculiar to that occupation, and its latter exponents say obtains in agriculture, and in the extraction of limited natural agents, such as coal, shows itself in all modes of production, and must continue to do so, even did we discover some means of producing wealth by solidifying atmospheric air or an all-pervading ether, which some modern scientists suppose. For this alleged "law of diminishing returns in agriculture" is nothing more nor less than the spacial law of material existence, the reversal or denial of which is absolutely unthinkable.

To see this, let us take a form of production widely differing from that of agriculture—the production of brick. Brick is usually made from clay, but can be made from other inorganic substances, such as shale, coal-dust, marble-dust, slag, etc., and no part of its production involves any use of the principle of increase that characterizes life. Nor can any of the substances used in brickmaking be considered as limited natural substances or agents by any classification that would not destroy the distinction by including the whole earth itself as a limited natural agent. The production of brick is clearly one of the forms of production which those who uphold the doctrine of "diminishing returns in agriculture," or in its extension to the doctrine of "diminishing returns in the use of limited natural agents," would consider a form of production that can be continued indefinitely by the increased application of labor without diminishing returns.

Yet we have only to think of it to see that what is called the law of diminishing returns in agriculture applies to the making of brick as fully as to the growing of beets. A single man engaged in making a thousand bricks would greatly waste labor if he were to diffuse his exertions over a square mile or a square acre, digging and burning the clay for one brick here, and for another some distance apart. His exertion would yield a much larger return if more closely concentrated in space. But there is a point in this concentration in space where the increase of exertion will begin to diminish its proportionate yield.

In the same superficial area required for the production of one brick, two bricks may be produced to advantage. But this concentration of labor in space cannot be continued indefinitely without diminishing the return and finally bringing production to a stop. To get the clay for a thousand bricks without use of more surface of the earth than is required to get the clay for one brick, would involve, even if it were possible at all, an enormous loss in the productiveness of the labor. And so if an attempt were made to put a thousand men to work in making brick on an area in which two men might work with advantage, the result would be not merely that the exertion of the thousand men could not produce five hundred times as much as the exertion of two men, but that it would produce nothing at all. Men so crowded would prevent each other from working.

Or let us take that part of the production of bricks that of all parts requires least space—that which consists merely in the storage of bricks after they are made, so as to have them in readiness when required.

Two bricks must occupy twice as much cubical space as one brick. But if placed one on top of the other, the two require for resting-place no more superficial area than the one; while, as it requires on the part of a man of ordinary powers practically no more exertion to lay down or take up two bricks on the same surface than to lay down or take up one, there would be a greater gain in the productiveness of labor so applied to the storage of brick than if applied to the storing of brick side by side on the surface of the ground. But this economy in the storage of brick could not be continued indefinitely. Though two bricks may be rested one on top of the other without any more use of superficial area than is required for the resting of one brick, this is not true of a thousand bricks, nor even of a hundred. Much less than a hundred bricks so placed as to rest upon the superficies required for the resting of one brick would become so unstable as to fall with the slightest jar or breeze. Before ten or even half a dozen bricks had been rested one on top of another it would become evident that any further extension of the perpendicular would require a further extension of base. And even with such extension of base as would permit of perpendicular solidity, a point would finally be reached where, even if the surface continued solid, the weight of the upper bricks would crush the lower bricks to powder. Thus it is no more possible indefinitely to store bricks on a given area than on a given area indefinitely to grow beets.

Up to a point, moreover, which is about waist-high for an ordinary man, it requires less exertion to place or take from place the last brick than the first brick, or in other words, labor at this point is more productive. But this point of greatest productiveness reached, the productiveness of labor begins to decline with the further application of labor on the same area, until the point of no return or non-productiveness is reached. The reaching of this point of no return to the further application of labor in the storing of bricks on a given area may be delayed by the invention and use of such labor-saving devices as the wheelbarrow and steam-engine, but it cannot be prevented. There is a point in the application of labor to the storage of bricks on any given area, whether a square foot or a square mile, where the application of successive "doses of labor" (to use the phrase of the writers who have most elaborately dwelt on this assumed "law of diminishing productiveness in agriculture") must cease to yield proportionate returns, and finally where they must cease to yield any return.

Thus the law of diminishing returns which has been held as peculiar to agriculture is as fully shown in the mere storage of bricks as it is in the growing of crops or the breeding of animals. It is quite as true that all the bricks now needed in the three kingdoms could not be stored on a single square yard, as it is that all the food needed in the three kingdoms could not be grown on a single acre. The point of greatest efficiency or maximum productiveness in the application of labor to land exists in all modes and all forms of production. It results in fact from nothing more nor less than the universal law or condition that all material existence, and consequently all production of wealth, requires space.

Nor has the spacial requirement of production merely regard to the material object of production; it has regard as well to the producer—to labor itself. Man himself is a material being requiring space for his existence even when in the most passive condition, and still more space for the movements necessary to the continuous maintenance of life and the exertion of his powers in the production of wealth. For an hour or two men may, as in listening to a speech or looking at a spectacle, remain crowded together in a space which gives them little more than standing-room. But to bring a few more into such a crowd would mean illness, death, panic. Nor in such narrow space as men may for a while safely stand, could life be maintained for twenty-four hours, still less any mode of producing wealth be carried on.

The division of labor permits the concentration of workers whose particular parts in production require comparatively little space, and by building houses one story above another in our cities we economize superficial area in furnishing dwelling and working places in much the same way as by storing bricks one upon another. Improvements in the manufacture of steel and in the utilization of steam and electricity have much increased the height to which such structures can be carried, and we already have in our large American cities buildings of over twenty stories in which production of some sort is carried on. But though the requirement of superficial area may thus be pressed back a little by making use of cubical area (and in the tallest buildings of New York and Chicago rent is estimated in cubic not in square feet) this is only possible to a slight degree. The intensive use of land shown in the twenty-story building is in fact made possible by the extensive use of land brought about by improvements in transportation, and every one of these monstrous buildings erected lessens the availability of adjoining land for similar purposes.

CHAPTER VIII.

THE RELATION OF TIME IN PRODUCTION.

SHOWING THAT ALL MODES OF PRODUCTION HAVE RELATION TO TIME.

Difference between apprehensions of space and time, the one objective, the other subjective—Of spirits and of creation—All production requires time—The concentration of labor in time.

AS space is the relation of things in extension, so time is the relation of things in sequence.

But time, the relation of sequence, seems when we think of it, to be, so to speak, wider than space, the relation of extension. That is to say, space is a quality or affection of what we call matter; and while we conceive of immaterial things which having no extension have no relation in space, we cannot conceive of even immaterial things as having no relation in sequence.

Our apprehension of space is through our senses, the direct impressions of which are uncertain and misleading, but which we habitually verify and correct and give some sort of exactness to, through other impressions of our senses. Our first and simplest measure of space is in the impression of relative distance produced through the sight, or in the feeling of exertion required to move ourselves or some other object from point to point, as by paces or stone's throw or bow-shot; and these give way to more exact measurements, such as by lines, inches, feet, miles, diameters of the earth or of the earth's orbit. Deprived of the senses, which make us cognizant of matter, it is impossible to see how we could have any impression or idea of space.

Our impression of time, however, is not primarily through our senses. Though we correct and verify and give some exactness to it through them, there is a purely subjective apprehension of time in our own mental impressions or thoughts, which do not come all at once, but precede or succeed one another, having to each other a relation of sequence. It is through this succession of mental impressions that we are in the first place and directly conscious of time. But while our direct consciousness of space must vary widely, our direct impressions of time are more variable still, since they depend upon the rapidity and intensity of mental impressions. We may seem to have lived through years in the intense activity of a vivid dream, and to be utterly unconscious of the passage of time in a sound sleep. And while we can conceive the impression of space to be very different on the part of a sloth and that of a greyhound, it may be that the brief day of an animalcule may seem as long to it as does a century of life to the larger elephant.

But the reason of man enables him to obtain more exact measures of sequence from the uniformities of natural phenomena, such as days or years, moons or seasons, and from the regularity of mechanical movement as by sand-glasses or dials, or by clocks or watches.

Time seems indeed to be necessary to and in some degree coincident with all perceptions of space. But space does not seem necessary to time. That is to say, we seem to be able to imagine an immaterial being, or pure intelligence, not limited by or having necessary consciousness of relations of extension, and this is the way in which we usually think of unembodied spirits, such as angels or devils; and of disembodied spirits, such as ghosts. But we cannot really think thus of them with regard to relations of sequence. We can indeed think of them as knowing nothing and regarding nothing of our measures of time—of a day being to them as a thousand years, or a thousand years as a day, for that these measures are only relative we can see for ourselves. But we can also see that in the realm of spirit there is and must be the same relation of preceding and succeeding, of coming before and coming after, as in the realm of matter; and that this relation of sequence or time is really clearer and closer to that in us which we must think of as our immaterial part than is that of extension or space to our physical parts.

We usually think of creation, the bringing into existence by a power superior to and anterior to that of man, as taking place at once as by the Divine fiat: "God said, Let there be light: and there was light." But it would seem on analysis, that in this way of thinking we are considering rather the mental action which we conceive of as in itself immaterial—which our experience so far as it goes, and our reason so far as it can reach, teach us must lie back of all material expression—than of the material expression itself. All speculations and theories of the origin of the cosmos, all religions which are their popular expression, conceive of the appearance of material phenomena as in order or sequence, and consequently in time. Save in its childlike measurement of time by days, the ancient Hebrew account of the genesis of the material world recognizes this necessary order or sequence as fully as do modern scientists, for whose almost as vague measurements millenniums are too short. And so far as we can see, thought itself is in sequence and requires time, and its continued exertion brings about weariness. It, at any rate, seems to me that if we consider the essential and not merely the crude expression of the Hebrew scripture that in six days God created the heavens and the earth and rested on the seventh, it may embody a deep truth—the truth that exertion, mental as physical, requires a season of rest.

But, all such speculations aside, it is certain that all production of wealth takes place in sequence and requires time. The tree must be felled before it can be hewn or sawed into lumber; lumber must be seasoned before it can be used in building or wrought into the manifold articles made of wood. Ore must be taken from the vein before it can be smelted into iron, or from that form turned into steel or any of the manifold articles which by subsequent processes are made from iron or steel. Seeds must be planted before they can germinate; there must be a considerable interval of time before the young shoots can show themselves above the ground; then a longer interval before they can grow and ripen and produce after their order; grain must be harvested and ground before it can be converted into meal or flour or changed by labor from that form into other forms which gratify desire, all of which, like fermenting and baking, require time. So, in exchanging, time is required even for the concurrence and expression of human wills which result in the agreement to exchange, and still more time for the actual transference of things which completes the exchange. In short, time is a necessary element or condition in all exertion of labor in production.

Now, from this necessary element or condition of all production, time, there result consequences similar to those which result from the necessary element or condition of all production, space. That is to say, there is a law governing and limiting the concentration of labor in time, as there is a law governing and limiting the concentration of labor in space. Thus there is in all forms of production a point at which the concentration of labor in time gives the largest proportionate result; after which the further concentration of labor in time tends to a diminution of proportionate result, and finally to prevent result.

Thus there is a certain degree of concentration of labor in time (intensity of exertion), by which the individual can in any productive occupation accomplish on the whole the largest result. But if a man work harder than this, endeavoring to concentrate more exertion in a shorter time, it will be to the relative and finally to the absolute loss of productiveness—a principle which gives its point to the fable of the hare and the tortoise.

And so, if I go to a builder and say to him, "In what time and at what price will you build me such and such a house?" he would, after thinking, name a time, and a price based on it. This specification of time would be essential, and would involve a certain concentration of labor in time as the point of largest return or least cost. This I would soon find if, not quarreling with the price, I ask him largely to lessen the time. If I be a man like Beckford—the author of "Vathek," for whom Fonthill was built by relays of workmen, who lighted up the night with huge fires—a man to whom cost is nothing and time everything, I might get the builder somewhat to reduce the time in which he would agree, under bond, to build the house; but only by greatly increasing the price, until finally a point would be reached where he would not consent to build the house in less time no matter at what price. He would say: "Although I get bricks already made, and boards already planed, and stairs and doors, and sashes and blinds, and whatever else may be obtained from the mill, and no matter how many men I put on and how much I disregard economy, the building of a house requires time. Cellar cannot be dug and foundations raised, and walls built and floors laid, and roof put on, and partitioning and plastering, and plumbing, and painting and papering be done all at once, but only one after another, and at the cost of time as well as labor. The thing is impossible."

And so, although the concentration of labor in agriculture may with decreasing efficiency hasten beyond the normal point the maturity of vegetables or fruit or even of animals, yet the point of absolute non-productiveness of further applications of labor is soon reached, and no amount of human exertion applied in any way we have yet discovered could bring wheat from the seed to the ear, or the chick from the egg to the laying hen, in a week.

The importance in political economy of this principle that all production of wealth requires time as well as labor we shall see later on; but the principle that time is a necessary element in all production we must take into account from the very first.

CHAPTER IX.

COÖPERATION—ITS TWO WAYS.

SHOWING THE TWO WAYS OF COÖPERATION.

Coöperation is the union of individual powers in the attainment of common ends—Its ways and their analogues: (1) the combination of effort; (2) the separation of effort—Illustrations: of building houses, of joint-stock companies, etc.—Of sailing a boat—The principle shown in naval architecture—The Erie Canal—The baking of bread—Production requires conscious thought—The same principle in mental effort—What is on the one side separation is on the other concentration—Extent of concentration and specialization of work in modern civilization—The principle of the machine—Beginning and increase of division of labor—Adam Smith's three heads—A better analysis.

COÖPERATION means joint action; the union of efforts to a common end. In recent economic writings the word has been so much used in a narrower sense that its meaning in political economy is given in the latest American dictionary (the Standard) as "a union of laborers or small capitalists for the purpose of advantageously manufacturing, buying and selling goods, and of pursuing other modes of mutual benefit; also, loosely, profit-sharing."

This is a degradation of a word that ought not to be acquiesced in, either in the interests of the English language or in the interests of political economy, and at the risk of being misunderstood by those who have become accustomed to associate it with trivial schemes of profit-sharing or namby-pamby "reconciliations" of capital and labor, I shall use it as an economic term in its full meaning—understanding by coöperation that union of individual powers in the attainment of common ends which, as already said (Book I., Chapter V.), is the means whereby the enormous increase of man's power that characterizes civilization is secured.

All increase in the productive power of man over that with which nature endows the individual comes from the coöperation of individuals. But there are two ways in which this coöperation may take place.

1. By the combination of effort. In this way, individuals may accomplish what exceeds the full power of the individual.

2. By the separation of effort. In this way, the individual may accomplish for more than one what does not require the full power of the individual.

This first way of coöperation may be styled the combination of labor, though perhaps the most distinctive term that could be used for it would be, the multiplication of labor, since the second way is well known by the term Adam Smith adopted for it, "the division of labor."

The one, the combination of labor, is analogous to the application in mechanics of that principle of the lever by which larger masses are moved in shorter distance or longer time, as in the crowbar. The other, the division of labor, is analogous to the application of that principle of the lever by which smaller masses are moved in longer distance or shorter time, as in the oar.

To illustrate: The first way of coöperation, the combination of labor, enables a number of men to remove a rock or to raise a log that would be too heavy for them separately. In this way men conjoin themselves, as it were, into one stronger man.

Or to take an example so common in the early days of American settlement that "log-rolling" has become a term for legislative combination: Tom, Dick, Harry and Jim are building near each other their rude houses in the clearings. Each hews his own trees, but the logs are too heavy for one man to get into place. So the four unite their efforts, first rolling one man's logs into place and then another's, until the logs of all four having been placed, the result is the same as if each had been enabled to concentrate into one time the force he could exert in four different times. Examples of the same principle in a more elaborate state of society are to be found in the formation of joint-stock companies—the union of many small capitals to accomplish works such as the building of railroads, the construction of steamships, the erection of factories, etc., which require greater capitals than are possessed by one man.

But while great advantages result from the ability of individuals, by the combination of labor, to concentrate themselves as it were into one larger man, there are other times and other things in which an individual could accomplish more if he could divide himself, as it were, into a number of smaller men.

Thus in sailing a boat, one man of extraordinary strength would be equal to two men of half his strength only in such exertions as rowing, hoisting the heavier sails, or the like. In other things, two men of ordinary strength would be able to do far more than the one man of double strength, since where he would have to stop one thing to do another, they could do both things at once. Thus while he would have to anchor in order to rest, they could move on without stopping, one sailing the boat while the other slept. There was a King Alphonso of Castile, celebrated by Emerson, who wished that men could be concentrated nine into one. But the loss of available power that would thus result would soon be seen. How often now when beset by calls or duties which require, not so much strength as time, does the thought occur, "I wish I could divide myself into half a dozen." What the division of labor does, is to permit men, as it were, so to divide themselves, thus enormously increasing their total effectiveness.

To illustrate from the example used before: While at times Tom, Dick, Harry and Jim might each wish to move logs, at other times they might each need to get something from a village distant two days' journey. To satisfy this need individually would thus require two days' effort on the part of each. But if Tom alone goes, performing the errands for all, and the others each do half a day's work for him, the result is that all get at the expense of half a day's effort on the part of each what otherwise would have required two days' effort.

It is in this manner that the second way of coöperation, the separation of effort, or to continue the term adopted by Adam Smith and sanctioned by long usage, the division of labor, saves labor; that is to say, permits the accomplishment of equal results with less exertion, or of larger results with equal exertion. But out of this primary saving of exertion arise other savings of exertion.

Let me illustrate from a domain outside of political economy the general principle from which these gains proceed. Nothing, perhaps, better shows the flexibility of the human mind than naval architecture. Yet, from the rude canoe to the monster ironclad, in all the endless variety of form that men have given to vessels intended to be propelled through the water, one principle always obtains. We always make such vessels longer than they are broad. Why is it that we do so? It is that a vessel moving through the water has two main points of resistance to overcome—(1) the displacement of the water at her bow, the resistance to which is shown by the ripple or wave that arises there, and (2) the replacement of the water at her stern, the resistance to which is shown by the suction or wake or "dead water" that she drags after her. In addition she must also overcome skin friction, shown, if one looks over the side of a vessel moving in smooth water, by the thin line of "dead water" or small ripples at her sides. But this, area for area, is slight as compared with the force required for displacement and replacement.

When the Erie Canal was first built its locks were constructed to accommodate boats of a certain length. The enlargement of these locks so as to admit boats of double that length is now going on, but is not yet entirely completed, so that to pass through the entire canal, boats of the shorter length must still be used. Each of these boats is usually pulled by two horses or mules. But whoever passes over the railroads that parallel this great waterway will notice that for much of the distance the boats are now run in pairs, the bow of one boat being fastened to the stern of its predecessor, and that instead of four horses for the two boats only three are used. What makes this economy possible is that the displacement for the two boats is mainly borne by the first boat, and the replacement for the two is mainly borne by the second boat. As the additional force required to move two boats instead of one is thus not much more than the additional skin friction, three animals suffice instead of four. If the boats were so constructed as to fit closely together the economy would be still greater.

Now, what we do in building a vessel is virtually to place one cross-section behind another cross-section so that the whole may be moved with no more resistance of displacement and replacement than would be required to move any one cross-section. The principle is the same as that which would prompt us if we had to carry two bodies through a wall, to carry the second through the hole that it would be necessary to make for the first, instead of making another hole. In addition to this the increase of length without increase of width which results virtually from the placing of the cross-sections behind each other, permits the graduation or sharpening of entrance and egress, thus allowing displacement and replacement to be effected in longer times or more gradually, and with lessened resistance; although the fact that resisting surface does not increase proportionately to increase in cubical capacity, enables the large vessel to outstrip the small vessel with the same proportionate expenditure of power, even if built on the same lines.

Now these principles, or rather this principle, for at bottom they are one, have their analogues in our making of things. Just as ten thousand tons can be transported in one vessel at much greater speed or with much less expenditure of power than in ten thousand vessels of one ton each, so can production be facilitated and economized by doing together things of like kind that are to be done.

Take for instance the baking of bread. To bake a loaf of bread requires the application of a certain amount of heat for a certain time to a certain amount of dough. To heat an oven to this point requires a certain expenditure of fuel; to maintain it for this time a certain other expenditure of fuel; and a certain expenditure of fuel is lost in the cooling of the oven after the bread is baked. To bake one loaf of bread in an ordinary oven thus requires a much greater relative expenditure of fuel than is required to bake at one time as many loaves as the oven will hold; and a larger oven will bake more loaves with a proportionately less expenditure of fuel than a smaller one, since the loss of heat that escapes from the work of baking is relatively less; and if one batch of bread is succeeded by another batch without suffering the oven to cool, another great relative saving is made. So that the concentration of the work of baking bread effects a great saving of labor in the item of fuel alone. And it is so with other items.

The saving thus made by the concentration of work arises not only from physical laws but from mental laws as well. All our doing or accomplishing of things, except those that may be referred to instinct, require in the first place the exertion of conscious thought. We see this in the child as it learns to walk, to talk, to read and write. We see this as adults when we begin to do things new to us, as to speak a foreign tongue, to write shorthand, or use a typewriter or a bicycle. But as we do the same things again and again, the mental exertion becomes less and less, until we come to do them automatically and without consciously thinking of how we do them.

Now the result of what regarded from the standpoint of the whole or industrial organism is the separation of effort or division of labor in the production of wealth, is that the individual does fewer things but does them oftener. It is thus from the standpoint of the individual the concentration of effort or of labor, and so from the standpoint of the things to be done it involves a similar concentration in place and time, thus securing the saving of effort or increased efficiency of exertion which, to recur to our illustration, comes from doing one thing behind another and on a large instead of on a small scale.

Thus, when instead of each individual or each family endeavoring to hunt, fish, obtain vegetables, build habitations and make clothing or tools, for the satisfaction of their own needs, some devote themselves to doing one thing and some to doing another of the things required for the satisfaction of the general needs, what is the separation of function from the standpoint of the all or industrial whole is the concentration of function in its units, and special trades and vocations are developed.

And as the social organism grows by increase in numbers or the widening of the circle of exchanges, or both, this differentiation of function between its units tends constantly to increase, augmenting the efficiency of the productive powers of man to a degree to which we can assign no limits, and of which the marvelous increase in productive power which so strikingly characterizes our modern civilization affords but a faint forecast.

In civilized society where the division of labor has been carried to great lengths, we are so used to it that it is hard to realize how much we owe to it, and how utterly different our life would be without it. But as one tries to think to what we should be reduced without division of labor, he will see how large is the part it plays in the production of wealth—so large, indeed, that without it man as we know him could not exist. Take for instance the providing of clothing. If each one had to make his own clothing from the raw material, he could get nothing better than leaves or skins. Even with all the advantages which the division of labor gives in the making of cloth, of needles, thread, buttons, etc., let any one unused to it set himself to the making of a garment. He will soon realize how hard it is to make the first one; how much easier and better the second is made than the first, the third than the second, and so on, until the process ceases to require thought and becomes automatic. When by means of the division of labor, the making of clothing is so far concentrated that the clothing for some dozens or scores of men can be made together, then individuals can devote themselves solely to the making of clothes, with greatly increased economy. As the concentration of clothes-making proceeds further, and the making of clothes for hundreds, thousands, tens of thousands, and even hundreds of thousands of individuals is by the development of the ready-made clothing industry brought together, greater and greater economies become possible. Separate individuals devote themselves to the making of particular garments, and then to the making of particular parts or to particular processes. Instead of one tailor cutting out a garment with a pair of shears and then proceeding to make it in all its parts, cutters who do nothing else cut out scores of garments at once with great knives; the operations of basting, lining, buttonholing, etc., are performed by different people who devote themselves to doing these things alone, and whose work is aided by powerful machines, the use of which becomes possible with the larger scale and greater continuity of employment this concentration permits.

It is this concentration and specialization of work, with the division of labor, that brings about the development of labor-saving machinery of all kinds. The essential quality of the machine is its adaptation for the doing of certain special things. The human body considered as a machine is of all machines that which is best adapted for the doing of the greatest variety of things. But for doing only one thing, for the increase of quantity at the expense of variety, man is able to make machines which within a narrow range are far superior to the tools nature gives him. And the same principle governs the employment of forces other than the force he can command in his muscles. The utilization of winds and tides and currents and falling streams, of steam and of electricity, and chemical attractions and repulsions, is dependent on this concentration.

Thus the division of labor involves and proceeds from the concentration of effort for the satisfaction of desires. It begins when there are two individuals who coöperate; it increases and becomes productive of greater and greater economies with the increase of the number who thus coöperate.

Adam Smith, who begins his "Wealth of Nations" by considering how coöperation increases the productive powers of mankind, which he styles "the division of labor," refers to the economy which it produces under three heads:

1. The increased dexterity of workmen.

2. The saving of time by the greater continuity of employment.

3. The economy effected by the use of machinery.

But on a larger and fuller survey we may perhaps best analyze the advantages that result from the coöperation of labor as follows:

A. The combination of labor permits a number of individuals by direct union of their powers to accomplish what severally would be impossible.

B. The division of labor, with the concentration and coöperation it involves, permits the doing for many (or a larger number) of what may with a less expenditure be done by one (or by a smaller number):

1. By the saving of time and effort, as in the preceding illustration, where one man goes on a journey which to accomplish severally four men would have to make.

2. By utilizing the differing powers of individuals, as where those who excel in physical strength devote themselves to things requiring physical strength, while those who are inferior in physical strength do the things which require less physical strength, but for which they are otherwise just as capable, thus producing the same net results as would a bringing up of all to the highest level of physical strength; or where those who excel in other qualities do the things for which such qualities are best adapted, thus practically bringing up the level of the accomplishment of all to that of the highest qualities of each.

3. By increasing skill, consequent upon those who do a larger amount of that same kind of work being able to acquire facility in it.

4. By accumulating knowledge. The same tendency which increases the incommunicable knowledge called skill, also tends to increase the communicable knowledge properly so called, which consists in a knowing of the relations of things to other external things, and which constitutes a possession of the economic body or Greater Leviathan, transferable by writing or similar means.

5. By utilizing the advantages of doing things on a large scale instead of on a small scale, and of doing them successively instead of separately.

6. By utilizing the natural forces, and by the invention and use of machines and of improved processes, for the use of which the large scale of production gives advantages.

CHAPTER X.

COÖPERATION—ITS TWO KINDS.

SHOWING THE TWO KINDS OF COÖPERATION, AND HOW THE POWER OF THE ONE GREATLY EXCEEDS THAT OF THE OTHER.

The kind of coöperation which, as to method of union or how of initiation, results from without and may be called directed or conscious coöperation—Another proceeding from within which may be called spontaneous or unconscious coöperation—Types of the two kinds and their analogues—Tacking of a full-rigged ship and of a bird—Intelligence that suffices for the one impossible for the other—The savage and the ship—Unconscious coöperation required in ship-building—Conscious coöperation will not suffice for the work of unconscious—The fatal defect of socialism—The reason of this is that the power of thought is spiritual and cannot be fused as can physical force—Of "man power" and "mind power"—Illustration from the optician—Impossibility of socialism—Society a Leviathan greater than that of Hobbes.

WE have seen that there are two ways or modes in which coöperation increases productive power. If we ask how coöperation is itself brought about, we see that there is in this also a distinction, and that coöperation is of two essentially different kinds. The line of distinction as to what I have called the ways of coöperation, and have in the last chapter considered, is as to the method of action or how of accomplishment; the line of distinction as to what I shall call the kinds of coöperation, and am about in this chapter to consider, is as to the method of union or how of initiative.

There is one kind of coöperation, proceeding as it were from without, which results from the conscious direction of a controlling will to a definite end. This we may call directed or conscious coöperation. There is another kind of coöperation, proceeding as it were from within, which results from a correlation in the actions of independent wills, each seeking but its own immediate purpose, and careless, if not indeed ignorant, of the general result. This we may call spontaneous or unconscious coöperation.

The movement of a great army is a good type of coöperation of one kind. Here the actions of many individuals are subordinated to and directed by one conscious will, they becoming, as it were, its body and executing its thought. The providing of a great city with all the manifold things which are constantly needed by its inhabitants is a good type of coöperation of the other kind. This kind of coöperation is far wider, far finer, far more strongly and delicately organized, than the kind of coöperation involved in the movements of an army, yet it is brought about not by subordination to the direction of one conscious will, which knows the general result at which it aims; but by the correlation of actions originating in many independent wills, each aiming at its own small purpose without care for or thought of the general result.

The one kind of coöperation seems to have its analogue in those related movements of our body which we are able consciously to direct. The other kind of coöperation seems to have its analogue in the correlation of the innumerable movements, of which we are unconscious, that maintain the bodily frame—motions which in their complexity, delicacy and precision far transcend our powers of conscious direction, yet by whose perfect adjustment to each other and to the purpose of the whole that coöperation of part and function that makes up the human body and keeps it in life and vigor is brought about and supported.

A beautiful instance of coöperation of the first kind is furnished by the tacking of a square-rigged ship under full sail. The noble vessel, bending gracefully to the breeze, under her cloud of canvas, comes driving along, cleaving white furrows at her bow and leaving a yeasty wake at her stern. Suddenly her jibs fly free and her spanker flattens, as she curves towards the wind; her foreyards round in and their sails begin to shake, and at length, as what were their weather braces are hauled taut, to fill on the other side. The after sails that at first held the wind as before, begin in their turn to spill; then their yards are shifted, and they too take the wind on a different side; and with every sheet and tack in its new place the vessel gathering again her deadened headway, begins to drive the foam from her bow as she bends on the other side to cut her way in a new direction. So harmonious are her movements, so seemingly instinct with life, that the savage who sees for the first time such a vessel beating along the coast might take her for a great bird, changing its direction with the movement of its wings as do sea-gull and albatross.

And between ship and bird there are certain resemblances. Both are structures in which various parts are combined into a related whole and distinct motions are correlated in harmonious action. And in both movement is produced by the varying angles at which flat surfaces are by a mechanism of joints and ligaments exposed to the impact of air. In a bird, however, the parts in their motions obey instinctively and unconsciously the promptings of the conscious will. But in the ship the motions of the parts are produced by the distinct action of a number of conscious wills, ranging from one or two dozen in a merchant vessel to several hundred in an old-fashioned ship of war. Their coöperation is produced, not instinctively and unconsciously, but by intelligent obedience to the intelligent orders of one directing will, which prescribes to every man his place and function, directing when, how, and by whom, each motion shall be made. The bird veers, because when it wills to veer, nerve and tendon directly respond with the necessary motions. The ship tacks because the separate wills that manage her rudder and sails consciously obey the successive commands which prescribe each of the necessary motions from the first order, "Full for stays!" to the last, "Belay all!" A series of intelligent directions, consciously obeyed by those to whom they are addressed, bring about and correlate the movements of the parts.

Nor could the manœuvers of a ship be carried on without such intelligent direction. Any attempt to substitute independent action, no matter how willing, for responsive obedience to intelligent direction would be certain ere long to result as in the traditional coasting schooner, manned by two—captain and mate—where the captain who was steering, irritated by some gratuitous advice of the mate who was tending jib-sheets, yelled out to him, "You run your end of this schooner and I'll run mine!" Whereupon there was a rattle of chain at the bow, and the mate yelled back, "Captain, I've anchored my end of this schooner; you can run your end where you choose!"

Now, much of the coöperation of man in producing social effects is of the nature of that by which a ship is sailed. It involves the delegation to individuals of the power of arranging and directing what others shall do, thus securing for the general action the advantages of one managing and correlating intelligence. But while coöperation of this kind is indispensable to producing certain results by conjoined action, it is helpless or all but helpless to bring about certain other results involving a longer series and more complicated and delicate actions and adjustments.

To continue our illustration: The bird structurally is a machine as the ship is a machine, which the conscious will of the bird, controlling certain voluntary movements, causes to rise or fall, to sweep in this direction or in that, to be carried with the gale or to tack in its teeth, in short to execute all the movements, sometimes swift and sometimes slow, but nearly always graceful, of which this bird machine is capable. But the conscious will that controls the voluntary motions of the bird; the intelligence that is the captain of this aërial craft, will not account for the machine itself; for its consummate arrangements and adjustments and adaptions. These not merely infinitely transcend the intelligence of the bird, but of the highest human intelligence. The union of lightness with strength, of rigidity with flexibility, of grace with power; the appropriateness of material, the connection and relation of parts, the economies of space and energy and function, the applications of what are to us the most complex and recondite of physical laws, make the bird as a machine, as far superior to the best and highest machines of man's construction, as the paintings of the great master are to the rude slate-drawings of the prattling child.

The bird is not a construction as man's machines are constructions. It was not built, but grew. Its first tangible form, as far as we can trace it, was a limy envelop containing a substance called the yolk, swimming in a sticky fluid, the white. Under certain conditions and without external influence except that of gentle and continued heat, the molecules of the contained substance began, by some influence from within, and seemingly, of themselves, to range themselves into cells, and cells to form into tissue and bone, and turning in related order into heart and lungs, backbone and head, stomach and bowels, brain and nerve, wings and feet, skin and feathers, until at length a tiny living thing pecked its way out, leaving an empty shell, and with a little eating and sleeping, a little hardening of gristle and lengthening of feathers, the "it" of it, the new captain of the new air-ship, began to try rudder and sails and paddles, until having "learned the ropes," and got accustomed to the measurement of distance and the "feel" of motion, it started off boldly to skim and to soar, to get food and digest it, to live its life and propagate its kind.

The veriest savages must at times ponder over the mystery of the egg, as we civilized men at times ponder over the mystery of common things—for to them as to us it would be an insoluble mystery. But it is the ship, not the bird, that would most excite their wonder and admiration, for the savage would see in the ship as soon as he came close to it, not a thing that grew, but a thing that was made—a higher expression of the same power which he himself exercises in his own rude constructions. He would see in it, when he came to look closely, but a vastly greater and better canoe, and would wonder and admire as he who has begun to paint stands in wonder and admiration before the picture of a master, which one who knew nothing of the difficulties of the art would pass with little notice. As the savage would understand the kind of coöperation called into play in the managing of a vessel, so would he attribute the building of the vessel to coöperation of the same kind. Since a larger canoe than one man can build may be built by the same man if he can unite the exertions of others in cutting, rolling, hewing and hollowing a great log, so would it seem to our savage that it was in this way that the ship of civilization was built. And the admiration which the ship would excite in him would be an admiration of the men who sailed it, whom he would naturally take to be the men who built it, or at least to be men who could build it. The superiority of the ship to the rude canoes with which he was familiar he would attribute to superiority of their personal qualities —their greater knowledge and skill and power. They would indeed seem to him at first as very gods.

Yet the savage would be wrong. The superiority of the ship does not indicate the superiority of individual men. If driven ashore with the loss of their ship and all its contents, these men would be more helpless than so many of his own people, and would find it more difficult to make even a canoe. Even if they had saved tools and stores, it would be only after long toil that they could succeed in building some rude, small craft unfitted for a long voyage and rough weather, and not in any respect comparable with their ship. For a modern ship *is* rather a growth than a direct construction in that as between the kind of coöperation required for its production and that which suffices for that of a canoe, there is a difference which suggests something not altogether unlike the difference between a work of nature and a work of man.

The coöperation required in the making of a large canoe or in the sailing of a ship is exceedingly simple as compared to that involved in the construction and equipment of a well-found, first-class ship. The actual putting together, according to the plans of the naval architect, of the separate parts and materials which compose such a ship, would require, after they had been assembled, some directed coöperation. But if coöperation of this kind could suffice for even putting the parts together after they had been made and assembled, how could it suffice for making those various parts from the forms in which nature offers their material, and assembling them in the place where they were to be put together?

Consider the timbers, the planks, the spars; the iron and steel of various kinds and forms; the copper, the brass, the bolts, screws, spikes, chains; the ropes, of steel and hemp and cotton; the canvas of various textures; the blocks and winches and windlasses; the pumps, the boats, the sextants, the chronometers, the spy-glasses and patent logs, the barometers and thermometers, charts, nautical almanacs, rockets and colored lights; food, clothing, tools, medicines and furniture, and all the various things, which it would be tiresome fully to specify, that go to the construction and furnishing of a first-class sailing-ship of modern type, to say nothing of the still greater complexity of the first-class steamer. Directed coöperation never did, and I do not think in the nature of things it ever could, make and assemble such a variety of products, involving as many of them do the use of costly machinery and consummate skill, and the existence of subsidiary products and processes.

When a ship-builder receives an order for such a ship as this he does not send men into the forest, some to cut oak, others to cut yellow pine, others to cut white pine, others to cut hickory and others still to cut ash and lignum-vitæ; he does not direct some to mine iron ore, and others copper ore, and others lead ore, and others still to dig the coal with which these ores are to be smelted, and the fire-clay for the smelting-vessels; some to plant hemp, and some to plant cotton, and others to breed silkworms; some to make glass, others to kill beasts for their hides and tallow, some to get pitch and rosin, oil, paint, paper, felt and mercury. Nor does he attempt to direct the manifold operations by which these raw materials are to be brought into the required forms and combinations, and assembled in the place where the ship is to be built. Such a task would transcend the wisdom and power of a Solomon. What he does is to avail himself of the resources of a high civilization, for without that he would be helpless, and to make use for his purpose of the unconscious coöperation by which without his direction, or any general direction, the efforts of many men, working in many different places and in occupations which cover almost the whole field of a minutely diversified industry, each animated solely by the effort to obtain the satisfaction of his personal desires in what to him is the easiest way, have brought together the materials and productions needed for the putting together of such a ship.

He buys of various dealers in such things, knees, beams, planking, spars, sails, cables, ropes, boats, lanterns, flags, nautical instruments, pumps, stoves; and he probably contracts for various parts of the work of putting together the hull, such as calking, sheathing, painting, etc.; of making the sails and rigging the spars. And each of these separate branches of collation and production will be found on inquiry to reach out and ramify into other branches having necessary relations with still other branches. So far from any lifetime sufficing to acquire or any single brain being able to hold, the varied knowledge that goes to the building and equipping of a modern sailing-ship, already becoming antiquated by the still more complex steamer, I doubt if the best-informed man on such subjects, even though he took a twelvemonth to study up, could give even the names of the various separate divisions of labor involved.

A modern ship, like a modern railway, is a product of modern civilization; of that correlation of individual efforts in which what we call civilization essentially consists; of that unconscious coöperation which does not come by personal direction, as it were from without, but grows, as it were from within, by the relation of the efforts of individuals, each seeking the satisfaction of individual desires. A mere master of men, though he might command the services of millions, could not make such a ship unless in a civilization prepared for it. A Pharaoh that built pyramids, a Genghis Khan who raised mounds of skulls, an Alexander, a Cæsar, or even a Henry VIII. could not do it.

The kind of coöperation which I have illustrated by the tacking of a ship is a very simple matter. It could be readily taught, the difficulties of language aside, to Malays, or Somalis, or Hindus, or Chinamen, or to the men who manned the Roman galleys or the viking ships. But that kind of coöperation which is involved in the making of such a ship is a much deeper and more complex matter. It is beyond the power of conscious direction to order or bring about. It can no more be advanced or improved by any exertion of the power of directing the conscious actions of men than the conscious will of the individual can add a cubit to his stature. The only thing that conscious direction can do to aid it is to let it alone; to give it freedom to grow, leaving men free to seek the gratification of their own desires in the ways that to them seem best. To attempt to apply that kind of coöperation which requires direction from without to the work proper for that kind of coöperation which requires direction from within, is like asking the carpenter who can build a chicken-house to build a chicken also.

This is the fatal defect of all forms of socialism—the reason of the fact, which all observation shows, that any attempt to carry conscious regulation and direction beyond the narrow sphere of social life in which it is necessary, inevitably works injury, hindering even what it is intended to help.

And the rationale of this great fact may, I think, at least in some measure, be perceived when we consider that the originating element in all production is thought or intelligence, the spiritual not the material. This spiritual element, this intelligence or thought power as it appears in man, cannot be combined or fused as can material force.

Two men may pull or push twice as much as one man, and the physical force of one hundred thousand men properly brought to bear will one hundred thousand times exceed the physical force of a single man. But intelligence cannot be thus aggregated. Two men cannot see twice as far as one man, nor a hundred thousand determine one hundred thousand times as well. If it be true that "In a multitude of counselors there is wisdom," it is only in the sense that in a large comparison of views and opinions eccentricities and aberrations are likely to be eliminated. But in this elimination the qualities necessary for superior judgment and prompt direction are also lost. No one ever said, "In a multitude of generals there is victory." On the contrary the adage is, "One poor general is better than two good ones."

In the first kind of coöperation, as for example, when ten men pull on the same rope in the same way in obedience to the direction of one man, there is a utilization of the physical force of ten at the direction of the mental force of one. But there is at the same time a loss or rather non-utilization of the mental force of ten. The result can be no greater than if the ten men who are pulling were for the time utterly devoid of intelligence—mere automata. And we can readily conceive of such extensions in the applications of machinery to the utilization of natural physical forces that the captain of a ship might by touching an electrical keyboard, so give responsive motion to rudder, sheets and braces, as to tack ship without a crew, which would be a long approach in the mechanism of a ship to the mechanism of a bird.

But in the kind of coöperation that I have called spontaneous, where the direction comes from within, what is utilized in production is not merely the sum of the physical power of the units, but the sum of their intelligence. If I may be permitted to use for a moment the term "man power" and symbol M as expressing the physical force which one individual can exert, and the term "mind power" and symbol M′ as suggesting quantitatively the individual power of intelligence or thought, the best possible result of the exertion of one hundred thousand men in coöperation of the first kind would be 100,000 man power × 1 mind power or 100,000 MM′; while of the same number of men employed in the second kind of coöperation it would be 100,000 man power × 100,000 mind power or 10,000,000,000 MM′.

The illustration is clumsy, but it may serve to suggest the enormous difference which we see developed in the two kinds of coöperation, and which as it seems to me arises at least in important part from the fact that while in the second kind of coöperation the sum of intelligence utilized is that of the whole of the coöperating units, in the first kind of coöperation it is only that of a very small part.

In other words it is only in independent action that the full powers of the man may be utilized. The subordination of one human will to another human will, while it may in certain ways secure unity of action, must always where intelligence is needed, involve loss of productive power. This we see exemplified in slavery and where governments have undertaken (as is the tendency of all government) unduly to limit the freedom of the individual. But where unity of effort, or rather combination of effort, can be secured while leaving full freedom to the individual, the whole of productive power may still be utilized and the result be immeasurably greater.

The hardening of muscular tissue, which comes to us as the years of our lives go by, has deprived the delicate mechanism which once adequately moved the lenses of my eyes of what opticians call their power of accommodation, so that to my natural sight printed pages that I once read comfortably are now indistinguishably confused. By piercing a small pinhole in a piece of cardboard and holding it close to one of my eyes, while I shut the other, I can cut off from my vision so many of the rays of light that the few which reach my retina do not interfere with each other, and I can thus see the same printed page for a few moments distinctly. But this is by the sacrifice of otherwise available rays of light. Now by means of a properly ground pair of spectacles which deflect so as to utilize for the eyes the interfering rays of light I can use them all.

To attempt in social affairs to secure by coöperation of the first kind that alignment of effort which by natural law belongs to coöperation of the second kind, is like attempting to secure by cardboard and pinholes the definiteness of vision that can be far better secured by spectacles. Such is the attempt of what is properly called socialism.

Imagine an aggregation of men in which it was attempted to secure by the external direction involved in socialistic theories that division of labor which grows up naturally in society where men are left free. For the intelligent direction thus required an individual man or individual men must be selected, for even if there be angels and archangels in the world that is invisible to us, they are not at our command.

Taking no note of the difficulties which universal experience shows always to attend the choice of the depositaries of power, and ignoring the inevitable tendency to tyranny and oppression, of command over the actions of others, simply consider, even if the very wisest and best of men were selected for such purposes, the task that would be put upon them in the ordering of the when, where, how and by whom that would be involved in the intelligent direction and supervision of the almost infinitely complex and constantly changing relations and adjustments involved in such division of labor as goes on in a civilized community. The task transcends the power of human intelligence at its very highest. It is evidently as much beyond the ability of conscious direction as the correlation of the processes that maintain the human body in health and vigor is beyond it.

Aristotle, Julius Cæsar, Shakespeare, Newton, may be fairly taken as examples of high-water mark in the powers of the human mind. Could any of them, had the control of the processes that maintain the individual organism been relegated to his conscious intelligence, have kept life in his body a single minute? Newton, so the tradition runs, stopped his tobacco-bowl with his lady's finger. What would have become of Newton's heart if the ordering of its beats had been devolved on Newton's mind?

This mind of ours, this conscious intelligence that perceives, compares, judges and wills, wondrous and far-reaching as are its powers, is like the eye that may look to far-off suns and milky ways, but cannot see its own mechanism. This body of ours in which our mind is cased, this infinitely complex and delicate machine through which that which feels and thinks becomes conscious of the external world, and its will is transmuted into motion, exists only by virtue of unconscious intelligence which works while conscious intelligence rests; which is on guard while it sleeps; which wills without its concurrence and plans without its contriving, of which it has almost no direct knowledge and over which it has almost no direct control.

And so it is the spontaneous, unconscious coöperation of individuals which, going on in the industrial body, the Greater Leviathan than that of Hobbes, conjoins individual efforts in the production of wealth, to the enormous increase in productive power, and distributes the product among the units of which it is composed. It is the nature and laws of such coöperation that it is the primary province of political economy to ascertain.

CHAPTER XI.

THE OFFICE OF EXCHANGE IN PRODUCTION.

SHOWING THAT IN MAN THE LACK OF INSTINCT IS SUPPLIED BY THE HIGHER QUALITY OF REASON, WHICH LEADS TO EXCHANGE.

The coöperation of ants and bees is from within and not from without; from instinct and not from direction—Man has little instinct; but the want supplied by reason—Reason shows itself in exchange—This suffices for the unconscious coöperation of the economic body or Greater Leviathan—Of the three modes of production, "exchanging" is the highest—Mistake of writers on political economy—The motive of exchange.

IT is a curious fact, having in it suggestions that it would lead beyond our purpose to follow, that the living things that come nearest to the social organization of man are not those to whom we are structurally most allied, but those belonging to a widely separated genus, that of insects. The coöperation by which ants and bees build houses and construct public works, procure and store food, make provision for future needs, rear their young, meet the assaults of enemies and confront general dangers, gives to their social life a striking superficial likeness to that of human societies, and brings them in this apparently far closer to us than are animals to whom we are structurally more akin.

The coöperation by which the social life of such insects is carried on seems at first glance to be of the kind I have called directed coöperation, in which correlation in the efforts of individual units is brought about, as it were from without, by such subordination of some of the units to other units as secures conscious obedience in response to intelligent direction. The republican monarchy of the bees has its queen, its drones, its workers; the ants range themselves for march, for battle, or for work, in militant or industrial armies.

Yet closer observation shows that this is more in seeming than in fact, and that the great agency in the correlation of effort which the insects show is something which impresses the units not from without but from within their own nature, the force or power or impulse that we call instinct, which operating directly on the individual unit, brings each, as it were, of its own volition, to its proper place and function with relation to the whole, in something of the same way in which the vital or germinative force operates within the egg-shell to bring the separate cells into relations that result in the living bird.

Now of this power or impulse that we call instinct conscious man has little. While the involuntary and unconscious functions of his bodily frame may be ordered and maintained by it or something akin to it, and while it may in the same way furnish the sub-stratum of what we may call his mental frame, yet instinct, so strong in the orders of life below him, seems with man to fade and withdraw as the higher power of reason assumes control. What of instinct he retains would not suffice even for such social constructions as those of ants or bees or beavers. But reason, which in him has superseded instinct, brings a new and seemingly illimitable power of uniting and correlating individual efforts, by enabling and disposing him to exchange with his fellows. The act of exchange is that of deliberately parting with one thing for the purpose and as a means of getting another thing. It is an act that involves foresight, calculation, judgment—qualities in which reason differs from instinct.

All living things that we know of coöperate in some kind and to some degree. So far as we can see, nothing that lives can live in and for itself alone. But man is the only one who coöperates by exchanging, and he may be distinguished from all the numberless tribes that with him tenant the earth as the exchanging animal. Of them all he is the only one who seeks to obtain one thing by giving another. A dog may prefer a big bone to a little bone, and where it cannot hold on to both, may keep one in preference to the other. But no dog or other animal will deliberately and voluntarily give up one desirable thing for another desirable thing. When between two desired things the question "Which?" is put to it, its answer is always the answer of the child, "Both," until it is forced to leave the one in order to hold the other. No other animal uses bait to attract its prey; no other animal plants edible seeds that it may gather the produce. No other animal gives another what it itself would like to have in order to receive in return what it likes better. But such acts come naturally to man with his maturity, and are of his distinguishing principle.

Exchange is the great agency by which what I have called the spontaneous or unconscious coöperation of men in the production of wealth is brought about, and economic units are welded into that social organism which is the Greater Leviathan. To this economic body, this Greater Leviathan, into which it builds the economic units, it is what the nerves or perhaps the ganglions are to the individual body. Or, to make use of another illustration, it is to our material desires and powers of satisfying them what the switchboard of a telegraph or telephone or other electric system is to that system, a means by which exertion of one kind in one place may be transmuted into satisfaction of another kind in another place, and thus the efforts of individual units be conjoined and correlated so as to yield satisfactions in most useful place and form, and to an amount enormously exceeding what otherwise would be possible.

Of the three modes of production which I have distinguished as adapting, growing and exchanging, the last is that by which alone the higher applications of the modes of adapting and growing are made available. Were it not for exchange the coöperation of individuals in the production of wealth could go no further than it might be carried by the natural instincts that operate in the formation of the family, or by that kind of coöperation in which individual wills are made subordinate to another individual will. These it is evident would not suffice for the lowest stage of civilization. For not only does slavery itself, which requires that the slaves shall be fed and clothed, involve some sort of exchange, though a very inadequate one, but the labor of slaves must be supplemented by exchange to permit the slave-owner to enjoy any more than the rudest satisfactions. It was only by exchanging the produce of their labor that the American slave-owner could provide himself with more than his slaves themselves could obtain from his own plantation, and a slave-based society in which there was no exchanging could hardly carry the arts further than the construction of the rudest huts and tools. When we speak of pyramids and canals being constructed by enforced labor we are forgetting the great amount of exchanging which was involved in such work.

Many if not most of the writers on political economy have treated exchange as a part of distribution. On the contrary, it properly belongs to production. It is by exchange and through exchange that man obtains and is able to exert the power of coöperation which with the advance of civilization so enormously increases his ability to produce wealth.

The motive of exchange is the primary postulate of political economy, the universal fact that men seek to gratify their desires with the least exertion. This leads men by a universal impulse to seek to gratify their desires by exchange wherever they can thus obtain the gratification of desire with less exertion than in any other way; and by virtue of the natural laws, both physical and mental, explained in Chapter II. of this Book, this is from the very origin of human society, and increasingly with its advance, the easiest way of procuring the satisfaction of the greatest number of desires.

And in addition to the laws already explained there is another law or condition of nature related to man which is taken advantage of to the enormous increase of productive power in exchange.[1]

---

[1] A note, "Leave six pages," written in pencil, appears on the last page of this chapter in the MS. The indications are that it was intended not for this, but for the next succeeding chapter, which was left unfinished. — H. G., Jr.

CHAPTER XII.

OFFICE OF COMPETITION IN PRODUCTION.

SHOWING THAT COMPETITION BRINGS TRADE, AND CONSEQUENTLY SERVICE, TO ITS JUST LEVEL.

["Competition is the life of trade" an old and true adage—The assumption that it is an evil springs from two causes—one bad, the other good—The bad cause at the root of protectionism—Law of competition a natural law—Competition necessary to civilization.][1]

THAT "competition is the life of trade," is an old and true adage. But in current thought and current literature there is so much assumption that competition is an evil that it is worth while to examine at some length its cause and office in the production of wealth.

Much of this assumption that competition is an evil and a wrong that should be restricted and indeed abolished in the higher interests of society springs from the desire of men unduly to profit at the expense of their fellows by distorting natural laws of the distribution of wealth. This is true of the form of socialism which was known in the time of Adam Smith as the mercantile system or theory, and which still exists with but little diminished strength under the general name of protectionism. Much of it again has a nobler origin, coming from a righteous in-

[1] No summary of this chapter appears in the MS. The summary here presented and inclosed by brackets is supplied for the reader's convenience. —H. G., Jr.

dignation with the monstrous inequalities in the existing distribution of wealth throughout the civilized world, coupled with a mistaken assumption that these inequalities are due to competition.

I do not propose here to treat either of protectionism or socialism proper, my purpose being not that of controversy or refutation, but merely that of discovering and explaining the natural laws with which the science of political economy is concerned. But the law of competition is one of these natural laws, without an understanding of which we cannot fully understand the economy or system by which that Intelligence to which we must refer the origin and existence of the world has provided that the advance of mankind in civilization should be an advance towards the general enjoyment of literally boundless wealth.

The competition of men with their fellows in the production of wealth has its origin in the impulse to satisfy desires with the least expenditure of exertion.

Competition is indeed the life of trade, in a deeper sense than that it is a mere facilitator of trade. It is the life of trade in the sense that its spirit or impulse is the spirit or impulse of trade or exchange.

CHAPTER XIII.

OF DEMAND AND SUPPLY IN PRODUCTION.[1]

[1] No more than the title of this chapter was written. The reader will find the subject of demand and supply in production treated in "Progress and Poverty" and in "Social Problems."—H. G., Jr.

CHAPTER XIV.

ORDER OF THE THREE FACTORS OF PRODUCTION.

SHOWING THE AGREEMENT OF ALL ECONOMISTS AS TO THE NAMES AND ORDER OF THE FACTORS OF PRODUCTION.

Land and labor necessary elements in production—Union of a composite element, capital—Reason for dwelling on this agreement as to order.

ALL economists give the factors of production as three—land, labor and capital. And without exception that I know of, they name them in this order. This, indeed, is the natural order; the order of their appearance. The world, so far as political economy takes cognizance of it, began with land. Reason tells us that land, with all its powers and potentialities, including even all vegetable and animal life, existed before man was, and must have existed before he could be. But whether still "formless and void," or already instinct with the lower forms of life, so long as there was in the world only the economic element land, production in the economic sense could not be, and there was no wealth. When man appeared, and the economic element labor was united to the economic element land, production began, and its product, wealth, resulted. At length (for in the myths and poems in which mankind have expressed all the wisest could tell of our far beginnings they have always loved to picture a golden age devoid of care), or more probably almost immediately (for the very first of our race must have possessed that reason which is the distinguishing quality of man), the greater power that could be gained by using wealth in aid of labor was seen, and a third factor of production, capital, appeared.

But between this third factor and the two factors which precede it, a difference in nature and importance is to be noted. Land and labor are original and necessary factors. They cannot be resolved into each other, and they are indispensable to production, being necessary to production in all its modes. But capital is not an original factor. It is a compound or derivative factor, resulting from the union of the two original factors, land and labor, and being resolvable on final analysis into a form of the active factor, labor. It is not indispensable to production, being necessary, as before explained, not in *all* modes of production, but only in *some* modes. Nevertheless, the part that it bears in production is so separable, and the convenience that is served by distinguishing it from the original factors is so great, that it has been properly recognized by the earliest and by all subsequent writers in political economy as a separate factor; and the three elements by whose union wealth is produced in the civilized state are given by the names and in the order of (1) land, (2) labor, and (3) capital.

It may seem to the reader superfluous that I should lay such stress upon the order of the three factors of production, for it is not more self-evident that the mother must precede the child than that land must precede labor, and that labor must precede capital. But I dwell upon this question of order because it is the key to confusions which have brought the teaching of the science of political economy to absurdity and stultification. Such of these writers as have condescended to make any definitions of the terms they use have indeed in these definitions recognized the natural order of the three factors of production. But whoever will follow them will see that without seeming conscious of it themselves they soon slip into a reversal of this order, and, literally making the last first, proceed to assume that capital is the prime factor in production. Socialism, which gives such undue prominence to capital and yet is so completely at sea as to the real nature and functions of capital has the root of its absurdities in the teachings of the scholastic economists.

But the results of this confusion as to the nature and order of the factors of production will be more fully treated when we come to consider the distribution of wealth. All that it is necessary to do here is to point out the true order of the factors of production and to make clear what they are. Let us proceed to consider them one by one.

CHAPTER XV.

THE FIRST FACTOR OF PRODUCTION—LAND.

SHOWING THAT LAND IS THE NATURAL OR PASSIVE FACTOR IN ALL PRODUCTION.

The term "land"—"Landowners"—Labor the only active factor.

MAN produces by drawing from nature. Land, in political economy, is the term for that from which he draws—for that which must exist before he himself can exist. In other words, the term land in political economy means the natural or passive element in production, and includes the whole external world accessible to man, with all its powers, qualities and products, except perhaps those portions of it which are for the time included in man's body or in his products, and which therefore temporarily belong to the categories, man and wealth, passing again in their re-absorption by nature into the category, land.

The original and ordinary meaning of the word, land, is that of dry superficies of the earth as distinguished from water or air. But man, as distinguished from the denizens of the water or the air, is primarily a land animal. The dry surface of the earth is his habitat, from which alone he can venture upon or make use of any other element, or obtain access to any other material thing or potency. Thus, as a law term, land means not merely the dry superficies of the earth, but all that is above and all that mãy be below it, from zenith to nadir. For the same reason the word land receives like extension of meaning when used as a term of political economy, and comprises all having material form that man has received or can receive from nature, that is to say, from God.

Thus the term "land" in political economy means the natural or passive factor, on which and by or through which labor produces, and can alone produce.

But that land is only a passive factor in production must be carefully kept in mind. It is a thing, but not a person, and though the tendency to personification leads not merely in poetry but in common speech to the use of phrases which attribute sentiment and action to land, it is important to remember that when we speak of a smiling, a sullen, or an angry landscape, of a generous or a niggard land, of the earth giving or the earth receiving, or rewarding or denying, or of nature tempting or forbidding, aiding or preventing, we are merely using figures of speech more forcibly or more gracefully to express our own feelings by reflection from inanimate objects. In the production of wealth land cannot act; it can only be acted upon. Man alone is the actor.

Nor is this principle changed or avoided when we use the word land as expressive of the people who own land. Landowners, as landowners, are as purely passive in production as land itself; they take no part in production whatever. When Arthur Young spoke of the "magic of property turning sands to gold" he was using a figure of speech. What he meant to say was that the effect of security in the enjoyment of the produce of labor on land was to induce men to exert that labor with more assiduity and intelligence, and thus to increase the produce. Land cannot know whether men regard it as property or not, nor does that fact in any degree affect its powers. Sand is sand and gold is gold, and the rain falls and the sun shines, as little affected by the moral considerations that men recognize as the telegraph-wire is affected by the meaning of the messages that pass through it, or as the rock is affected by the twitter of the birds that fly over it.

I speak of this because although their definition of land as a factor in production is precisely that which I have given, there is to be found in the accepted treatises on political economy a constant tendency to the assumption that landowners, through their ownership of land, contribute to production.

That the persons whom we call landowners may contribute their labor or their capital to production is of course true, but that they should contribute to production as landowners, and by virtue of that ownership, is as ridiculously impossible as that the belief of a lunatic in his ownership of the moon should be the cause of her brilliancy.

We could not if we would, and should not if we could, utterly eschew metaphors; but in political economy we must be always careful to hold them at their true meaning.

CHAPTER XVI.

THE SECOND FACTOR OF PRODUCTION—LABOR.

SHOWING THAT LABOR IS THE HUMAN OR ACTIVE FACTOR IN ALL PRODUCTION.

The term labor—It is the only active factor in producing wealth, and by nature spiritual.

ALL human actions, or at least all conscious human actions, have their source in desire and their end or aim in the satisfaction of desire. The intermediary action by which desire secures its aim in satisfaction, is exertion. The economic term for this exertion is labor. It is the active, and from the human standpoint, the primary or initiative, factor in all production—that which being applied to land brings about all the changes conducive to the satisfaction of desire that it is possible for man to make in the material world.

In political economy there is no other term for this exertion than labor. That is to say, the term labor includes all human exertion in the production of wealth, whatever its mode. In common parlance we often speak of brain labor and hand labor as though they were entirely distinct kinds of exertion, and labor is often spoken of as though it involved only muscular exertion. But in reality any form of labor, that is to say, any form of human exertion in the production of wealth above that which cattle may be applied to doing, requires the human brain as truly as the human hand, and would be impossible without the exercise of mental faculties on the part of the laborer.

Labor in fact is only physical in external form. In its origin it is mental or on strict analysis spiritual. It is indeed the point at which, or the means by which, the spiritual element which is in man, the Ego, or essential, begins to exert its control on matter and motion, and to modify the material world to its desires.

As land is the natural or passive factor in all production, so labor is the human or active factor. As such, it is the initiatory factor. All production results from the action of labor on land, and hence it is truly said that labor is the producer of all wealth.

CHAPTER XVII.

THE THIRD FACTOR OF PRODUCTION—CAPITAL.

SHOWING THAT CAPITAL IS NOT A PRIMARY FACTOR, BUT PROCEEDS FROM LAND AND LABOR, AND IS A FORM OR USE OF WEALTH.

Capital is essentially labor raised to a higher power—Where it may, and where it must aid labor—In itself it is helpless.

THE primary factors of production are labor and land, and from their union all production comes. Their concrete product is wealth, which is land modified by labor so as to fit it or better fit it for the satisfaction of human desires. What is usually distinguished as the third factor of production, capital, is, as we have seen, a form or use of wealth.

Capital, which is not in itself a distinguishable element, but which it must always be kept in mind consists of wealth applied to the aid of labor in further production, is not a primary factor. There can be production without it, and there must have been production without it, or it could not in the first place have appeared. It is a secondary and compound factor, coming after and resulting from the union of labor and land in the production of wealth It is in essence labor raised by a second union with land to a third or higher power. But it is to civilized life so necessary and important as to be rightfully accorded in political economy the place of a third factor in production. Without the use of capital man could raise himself but little above the level of the animals.

I have already, in Chapter II. of this Book, generalized the various modes of production into three, adapting, growing and exchanging. Now in the first of these modes, which I have called adapting, the changing of natural products either in form or in place so as to fit them for the satisfaction of human desires, capital may aid labor, and in the higher forms of this mode must aid labor. But it is not absolutely necessary, to the lower forms at least. Some of the smaller and less powerful animals might be taken and the natural fruits and vegetables obtained, some rude shelter and clothing produced, and even some rude forms of wealth adapted from the mineral world, without the application of capital.

But in the second and third of these modes, those namely of growing and exchanging, capital must aid labor, or *is* indispensable. For there can be no cultivation of plants or breeding of animals, unless vegetables or animals previously brought into the category of wealth are devoted not to the consumption that gives direct satisfaction to desire, but to the production of more wealth; and there can be no exchanging of wealth until some wealth is applied by its owners, not to consumption, but to exchange for other wealth or for services.

It is to be observed that capital of itself can do nothing. It is always a subsidiary, never an initiatory factor. The initiatory factor is always labor. That is to say, in the production of wealth labor always uses capital, is never used by capital. This is not merely literally true, when by the term capital we mean the thing capital. It is also true when we personify the term and mean by it not the thing capital, but the men who are possessed of capital. The capitalist pure and simple, the man who merely controls capital, has in his hands the power of assisting labor to produce. But purely as capitalist he cannot exercise that power. It can be exercised only by labor. To utilize it he must himself exercise at least some of the functions of labor, or he must put his capital, on some terms, at the use of those who do.

I speak of this because it is the habit, not only of common speech but of many writers on political economy, to speak as though capital were the initiatory factor in production, and as if capital or capitalists employed labor; whereas in fact, no matter what the form of the arrangement for the use of capital, it is always labor that starts production and is aided by capital; never capital that starts production and is aided by labor.

It cannot be too clearly kept in mind that labor is the only producer either of wealth or of capital. Appropriation can produce nothing. Its sole power is that of affecting distribution under penalty of preventing production. This may put wealth or capital in the hands of the appropriator, by taking it from others; but can never bring it into existence.

BOOK IV

THE DISTRIBUTION OF WEALTH

For "Mars is a tyrant," as Timotheus expresses it; but justice, according to Pindar, "is the rightful sovereign of the world." The things which Homer tells us kings receive from Jove are not machines for taking towns or ships with brazen beaks, but law and justice; these they are to guard and cultivate. And it is not the most warlike, the most violent and sanguinary, but the justest of princes, whom he calls the disciple of Jupiter. —*Plutarch, Demetrius.*

CONTENTS OF BOOK IV.

THE DISTRIBUTION OF WEALTH.

CHAPTER III.

THE COMMON PERCEPTION OF NATURAL LAW IN DISTRIBUTION.

SHOWING THE COMMON AND INERADICABLE PERCEPTION OF NATURAL LAWS OF DISTRIBUTION.

CHAPTER IV.

THE REAL DIFFERENCE BETWEEN LAWS OF PRODUCTION AND OF DISTRIBUTION.

SHOWING THAT DISTRIBUTION HAS REFERENCE TO ETHICS, WHILE PRODUCTION HAS NOT.

CHAPTER V.

OF PROPERTY.

SHOWING THAT PROPERTY DEPENDS UPON NATURAL LAW.

CHAPTER VI.

CAUSE OF CONFUSION AS TO PROPERTY.

SHOWING WHY AND HOW POLITICAL ECONOMISTS FELL INTO SUCH CONFUSIONS WITH REGARD TO PROPERTY.

INTRODUCTION TO BOOK IV.

IN accordance with the earlier usage I have planned the division of political economy for purposes of investigation into three grand divisions: I.—The nature of wealth. II.—The laws of production. III.—The laws of distribution. Having passed through the first two grand divisions, having seen the nature of wealth and the laws of its production, we proceed now to the laws of distribution.

In the branch of political economy to which we now turn lies the heart of all economic controversies. For all disputes as to the nature of wealth and all disputes as to the production of wealth will be found at last to have their real ground in the distribution of wealth. Hence, this, as we shall find, is the part of political economy most beset with confusions. But if we move carefully, making sure as we go of the meaning of the words we use, we shall find no real difficulty.

CHAPTER I.

THE MEANING OF DISTRIBUTION.

SHOWING THE MEANING AND USES OF THE WORD DISTRIBUTION; THE PLACE AND MEANING OF THE ECONOMIC TERM; AND THAT IT IS CONCERNED ONLY WITH NATURAL LAWS.

Derivation and uses of the word—Exchange, consumption and taxation not proper divisions of political economy—Need of a consideration of distribution—It is the continuation and end of what begins in production, and thus the final division of political economy—The meaning usually assigned to distribution as an economic term, and its true meaning.

THE word distribution comes from the Latin, *dis*, asunder, and *tribuo*, to give, or *tribuere*, to allot.

The common meaning of distribution differs from that of division by including with the idea of a separation into parts the idea of an apportionment or allotment of these parts, and is that of a division into or a division among.

Thus the distribution of work, or duty, or function is the assignment to each coöperator of a separate part in securing an aggregate result; the distribution of food, or alms, or of a trust fund, involves the allotment of a proper portion of the whole to each of the beneficiaries; the distribution of gas, or water, or heat, or electricity, through a building or city, means the causing of a flow to each part of its proper quota; the distribution of rocks, plants or animals over the globe involves the idea of causes or laws which have brought them to the places where they are found; the distribution of weight or strain in a building or structure involves the idea of a division of the aggregate mass or pressure among the various parts; distribution in logic is the application of a term to all members of a class taken separately, so that what is affirmed or denied of the whole is not merely affirmed or denied of them all collectively, but of each considered independently; the distribution of things into categories, or species, or genera, in the sciences is the cataloguing of them with reference to their likeness or unlikeness in certain respects of form, origin or quality.

What is called the distribution of mail in a post-office is the reverse, or complement, of what is called the collection of mail. It consists of the separation into pouches or bags according to the common destination of the mail matter brought in for transmission, or of a similar separation of the mail matter received for delivery.

What is called the distribution of type in a printing-office is the reverse, or the complement, of what is called the composition of type. In composition the printer places into a "stick" the letters and spaces in the sequence that forms words. One line composed and "justified" by such changes in spacing as bring it to the exact "measure," he proceeds to compose another line. When his stick contains as many lines as it will conveniently hold he "empties" it on a "galley," from which this "matter" is finally "imposed" in a "form." As many impressions as are desired having been made from the "form" upon paper (or upon a "matrix" if any process of stereotyping is used), what until put to its destined use of printing was "live matter" becomes in the terminology of the printing-office "dead matter," and that the movable types may be used again in composition the printer proceeds to distribute them. If the matter has been thrown into "pi" by an accident which disarranges the order of the letters in words, "distribution" is a very tedious operation, since each letter has to be separately noted. But if not, the compositor, now become distributor, takes in his left hand so that he can read as much of the "dead matter" as he can conveniently hold, and beginning at the right end of the upper line lifts with the forefinger and thumb of his right hand a word or words, reading with a quick glance as he does so, and moving his hand over the case, releases each letter or space or "quad" (blank) over its appropriate box, from which they may be readily taken for renewed composition.

This is the system of composing and distributing type in use from the time of Gutenberg to the present day. But printing-machines are now (1896) rapidly beginning to supersede hand-work. In these, composition takes place by touches on a keyboard, like that of a typewriter. In the type-using machines the touch on a key brings the letter into place, justification is made afterwards by hand, and distribution is accomplished by revolving the type around a cylinder where by nicks on its body it is carried to its appropriate receptacle. In the type-casting machines, each type is cast as the key is touched, and instead of being distributed is re-melted. In the line-making machines, or linotypes, the composition is of movable matrices, the line is automatically justified by wedges which increase or diminish the space between the words, and is cast on the face of a "slug" by a jet of molten metal. In these there is no distribution; the slugs when no longer needed being thrown into the melting-pot.

As has already been observed, the distribution of wealth in political economy does not include transportation and exchange, as most of the standard economic writers assume. Nor yet is there any logical reason for treating exchange as a separate department in political economy, as is done by those writers who define political economy as the science which teaches of the laws which regulate the production, distribution and *exchange* of wealth, or as they sometimes phrase it, of the production, *exchange* and distribution of wealth. Transportation and exchange are properly included in production, being a part of the process in which natural objects are by the exertion of human labor better fitted to satisfy the desires of man.

Nor yet again is there any logical reason in the division of the field of the science of political economy for following that department which treats of the distribution of wealth with other departments treating of the consumption of wealth or of taxation, as is done by some of the minor and more recent writers. Taxation is a matter of human law, while the proper subject of science is natural law. Nor does the science of political economy concern itself with consumption. It is finished and done—the purpose for which production began is concluded when it reaches distribution.

The need of a consideration of the distribution of wealth in political economy comes from the coöperative character of the production of wealth in civilization. In the rudest state of humanity, where production is carried on by isolated human units, the product of each unit would in the act of production come into possession of that unit, and there would be no distribution of wealth and no need for considering it.* But in that higher state of humanity where separate units, each moved to action by the motive of satisfying its individual desires, coöperate to production, there necessarily arises when the product has been obtained, the question of its distribution.

Distribution is in fact a continuation of production—the latter part of the same process of which production is the

---

* Book I., Chapter I.

first part. For the desire which prompts to exertion in production is the desire for satisfaction, and distribution is the process by which what is brought into being by production is carried to the point where it yields satisfaction to desire—which point is the end and aim of production.

In a logical division of the field of political economy, that which relates to the distribution of wealth is the final part. For the beginning of all the actions and movements which political economy is called on to consider is in human desire. And their end and aim is the satisfaction of that desire. When this is reached political economy is finished, and this is reached with the distribution of wealth. With what becomes of wealth after it is distributed political economy has nothing whatever to do. It can take any further account of it only should it be reëntered in the field of political economy as capital, and then only as an original and independent entry. What men choose to do with the wealth that is distributed to them may be of concern to them as individuals, or it may be of concern to the society of which they are a part, but it is of no concern to political economy. The branches of knowledge that consider the ultimate disposition of wealth may be instructive or useful. But they are not included in political economy, which does not embrace all knowledge or any knowledge, but has as a separate science a clear and well-defined field of its own.

If, moved by a desire for potatoes, I dig, or plant, or weed, or gather them, or as a member of the great coöperative association, the body economic, in which civilization consists, I saw or plane, or fish or hunt, or play the fiddle, or preach sermons for the satisfaction of other people who in return will give me potatoes or the means of getting potatoes, the whole transaction originating in my desire for potatoes is finished when I get the potatoes, or rather when they are put at my disposal at the place contemplated in my desire. Whether I then choose to boil, bake, roast or fry them, to throw them at dogs or to feed them to hogs, to plant them as seed, or to let them decay; to trade them off for other food or other satisfactions, or to transfer them to some one else as a free gift or under promise that by and by he will give me other potatoes or other satisfactions, is something outside of and beyond the series of transactions which originating in my desire for potatoes was ended and finished in my getting potatoes.

As a term of political economy, distribution is usually said to mean the division of the results of production among the persons or classes of persons who have contributed to production. But this as we shall see is misleading, its real meaning being the division into categories corresponding to the categories or factors of production.

In entering on this branch of our inquiry, it will be well to recall what, in Book I., I have dwelt upon at length, and what is here particularly needful to keep in mind, that the laws which it is the proper purpose of political economy to discover are not human laws, but natural laws. From this it follows that our inquiry into the laws of the distribution of wealth is not an inquiry into the municipal laws or human enactments which either here and now, or in any other time and place, prescribe or have prescribed how wealth shall be divided among men. With them we have no concern, unless it may be for purposes of illustration. What we have to seek are those laws of the distribution of wealth which belong to the natural order—laws which are a part of that system or arrangement which constitutes the social organism or body economic, as distinguished from the body politic or state, the Greater Leviathan that makes its appearance with civilization and develops with its advance. These natural laws are in all times and places the same, and though they may be crossed by human enactment, can never be annulled or swerved by it.

It is more needful to call this to mind, because in what have passed for systematic treatises on political economy the fact that it is with natural laws, not human laws, that the science of political economy is concerned, has in treating of the distribution of wealth been utterly ignored, and even flatly denied.

CHAPTER II.

THE NATURE OF DISTRIBUTION.

SHOWING THE FALLACY OF THE CONTENTION THAT DISTRIBUTION IS A MATTER OF HUMAN LAW; THAT THE NATURAL LAWS OF DISTRIBUTION ARE MANIFEST NOT ON WEALTH ALREADY PRODUCED, BUT ON SUBSEQUENT PRODUCTION; AND THAT THEY ARE MORAL LAWS.

John Stuart Mill's argument that distribution is a matter of human law—Its evidence of the unscientific character of the scholastic economy—The fallacy it involves and the confusion it shows—Illustration from Bedouin and from civilized society—Natural laws of distribution do not act upon wealth already produced, but on future production—Reason of this—Illustration of siphon and analogy of blood.

MILL'S "Principles of Political Economy" is, I think, even at the present day entitled to the rank of the best and most systematic exposition of the scholastically accepted political economy yet written, and as I wish to present in their very strongest form the opinions that I shall controvert, I quote from it the argument from which it is assumed that the laws of distribution with which political economy has to deal are human laws. Mill opens with this argument the second grand division of his work, Book II., entitled "Distribution," which follows his introductory and the thirteen chapters devoted to "Production," and thus states the fundamental principle on which he endeavors to conduct his whole inquiry into distribution, the principle that distribution is a matter of human institution solely:

The principles which have been set forth in the first part of this treatise, are, in certain respects, strongly distinguished from those, on the consideration of which we are now about to enter. The laws and conditions of the production of wealth, partake of the character of physical truths. There is nothing optional or arbitrary in them. Whatever mankind produce, must be produced in the modes, and under the conditions, imposed by the constitution of external things, and by the inherent properties of their own bodily and mental structure. . . .

But it is not so with the Distribution of Wealth. That is a matter of human institution solely. The things once there, mankind, individually or collectively can do with them as they like. They can place them at the disposal of whomsoever they please, and on whatever terms. Further, in the social state, in every state except total solitude, any disposal whatever of them can only take place by the consent of society, or rather of those who dispose of its active force. Even what a person has produced by his individual toil, unaided by any one, he cannot keep, unless by the permission of society. Not only can society take it from him, but individuals could and would take it from him, if society only remained passive; if it did not either interfere *en masse*, or employ and pay people for the purpose of preventing him from being disturbed in the possession. The distribution of wealth, therefore, depends on the laws and customs of society. The rules by which it is determined, are what the opinions and feelings of the ruling portion of the community make them, and are very different in different ages and countries; and might be still more different, if mankind so chose.

The opinions and feelings of mankind, doubtless, are not a matter of chance. They are consequences of the fundamental laws of human nature, combined with the existing state of knowledge and experience, and the existing condition of social institutions and intellectual and moral culture. But the laws of the generation of human opinions are not within our present subject. They are part of the general theory of human progress, a far larger and more difficult subject of inquiry than political economy. We have here to consider, not the causes, but the consequences, of the rules according to which wealth may be distributed. Those, at least, are as little arbitrary, and have as much the character of physical laws, as the laws of production. Human beings can control their own acts, but not the consequences of their acts either to themselves or to others. Society can subject the distribution of wealth to whatever rules it thinks best; but what practical results will flow from the operation of those rules, must be discovered, like any other physical or mental truths, by observation and reasoning.

We proceed, then, to the consideration of the different modes of distributing the produce of land and labor which have been adopted in practice or may be conceived in theory.*

In all the dreary waste of economic treatises that I have plodded through, this, by a man I greatly esteem, is the best attempt that I know of to explain what is really meant in political economy by laws of distribution. And it is no small evidence of Mill's superiority to those who since the time of Adam Smith had preceded him, and to those who since his own time have followed him, in treatises which bear the stamp of authority in our schools and colleges, that he should feel it incumbent on him even to attempt this explanation. But this attempt brings into clear relief the unscientific character of what had passed and yet still passes as expositions of the science of political economy. In it we are deliberately told that the laws which it is the object of political economy to discover, are, in the first part of its inquiries, natural laws, but that in the later and practically more important part of those inquiries, they are human laws! Political economy of this sort is as incongruous as the image that troubled Nebuchadnezzar, with its head of fine gold and its feet part of iron and part of clay, for in the first part its subject-matter is natural law, and in the last and practically more important, it is human law.

Let us examine this argument carefully, for it is made on behalf of the current political economy by a man who from his twelfth year had been carefully trained in systematic logic and who before he wrote this had won

* Book II., Chapter I., Sec. 1, "Principles of Political Economy."

the highest reputation as a logician, by a great work on systematic logic, that is repeated and accepted to this day by professors of political economy in universities and colleges that make systematic logic a part of their curriculum.

To make this examination is to see that the plausibility of the argument comes from the leading proposition—"The things once there, mankind individually or collectively can do with them as they like." It is evidently this that in the mind of Mill himself and in the minds of the professors and students who have since gone over his "Principles of Political Economy," has seemed to prove beyond peradventure that though the laws of production may be natural laws, the laws of distribution are human laws. For in itself this proposition is a self-evident truth. Nothing, indeed, can be clearer than that "the things once there, mankind individually or collectively can do with them as they like"—that is to say, wealth once produced, human law may distribute it as human will may ordain.

Yet while this proposition that things once there mankind can do with them as they like, is in itself irrefutable, the argument in which it is introduced is an egregious instance of the fallacy called by the logicians *petitio principii*, or begging the question. The question that Mill is arguing is whether what is called in political economy the distribution of wealth is a matter of natural law or a matter of human law, and what he does is to cite the fact that in what is called in human law the distribution of wealth, mankind can do as they like, and assume from that that the distribution of wealth in the economic sense of the term is a matter of human law—"a matter of human institution solely."

Such a fallacy could not have been proposed by Mill, himself a trained logician, nor could it have passed current with the trained logicians who since his time, leaving their logic behind them, have written treatises on political economy, had it not been for the fact that in the scholastic political economy the real nature of the distribution of wealth has been slurred over and the question of what natural laws may have to do with it utterly ignored. Let us endeavor to settle this:

The original meaning of the word distribution is that of a division into or among. Distribution is thus an action, presupposing an exertion of will, and involving a power of giving that will effect. Now as to things already there, that is to say with wealth that has been already produced, it is perfectly clear that their division or distribution among men is determined entirely by human will backed by human force. With such a distribution nature is not concerned and in it she takes no part. Things already there, wealth already produced, belong to nature only in what logicians would call their accident, matter. But while still subject to material laws, such as the law of gravitation, who shall possess or enjoy them is a matter purely of human will and force. Mankind can place them at the disposal of whomsoever they please and on whatever terms.

Thus, distribution in this sense, the distribution of things already in existence, is indeed a matter solely of human will and power. If I would know the law of distribution in this sense of human law, I cannot look to political economy, but where settled institutions have not grown up or are discarded, must look to the will of the strongest. Where in civilized society it is human institutions that decide among whom wealth shall be divided, as for instance in case of an insolvent, in case of the estate of a deceased person, or in case of controverted ownership, the municipal law governing such distribution is to be found recorded in written or printed statutes, in the decisions of judges or in traditions of common use and wont. It is in cases of dispute authoritatively expounded by courts, and is carried into effect by sheriffs or constables or other officials having at their back the coercive power of the state, with its sanctions of seizure of property and person, fine, imprisonment and death.

But from its very rudest expression, where what obtains is

> "The good old rule,
> . . . . . . the simple plan,
> That they should take who have the power,
> And they should keep who can,"

to societies where the most elaborate machinery for declaring and enforcing human laws of distribution exists, such laws of distribution always are and always must be based upon human will and human force.

How then can we talk of natural laws of distribution? Laws of nature are not written or printed, or carved on pillars of stone or brass. They have no parliaments, or legislatures, or congresses to enact them, no judges to declare them, no constables to enforce them. What then can we really mean by natural laws of the distribution of wealth? What is the mode or method by which without human agency wealth may be said to be distributed by natural law, and without human agency, among individuals or classes of individuals? Here is the difficulty that not having been cleared up in economic works has given plausibility to the assumption into which the scholastic economy has fallen in assuming that the only laws of distribution with which political economy can deal are not natural laws at all, but only human laws—an assumption that must bring any science of political economy to an end with production.

Laws of nature, as was explained in the first part of this work (Book I., Chapter VIII.), are the names which we give to the invariable uniformities of coexistence and sequence which we find in external things, and which we call *laws* of nature because our reason apprehends in them the evidence of an originating will, preceding and superior to human will. Let us call in the aid of that most potent instrument of political economy, imaginative experiment, to see if we do not find evidences of such laws of nature, the only laws with which a true science of political economy can deal, in the matter of the distribution of wealth:

A shifting of desert sands reveals to a roving tribe wealth produced in a long dead civilization—rings, coins, bracelets, precious stones and delicately carved marbles. The things *are* there. They have been produced. The tribesmen individually or collectively can do with them as they like—can place them at the disposal of whomsoever they please, and on whatever terms. Nature will not interfere. The desert sand and desert sky, the winds that sweep across it, the sun and moon and stars that look down on it, the living things that prowl or crawl over it, will make no remonstrance whatever the tribesmen may choose to do with this wealth that is there—that has already centuries ago been produced.

But things freshly produced this day or this minute are as truly *here* as things produced centuries ago. Why should not mankind individually or collectively do with them also as they like; place them at the disposal of whomsoever they please and on whatever terms they choose? They could do so with no more remonstrance from the things themselves or from external nature than would attend the rifling of Egyptian tombs by Bedouins. Why should not civilized men rifle the products of farm or mine or mill as soon as they appear? Human law interposes no objection to such collective action, for human law is but an expression of collective human will, and changes or ceases with the changes in that will. Natural law, so far as it is comprehended in what we call physical law, interposes no objection—the laws of matter and energy in all their forms and combinations pay no heed whatever to human ownership.

Yet it needs no economist to tell us that if in any country the products of a living civilization were treated as the Bedouins treat the products of a dead civilization, the swift result would be fatal to that civilization—would be poverty, famine and death to the people individually and collectively. This result would come utterly irrespective of human law. It would make no difference whether the appropriation of "things once there" without regard to the will of the producer were in defiance of human law or under the sanctions of human law; the result would be the same. The moment producers saw that what they produced might be taken from them without their consent, production would cease and starvation begin. Clearly then, this inevitable result is not a consequence of human law, but a consequence of natural law. Not a consequence of the natural laws of matter and motion, but a consequence of natural laws of a different kind—laws no less immutable than the natural laws of matter and motion.

For natural law is not all comprehended in what we call physical law. Besides the laws of nature which relate to matter and energy, there are also laws of nature that relate to spirit, to thought and will. And should we treat the present products of farm or mine or mill or factory as we may treat the products of a dead civilization, we shall feel the remonstrance of an immutable law of nature wherever we come in conflict with the moral law. This is not to say that any division of wealth that mankind individually or collectively may choose to make will be interfered with or prevented. Things once here, once in existence in the present, are absolutely in the control of the men of the present, and "they can place them at the disposal of whomsoever they please and on whatever terms." Any remonstrance of the moral law of nature to their action will not show itself in, or in relation to, these identical things. But it will show itself in the future—in checking or preventing the production of such things. Things once produced *are* then and there already in existence, and may be distributed as mankind may will. But the things on which the natural laws of distribution exert their control are not things already produced, but things which are being, or are yet to be, produced.

In other words, production in political economy is not to be conceived of as something which goes on for a while and then stops, when its product wealth has been brought into being; nor is it to be conceived of as something related only to a production that is finished and done. Both production and distribution are properly conceived of as continuous, resembling not the drawing of water in a bucket but the drawing of water through a pipe—or better still, in the conveyance of water over an elevation by means of a bent pipe or siphon, of which the shorter arm may stand for production and the longer for distribution. It is in our power to tap this longer arm of the pipe at any point below the highest. and take what water is *already there.* But the moment we do so, the continuity of the stream is at an end, and the water will cease to flow.

Production and distribution are in fact not separate things, but two mentally distinguishable parts of one thing—the exertion of human labor in the satisfaction of human desire. Though materially distinguishable, they are as closely related as the two arms of the siphon. And as it is the outflow of water at the longer end of the siphon that is the cause of the inflow of water at the shorter end, so it is that distribution is really the cause of production, not production the cause of distribution. In the ordinary course, things are not distributed because they have been produced, but are produced in order that they may be distributed. Thus interference with the distribution of wealth is interference with the production of wealth, and shows its effect in lessened production.

To use again the analogy supplied by our material frames. Blood stands in the same relation to the physical body that wealth does to the social body, distributing throughout all parts of the physical frame potentialities akin to those which wealth carries through the social frame. But though the organs that distribute this vital current are different from the organs that produce it, their relations are so intimate that seriously to interfere with the distribution of the blood is necessarily to interfere with its production. Should we say of the blood that passes into the great pumping station, the heart, "It has been produced; it is here, and we may do with it as we please!" and acting on the word, divert it from its course through the organs of distribution—at once the great pump ceases to beat and the organs that produce blood lose their power and begin to decompose.

And as to pierce the heart and divert the blood that has been produced from the natural course of its distribution is to bring about the death of the physical organism most swiftly and certainly, so to interfere with the natural laws of the distribution of wealth is to bring about a like death of the social organism. If we seek for the reason of ruined cities and dead civilizations we shall find it in this.

CHAPTER III.

THE COMMON PERCEPTION OF NATURAL LAW IN DISTRIBUTION.

SHOWING THE COMMON AND INERADICABLE PERCEPTION OF NATURAL LAWS OF DISTRIBUTION.

Mill's admission of natural law in his argument that distribution is a matter of human law—Sequence and consequence—Human will and the will manifest in nature—Inflexibility of natural laws of distribution—Human will powerless to affect distribution—This shown by attempts to affect distribution through restriction of production—Mill's confusion and his high character.

IT would seem impossible for a man of the logical acumen and training of John Stuart Mill to accept in deference to preconceived opinion, and to justify by such a transparent fallacy, such an incongruous conclusion as that while the laws of political economy relating to production are natural laws, the laws relating to distribution are human laws, without at least a glance towards the truth. And such a sidelong glance we find in the latter part of the argument which in the last chapter was given in full.

To bring this more clearly into view let me print it again, supplying the elisions in brackets, and emphasizing with italics words to which I would direct special attention:

We have here [in political economy] to consider, not the causes, but the *consequences*, of the [human] rules according to which wealth may be distributed. Those [*consequences*], at least, are as little arbitrary, and have as much the character of physical laws, as the laws of production. Human beings can control their own acts, but not the *consequences* of their acts either to themselves or to others. Society can subject the distribution of wealth to whatever rules it thinks best; but what *practical results* will flow from the operation of those rules, must be discovered, like any other physical or mental truths, by observation and reasoning.

Here we have, what would hardly be expected from the author of "Mill's System of Logic," an example of that improper use of the word consequence where sequence is really meant, which I referred to in Chapter VIII. of Book I.

To recall what was there said: A sequence is that which follows. To say that one thing is a sequence of another is to say that it has to its antecedent a relation of succession or coming after, but is not necessarily to say that this relation is invariable or causal. But a *con*sequence is that which follows *from*. To say that one thing is a consequence of another is really to say that it has to its antecedent not merely a relation of succession, but of invariable succession—the relation namely of effect to cause.

Our disposition to prefer the stronger word leads in common speech to the frequent use of consequence where merely sequence is really meant, or to speak of a result as the consequence of what we know can be only one of the causal elements in bringing it about. If a boy break a window-pane in throwing a stone at a cat, or a man is drowned in going in to swim, we are apt to speak of the one thing as a consequence of the other, though we know that stones are constantly thrown at cats without breaking windows and that men go in to swim without being drowned, and that the result in the particular case was not due to the human action alone, but to the concurrence with it of other causes, such as the force and direction of wind or tide, the attraction of gravitation, etc. This tendency to a loose use of the word consequence is of little or no moment in common speech, where what is really meant is well understood; but it becomes a fatal source of confusion in philosophical writing, where exactness is necessary, not merely that the writer be understood by the reader, but that he may really understand himself.

Now, what are the things which Mill here speaks of as consequences of human rules according to which wealth may be distributed: the things which (and not the causes of the human rules) we have, he says, to consider in political economy, and which he tells us have as much the character of physical laws as the laws of production, and "must be discovered, like any other physical or mental truths, by observation and reasoning"? They follow, and are thus sequences of human action, or as Mill subsequently speaks of them, "practical results," appearing as invariable uniformities in the actual outcome of man's efforts to regulate the distribution of wealth. But though sequences they clearly are not con-sequences of human action. To say that human beings can control their own acts but not what *follows from* those acts would be to deny the laws of causation. Since these invariable uniformities appearing in the practical results or sequences of man's action cannot be related as effects to man's action as cause, they are not properly con-sequences of man's action, but con-sequences of something independent of man's action.

The truth that Mill vaguely perceives and confusedly states in these sentences is in direct contradiction of his assertion that the distribution of wealth is a matter of human institution solely. It is, that the distribution of wealth is *not* a matter of human institution solely, and does *not* depend upon the laws and customs of society alone; that though human beings may control their own acts towards the distribution of wealth, and frame for their action such laws as the ruling portion of the community may wish, yet the practical results will not depend on this human action alone, but on that as combined with and dominated by another more permanent and powerful element—a something independent of human action that modifies the practical results of human action towards the distribution of wealth, as gravitation modifies the flight of a cannon ball.

Now these invariable sequences which come out in the practical results of man's action, and which we know only as effects, and cannot relate to man's action as cause, we are compelled by the mental necessity which demands a cause for every effect to refer to a causal antecedent in the nature of things, which, as explained in Book I., we call a law of nature. That is to say, invariable uniformities, modifying the effects of all human action, such as Mill confusedly recognizes in these sentences, are precisely what, apprehending them as manifestations of a higher than human will, we style laws of nature, or natural laws.

Mill's own definition of a law of nature ("System of Logic," Book III., Chapter IV.) is a uniformity in the course of nature, ascertained by what is regarded as a sufficient induction, and reduced to its most simple expression. Thus if observation and reasoning discover in the actual phenomena or practical results of man's action in the distribution of wealth uniformities which swerve or destroy the effect of human action not in exact conformity with them, these are the natural laws of distribution as clearly as similar sequences or uniformities which observation and reasoning discover in the phenomena of production are the natural laws of production. And what Mill is vaguely thinking of and confusedly writing about are clearly the very natural laws of distribution which he says do not exist.

In truth, the distribution of wealth is no more "a matter of human institution solely" than is the production of wealth. That human beings can control their own acts is true in one case as in the other, only in the same sense and to the same degree. Our will is free. But human will can only affect external nature by taking advantage of natural laws, which in the very name we give them carry the implication of a higher and more constant will. A boy may throw a stone or an artilleryman fire a cannon ball at the moon. If the result depended solely on the human action, both ball and stone would reach the moon. But the governance of natural law—without conformity to which even such action as throwing a stone or firing a cannon ball cannot take place—continuing to modify results, brings both to the ground again, the one in a few feet and the other in a few thousand feet.

And the natural laws which political economy discovers, whether we call them laws of production or laws of distribution, have the same proof, the same sanction and the same constancy as the physical laws. Human laws change, but the natural laws remain, the same yesterday, to-day and to-morrow, world without end; manifestations to us of a will that though we cannot obtain direct knowledge of it through the senses, we can yet see never slumbers nor sleeps and knows not change in jot or tittle.

If I can prove that this inflexibility to human effort is characteristic of the laws of distribution that political economy seeks to discover, I have proved finally and conclusively that the laws of distribution are not human laws, but natural laws. To do this it is only necessary to appeal to facts of common knowledge.

Now the three great laws of distribution, as recognized by all economists, though they are sometimes placed in different order, are the law of wages, the law of interest and the law of rent. Into these three elements or factors, the entire result of production is by natural law distributed. Now I do not of course mean to say that human law may not take from the part which under the natural law of distribution might be enjoyed by one man or set of men and give it to another, for as I have already said all wealth or any wealth from the moment it is produced is entirely at the disposition of human law, and mankind can do with it as they please. What I mean to say is that human law is utterly powerless directly to alter distribution, so that the laborer as laborer will get more wages or less wages, the capitalist as capitalist more interest or less interest, or the landowner as landowner more rent or less rent, or in any way alter the conditions of distribution fixed by natural law under existing industrial conditions. This has been tried again and again by the strongest governments, and is to some extent still being tried, but always unavailingly.

In England, as in other countries, there have been at various times attempts to regulate wages by law, sometimes to decrease them and sometimes to increase them below or above the level fixed at the time by natural law. But it was found that in the one case no law could prevent the laborer from asking and the employer from paying more than this legal rate when the natural law, or as we usually say the equation of demand and supply, made wages higher, and that no law, even when backed by grants in aid of wages, as was done in England during the beginning of this century, could in the opposite case keep wages at a higher rate. So it has proved with interest. There have been numberless attempts to keep down interest, and the State of New York retains to this day on her statute-book a law limiting, though with considerable holes, the rate of interest to six per cent. But such laws never have succeeded and do not now succeed in keeping interest below the natural rate. Lenders receive and borrowers pay that rate in the form of sales, premiums, discounts and bonuses, where the law forbids them to do it openly. So, too, in the case of rent. The British Parliament has recently attempted to reduce agricultural rent in certain cases in Ireland by instituting officials with power to fix "fair rents"—what should be paid by the tenant to the landlord. They have in many cases cut down the income of certain of the landlords, but they have not lessened rent. They have merely divided what before went to the landlord between him and the existing tenant, and a new tenant must pay, part in rent to the landlord and part in tenant right to the existing tenant, as much for the use of the land as it would have commanded if this attempt to reduce rent had not been made.

And so it has been with attempts of human law to fix and regulate prices, which involve the same great laws of distribution in combined forms. Human law is always potent to do as mankind will with what has been produced, but it cannot directly affect distribution. That it can reach only through production.

Nothing indeed could be more inconsistent with common perceptions than this notion into which the scholastic economists have fallen, that the distribution of wealth is *less* a matter of natural law than the production of wealth. The fact is (the reason of the fact will be considered hereafter) that the common perceptions of men recognize the immutability of the natural laws of distribution more quickly and more certainly than of the natural laws of production. If we look over the legislation by which the ruling portion of our communities have striven to affect the distribution of wealth, we shall find that (as if conscious of its hopelessness) they have seldom if ever tried directly to affect the distribution of wealth; but have tried to affect distribution indirectly through production.

An English Elizabeth or James wishes to alter the practical outcome of the distribution of wealth in favor of an Essex or Villiers, and to accomplish this imposes restrictions upon the production of gold lace or playing cards. A Russian Czar desires to alter the distribution of wealth in favor of one of his boyars, and seeks that end by making a tract of land the property of his favorite and forbidding peasants to leave it, thus preventing them from engaging in production except on his terms. Or, to come nearer the present in time and place, a Carnegie or a Wharton wishes to alter distribution in his favor so largely that he may play at building libraries and endowing schools of political economy (?); he seeks his end by getting Congress to restrict the production of iron, steel or nickel, by imposing a duty upon importation.

But it is not alone in the sentences I have reprinted that Mill shows an undefined consciousness that the laws of the distribution of wealth which it is the proper business of political economy to discover are natural laws, not human laws. Though he does not retract his statement that "the distribution of wealth depends on the laws and customs of society," and formally proceeds "to the consideration of the different modes of distributing the produce of land and labor which have been adopted in practice or may be conceived in theory," yet we find him afterwards (Book II., Chapter III., Sec. 1) speaking of laws according to which "the produce distributes itself by the spontaneous action of the interests of those concerned." If there be laws according to which produce *distributes itself*, they certainly cannot be human laws. King Canute, we are told, once tried by edict to turn back the tide; but who has ever dreamed that produce, whether houses or metals or wheat or hay, or even pigs or sheep, could by ukase or irade, act of Parliament or resolution of Congress, be made to *distribute itself?*

The truth is that in the long discussion of the distribution of wealth, which in John Stuart Mill's "Principles of Political Economy" succeeds to what I have quoted, he neither follows what he formally states, that distribution is a matter of human institution solely, and depends on the laws and customs of society; nor yet does he follow what he confusedly admits, that it is a matter of natural law. Passing to a consideration of the origin of private property in human law, and beginning with Communism and Socialism, the Moravians, the Rappists, the followers of Louis Blanc and Cabet, St. Simonism and Fourierism, he rambles along, mixing what properly belongs to the science of political economy with discussions of competition and custom, slavery, peasant proprietors, metayers, cottiers, the means of abolishing cottier tenancy and popular remedies for low wages, without either clearly giving the laws of distribution or saying what they are. And the reader who wishes to discover what the ablest and most systematic of scholastic economists takes to be the laws of distribution of wealth must after going through this mass of dissertation keep on through some forty chapters or 600 pages more, and finally fish them out for himself—only to find when he gets them or thinks that he gets them, that they do not correlate with each other.

As I have said, I only speak of John Stuart Mill as the best example of what has passed as the scientific exposition of political economy. The same absence of a really scientific method—that is to say the same want of order and precision—will be found in the treatment of distribution in all the treatises of the school of economists, now called the Classical school, of which Mill may be deemed the culmination. And it is to be found in even worse degree in the so-called Historical and Austrian schools which have within recent years succeeded the school of Mill in all our great universities. They are indeed so far behind the predecessors at whom they affect to sneer, that they make no attempt even at order and precision. Whoever would have an economic contrast suggested to him like that of Hamlet's "Hyperion to a Satyr," let him compare John Stuart Mill's "Principles of Political Economy" with the most pretentious of recent "Principles of Economics."

CHAPTER IV.

THE REAL DIFFERENCE BETWEEN LAWS OF PRODUCTION AND OF DISTRIBUTION.

SHOWING THAT DISTRIBUTION HAS REFERENCE TO ETHICS, WHILE PRODUCTION HAS NOT.

The laws of production are physical laws; the laws of distribution moral laws, concerned only with spirit—This the reason why the immutable character of the laws of distribution is more quickly and clearly recognized.

MILL is clearly wrong in the distinction which he seeks to draw between the production of wealth and the distribution of wealth with regard to the kind of laws which it is the proper business of these departments of political economy to discover.

But there is an important difference between them which, although he has failed to distinguish it, probably lies in vague way at the bottom of the notion that the laws of production and the laws of distribution are different kinds of laws. It is, that the branch of the science which treats of the distribution of wealth is that in which the relations of political economy to ethics are clearer and closer than in that branch which treats of production.

In short, the distinction between the laws of production and the laws of distribution is not, as is erroneously taught in the scholastic political economy, that the one set of laws are natural laws, and the other human laws. Both sets of laws are laws of nature. The real distinction is pointed out in the last chapter, that the natural laws of production are physical laws and the natural laws of distribution are moral laws. And it is this that enables us to see in political economy more clearly than in any other science, that the government of the universe is a moral government, having its foundation in justice. Or, to put this idea into terms that fit it for the simplest comprehension, that the Lord our God is a just God.

In considering the production of wealth we are concerned with natural laws of which we can only ask what is, without venturing to raise the question of what ought to be. Even if we can imagine a world in which beings like ourselves could maintain an existence and satisfy their material desires in any other way than by the application of labor to land under relations of uniform sequence not substantially different from those invariable sequences of matter and motion and life and being which we denominate physical laws, we cannot venture to apply to these physical laws, of which we can primarily say only that they exist, any idea of ought. Even in matters as to which we can imagine considerable differences between the physical uniformities that we observe in this world and those that might exist in a world in other respects resembling this—such for instance as might be brought about by a change in the distance of our earth from the sun, or in the inclination of its axis to the ecliptic, or in the density of its atmospheric envelop; or even by a change in such uniformities as seem to us to involve exceptions to a more general uniformity, like that exception to the general law of the contraction of water in cooling which causes it at the freezing-point to expand—there is nothing that has any reference to right or justice, or that arouses in us any perception of ought or duty.

For the perception of right or justice, the recognition of ought or duty, has no connection with or relation to two of the three elements or categories into which we may by analysis resolve the world as it is presented in consciousness to our reasoning faculties. That is to say, right or justice, ought or duty, do not and cannot have any relation either to matter or to energy, but only to spirit. They presuppose conscious will, and cannot be extended beyond the limits in which we recognize or assume a will having freedom to act.

Thus is it that in considering the nature of wealth or the production of wealth we come into no direct and necessary contact with the ethical idea, the idea of right or justice. It is only when and as we endeavor to pierce behind the invariable uniformities of matter and motion to which we give the name of laws of nature and recognize them in our thought as manifestations of an originating or creative spirit, for which our common name is God, in its dealing with other, and though inferior, essentially spiritual beings, that the idea of right or justice can have any place in that branch of political economy which deals with the nature of wealth or the laws of its production.

But the moment we turn from a consideration of the laws of the production of wealth to a consideration of the laws of the distribution of wealth the idea of ought or duty becomes primary. All consideration of distribution involves the ethical principle; is necessarily a consideration of ought or duty—a consideration in which the idea of right or justice is from the very first involved. And this idea cannot be truly conceived of as having limits or being subject to change, for it is an idea or relation, like the idea of a square or of a circle or of parallel lines, which must be the same in any other world, no matter how far separated in space or time, as in this world. It is not without reason that in our colloquial use of the words we speak of a just man as "a square man" or "a straight man." As Montesquieu says:

> Justice is a relation of congruity which really subsists between two things. This relation is always the same, whatever being considers it, whether it be God, or an angel, or lastly a man.

This I take to be the reason of the fact which in Chapter II. of this Book was referred to—that the immutable character of the laws of distribution is even more quickly and clearly recognized than the immutable character of the laws of production. Princes, politicians and legislatures attempt to influence distribution, but they always try to do it, not by aiming at distribution directly but by aiming at distribution indirectly, through laws that directly affect production.

CHAPTER V.

OF PROPERTY.

SHOWING THAT PROPERTY DEPENDS UPON NATURAL LAW.

The law of distribution must be the law which determines ownership—John Stuart Mill recognizes this; but extending his error treats property as a matter of human institution solely—His assertion quoted and examined—His utilitarianism—His further contradictions.

SINCE the distribution of wealth is an assignment of ownership, the laws of distribution must be the laws which determine property in the things produced. Or to put it in another way, the principle which gives ownership must be the principle which determines the distribution of wealth. Thus what we may speak of in political economy as the law of property and the law of distribution are not merely laws of the same kind, springing from the same principle, but are in reality different expressions of the same fundamental law. Hence, in considering the origin and basis of property we come again to the question, is it the law of nature or the laws of man that it is the office of the science of political economy to discover? To say that the distribution of wealth is "a matter of human enactment solely" is to say that property can have no other basis than human law; while to admit any basis of property in laws of nature is to say that the distribution of wealth is a matter of natural law.

It is another evidence of the superiority of John Stuart Mill in logical acumen that he seems to have been the only one of the accredited economic writers who has recognized this necessary relation between the laws of distribution and the origin of property. From the introductory section of his Book "Distribution," the section I have already quoted in full, he proceeds at once to a consideration of the origin of property, and indeed the first two chapters of the Book are entitled "Of Property."

But he is consistent in error. The same want of discrimination that leads him to treat distribution as a matter of human institution solely, leads him to treat property as a matter of human institution solely. Hence, his consideration of property does not, as it should, help him to see the incongruity of the notion that while the laws of production are natural laws the laws of distribution are human laws; but gives to that error such seeming plausibility as one error may give to another. Contradictions and confusions are however as marked in his discussion of property as in his discussion of distribution.

This is shown in the introductory paragraph of his treatment of property, Book II., Chapter I., Sec. 2, which is as follows.

> Private property, as an institution, did not owe its origin to any of those considerations of utility, which plead for the maintenance of it when established. Enough is known of rude ages, both from history and from analogous states of society in our own time, to show, that tribunals (which always precede laws) were originally established, not to determine rights, but to repress violence and terminate quarrels. With this object chiefly in view, they naturally enough gave legal effect to first occupancy, by treating as the aggressor the person who first commenced violence, by turning, or attempting to turn, another out of possession. The preservation of the peace, which was the original object of civil government, was thus attained; while by confirming, to those who already possessed it, even what was not the fruit of personal exertion, a guarantee was incidentally given to them and others that they would be protected in what was so.

All this I deny. It is in fact blank contradiction. Let the reader look over and consider it. In the first sentence we are told that private property did not originate in considerations of utility. In the second, that "tribunals (which always precede laws) were originally established, not to determine rights, but to repress violence and terminate quarrels." In the third, that they did this by treating as the aggressor the person who first commenced violence. In the fourth, that the preservation of the peace was the original object of such tribunals, and that by securing possession where there was no right they incidentally secured possession where there was right.

Thus, the first sentence asserts that private property did not originate in considerations of utility, and the three succeeding sentences that it did. For when all consideration of right is eliminated what remains as a reason for the preservation of the peace by the repression of violence and the termination of quarrels, if not the consideration of utility? What Mill tells us, is that society originally acted on the principle of the schoolmaster who says, "If I find any fighting I will not stop to ask the right or wrong, but will flog the boy who struck the first blow, *for* I cannot have the school thrown into disorder." If this is not a substitution of the principle of utility for the principle of right, what is it? And to this contradiction of himself, Mill adds that by confirming wrongful possession, society incidentally guarantees rightful possession!—something in the nature of things as impossible as that two railway trains should pass each other on a single track.

The fact is that Mill in his consideration of property is caught in the toils of that utilitarian philosophy which seeks to make the principle of expediency take the place of the principle of justice. Men can no more do this consistently than they can live without breathing, and Mill in his very attempt to base the institution of property on human law is driven despite himself into recognizing the moral law, and into talking of right and wrong, of ought and ought not, of just and unjust. Now these are terms which imply a natural law of morality. They can have no meaning whatever if expediency be the basis of property and human law its warrant.

The contradictions of this paragraph are shown through the whole consideration of property it introduces. While he strives to treat property as a matter of human institution solely, yet over and over again we find Mill forced to abandon this position and appeal to something superior to human institution—to right or justice.

Thus, in what follows the paragraph I have quoted, we find statements utterly contradictory of the notion that property has its origin in expediency and is determined by human enactment.

In the very next section to that in which we are told that the origin of property is not in justice but in expediency, not in the desire to determine rights, but the desire to repress violence, we are told (the italics being mine):

> The social arrangements of modern Europe commenced from a distribution of property which was the result, not of *just* partition, or acquisition by industry, but of conquest and violence: and notwithstanding what industry has been doing for many centuries to modify the work of force, the system still retains many and large traces of its origin. The laws of property have never yet conformed to the principles on which the *justification* of private property rests. They have made property of things which never *ought* to be made property, and absolute property where only a qualified property *ought* to exist.

Here we are told that, as a matter of fact, human laws of property did not originate in the expediency of repressing violence, but in violence itself; that they have never conformed to what we can only understand as the natural law of property, but have violated that natural law, by treating as property things that under it are not property. For to say that a human law *ought* to be different from what the legislature enacts is to say that there is a natural law by which human laws are to be tested.

What indeed that natural law of property is by which all human enactments are to be tested, Mill a little later shows himself to be conscious of, for he says:

> Private property, in every defense made of it, is supposed to mean the guarantee to individuals of the fruits of their own labor and abstinence.

And this basis of a natural right of property—a right which is unaffected by and independent of all human enactments—is still further on even more definitely and clearly stated:

> The institution of property, when limited to its essential elements, consists in the recognition, in each person, of a *right* to the exclusive disposal of what he or she have produced by their own exertions, or received, either by gift or by fair agreement, without force or fraud, from those who produced it. The foundation of the whole is, the *right* of producers to what they themselves have produced.
>
> The *right* of property includes, then, the freedom of acquiring by contract. The *right* of each to what he has produced, implies a *right* to what has been produced by others, if obtained by their free consent.

After thus conceding everything to natural law, Mill becomes concerned again for human law, and appeals to the "categorical imperative" of Kant, the *ought* of moral law, to give sanction under certain circumstances to human law, declaring that:

> Possession which has not been legally questioned within a moderate number of years, *ought* to be, as by the laws of all nations it is, a complete title.

Then, recognizing for a moment the incongruity of making legal possession—that is to say possession by virtue of human law—equivalent to possession by virtue of natural law, he continues:

> It is scarcely needful to remark, that these reasons for not disturbing acts of injustice of old date, cannot apply to *unjust* systems or institutions; since a bad law or usage is not one bad act, in the remote past, but a perpetual repetition of bad acts, as long as the law or usage lasts.

Now property, Mill himself has always spoken of as a system or institution, which it certainly is. And he has just before stated that the existing systems or institutions of property have their source in violence and force, and therefore are certainly in his own view unjust and bad. Hence what he tells us here is in plain English that the sanction of prescription cannot be pleaded in defense of property condemned by the natural or moral law. This is perfectly true, but it is in utter contradiction of the notion that property is a matter of human law.

CHAPTER VI.

CAUSE OF CONFUSION AS TO PROPERTY.

SHOWING WHY AND HOW POLITICAL ECONOMISTS FELL INTO SUCH CONFUSIONS WITH REGARD TO PROPERTY.

Mill blinded by the pre-assumption that land is property—He all but states later the true principle of property, but recovers by substituting in place of the economic term "land," the word in its colloquial use—The different senses of the word illustrated from the shore of New York harbor—Mill attempts to justify property in land, but succeeds only in justifying property in wealth.

LET us pause a moment before we go further in our examination of Mill's reasoning. What is it that so perplexes this trained logician and honestly minded man, involving him in such utter contradictions and confusions when he endeavors to trace the basis of property? It is evidently the same thing that has prevented all the scholastic economists, both those who preceded and those who have succeeded him, from giving any clear and consistent statement of the laws of distribution or of the origin of property. This is a pre-assumption they cannot bring themselves to abandon—the pre-assumption that land must be included in the category of property and a place found in the laws of distribution for the income of landowners. Since natural law can take no cognizance of the ownership of land, they are driven in order to support this pre-assumption to treat distribution and property as matters of human institution solely.

Mill, who though befogged by his utilitarian philosophy is in many respects the superior of all these writers, starts on his investigation of distribution and property with the same pre-assumption, or, to use our colloquial phrase, with the same "string tied to his leg." He had been, as they all have been—from the really great Adam Smith to the most recent purveyors of economic nonsense in Anglo-German jargon—accustomed to regard property in land as the most certain, most permanent, most tangible, of all property—that which the lawyers call *real* property, and which in common speech, where the unqualified word "property" usually means landed property, is recognized as the highest expression of ownership. And his logic was not strong enough to permit him even at its call to lay rude hands upon what to Englishmen of his class and time was the most sacred of institutions—what the very Ark of the Covenant was to the pious Jew. He did indeed, come so near questioning it as to excite the dismay of his contemporaries who deemed him a radical of radicals for utterances that squint towards the truth. But he always draws back from uttering it.

The real basis of property, the real fundamental law of distribution, is so clear that no one who attempts to reason can utterly and consistently ignore it. It is the natural law which gives the product to the producer. But this cannot be made to cover property in land. Hence the persistent effort to find the origin of property in human law and its base in expediency. It is evident, even where Mill speaks of property generally, as he has done in what I have to this point commented on, that the real cause of his contradictions and confusions is that he has always in mind property in land. But the failure of the attempt to bring this species of property under the only possible justification of property, the right of the producer to the product, is even more painfully clear when he comes, as he does in Chapter II., Sec. 3, specifically to treat of it.

He begins this by another admission of the truth utterly inconsistent with the derivation of property from expediency; saying:

> Nothing is implied in property but the right of each to his (or her) own faculties.

And then after some long disquisitions on bequest and inheritance which I will not comment on here lest it might divert the reader from the main subject, he continues again:

> The essential principle of property being to assure to all persons what they have produced by their labor and accumulated by their abstinence, this principle cannot apply to what is not the produce of labor, the raw material of the earth.

Abstinence is not a doing but a not doing, a refraining from consuming. The essential principle of property being to assure to all persons what they have produced by their labor, this of course includes what having been produced by labor is afterwards accumulated by abstinence. These words "and accumulated by their abstinence" are superfluous, having no weight or place in the argument, but their introduction is significant of the disposition to assume that capital rather than labor is the active factor in production.

But though a little superfluous in phrase, this statement is true and clear. In the conflict going on in Mill's mind the perception of a basis of property in natural law seems, in the admission that the principle of property *cannot* apply to land, to have finally conquered both the notion that its basis is in human law and the pre-assumption from which the notion comes.

But this is hardly for a moment. In the next sentence, not paragraph, and on the very same line in the printed page, the pre-assumption that has confused him asserts its power and Mill proceeds to argue that the principle of property *does* apply to land. He does this by what is in reality, though doubtless unconsciously to him, a juggle with words. But as his argument is the stock argument of the scholastic economists, I will quote it in full, distinguishing by italics the sentence already given:

> *The essential principle of property being to assure to all persons what they have produced by their labor and accumulated by their abstinence, this principle cannot apply to what is not the produce of labor, the raw material of the earth.* If the land derived its productive power wholly from nature, and not at all from industry, or if there were any means of discriminating what is derived from each source, it not only would not be necessary, but it would be the height of injustice, to let the gift of nature be engrossed by individuals. The use of the land in agriculture must indeed, for the time being, be of necessity exclusive; the same person who has plowed and sown must be permitted to reap; but the land might be occupied for one season only, as among the ancient Germans; or might be periodically redivided as population increased: or the State might be the universal landlord, and the cultivators tenants under it, either on lease or at will.
>
> But though land is not the produce of industry, most of its valuable qualities are so. Labor is not only requisite for using, but almost equally so for fashioning, the instrument. Considerable labor is often required at the commencement, to clear the land for cultivation. In many cases, even when cleared, its productiveness is wholly the effect of labor and art. The Bedford Level produced little or nothing until artificially drained. The bogs of Ireland, until the same thing is done to them, can produce little besides fuel. One of the barrenest soils in the world, composed of the material of the Goodwin Sands, the Pays de Waes in Flanders, has been so fertilized by industry, as to have become one of the most productive in Europe. Cultivation also requires buildings and fences, which are wholly the produce of labor. The fruits of this industry cannot be reaped in a short period. The labor and outlay are immediate, the benefit is spread over many years, perhaps over all future time. A holder will not incur this labor and outlay when strangers and not himself will

be benefited by it. If he undertakes such improvements, he must have a sufficient period before him in which to profit by them; and he is in no way so sure of having always a sufficient period as when his tenure is perpetual.

These are the reasons which form the justification in an economical point of view, of property in land.

This argument begins by asserting that the principle of property *cannot* apply to land; it ends by asserting that it *does*. The language is loose, for Mill indulges in a practice dangerous where exactness is important, the use of paraphrases for economic terms, such as "raw material of the earth" and "gift of nature" for land; "industry" for labor, and "valuable qualities"* for useful qualities, or productive powers. But carefully to consider these reasons which are held to justify the unjustifiable, is to see that their plausibility is brought about by the same way that a juggler seems to change a watch into a turnip—the substitution of one thing for another thing while attention is distracted. In this case the substitution is of one sense of a word for another different sense of the same word.

The word land, as before explained, has two senses. One of these is that of the dry and solid superficies of the globe as distinguished from water or air, or that of the cultivatable matter of the earth as distinguished from rock or sand or ice or bog. In this sense we frequently speak of "improved land" or "made land." The other, the economic sense of the word, is that of the natural or passive element in production, including the whole external world, with all its powers, qualities and products, as distinguished from the human or active element, labor, and its sub-element, capital. In this sense we cannot

* Value in political economy should be restricted to value in exchange, and the only sense in which land or other natural objects or their qualities may be said to have value in themselves is that of value in use. (See Book II., Chapter X.)

speak of "improved land" or "made land." Such phrases would involve contradiction in terms.

Now in the reasoning just quoted Mill slips from one to the other of these two senses of the word land, not merely in the same connection, but in the same sentence, and even as between the noun and its pronoun without notice to the reader and seemingly without consciousness on his own part.

The first suggestion of this substitution comes in the *ifs* of the second sentence. *If*, says Mill, land derived its productive power wholly from nature and not at all from labor, or *if* there were any means of discriminating what is derived from each source, it would be the height of injustice to let land be engrossed by individuals.

Why these *ifs?* Mill is here writing as a political economist, in a work entitled "Principles of Political Economy," and for the purpose in this particular place of discovering whether there is any justification from an economic point of view of property in land. Land, as a term of political economy, *means* that element of productive power derived from nature and not at all from labor. It has and can have no other meaning. The first principle of political economy is the distinction between the productive power derived wholly from nature, for which its term is land, and the productive power derived from human exertion, for which its term is labor. Where the reason can find no "means of discriminating what is derived from each source," political economy becomes impossible, and to confuse this discrimination is to abandon political economy.

This is precisely what Mill does, when he goes on in the first sentence of the next paragraph to tell us that "though *land* is not the produce of industry, most of *its* valuable qualities are so." He is abandoning political economy by dropping in the pronoun the sense in which he uses the word land in the noun, and falling with seeming unconsciousness into the vague sense of common speech. When he says that land is not the produce of industry he uses the word in the economic sense. But when he says that qualities of land are the produce of labor he is using the word in that loose ordinary sense in which we speak of "improved land" or "made land." For what single quality of land in the economic sense of the word is the produce of labor? Is it gravitation? Is it extension? Is it cohesion? Is it chemical affinities or repulsions? Is it the qualities shown in generation and germination and growth? Why, Mill himself in the first chapter of the first book of his "Principles of Political Economy" declares that the primary power of labor, that by which man can alone act on the external world, consists in that power of muscular contraction by means of which he can to some slight extent move or arrest the motion of matter, adding:

> Labor, then, in the physical world, is always and solely employed in putting objects in motion; the properties of matter, the laws of nature, do all the rest.

These properties of matter, these laws of nature which when labor changes things in place do all the rest, are qualities of land in the economic sense of the word land. Mill does not mean that *they* are ever the produce of industry? He cannot mean that. The fact is, that abandoning the economic sense of the word land, he resorts to that loose colloquial sense of the word in which we speak of "improving land" or "making land." And it is with illustrations of "improved land" and "made land" that he goes on to show how the qualities of land are products of labor.

Let me too do a little illustrating, for the confusions to which Mill succumbed are in these closing years of the century being crammed into the minds of young people by a thousand "professors of political economy:"

I am writing these pages on the shore of Long Island, where the Bay of New York contracts to what is called the Narrows, nearly opposite the point where our legalized robbers, the Custom-House officers, board incoming steamers to ask strangers to take their first American swear, and where if false oaths really colored the atmosphere the air would be bluer than is the sky on this gracious day. I turn from my writing-machine to the window, and drink in, with a pleasure that never seems to pall, the glorious panorama.

"What do you see?" If in ordinary talk I were asked this, I should of course say, "I see land and water and sky, ships and houses and light clouds, and the sun, drawing to its setting, over the low green hills of Staten Island, and illuminating all."

But if the question refer to the terms of political economy, I should say, "I see land and wealth." Land, which is the natural factor of production; and wealth, which is the natural factor so changed by the exertion of the human factor, labor, as to fit it for the satisfaction of human desires. For water and clouds, sky and sun, and the stars that will appear when the sun is sunk, are, in the terminology of political economy, as much land as is the dry surface of the earth to which we narrow the meaning of the word in ordinary talk. And the window through which I look; the flowers in the garden; the planted trees of the orchard; the cow that is browsing beneath them; the Shore Road under the window; the vessels that lie at anchor near the bank, and the little pier that juts out from it: the trans-Atlantic liner steaming through the channel; the crowded pleasure-steamers passing by; the puffing tug with its line of mud-scows; the fort and dwellings on the opposite side of the Narrows; the lighthouse that will soon begin to cast its far-gleaming eye from Sandy Hook; the big wooden elephant of Coney Island; and the graceful sweep of the Brooklyn Bridge, that may be discovered from a little higher up; all alike fall into the economic term wealth—land modified by labor so as to afford satisfaction to human desires. All in this panorama that was before man came here, and would remain were he to go, belongs to the economic category land; while all that has been produced by labor belongs to the economic category wealth, so long as it retains its quality of ministering to human desire.

But on the hither shore, in view from the window, is a little rectangular piece of dry surface, evidently reclaimed from the line of water by filling in with rocks and earth. What is that? In ordinary speech it is land, as distinguished from water, and I should intelligibly indicate its origin by speaking of it as "made land." But in the categories of political economy there is no place for such a term as "made land." For the term land refers only and exclusively to productive powers derived wholly from nature and not at all from industry, and whatever is, and in so far as it is, derived from land by the exertion of labor, is wealth. This bit of dry surface raised above the level of the water by filling in stones and soil, is, in the economic category, not land, but wealth. It has land below it and around it, and the material of which it is composed has been drawn from land; but in itself it is, in the proper speech of political economy, wealth; just as truly as the ships I behold are not land but wealth, though they too have land below them and around them and are composed of materials drawn from land.

Now here is the evident confusion in Mill's thought, which he has perplexed by dropping from the terminology of political economy to the language of ordinary speech.

The Bedford Level, which is land that has been drained; the cultivatable bog of Ireland, which is land that has had a coating of soil put on it; the improved farms he refers to, which are land cleared or manured by labor, belong all of them to the same economic category as the little piece of "made land" visible from my window. In the qualities that he is considering in them they are all of them in the economic meaning not land at all, but wealth; not the free gift of nature, but the toil-earned produce of labor. In this, and so far as these qualities go, but no further—that is, in so far as they are wealth, not land, they are property; not because human agency can add any qualities to the natural factor, land; but because of the natural law of property, which gives to the producer the ownership of what his labor has produced.

Mill seems to think that he has shown the justification of property in land, but the reasons he gives only justify property in the produce of labor; thus in his own case adding a signal instance of the truth of what he has before said that "in every defense made of it, property is supposed to mean the guarantee to individuals of the fruits of their own labor."

BOOK V.

MONEY—THE MEDIUM OF EXCHANGE AND MEASURE OF VALUE

CONTENTS OF BOOK V.

MONEY—THE MEDIUM OF EXCHANGE AND MEASURE OF VALUE.

CHAPTER III.

MEDIUM OF EXCHANGE AND MEASURE OF VALUE.

SHOWING HOW THE COMMON MEDIUM OF EXCHANGE BECOMES THE COMMON MEASURE OF VALUE, AND WHY WE CANNOT FIND A COMMON MEASURE IN LABOR.

CHAPTER IV.

THE OFFICE OF CREDIT IN EXCHANGES.

SHOWING THAT THE ADVANCE OF CIVILIZATION ECONOMIZES THE USE OF MONEY.

CHAPTER V.

THE GENESIS OF MONEY.

SHOWING THAT THE LAW OF GRATIFYING DESIRES WITH THE LEAST EXERTION PROMPTS THE USE FROM TIME TO TIME OF THE MOST LABOR-SAVING MEDIUM AVAILABLE.

CHAPTER VI.

THE TWO KINDS OF MONEY.

SHOWING THAT ONE ORIGINATES IN VALUE FROM PRODUCTION AND THE OTHER IN VALUE FROM OBLIGATION.

INTRODUCTION TO BOOK V.

THIS Book is really in the nature of a supplement to Book II., "The Nature of Wealth." In my first draft of arrangement, a matter of much perplexity, the discussion of money was to have followed the discussion of value, with which it is so intimately connected; or at least, to have followed the discussion as to the definition of wealth. But to have given to the subject of money in Book II. the thorough treatment which present confusions seem to require would not only have disproportionately expanded that Book, but would have made needful the anticipation of some of the conclusions more logically and conveniently reached in Book III. and Book IV. I therefore finally determined as the best arrangement for the reader of this work to answer briefly in the last chapter of Book II. the question as to the relation of money to wealth which the conclusion of the discussion of the nature of wealth would be certain to bring, and to defer a fuller discussion of the subject of money until after the production and distribution of wealth had both been treated. This point has now been reached, and continuing as it were Chapter XXI. of Book II., "The Nature of Wealth," I proceed to the discussion of the medium of exchange and measure of value.

CHAPTER I.

CONFUSIONS AS TO MONEY.

SHOWING THE DIVERGENCE IN COMMON THOUGHT AND AMONG ECONOMISTS AS TO MONEY.

Present confusions as to money—Their cause—How to disentangle them.

THERE is no social idea or instrument with which civilized men are more generally and personally familiar than money. From early infancy to latest age we all use it in thought and speech and daily transactions, without practical difficulty in distinguishing what is money from what is not money. Yet as to what it really is and what it really does, there are both in common thought on economic subjects and in the writings of professed economists the widest divergences. This is particularly obvious in the United States at the time I write. For twenty years the money question has been under wide discussion, and before that, has had similar periods of wide discussion from the very foundation of the American colonies, to say nothing of the discussion that has gone on in Europe. Yet the attitude of Congress, of the State legislatures, of the political parties, and the press, shows that nothing like any clear conclusion as to first principles has yet been arrived at. As for the vast literature of the subject which has been put into print within recent years any attempt to extract from it a consensus of opinion as to the office and laws of money is likely to result in the feeling expressed by an intelligent man who recently made this attempt, that "The more one reads the more he feels that any sure knowledge on the question is beyond his comprehension."

The very latest American cyclopedia (Johnson's, 1896) gives this definition: "Money is that kind of currency which has an intrinsic value, and which thus if not used as currency would still be wealth." Thus, there are some who say that money really consists of the precious metals, and that whatever may be locally or temporarily or partially used as money can be so used only as a representative of these metals. They hold that the paper money which now constitutes so large a part of the currency of the civilized world derives its value from the promise, expressed or implied, to redeem it in one or another of these metals, and by way of assuring such redemption vast quantities of these precious metals are kept idly in store by governments and banks.

Of those who take this view, some hold that gold is the only true and natural money, in the present stage of civilization at least; while others hold that silver is as much or even more entitled to that place, and that the gravest evils result from its demonetization.

On the other hand there are those who say that what makes a thing money is the edict or fiat of government that it shall be treated and received as money.

And again, there are others still who contend that whatever can be used in exchange to the avoidance of barter is money, thus including in the meaning of the term, notes, checks, drafts, etc., issued by private parties, as fully as the coins or notes issued by governments or banks.

Much of the contradiction and confusion which exists in popular thought proceeds from the pressure of personal interests brought into the question by the relation of debtor and creditor. But the confusions which prevail among professed economists have a deeper source. They evidently result from the confusions which prevail in economic thought and teaching as to the nature of wealth and the cause of value. Money is the common measure of value, the common representative and exchanger of wealth. Unless we have clear ideas of the meaning of value and the nature of wealth, it is manifest therefore that we cannot form clear ideas as to the nature and functions of money. But since we have cleared up in the preceding chapters the meaning of the terms value and wealth, we are now in a position to proceed with an inquiry into the nature, functions and laws of money. It is unnecessary to waste time with any attempt to disentangle the maze of contradictory statements of fact and confusions of opinion with which the current literature of the subject is embarrassed. The true course of all economic investigation is to observe and trace the relation of those social phenomena that are obvious now and to us. For economic laws must be as invariable as physical laws, and as the chemist or astronomer can safely proceed only from relations which he sees do here and now exist to infer what has existed or will exist in another time and place, so it is with the political economist.

Yet we find, if we consider them, that these divergences in the definition of money spring rather from differences of opinion as to what ought to be considered and treated as money, than from differences as to what, as a matter of fact, money actually is. The men who differ most widely in defining money find no difficulty in agreeing as to what is meant by money in daily transactions. Since we cannot find a consensus of opinion among economists, our best plan is to seek it among ordinary people. To see what usually is meant by money we have only to note the essential characteristics of that which we all agree in treating as money in our practical affairs.

After we have seen what money really is, and what are the functions it performs, we shall then be in a position to determine what are the best forms of money.

CHAPTER II.

THE COMMON UNDERSTANDING OF MONEY.

SHOWING THAT THE COMMON USE OF MONEY IS TO BUY THINGS WITH, AND THAT ITS ESSENTIAL CHARACTER IS NOT IN ITS MATERIAL BUT IN ITS USE.

The use of money to exchange for other things—Buying and selling—Illustration of the travelers—Money not more valuable than other things, but more readily exchangeable—Exchanges without money—Checks, etc., not money—Different money in different countries—But money not made by government fiat—Does not necessarily consist of gold and silver—Or need intrinsic value—Its essential quality and definition.

WHEN we are confused as to the true meaning of an economic term, our best plan is to endeavor to obtain a consensus of opinion as to what the thing really is; what function it really performs.

If I have agreed to pay money to another the common understanding of what money is will not hold my agreement fulfilled if I offer him wood, or bricks, or services, or gold or silver bullion, even though, as closely as can be estimated, these may be of equal value to the money promised. My creditor might take such things in lieu of what I had agreed to pay. But he would be more likely to object, and his objection if fully expressed would amount to this: "What you agreed to pay me was money. With money I can buy anything that any one has to sell, and pay any debt I owe. But what you offer me is not money. It is something I would be willing to take if I happened to have any personal use for it. But I have no personal use for it, and to get any one to give me for it what I may want I must find some one who wants this particular thing and make a trade with him. What you propose would therefore put on me trouble, risk and loss not contemplated in our agreement." And the justice of this objection would be recognized by all fair men.

In this—in the ease with which it may be passed from hand to hand in canceling obligations or transferring ownership—lies the peculiar characteristic of money. It is not the intrinsic nature of the thing, but the use to which it is applied that gives its essential character to money, and constitutes the distinction between it and other things. Even children recognize this. I make friends with a little one of four or five, and, showing it a stick of candy, ask what that is for? it will say, "That is to eat." If I show a hat or a pair of shoes, it will say, "That is to wear." If I show a toy, it will say, "That is to play with." But if I show a piece of money, it will say, even though to it as yet all money may be pennies, "That is to buy things with."

Now, in this, the little child will give a definition of money that, whatever may be our monetary theories, we all practically recognize. The peculiar use of money—what as money "it is for"—is that of buying other things. What by virtue of this use is money, may or may not have capability for any other use. That is not material. For so long as a thing is reserved to the use of buying things any use inconsistent with this use is excluded.

We might, for instance, apply sticks of candy to the use of buying things. But the moment a stick of candy was applied to the use of being eaten its use in buying things would end. So, if a greenback be used to light a cigar, or a gold coin converted to the use of filling teeth, or of being beaten into gold-leaf, its use as money is destroyed. Even where coins are used as ornaments, their use as money is during that time prevented.

In short, the use of money, no matter of what it be composed, is not directly to satisfy desire, but indirectly to satisfy desire through exchange for other things. We do not eat money nor drink money nor wear money. We pass it. That is to say, we buy other things with it. We esteem money and seek it, not for itself, but for what we may obtain by parting with it, and for the purpose of thus parting with it. This is true even where money is hoarded, for the gratification which hoarding gives is the consciousness of holding at command that with which we may readily buy anything we may wish to have.

The little child I have supposed would probably not know the meaning of the word exchange, which is that of the voluntary transfer of desired things for desired things. But it would know the thing, having become familiar with it in the little exchanges that go on between children—in the giving of marbles for tops, of candy for toys, or in transactions based on "I will do this for you, if you will do that for me." But such exchanges it would probably speak of as trades or swaps or promises, reserving the words buying or selling to exchanges in which money is used.

In this use of words the child would conform to a practice that has become common among careful writers. In the wider sense, buying and selling merely distinguish between the giver and receiver in exchange; and it is in this wider sense that Adam Smith uses the words, and as in poetry or poetical expression we continue to use them. But both in ordinary usage and in political economy we now more generally confine the words buying and selling to exchanges in which money is given or promised, speaking of an exchange in which money is not involved, as a barter or trade, or simply an exchange. It is where money is one of the things exchanged that the transaction is called a purchase and sale; the party who gives money for another thing being termed the buyer, and the party who gives the other thing for the money being termed the seller.

In this usage, we habitually treat money as though it were the more notable or more important side of exchanges in which things not money are given for money—that side of exchange from which or towards which the initiative impulse proceeds. And there is another usage which points in the same direction. Among the masses of our people at least, and I presume the same usage obtains in all countries, good manners is held to require that where money passes in a transaction of exchange, the receiver of the money should by some such phrase as "Thank you," indicate a sense of benefit or obligation.

The reason of both these usages is, I think, to be found in the fact that money is the thing in which gain or profit is usually estimated; the thing which can usually be most readily and certainly exchanged for any other thing. Thus whatever difficulty there may be in exchanging particular commodities or services for other commodities or services is generally most felt in exchanging them for money. That exchange once made, any subsequent exchange of the money for the things that are the ultimate objects of desire is comparatively easy. It is this that makes it seem to those who do not look closely, that what is sought in exchange is money, and that he who gets money in return for other things, is in a better position than he who gets other things in return for money.

To see in what money really differs from other things having exchangeable or purchasing power let us imagine a number of men to undertake a journey through a country where they have no personal acquaintance. Let them for instance start from New York, in pleasant weather, to make a leisurely trip by the highroads for one to two hundred miles. Let them for the defrayal of the expenses of the journey provide themselves with exchangeable things of different kinds. Imagine one to have a valuable horse; another some staple commodity, such as tobacco or tea; another gold and silver bullion; another a check or bill of exchange, or a check-book; and a fifth to have current money. These things might have value to the same amount, but at the first stop for rest and refreshment the great difference between them as to readiness of convertibility would be seen.

The only way the man with the horse could pay for the slightest entertainment for man or beast, without selling his horse for money, or bartering for things that might be very inconvenient to carry, would be by trading him for a less valuable horse. It is clear that he could not go far in this way, for, to say nothing of the delays incident to horse trades, he would, if he persisted in them under pressure of his desire to go on, soon find himself reduced to an animal that could hardly carry himself.

Though of all staple commodities, tobacco and tea are probably those most readily divisible and easily carried, the tourist who tried to pay his way with them would find much difficulty. If not driven to sell his stock outright for what money he could get, he would virtually have to convert his pleasure excursion into a peddling trip; and, to say nothing of the danger he would run of being arrested for infringement of Federal or local license laws, would be put to much delay, loss and annoyance in finding those willing to give the particular things he needed for the particular things he had.

And while gold and silver are of all commodities those which have the most uniform and staple value, yet the man who had started with bullion would, after he had left the city, hardly find any one who could tell their real value or was willing to take them in return for commodities or service. To exchange them at all at anything like a reasonable rate he would have to hunt up some village jeweler who could test and weigh them, and who, though he might offer to give him a clock or a trinket, or to repair his watch in exchange, would hardly have the commodities or service our traveler needed at his disposal. To get what he wanted for what he had to give without recourse to money he would be driven to all sorts of intermediate exchanges.

As for the man with the check-book, or check or bill of exchange, he would find himself the worst off of all. He could make no more use of them where he was not known than of so much blank paper, unless he found some one who could testify to his good credit or who would go to the expense of telegraphing to learn it. To repeat this at every stopping-place, as would be necessary if his trip were to be carried through as it had been begun, would be too much for the patience and endurance of an ordinary man.

But the man with the money would find no difficulty from first to last. Every one who had any commodity to exchange or service to render would take his money gladly and probably say "Thank you" on receiving it. He alone could make the journey he set out to make, without delay or annoyance or loss on the score of exchanges.

What we may conclude from this little imaginative experiment is not that of all things money is the most valuable thing. That, though many people have in a vague way accepted it, would involve a fallacy of the same kind that is involved in the assumption that a pound of lead is heavier than a pound of feathers. What we may safely conclude from our experiment is, that of all exchangeable things money is the most readily exchangeable, and indeed that this ready exchangeability is the essential characteristic of money.

Yet we have but to extend our illustration so as to imagine our travelers taking with them beyond this country that same money they had found so easily exchangeable here, to see that money is not one substance, nor in all times and places the same substance.

What is money in the United States is not money in England. What is money in England is not money on the Continent. What is money in one of the Continental states may not be money in another, and so on. Although in places in each country much resorted to by travelers from another country, the money of the two countries may circulate together, as American money with English money in Bermuda; or Canadian money with American money at Niagara Falls; or Indian money, English money, French money and Egyptian money at Port Said; yet the traveler who wishes to pass beyond such monetary borders with what will readily exchange for the things he may need must provide himself with the money of the country. The money that has served him in the country he has left becomes in a country using a different money a mere commodity the moment he leaves the monetary border, which he will find it advantageous to exchange with some dealer in such commodities for money of the country.

Is money therefore a matter of mere governmental regulation? That is to say, can governmental statute or fiat, as is to-day contended by many, prescribe what money shall be used and at what rate it shall pass?

It is unnecessary for those of us who lived in or visited California between the years 1862 and 1879, to look further than our own country and time to see that it cannot. During those years, while the money of the rest of the Union was a more or less depreciated paper, the money of that State, and of the Pacific coast generally, was gold and silver. The paper money of the general government was used for the purchase of postage stamps, the payment of internal revenue dues, the satisfaction of judgments of the Federal courts, and of those of the State courts where there was no specific contract, and for remittances to the East. But between man and man, and in ordinary transactions, it passed only as a commodity.

If it be said that governmental power was not fully exerted in this case; that the United States government dishonored its own currency in making bonds payable and Custom-House dues receivable only in gold, and that the California specific contract law virtually gave the recognition of the State courts only to gold and silver, we may turn to such examples as that of the Confederate currency; as that of the Continental currency; as that afforded by Colonial currencies prior to the Revolution; as that of the French assignats; or to that comical episode in which the caustic pen of Dean Swift, writing under an assumed name, balked the whole power of the British government in its effort to induce the Irish people to accept what was really a better copper money than that they were using.

Government may largely affect the use of money, as it may largely affect the use of language. It may enact what money shall be paid out and received by government officials, or recognized in the courts, as it may prescribe in what language government documents shall be printed or legislative or legal proceedings held, or scholars in the public schools be taught. But it can no more prescribe what shall be used as the common medium of exchange between man and man in transactions that depend on mutual consent than it can prescribe in what tongue mothers shall teach their babes to lisp. In all the many efforts that governments, limited or absolute, have made to do this, the power of government has signally failed.

Shall we say then, as do many who point out this impotency of mere government fiat, that the exchange value of any money depends ultimately upon its intrinsic value; that the real money in the world, the only true and natural money, is gold and silver, one or both—for the metal-moneyists differ as to this, being divided into two opposing camps—the monometallists and the bimetallists?

This notion is even more widely opposed to facts than is that of the fiatists. Gold and silver have for the longest time and over the widest area served, and yet do serve, as material for money, and sometimes have served, and in some places yet do serve, as money. This was the case, to some extent, in the early days of the California diggings, when every merchant or hotel-keeper or gambler or bar-tender was provided with a bottle of acid and a pair of scales, and men paid for goods or food or lodging or drinks or losses out of buckskin bags in which they carried gold dust or nuggets. This is to some extent still the case in some parts of Asia, where, as was once the case in parts of Europe, even gold and silver coin passes by weight. But gold and silver are not the money of the world. The traveler who should attempt to go round the world paying his expenses with gold and silver bullion would meet the same difficulty or something like the same difficulty that he would meet in the country around New York. Nor would he obviate that difficulty by taking instead of bullion, gold and silver coin. Except in a few places, such as Bermuda or the Hawaiian Islands, they too would become commodities not easily exchangeable when he left the United States.

The truth is that there is no universal money and never yet has been, any more than there is or has been in times of which we have knowledge a universal language.

As for intrinsic value, it is clear that our paper money, which has no intrinsic value, performs every office of money—is in every sense as truly money as our coins, which have intrinsic value; and that even of our coins, their circulating or money value has for the most part no more relation to intrinsic value than it has in the case of our paper money. And this is the case to-day all over the civilized world.

The fact is that neither the fiat of government nor the action of individuals nor the character or intrinsic value of the material used, nor anything else, can make money or mar money, raise or lessen its circulating value, except as it affects the disposition to receive it as a medium of exchange.

In different times and places all sorts of things capable of more or less easy transfer have been used as money. Thus in San Francisco in the early days, when the sudden outflow of gold from the mines brought a sudden demand for money which there was no ready means of supplying, bogus coins, known to be bogus, passed from hand to hand as money; and in New York at the beginning of the Civil War, when there was a great scarcity of circulating medium, owing to the withdrawal of gold and silver from circulation, postage stamps, car tickets, bread tickets, and even counterfeit notes, known to be counterfeit, passed from hand to hand as money.

Shall we say then that they are right who contend that a true definition of money must include everything that can be used in exchange to the avoidance of barter?

Clearly, we cannot say this, without ignoring a real and very important distinction—the distinction between money and credit. For a little consideration will show that the checks, drafts, negotiable notes and other transferable orders and obligations which so largely economize the use of money in the commercial world to-day, do so only when accompanied by something else, which money itself does not require. That something else is trust or credit. This is the essential element of all devices and instruments for dispensing with the mediumship of money without resort to barter. It is only by virtue of it that they can take the place of the money which in form they are promises to pay.

When I give money for what I have bought, I pay my debt. The transaction is complete. But I do not pay my debt when I give a check for the amount. The transaction is not complete. I merely give an order on some one else to pay in my place. If he does not, I am still responsible in morals and in law. As a matter of fact no one will take a check of mine unless he trusts or credits me. And though an honest face, good clothes and a manifest exigency might enable me to pass a small check upon one who did not know me, without the guarantee of some one he did know, I could as readily, and perhaps more readily, get him to trust me outright. So, I cannot, except to one who knows me or to whom I am identified as a man of good credit, pass the check of another or his note or draft or bill of exchange in my favor, and without guaranteeing it by indorsement. Even then I do not make a payment; I merely turn over with my own guarantee an order for payment.

Thus there is a quality attaching to money, in common apprehension, which clearly distinguishes it from all forms of credit. It is, so far as the giver of the money is concerned, a final closing of the transaction. The man who gives a check or bill of exchange must guarantee its payment, and is liable if it be not paid; while the drawer on the other hand retains the power at any time of stopping payment before that has been actually made. Even the man who gives a horse or other commodity in exchange must, save as to certain things and with the observance of certain requirements, guarantee title, and that it shall possess certain qualities expressed or implied. But in the passing of money the transaction is closed and finished, and there can be no further question or recourse. For money is properly recognized by municipal law as the common medium of exchange.

All such things as checks, drafts, notes, etc., though they largely dispense with and greatly economize the use of money, do so by utilizing credit. Credit as a facilitator of exchange is older than money and perhaps is even now more important than money, though it may be made into money, as gold may be made into money. But though it may be made into money, it is not in itself money, any more than gold of itself is money, and cannot, without confusion as to the nature and functions of money, be included as money.

What then shall we say that money is?

Evidently the essential quality of money is not in its form or substance, but in its use.

Its use being not that of being consumed, but of being continually exchanged, it participates in and facilitates other exchanges as a medium or flux, serving upon a larger scale the same purpose of keeping tally and facilitating transfers as is served by the chips or counters often used in games of chance.*

This use comes from a common or usual consent or disposition to take it in exchange, not as representing or promising anything else, but as completing the exchange.

---

* It is most important that this purely representative character of money should be thoroughly understood and constantly kept in mind, for from the confusion resulting from the confounding of money with wealth have flown the largest and most pernicious results. It was the basis of that anti-social theory of international exchanges which has cost European civilization such waste of labor and drain of blood, formerly known as the mercantile system and which survives in the protectionism of to-day. And it is at the bottom of those theories prevalent in the United States to-day which seek to increase wealth by increasing money.

The only question any one asks himself in taking money in exchange is whether he can, in the same way, pass it on in exchange. If there is no doubt of that, he will take it; for the only use he has for money is to pass it on in exchange. If he has doubt of that, he will take it only at a discount proportioned to the doubt, or not take it at all.

What then makes anything money is the common consent or disposition to accept it as the common medium of exchange. If a thing has this essential quality in any place and time, it is money in that place and time, no matter what other quality it may lack. If a thing lacks this essential quality in any place and time, it is not money in that place and time, no matter what other quality it may have.

To define money:

Whatever in any time and place is used as the common medium of exchange is money in that time and place.

There is no universal money. While the use of money is almost as universal as the use of languages, and it everywhere follows general laws as does the use of languages, yet as we find language differing in time and place, so do we find money differing. In fact, as we shall see, money is in one of its functions a kind of language —the language of value.

CHAPTER III.

MEDIUM OF EXCHANGE AND MEASURE OF VALUE.

SHOWING HOW THE COMMON MEDIUM OF EXCHANGE BECOMES THE COMMON MEASURE OF VALUE, AND WHY WE CANNOT FIND A COMMON MEASURE IN LABOR.

Money is most exchanged—Why not measure value by labor?—Smith's unsatisfactory answer—The true answer—Labor can afford no common measure, and commodities are preferably taken—Survivals of common measures—Difference in common measures does not prevent exchange.

I HAVE in the last chapter defined money as whatever is at any time and place used as the common medium of exchange. This is indeed the primary quality of money. But proceeding from this use as a common medium of exchange, money has another and closely conjoined use—that of serving as a common measure of value.

The reason of this is that the use of money as a common medium of exchange, which causes it to be esteemed for exchange and not for consumption, makes it of all exchangeable things that which in civilized societies is often and most commonly exchanged. A given portion of wood or coal, for instance, may be used by the producer and thus not be exchanged at all; or it may be exchanged once or perhaps even half a dozen times between cutting or mining and its reaching in the hands of the consumer the ultimate end for which it was produced, the combustion that supplies heat. So it is with potatoes or wheat or corn. The majority of horses are probably not exchanged at all during their working days, and it would be a much exchanged horse who should have six owners during his life. Cotton and wool and hemp and silk may pass from one to half a dozen exchanges before they assume the form of cloth or rope, and in that form may pass through from two to half a dozen more exchanges before reaching the consumer. And so with lumber or iron or most of the forms of paper, meat or leather. Not only is the ultimate purpose of the exchanges of such things destructive consumption, but they are mainly composed of things which if not soon consumed will wear out or decay.

Money, on the other hand, is not produced for the purpose of being consumed, but for the purpose of being exchanged. This, not consumption, is its use. And we always seek for its substance materials least subject to wear and decay, while it is usually carefully guarded by whoever for the moment may be in its possession. And further while an article of money may frequently pass through more hands in a single day than ordinary articles of wealth are likely to pass through during the whole period of their existence, the use of money in thought and speech as a symbol of value brings it to the constant notice of those who do not often tangibly use it. Thus it is that the value of the money which is the common medium of exchange in any community becomes to the people of that community better known than the value of anything else, and hence is most readily and constantly chosen to compare the value of other things.

But here may arise a question, which I wish thoroughly to answer: If, as explained in Book II., value is in itself a relation to labor, why can we not find not merely a common measure of value, but an exact and final measure of value in labor itself?

This is a question that perplexes a great many of the monetary theories that have been broached in the United States without finding scholastic recognition, and it is raised but not satisfactorily answered by Adam Smith.

In a passage previously quoted in full* Adam Smith says: "But though labor be the real measure of the exchangeable value of all commodities, it is not that by which their value is commonly estimated." And then goes on to explain the reason of this.

But in the attempt to explain this fact Adam Smith falls into confusion through the slipperiness of his terms and misses the true reason. While he says in effect that the time of exertion will not measure the quality of exertion, he yet, almost in the same breath, uses time as the measure of exertion, saying that "every commodity is . . . more frequently exchanged for and thereby compared with other commodities than with labor," that "it is more natural therefore to estimate its exchangeable value by the quantity of some other commodity than by that of the labor which it can purchase," and that "the greater part of the people too understand better what is meant by the quantity of a particular commodity than by a quantity of labor," thus ignoring what he had just shown, that it is the labor (in the sense of exertion) that their possession will save which determines the value of all commodities. His attempted explanation of the fact that the real measure of value is not the common measure of value, amounts to nothing more than that it is more usual to measure value by commodities than by labor. This is no explanation of the fact; it is merely a statement of the fact. We cannot explain a custom or habit by saying that it is natural or showing that it is usual. The very thing to be explained is why it seems natural and has become usual.

---

* Page 231.

Yet in the light of our previous investigation the reason why the real measure of value cannot serve as a common measure of value is clear. It lies in the human constitution. We become conscious of exertion through the "toil and trouble" it involves—the feeling of effort and at length of irksomeness and repugnance that attends its continuance. Now feeling is an affection or condition of the individual perception or Ego, which can find objective manifestation only through action. Even the mother can know the feelings of the babe only through its actions. If she can tell that it is hungry or sleepy or in pain, or is satisfied and happy, it is only in this way.

As we have seen, labor in the sense of exertion, is the true, ultimate and universal measure of value; what anything will bring in exchange being always based upon an estimate of the toil and trouble attendant upon the exertion which the possession of that thing will save.

But this is an estimate which, though each may make it for himself, he cannot convey to another directly, since the feeling of weariness or repugnance, the dislike of "toil and trouble," which constituting the resistance to, is the measure of, exertion, can, in our normal condition at least, be conveyed to, or expressed by one to another only through the senses.

We make such estimates continually in our own minds, for memory which registers the experience of the individual permits us to compare the exertion it has required to do or procure one thing with what it has required to do or procure another thing. But to express to another person my idea of the amount of exertion required to do or procure a particular thing there must be something that will serve us as a mutual measure of the resistance to exertion, that is to say the "toil and trouble" that exertion involves.

Thus, to convey to one ignorant of swimming some idea of the exertion it requires, I must compare it with some exertion with which we are both familiar, such as walking. Or, if a stranger wishes to know of me what exertion he will have to make to walk to a certain point, I will tell him, if I know it, the distance, and give some idea of the character of the road, for he will have some idea of the exertion required to walk a given distance on an ordinary road. If he be a Frenchman accustomed to meters and kilometers, which neither of us can translate into feet and miles, I will still be able to convey to him my idea by saying, so many minutes' or hours' walk, for all men have some idea of the exertion required to walk for a certain time. If we could find no common nomenclature of time, I could still give him some idea by pointing to the dial of my watch or to the sun, or by finding from whence he had come, and making him understand that the distance he had yet to go was longer or shorter, and the road harder or easier. But there must be some point of mutual knowledge which will furnish us with a common measure, for me to make myself intelligible to him at all.

So reversely, a common experience of required exertion will, in the absence of a more exact measure, give some idea of distance or area, as

> A bowshot from her bower eaves,
> He rode between the barley sheaves,

or,

> They gave him of the corn-land
>   That was of public right,
> As much as two strong oxen
>   Could plow from morn to night.

Now while exertion is always the real measure of value, to which all common measures of value must refer, yet to get a common measure of value, which will enable us to express from one to another both quantity and quality (duration and intensity) of exertion, we must take some result of exertion, just as to find a common measure of heat, light, expansive force or gravitation we must take some tangible manifestation of those forms of energy. It is because commodities, being the results of exertion, are tangible manifestations of exertion that they are generally and naturally used as common measures of value.

Even where exertion is expressed in time, there is always at least an implied reference to accomplishment or results. Where I hire a man to work for me by the day or week or month in occupations which show tangible result, as in digging or draining, in plowing or harvesting, in felling trees or chopping wood, it is always with a certain idea of the tangible result to be achieved, or in other words, of the intensity as well as of the duration of the exertion. If I find no result, I say that no work has been done; and if I find that the results are not such as should have come from a reasonable or customary intensity of exertion with a reasonable or customary knowledge or skill, I say that what I really agreed to pay for has not been accorded me. And disinterested men would support me.

On going ashore in San Francisco, a shipmate of mine, who could not tell a scythe from a marlinspike, hired out to a farmer in haying-time for $5 a day. At his first stroke with the scythe he ran it so deep in the ground that he nearly broke it in getting it out. Though he indignantly denounced such antiquated tools as out of fashion, declaring that he was used to "the patent scythes that turn up at the end," he did not really feel wronged that the farmer would not pay him a cent, as he knew that the agreement for day's labor was really an agreement for so much mowing.

In fact, the form of measuring exertion by time, at bottom, involves its measurement by result.

This we find to be true even where there is no definite result. If I hire a boatman or cabman to take me to a certain point, the distance, being known, affords a close idea of the exertion required, and it is the fairest, and to both parties usually the most agreeable way, that the stipulation shall be for that result, or as the cabmen in Europe say "by course?" which is a definite payment for a definite result. But even were I to take a boat or a cab without fixed idea of where I want to go, and agree to pay by the hour, there is an implied understanding as to the intensity of the exertion for which I am to pay. Either boatman or cabman would feel that he was not keeping his agreement fairly, and I would certainly feel so, were he, for the purpose of "putting in time," to row or drive at a snail's pace.

So strong is the disposition to take tangible results as the measure of exertion that even where quality is of more importance than quantity, as in literary work, the formal measurement is even in our best magazines and newspapers by the page or column, differences in quality, real or expected, being recognized partly in the readiness with which an article is accepted, and partly in a greater price per page or per column.

In short, while exertion, including both quantity and intensity, is always the true and final measure of value, it is only through the manifestations of exertion that any common measure of value can be had. Thus commodities being tangible expressions of exertion become the readiest common measures of value, and have since the beginning of human society been so used.

While any commodity, or for that matter any definite service, may be used as a common measure of value to the extent to which it is recognized as embodying or expressing a certain amount of exertion and thus having a definite, though not necessarily a fixed value, the tendency is always to use for this purpose the commodity whose value is most generally and easily recognized. And since the commodity which is used as *the* common medium of exchanges becomes in that use the commodity which is oftenest exchanged and whose value is most generally and easily recognized, whatever serves as *the* common medium of exchange tends in that to become *the* common measure of value, in terms of which the values of other things are expressed and compared. In societies which have reached a certain stage of civilization this is always money. Hence we may define money with regard to its functions as that which in any time and place serves as *the* common medium of exchange and *the* common measure of value.

It must be remembered, however, that of these two functions, use as the common medium of exchange is primary. That is to say, use as the common medium of exchange brings about use as the common measure of value, and not the reverse. But these two uses do not always exactly correspond.

Thus, in New York and its neighborhood one may still hear of shillings or York shillings (12½ cents) as a measure of small values. There is no such coin, this use of an ideal shilling being a survival from Colonial times. So, in Philadelphia one may hear of fips and levies; in New Orleans of picayunes and in San Francisco of bits, survivals of the Spanish coinage; and in the far Northwest of "skins," a purely ideal measure of value surviving from the time when the Hudson Bay Company bartered with the Indians for furs. During, and for some time after, the civil war two different common measures of value were in co-temporaneous use in the United States—paper money and gold. But since the resumption of specie payments, though paper money still constitutes the more largely used medium of exchange, gold alone has in this country become the common measure of value. And though gold, silver and paper are all largely, and generally co-temporaneously, used throughout the civilized world to-day as supplying the common medium of exchange, the great monetary division is between the countries which use gold as the common measure of value and the countries which use silver.

But it is still evident, as Adam Smith said, that labor (in the sense of exertion) is "the real measure of the exchangeable value of all commodities,"—"the only universal as well as the only accurate measure of value, or the only standard by which we can compare the values of all commodities in all times and in all places." For it is still true, as he said, that "the real price of everything, what everything really costs to the man who wants to acquire it, is the toil and trouble of acquiring it. What everything is really worth to the man who has acquired it, and who wants to dispose of it or exchange it for something else, is the toil and trouble which it can save to himself, and which it can impose upon other people."

Since labor is thus the real and universal measure of value, whatever any country may use as the common measure of value can impose little difficulty upon the exchanges of its people with the people of other countries using other common measures of value. Nor yet would any change within a country from one common measure of value to another common measure of value bring more than slight disturbance were it not for the effect upon credits or obligations. In this lies the main source of the controversies and confusions with which the "money question" is now beset.

Before going further it would therefore be well, at least so far as pertains to the idea of money, to examine the relations of credit to exchange.

CHAPTER IV.

THE OFFICE OF CREDIT IN EXCHANGES.

[SHOWING THAT THE ADVANCE OF CIVILIZATION ECONOMIZES THE USE OF MONEY.

Tendency to over-estimate the importance of money—Credit existed before the use of money began, and it is now and always has been the most important instrument of exchange—Illustration of shipwrecked men—Adam Smith's error as to barter—Money's most important use to-day is as a measure of value.] [1]

I HAVE sought to explain the common understanding of money and the part that it plays in exchanges by supposing a number of travelers. I did so because it is in such small and immediate exchanges as a traveler must make among strangers that the peculiar usefulness of money is most clearly felt. I did not mean to assume that the difficulties of barter in all places and times are so great as those that in the vicinity of New York at the close of the Nineteenth Century would attend the effort of a traveler to supply his personal needs by that means of exchange.

On the contrary there are even now parts of the world where a traveler might find a properly selected stock of commodities more readily and advantageously exchangeable than money itself, and the difficulties of barter have certainly increased not merely with the greater use of money, but with such modern appliances as post-offices,

[1] Heading not complete in MS. See Prefatory Note.—H. G., JR.

steamboats, railways, telegraphs and telephones, and with the greater concentration of population and exchanges that result from them. Even in our own civilization barter must have been a more efficient means of exchange in the times that preceded the great industrial development of the Nineteenth Century than it is now because people were more generally accustomed to it. The old traveling merchants and even the old foreign merchants, who sent their ships over the maritime world, were largely barterers, and the stated fairs of which we have now only faint survivals, but which formed so important a part in the industrial life of our ancestors, gave place and occasion for the meeting of those who wished to make a direct exchange of commodities for commodities or services for services that are wanting now.

The effect of the general adoption of the more elaborate and on a large scale more efficient methods of an advanced civilization is always to relegate to forgetfulness the simpler methods previously in use. We have become within a few years so accustomed to the electric telegraph that we are apt to think that without it men would be reduced in carrying messages to the means of transportation by land or water, and to forget that telegraphs were in use before electric telegraphing was dreamed of. The convenience of the lucifer match has made its use so universal, that most of us if thrown on our own resources without matches, would find it a most serious difficulty to light a pipe or make a fire. A hunting party of civilized men, if deprived by accident of their ammunition, might starve to death before they could kill game even where it was abundant. Yet at the beginning of this century lucifer matches were unknown, and men killed game before firearms were invented.

And so it is with money. Its use is so general in our high civilization and its importance so great that we are apt to over-estimate that importance and to forget that men lived and advanced before money was developed, and both to underrate the efficiency of the means of exchange other than that of money, and the amount of exchanging that even now goes on without any more use of money than that of a counter or denominator of values.

It is not only that the simplest form of exchange, the transfer of things desired in themselves for things desired in themselves, still to some extent continues; but the advance of civilization which in an early stage develops the use of money as a medium of exchange begins in later stages to develop means for dispensing with or much economizing this use of money. The exchanges between different countries are still carried on without the use of money, and so in great measure are domestic exchanges, even in the same locality. Not merely in the rural districts and in small transactions is there much exchanging without actual transfer of money, but in the greatest cities, the largest transactions, habitually spoken of and thought of as though they involved the transfer of money, really take place without it. The richer people in fact use comparatively little money, even in personal transactions, and I fancy that a man of good credit who kept a bank-account might, if he tried to, live from year's end to year's end, even in a great city like New York (and with less effort in a smaller place), without a penny of actual money passing through his hands. His income, if not received in small amounts, he would get in checks or similar transfers. His larger expenses he could of course pay for in checks, and even such things as newspapers, tickets for street-car lines or railways, or admission to theaters, postage-stamps, etc., he could with a little effort get in the same way.

Now all this economizing in the use of money, which we are accustomed to think of as, and indeed in some of its forms really is, the latest development of a civilization that for immemorial ages has been accustomed to the use of money, is really in essence a return to something that must have been in use for the facilitating of exchanges before money was developed among men. That something is what we call trust or credit. Credit is to-day and in our highest civilization the most important instrument of exchange; and that it must have been from the very first appearance of man on this globe the most important instrument of exchange, any one can see, if he will only discard the assumption that invalidates so much of our recent philosophy and philosophic history—the assumption that the progress of civilization is a change in man himself—and allow even prehistoric man the same reasoning faculties that all we know of man in historic times shows to belong to him as man.

Imagine a number of totally shipwrecked men swimming ashore in their buffs to an uninhabited island in a climate genial enough to enable them to support life. What would be their first exchanges? Would they not be based upon the various forms of the proposition, "I will do or get this for you, if you will do or get that for me?" Now, no matter where or how they got into this world, this must have been the position of the first men when they got here, and all that we can reason from with any certainty goes to show that these first men must have been essentially the same kind of men as we ourselves.

If there is any difference in priority between them, credit must, in the nature of things, have preceded barter as an instrument of exchange, and must at least from the very first have assisted barter. What more natural than that the man who had killed a deer, or made a large catch of fish, should be willing to give now while he had abundance in return for a promise expressed or implied that his neighbor when similarly fortunate would in the same way remember him? The organization of credit into more elaborate and finer forms goes on with the development of civilization, but credit must have begun to aid exchanges with the very beginnings of human society, and it is in the backwoods and new settlements rather than in the great cities that we will to-day find its direct forms playing relatively the most important part in exchanges.

In explaining the origin and use of money, Adam Smith much overrated the difficulties of barter, and in this he has been followed by nearly all the writers who have succeeded him. Of the condition before the use of the metals as money he says (Book I., Chapter IV. of the "Wealth of Nations"):

> One man, we shall suppose, has more of a certain commodity than he himself has occasion for, while another has less. The former consequently would be glad to dispose of, and the latter to purchase, a part of this superfluity. But, if this latter should chance to have nothing that the former stands in need of, *no exchange can be made between them.* The butcher has more meat in his shop than he himself can consume, and the brewer and the baker would each of them be willing to purchase a part of it. But they have nothing to offer in exchange, except the different productions of their respective trades, and the butcher is already provided with all the bread and beer which he has immediate occasion for. *No exchange can, in this case, be made between them.* He cannot be their merchant, nor they his customers; and they are all of them thus mutually less serviceable to one another. . . .
>
> . . . The man who wanted to buy salt, for example, and had nothing but cattle to give in exchange for it, must have been obliged to buy salt to the value of a whole ox, or a whole sheep, at a time. He could seldom buy less than this, because what he was to give for it could seldom be divided without loss; and if he had a mind to buy more, he must, for the same reasons, have been obliged to buy double or triple the quantity, the value, to wit, of two or three oxen, or of two or three sheep. If, on the contrary, instead of sheep or oxen, he had metals to give in exchange for it, he could easily proportion the quantity of the metal to the precise quantity of the commodity which he had immediate occasion for.

Though this explanation of the difficulties attending barter has been paraphrased by writer after writer since

Adam Smith, it is an exaggeration so gross as to be ridiculous. The differentiation of such trades as that of the butcher, brewer and baker, the fact that men habitually devote their labor to the production of more of certain commodities than they themselves can consume, implies a division of labor that could not possibly take place were exchange impossible under the circumstances that Adam Smith assumes. And it is evident that such circumstances would impose no insuperable difficulty to exchange even though a true money had not yet come into use. The butcher, with meat that he wanted to dispose of, would not have refused the exchange offered by the brewer and baker because he himself was already provided with all the bread and beer that he had immediate occasion for. On the contrary, he would say, "I have no immediate use for bread and beer because I am already supplied, but I will give you the meat you want on your promise to give me its equivalent in bread and beer when I call for them." Nor need he necessarily wait for his own supply of bread and beer to be exhausted before calling on the baker and brewer for the fulfilment of their promises, for since man's wants are not satisfied with meat, bread and beer alone, he might want from the tailor a coat, from the grazier a bullock, from the carpenter a house; and since they could not take from him at once full payment in such a perishable commodity as meat, he could help out his part of the exchange by telling the baker and brewer to give to them the bread and beer they had promised him.

That is to say, it is not necessary to an exchange that both sides of it shall be effected at once or with the same person. One part or side of the full exchange may be effected at once, and the effecting of the other part or side may be deferred to a future time and transferred to another person or persons by means of trust or credit. And by this simple and natural device, and without the intervention of money, salt could be exchanged for less quantities of beef or mutton than are likely to spoil before a single family could consume them. The truth is that the difficulties of incidence which Adam Smith speaks of here as if they were inseparable from barter are always avoided by the use of trust where trust is possible. It is only where there are no other exchanges going on and it is not probable that the parties concerned will come into contact directly or indirectly again, as in a desert or at sea, that owing to want of incidence no exchange can be made between them.*

It is really in exchange between those who are unknown to each other and do not expect to meet each other again that money performs its most indispensable office (as illustrated in Book V., Chapter II.). The use of money, by which the traveler can easily carry with him the means of supplying his needs, has greatly facilitated traveling; yet in the bill of exchange, the letter of credit, Cook's coupons, and the book of certified checks, which are so largely displacing money for the use of travelers, we come back again to the use of trust.

Trust or credit is indeed the first of all the instrumentalities that facilitate exchange. Its use antedates not merely the use of any true money, but must have been

---

* But even here there is often something of the nature of exchange, although it may lack the element of certainty. When a boy, passing through a street in Philadelphia during a sudden rain, I met a gentleman standing in a doorway and proffered him the shelter of my umbrella, going a little out of my way to take him to his destination. As we parted he said, "You and I are not likely to meet again, as I am a stranger here; but one good turn deserves another, and I will try to return your service to me by doing such a service for some one else, telling him to pass it along." Possibly that little kindly service, which I would have forgotten but for the impression his words made, may be "passing along" still. Both good and evil pass on as waves pass on. Yet I cannot but think that in the long run, good outlives evil. For as to the normal constitution of the human mind, evil must bring the wider and more permanent pain, the impulse to its perpetuation must meet the greater friction.

coeval with the first appearance of man. Truth, love, sympathy are of human nature. It is not only that without them man could never have emerged from the savage state, but that without them he could not have maintained himself even in a savage state. If brought on earth without them, he would inevitably have been exterminated by his animal neighbors or have exterminated himself.

Men do not have to be taught to trust each other, except where they have been deceived, and it is more often in our one-sided civilization, where laws for the collection of debts have weakened the moral sanction which public opinion naturally gives to honesty, and a deep social injustice brings about a monstrous inequality in the distribution of wealth, and not among primitive peoples, that the bond is oftenest required to back the simple word. So natural is it for men to trust each other that even the most distrustful must constantly trust others.

And trust or credit is not merely the first of the agencies of exchange in the sense of priority; it yet is, as it always has been, the first in importance. In spite of our extensive use of money in effecting exchanges, what is accomplished by it is small as compared with what is accomplished by credit. In international exchanges money is not used at all, while the great volume of domestic exchange is in every civilized country carried on by the giving and cancelation of credits. As a matter of fact the most important use of money to-day is not as a medium of exchange, though that is its primary use. It is that of a common measure of value, its secondary use. Not only this, but with the advance in civilization the tendency is to make use of credit as money; to coin, as it were, trust into currency, and thus to bring into use a medium of exchange better adapted in many circumstances to easy transfer than metallic money. The paper money so largely in use in all civilized countries as a common medium of exchange is in reality a coinage of credit or trust.

CHAPTER V.

THE GENESIS OF MONEY.

[SHOWING THAT THE LAW OF GRATIFYING DESIRES WITH THE LEAST EXERTION PROMPTS THE USE FROM TIME TO TIME OF THE MOST LABOR-SAVING MEDIUM AVAILABLE.

Money not an invention, but developed by civilization—It grows with the growth of exchanges—Exchange first of general commodities —Then of the more convenient commodities—Then of coin, whose commodity value comes to be forgotten—Illustration of the American trade dollar—The lessening uses of commodity money and extensions of credit money—Two elements in exchange value of metal coin: intrinsic, or value of the metal itself, and seigniorage—Meaning of seigniorage—Exchange value of paper money is seigniorage—Use of money not for consumption, but exchange—Proprietary articles as mediums of exchange—Mutilated coins—Debased coinage—When lessening metal value in coins does not lessen circulating value—This the reason why paper money exchanges equally with metal money of like denomination.] [1]

MONEY is not an invention, but rather a natural growth or development, arising in the progress of civilization from common perceptions and common needs. The same fundamental law of human nature which prompts to exchange, the law by which we seek to satisfy our desires with the least exertion, prompts us with the growth of exchanges to adopt as a medium for them the most labor-saving instruments available.

[1] The part of chapter heading within brackets not in MS.—H.G., JR.

All exchange is of services or commodities. But as commodities are in reality concrete services they afford from the first the readiest media of exchange, performing that office and serving as measures of value not only for other commodities but for direct services.

But commodities (under which name we include all movable products of labor, which, as such, have value so long as they retain the capacity of ministering to desire) greatly differ in their availability as media of exchange. Those best fitted for that use are those which are least perishable, which can be most easily passed from hand to hand and moved from place to place; which are most uniform in their articles and most homogeneous in their structure, so that they may be estimated with most certainty and divided and reunited with the least waste, and whose value is from their general use best known and most quickly recognized.

In proportion as these qualities are united in one commodity there is a natural tendency to its use as a medium for the exchange of other things, and this use tends again to the wider knowledge and quicker recognition of its value.

In primitive societies, or in the outposts of civilization where better means were not readily obtainable, skins, shells, salt, beads, tobacco, tea, blankets, and many other of the less perishable and more portable commodities, have in an imperfect way and to a limited extent been used as common media of exchange and common measures of value, thus becoming the money of the time and place.* But

---

* Adam Smith and most of the subsequent writers have included cattle in the list of things that have in rude times served this function. Smith says, Book I., Chapter IV., "Wealth of Nations":

"In the rude ages of society, cattle are said to have been the common instrument of commerce; and, although they must have been a most inconvenient one, yet in old times we find things were frequently valued according to the number of cattle which had been given in

the metals, and particularly the precious metals, so well fill all the requirements of a medium of exchange, that wherever they have become well known mankind have applied them to this use. At first they were doubtless weighed, and perhaps tested, with every passage from hand to hand; but as their use for purposes of exchange became more common, the same desire to economize labor which leads the baker to give his bread the form and shape of loaves or rolls, and the tobacconist or tea-dealer to put up his commodities into uniform packages, must soon have led to the running of the metals used as media of exchange into pieces of definite weight and purity, so that they may be passed from hand to hand without the trouble of weighing and testing them. To make these pieces of circular form, since that is the most convenient and the least subject to abrasion in handling, and to afford evidence that they yet retained their original substance by stamping their sides and edges, are obvious devices that seem to have

---

exchange for them. The armor of Diomede, says Homer, cost only nine oxen; but that of Glaucus cost an hundred oxen."

Although I have hitherto accepted this statement, closer consideration now convinces me that the inconvenience attaching to such a use of cattle never could have permitted them to take the place of money. As for the authority of Homer, the state of the arts assumed in the Iliad would imply the use of metal money, and the Marquis Gainier has contended that the oxen spoken of were really coins. But this supposition is not the only alternative to supposing that the allusions in Homer's poems are to be taken as indicating that cattle were in use as the common medium of exchange and common measure of value. In ordinary speech, and especially in poetry, which eschews the exactness of monetary terms, such things as cattle, lands. slaves, have always been used to convey a vague but striking idea of wealth or value; and it seems far more reasonable so to understand the references of ancient writers than to take them as proof that commodities so inconvenient to divide, preserve and transfer as cattle ever passed from the position of an article of exchange to that of its common medium and measure.

been adopted wherever sufficient skill in the arts had been attained and the metals were in this way used. And thus by a natural development in use, a commodity peculiarly adapted to the purpose becomes, in the shape of coined money, the commodity which serves as a medium of exchange and measure of value for all commodities and services, and which has been in use among peoples of the most advanced civilization for long ages and still remains in use, though not in exclusive use, to our day.

But while the first purpose of coinage is, we may safely assume, to save the trouble of weighing and testing the commodity which has become a common medium of exchange, the general use of these coins as giving evidence of weight and purity must gradually have the effect of transferring the quality of ready exchangeability from the commodity to the coin. The habit of weighing and testing passes away; even the amount of the commodity embodied in the coin is, by the great majority of those who use it, forgotten or not heeded; and the shape, size, color and devices of the coin become the things that give it circulation. An American Eagle, or ten-dollar piece, contains so many grains of gold of a certain fineness, and exchanges at the value of the gold. But not one in ten thousand of those who use this coin, and who know its value in relation to other things that they are in the habit of buying and selling, know how many grains of gold it contains. A man with a ten-dollar gold piece will find no difficulty in the United States in fairly exchanging it for anything he may happen to want, but he would find much difficulty in fairly exchanging the same quantity of gold in the shape of dust or of an ingot, anywhere except at a mint or with a bullion dealer.

A curious evidence of this tendency to accept the sign rather than the substance is given in the history of the American trade dollar. For many years much of the export of silver to China has been in the shape of Mexican dollars, the stamp of which has become known there as evidencing a certain weight of silver. Thinking that it might take the place in China of the Mexican coin the American government in 1874 coined what was called a trade dollar. It was a better finished and handsomer coin than the Mexican dollar, and contained a greater weight of silver. But the Chinese preferred a coin whose look they had become familiar with, to one that was new to them, even though the latter was of greater intrinsic value. The attempt was a failure, and after an instructive domestic experience, which it is not worth while to speak of here, the coinage of the trade dollar was stopped.

Now this transfer of ready exchangeability from the commodity to the coin, with the accompanying relegation of the commodity itself to the same position in exchange held by other commodities, which takes place as a result of the use of coin money, is a matter of great importance, leading ultimately to a complete change in the nature of the money used.

In the coinage of the precious metals the use of commodities as a medium of exchange seems to have reached its highest form. But the very same qualities which of all commodities best fit the precious metals for this use, attach or may attach in still higher degree to something which, having no material form, may be passed from person to person or place to place without inconvenience from bulk or weight, or danger of injury from accident, abrasion or decay. This something is credit or obligation. And as the advance of civilization goes on, the same tendency to seek the gratification of desire with the least exertion, which with a certain advance of civilization leads to the development of commodity money, leads with its further advance to the utilization of credit as money.

Movement in this direction may be distinguished along three lines: 1—The admixture in coinage of obligation value with production value. 2—The use of obligation or credit as representing an economizing commodity money. 3—The use of pure credit money.

We are here considering only money. Not only is credit a facilitator of exchange before money of any kind is developed, but the same social progress which shows itself in the development of money also shows itself in the extension of credit. If the use of money supersedes the use of credit in some exchanges, it is only where the use of credit is difficult and inconvenient; and in facilitating exchanges over wider areas than the use of the primitive forms of credit would have been equal to, it also increases that mutual knowledge and mutual desire to exchange that are necessary to the extension of credit. Although the primary and local function of money is that of affording a common medium of exchange, its secondary function of affording a common measure of values soon becomes of greater importance, and the extension of credits in our modern civilization is far more striking and important than the extensions in the use of money as a medium of exchange. Though the use of any particular money as a medium of exchange is still local, the money of any one country circulating only to a very limited extent in other countries, yet the development of credits has been such that the exchange of commodities to the ends of the earth and among peoples using different moneys as mediums of exchange, is conducted by means of it. But what we are considering now is not this development of commercial credits, but the way in which the use of commodity money passes into the use of credit money; or in other words, the way in which the coinage of production value into a convenient medium of exchange passes into the coinage of obligation values.

The demand for any metal in exchange is at first, like the demand for other things in exchange, a demand for consumption; and its value or rate of exchange, is determined by the cost of producing it in merchantable form. As one or another of the metals began to come into use as a medium of exchange, the largest demand for it would doubtless for some time still be for consumption, and any change in the form of the metal made to fit it for this new use would at first entail little or no greater cost than that of the ordinarily merchantable form. Thus the value of the metal used as money would at first be no greater than that of the same metal intended for consumption. But when coinage fairly began, something more of labor would be required to produce the stamped and finished coin than to produce the mere ingot of merchantable shape.

Hence there are, or may be, two elements in the exchange value of metal coin—(1) the intrinsic value, or value of the metal itself, which is governed by the cost of producing it in merchantable form; and (2) the cost of changing it from that form into the form of finished coin. This second element, the charge for coinage, is called seigniorage, from the idea that the coining of money has from the earliest times been deemed a function of the sovereign—the seignior or lord—as representative of organized society or the state.

There are two different ways in which it has been customary to pay for turning a merchantable material into a finished product. Thus: From time immemorial until the present when machinery has begun to revolutionize industrial methods, it was the custom for the man who wanted a suit of clothes to buy the material, take it to a tailor, and pay him for the work of making it into a suit. The tailor was not presumed to keep any of the cloth, and if he did so it was called "cabbage." During the same time it was, on the contrary, the universal custom for the miller to get his pay by keeping a part of the material brought him for conversion. The farmer or purchaser brought his grain to the mill, receiving back less than its equivalent in meal, the difference being the toll that the miller retained for the service of grinding. The manufacturer who is now succeeding both the old tailor and the old miller buys the material and sells the finished product.

Now the conversion of metal into coin seems always to have been paid for in the same way as the conversion of grain into meal or flour, by a toll or deduction in the return. This toll or seigniorage may be less or more than the actual cost of coinage. It is what the lord or state, who has the sole privilege of coinage, chooses to take for it; the difference between the rate at which metal is received or bought at the mint and the rate at which it is returned or issued in coin.

Had the coinage of metal into money been left to the free competition of individual enterprise, the charge for this conversion would have tended to the lowest point at which coin could be produced in sufficient quantities to supply the demand. But so far as we can see this has never been the case. The primary object of coinage being the certification of weight and fineness, that is obviously best assured by the stamp of the highest and most widely known authority, that of the sovereign or state. Where coinage is thus monopolized in the hands of the sovereign, the element of seigniorage in the value of coin may be eliminated altogether by the agreement or practice of the sovereign to return in coin the full amount of metal brought to his mints, as is to-day the case in some countries with some metals; or it may be extended so as to become the most important of the two elements in the value of coin by the refusal of the sovereign to coin on other terms and the exclusion or refusal of other coinage. Indeed, by the selection of some very cheap commodity for the material of coinage, it may become practically the only element of value. For, as Ricardo pointed out, the whole exchange value of paper money may be considered as a charge for seigniorage.

The reason of this fact that, the issuance of money being a monopoly, the element of intrinsic value may be partially or entirely eliminated without loss of usefulness, is to be found in the peculiar use of money. The use of other commodities is in consumption. The use of money is in exchange. Thus the intrinsic character of money is of no moment to him who receives it to circulate again. The only question that he is concerned with is as to the readiness of others to receive it from him when he wants in his turn to pass it on. And this readiness where coined money comes into use as the common medium of exchange is associated with coinage, which becomes the badge or stamp of circulation.

There are to-day certain commodities having a large and wide-spread sale in neatly put up packages under proprietary names, such as Pears' Soap, Colman's Mustard, Royal Baking Powder, and so on. The reputation as to quantity and quality of contents which has been secured for the packages bearing such a trade-mark gives their manufacturers proprietary profits often very considerable that are analogous to seigniorage. For a short time and to a small extent these profits might be increased by decreasing the quality of the goods. Those who bought them to sell again would at first be unconscious of the difference and would buy as before. But as soon as they reached the hands of purchasers for consumption, the difference would be detected and the demand would decline, for the demand of those who buy such things to sell again springs from the demand of those who buy for consumption.

But (and the expedients resorted to in times of sudden and acute monetary scarcity may suggest this) let us imagine some such proprietary packed article to pass into use as the medium of exchange. The increased demand caused by the new and wider use would enable the owners of the trade-mark, by restricting supply of which they would have exclusive control, to carry up the value of the article so far above that of the contained commodity that it would pass out of use for consumption. Yet so long as the demand for it as a medium of exchange continued, it would have use for that purpose, and the owners of the trade-mark could not merely keep up the price, but could with impunity reduce the quantity and quality of the contents of their packages to almost any extent. For since every acceptance of a thing in exchange is in reality a purchase of it, and every transfer of it in payment of an obligation or in return for any other thing is in reality a sale, the entire demand for an article used only as a medium of exchange would be with a view to subsequent sale—would be a demand of merchants or traders, who are not concerned with the intrinsic qualities of what they buy to sell again, but only with its salability.

In the illustration I have used, the possibility of lessening the quality or quantity of the packages without lessening their value as a medium of exchange, is dependent on their having passed out of use for consumption and the demand for them being entirely the demand for use in exchange. For, so long as any part of the demand was a demand for consumption, the lessening of commodity value would, by checking the total demand, operate at once to reduce value not merely of that part used for consumption, but that part used for exchange.

Now the first coined money being commodity money, the demand for it would be for a long time, in part at least, a demand for consumption. In the simpler stage of the arts, coin would be much more frequently than now beaten or melted into plate, adornments, ornaments, etc. And more important still perhaps, it would continue to be used as a commodity in the exchange with other countries. It is probable that the coinage of the more important sovereigns had a far wider area of diffusion when international commerce was much less than it is now. For, although the area of commerce was more limited than now, there was proportionately more of the area without any coinage of its own, and the development of credit as a medium of international exchanges, the use of coin in them as a conveniently portable commodity, was probably relatively greater than now.

Now, the demand for coin sent abroad, as American gold sent to England, like the demand for coin for use in the arts, is a demand for use in consumption and would quickly show itself in a lessening of aggregate demand and consequently of value, upon a reduction of the commodity value of coin, no matter how strictly the workmen of the mints were sworn to secrecy, as was the device of sovereigns who contemplated deteriorating their coinage.

But still more important is the fact that in order to keep up the value of coin while diminishing its intrinsic value it is necessary that the supply be strictly limited. But the sovereigns, whether princes or republics, who have resorted to the expedient of debasing their coinage have generally done so for the purpose of turning the same amount of metal into more coin, rather than that of keeping the same amount of coin in circulation with the use of less metal, or have been unable to resist the temptation to do this when they found opportunity.

That the circulating value of money need not necessarily depend on its intrinsic value, must have been clear to discerning men as soon as the habitual use of coined money had made its signs and emblems the accepted tokens of value, so that it passed from hand to hand without testing and usually without weighing. The fact that coins that had lost something of their intrinsic value by abrasion continued to pass current, must have made clipping and filling and sweating, early devices of the cunning, which raised figures and milled edges would not prevent, unless supplemented by such mercantile stipulation or legislative enactment as secured common agreement not to accept such coins. This of itself would show that the circulating value of a coin did not as a matter of fact depend upon the value of the material it contained.

Thus to the ministers and advisers of the sovereigns, who seem everywhere to have assumed from the first exclusive privilege of coining, it must have seemed an easy and safe economy to reduce the cost of the coin by substituting for its material some part of cheaper metal. Hence came those numerous and repeated reductions in the value of coins which are a marked feature in all monetary history; which have reduced the English pound sterling to but a fraction of its original equivalence to a pound troy, and in other countries have brought about a still greater difference.

So far as the principal and most important coinage is concerned, these attempts have from time to time ended in disaster, and in the final reunion of circulating value with commodity value, either by the rejection and withdrawal of the debased coin and a recoinage, or more frequently by the lowering of the circulating value to the level of the commodity value.

This, however, is not a necessary result of a debasement of coinage, as is so often assumed. A less valuable metal may be substituted in a coin for a more valuable metal without lessening the circulating value, *provided*—and this is the essential condition—it continues to be as hard for those who use the coin in exchanges to get the one as it was to get the other; or in other words that it continues to represent the same exertion.

For all exchange is really the exchange of labor, and the rate at which all things tend to exchange for all other things is determined by the relative difficulty of obtaining them. That a ten pound note of the Bank of England, having practically no intrinsic value, will exchange for ten gold sovereigns, having an intrinsic value of that amount of gold—that a five dollar note of the government of the United States, having no intrinsic value; five silver dollars, having an intrinsic value of something like two dollars and a half; and a five dollar piece, having an intrinsic value of five dollars, will exchange in this country for each other or for the same amount of commodities or services of any kind, is because the difficulty of getting these things, the quantity and quality of exertion ordinarily required to obtain them, is precisely the same. Should it become in the slightest degree harder to get one of these things than the others, this will show itself in a change of the rate at which they exchange. In this case we say that the one commands a premium or that the others bear a discount.

The difficulty of procurement which brings to the same value the gold coin, silver coin and notes spoken of, so that they will exchange for each other or for equal quantities of other things, is, though of the same intensity, of different kinds. In the gold coin, it is the difficulty of mining, refining and transporting the metal (for neither in Great Britain nor in the United States does the government make any charge or exact any seigniorage for the coinage of gold). In the silver coin, it is partly the difficulty of obtaining the metal and partly the difficulty imposed by the only terms on which the government will coin silver dollars—or in other words, by the seigniorage it demands. In the notes, it is the difficulty imposed by the restrictions on the issuance of such notes—or, as it may be considered, all seigniorage. What in short, gives to the paper notes or coins of small intrinsic value the same exchange value as the gold coin, is that the government concerned, which has the monopoly of coinage in its respective country, will not issue one of them on any less terms than it does the other, thus making them all to the individual equally hard to get.

What has everywhere caused the failure of the innumerable attempts to reduce the intrinsic value of the principal and important coin, without reducing its circulating value, is not the impossibility of the task, but the fact that the sovereigns who have attempted it did not, and perhaps could not, observe the necessary condition of success, the strict limitation of supply. But the purpose of the sovereigns, whether princes or republics, in debasing coinage has been, or under pressure of the temptation has become, not an attempt to make a less value in metal serve for the same quantity of coin, but to issue a greater quantity of coin on the same value in metal. Thus instead of restricting the supply of coin to the point where the demand for its use as a medium of exchange would keep up its exchange value irrespective of the lessening in its intrinsic value, they proceeded at once to increase supply on a falling demand, and met the inevitable depreciation of circulating value by fresh increase of supply, so that no matter how much the intrinsic value of the coin was reduced, its circulating value followed.

[Principle same as that which caused depreciation in French assignat, Continental money, etc.] [1]

It is this fall of circulating value with the fall of intrinsic value where it is not kept up by restriction of supply that has through succeeding depreciations reduced the English pound sterling to but a fraction of its original equivalence to a pound troy, and in other countries has brought about a still greater difference.

---

[1] Note in MS. indicating illustration to be developed by author. — H. G., JR.

CHAPTER VI.

THE TWO KINDS OF MONEY.

[SHOWING THAT ONE ORIGINATES IN VALUE FROM PRODUCTION, THE OTHER IN VALUE FROM OBLIGATION.

Money peculiarly the representative of value—Two kinds of money in the more highly civilized world—Commodity money and value from production—Credit money and value from obligation—Of credit money—Of commodity money—Of intrinsic value—Gold coin the only intrinsic value money now in circulation in the United States, England, France or Germany.] [1]

WHILE value is always one and the same power, that of commanding labor in exchange, there are as we have seen, with reference to its sources, two different kinds of value—that which proceeds from production and that which proceeds from obligation. Now money is peculiarly the representative of value—the common medium or flux through which things are exchanged with reference to their value, and the common measure of value. And corresponding to and proceeding from this distinction between the two kinds of value, there are, we find, two kinds of money in use in the more highly civilized world to-day—the one, which we may call commodity money, originating in the value proceeding from production; and the other, which we may call credit money, originating in the value proceeding from obligation.

This distinction has of course no relation to differences of denomination, such as those between English pounds,

[1] Merely the title in this heading appears in MS. — H. G., Jr.

French francs and American dollars. These are but differences of nomenclature. Nor yet does it coincide with differences in the material used as money, as for instance that between metal money and paper money. For while all paper money is credit money, all metal money is not commodity money. What I understand by commodity money is money which exchanges at its value as a commodity, that is to say, which passes current at no more than its "intrinsic value," or value of the material of which it is composed. Credit money is money which exchanges at a greater value than that of the material of which it is composed. In the one case the whole value for which the money exchanges is the value it would have as a commodity. In the other case the value for which the money exchanges is greater than its commodity value, and hence some part at least of its exchange value as money is given to it by credit or trust.

For instance, a man who exchanges ten dollars' worth of wheat for a coin containing ten dollars' worth of gold makes in reality a barter. He exchanges one commodity for an equal value of another commodity, crediting or trusting nobody, but having in the coin he has received a commodity which, irrespective of its use as money, has an equal value to that he gave. But the man who exchanges ten dollars' worth of wheat for a ten-dollar note receives for a commodity worth ten dollars what, as a commodity, has only the value of a bit of paper, a value practically infinitesimal. What renders him willing to take it as an equivalent of the wheat is the faith or credit or trust that he can in turn exchange it as money at the same valuation. If he drops the coin into the sea, he loses value to the extent of ten dollars, and the sum of wealth is lessened by that amount. If he burns the paper note, he suffers loss, to the value of ten dollars, but he alone; the sum of wealth is only infinitesimally lessened. Paper money is in truth of the same nature as the check or order of an individual or corporation except (and in this lies the difference that makes it money) that it has a wider and readier credit. The value of the coin of full intrinsic value, like the value of the wheat, is a value that comes from production. But the value of the paper money is, like the value of the check or order, a value from obligation.

The first money in use was doubtless a commodity money, and there are some countries where it is still the principal money, and places perhaps where it is the only money. But in the more highly civilized countries it has been very largely superseded by credit money. In the United States, for instance, the only commodity or intrinsic value money now in circulation is the gold coinage of the United States. Our silver dollars have an intrinsic or commodity value of only some fifty cents, and the value of our subsidiary coinage is still less. That they circulate in the United States at the same value as gold shows that their exchange value has no reference to their intrinsic value. They are in reality as much credit money as is the greenback or treasury note, the difference being that the stamp, which evidences their credit and thus secures their circulation, is impressed not on paper, but on a metallic material. The substitution of what is now the cheapest of metals, steel, or the utter elimination of intrinsic value, would not in the slightest lessen their circulating value. What is true of the United States in this respect is also true of England, of France, of Germany, and of all the nations that have adopted gold as the common measure of value. Their only commodity money is certain gold coins; their other coins being token or credit money. In the countries that have retained silver as the common measure of value the standard coin is generally commodity money, but the subsidiary coins, having less intrinsic value, are in reality credit money.

INDEX.